THIS BOOK BELONGS TO:

_____

PRESENTED BY:

_____

DATE:

_____

DEVOTIONS
from the WORLD *of*
MUSIC

PATRICK & BARBARA KAVANAUGH

Cook
COMMUNICATIONS

DEDICATION

This book is dedicated to all the wonderful, talented students
of the MasterWorks Festival.

Patrick and Barbara

Cook Communications Ministries, Colorado Springs, CO 80918
Cook Communications, Paris, Ontario
Kingsway Communications, Eastbourne, England

DEVOTIONS FROM THE WORLD OF MUSIC
© 2000 by Patrick and Barbara Kavanaugh for text.

All Scripture is taken from the *Holy Bible, New International Version.* Copyright © 1973, 1978, 1984 by the
International Bible Society. Used by permission of Zondervan Publishing House. All rights reserved.

Edited by Sue Reck and Jeannie Harmon
Designed by Boven Design Studio

CCM Magazine has generously given permission to use quotations from the following copyrighted issues: May 8 quotes were
originally published in "Plumb Line" by Wendy Lee Neutwig (May, 1999); June 14 quotes were originally published in "The
Art of Forgiveness" by James Long (January, 1998); June 21 quotes were originally published in "Saving Grace" by Lindy
Warren (September, 1998); June 22 quotes were originally published in "Fresh Horses" by Karly Randolph-Pitman (May,
1998); July 21 quotes were originally published in "Return of the Loving Dead" by Brian Quincey Newcomb (February, 1998);
July 27 quotes were originally published in "Golden Girl" by James Long (June, 1998); August 24 quotes were originally pub-
lished in "7 Days a Week" by Lucas Henderson (April, 1998); August 31 quotes were originally published in "Fast Times" by
Mike Parker (January, 1998); September 20 quotes were originally published in "In the Garden" by Melissa Riddle (December,
1998); September 24 quotes were originally published in "O, to be Rich" by James Long (November, 1995); October 1 quotes
were originally published in "Choir Girl" by Liz Kelly (November, 1998); October 13 quotes were originally published in "The
Rockford Files" by Gregory Rumburg (December, 1995); October 19 quotes were originally published in "Crystal's Cathedral"
by Anthony De Barros (May, 1998); November 21 quotes were originally published in "Prince of Steves" by Debra Atkins
(October, 1996); December 4 quotes were originally published in "Wade into the Talent Pool" by Holly Hamilton, (October,
1995). All these articles are copywritten by CCM Communications (For CCM Magazine subscription information, please call
800-333-9643), and are reprinted with permission.

First printing, 2000
Printed in the United States of America
04 03 02 01 00   5 4 3 2 1

Library of Congress Cataloging-in-Publication Data
Kavanaugh, Patrick.
    Devotions from the world of music/Patrick & Barbara Kavanaugh.
        p. cm.
    ISBN 0-7814-3347-9
    1. Christian life. 2. Devotional calendars. 3. Musicians—Miscellanea. I. Kavanaugh, Barbara. II. Title.
BV4501.2.K34 2000
242'.2—dc21

00-027298

Though there is only one way to God, Jesus Christ, there are many paths into His word. We can study it academically, meditatively, or devotionally. We can study it by theme, book, or according to chronology. We can approach it by character, by topic, or even (as most of us tend to do) haphazardly, letting the precious pages fall open to "see what the Lord has to say to us today." God honors all these paths to His Word because He cares more about the heart than the methodology.

The secret to any meaningful approach to Scripture is our ability to listen; to listen simply to the words of the text, to listen to the heart of the individual writer, to listen even to the silence between the words, for it is there often that God speaks to us.

Music teaches us how to listen. The writers of the Bible knew that. We know this because the Bible is so full of songs. Adams' first words to Eve are a song. There is, of course, the Psalter. The words of the prophets are songs as well, uttered originally to accompanying music. The New Testament is filled with bits and pieces of ancient hymns.

My friends, Patrick and Barbara, know how to listen. A lifetime of involvement with music has taught them well. The following devotions they have provided for us are a unique collection of Scripture and story. They originated in the lives of men and women all of whom made listening a lifestyle. Each one represents a different path into Scripture and therefore into the heart of God. Read then, and listen well.

Michael Card

LOOK FOR THESE SPECIAL FEATURES . . .

 **From the Score**—A key Scripture from God's Word.

 **From the Repertoire**—Glimpses from the pages of music history and how we can see God's principles at work in the world around us.

 **From the Conductor**—An action point or activity that will demonstrate to us personally our need to follow God, and show us how we can be a winner if we "practice" being like Him.

The crucible for silver and the furnace for gold, but man is tested by the praise he receives. –PROVERBS 27:21

On the first day of the year 1822, Ludwig van Beethoven (1770–1827) was elected an honorary member of Steiermark Musical Society. The composer was fifty-two years old and had already written eight symphonies, five piano concerti, an opera, dozens of sonatas, and a great deal of chamber music. Honors were not new to him. He had worked hard for decades, and he was now well known throughout the musical world.

Under the circumstances, Beethoven might have considered retirement. He was very deaf by that time and could never perform again on his beloved piano. Because he couldn't hear, it was hard for him to interact with other people. And to top it all off, his overall health was beginning to fail. No one would have blamed him if he had spent his declining years resting on his many laurels.

Yet Beethoven still had his greatest works to compose. Had he stopped in 1822, we would not have the Ninth Symphony, "Missa Solemnis," the late string quartets, and many other masterpieces that he produced in his last five years. Musically speaking, Beethoven chose to have no "declining years" and used his talent practically to his dying day.

Beethoven was always up early, composing several hours before breakfast. Never going anywhere without blank music paper, he was ready whenever an idea inspired him. His strong relationship with God gave him all the praise he needed. Concerning the world's recognition, Ludwig van Beethoven wrote, "I care nothing for it, because I have a higher goal."

Some of the greatest works throughout history were created by people who refused to let the praise of the world distract them from their purpose. Of course, we are all encouraged when we receive praise from our peers. There is no sin in this. But with praise comes a temptation. We need to be careful that we don't let praise itself become the reason we do things. It is our job to make certain that such praise never distracts us from what God wants us to do.

When was the last time you were publicly praised? Did it feel good? Did it go to your head? Are you craving more of the same? Ask God's help to work for His praises instead of man's.

Do you see a man skilled in his work? He will serve before kings; he will not serve before obscure men. –PROVERBS 22:29

This day in 1962 found four young British musicians feeling deeply discouraged. The previous day had been spent auditioning for Decca Records. It was their first experience with a professional record label, and they had given it everything they had. Now the frustrating announcement: Decca had turned them down in favor of another group—Brian Poole and the Tremeloes.

The four men's names were Paul McCartney, John Lennon, George Harrison, and Pete Best (who would later be replaced by Ringo Starr), and their group was called the Beatles. If they could have seen the future, they would find that within a very short time the Beatles would be on the top of the national charts. Indeed, these four young musicians would someday be recognized for creating the greatest band the world has ever seen.

But on January 2, 1961, none of them could have guessed their future. For all they knew, the Beatles might have just blown their only chance with a major record company. The future looked bleak, but they did the one thing they could still do. These young men worked hard on their music. They had no idea if another break might arrive, but the Beatles determined to be ready for it if it did. Eventually, new opportunities did arrive—and the rest is history.

Incidentally, Decca Records never did sign a contract with the Beatles. It was said that every Christmas the Decca executives would take those audition tapes out of the vault, and while listening again, they would weep over their missed chance to sign up the world's best-selling band!

When we face a roadblock or what seems like a dead end, God wants us to keep going and have the determination to not give up. As you can see from the Beatles' experience, determination pays off.

Do you know when your next big break will appear? Of course not. Are you ready for it today? How can you prepare so that you will be ready when it arrives?

You have taken off your old self with its practices and have put on the new self, which is being renewed in knowledge in the image of its Creator. —COLOSSIANS 3:9, 10

Keith Green sang and played piano in dozens of bars and clubs before he came to Christ. After his conversion, he dramatically turned away from his worldly background, choosing instead to use his musical gifts for spreading the Gospel. He became one of the most powerful voices in contemporary Christian music (CCM) until he was tragically killed in a plane crash in 1982.

Although Green had a burden for lost souls, he was also on a mission to encourage and challenge Christians to live more like Christ. Many of his albums—such as *He Who Has Ears to Hear* and *No Compromise*—contain songs that convict believers of our shortcomings and call us back to holiness. Like the prophets of old, he boldly spoke out against an easy, no-commitment Christianity. Green was even known to stop playing in the middle of his performance if he felt that worldliness rather than Christ was being exalted in any way.

A turning point in Green's life occurred at a party, attended by many ex-hippie Christians like himself. In the middle of the fun, one of the guys ran through the house naked ("streaking" was a fad in the 1970s), shouting, "Praise the Lord!" Green was horrified that this man apparently thought that becoming a Christian wouldn't change how he lived. Green decided right then and there to follow God with all his heart and to encourage those around him to do the same. Years after his death, Last Days Ministries, founded by Keith Green and his wife, Melody, continues to profoundly affect the Christian walk of thousands of young people around the world.

Take a moment to think about your daily habits. What bad attitudes or habits do you need to get rid of? Ask God to help you change these areas, and to be able to live a life worthy of the Gospel.

"Whoever exalts himself will be humbled, and whoever humbles himself will be exalted." –MATTHEW 23:12

On January 4, 1881, Johannes Brahms (1833–1897) received an honorary doctorate from the University of Breslau. It was on this same day that he premiered his *Academic Festival Overture,* composed for this occasion.

The master must have been amused and sensed the irony of this unsought honor. He had come from the most humble of beginnings. Born into poverty in the slums of Hamburg, his family could not afford a piano, even when Brahms' musical genius was becoming evident to everyone. He spent most of his youth playing piano in the lowliest Hamburg pubs, attempting to earn a few coins for his family.

The young Brahms took lessons from various teachers, yet his genius was mostly self-taught. In his "school of hard knocks," he learned more by doing than by studying. Brahms worked constantly. Some of his early compositions he threw in the trash, but gradually he mastered his calling and created works of great beauty. He never sought honors—though they came later. His desire was to strive for quality, and his work was rewarded.

Many years of mature composition passed before Brahms attempted to write a symphony. He would have nothing to do with such a noble musical endeavor unless he could create a masterpiece—and he did. Brahms' four symphonies are in a class by themselves. Only Beethoven's are performed more frequently today. Brahms' symphonies were not composed rashly, but with an attitude of humility and integrity.

Brahms was a man whose desire was to create excellence rather than celebrity, who was more concerned with the quality of his work than with the response of his peers. It was as if Brahms took the words of Jeremiah 45:5 to himself: "Should you then seek great things for yourself? Seek them not." Doubtless this composer—who claimed that he could always lay his hand on his Bible, even in the dark—also knew the proverb: "It is not good to eat too much honey, nor is it honorable to seek one's own honor" (Proverbs 25:27).

What means more to you, success or integrity? Pray that God will keep you focused, and help you to seek His glory rather than your own.

Do not follow the crowd in doing wrong. −EXODUS 23:2

Many Scriptures tell us to not "follow the crowd." We often see something that has brought someone else success, and then copy it to get the same results. But it doesn't always work out the second time. If we are stealing someone else's idea, we are not being original at all.

The great jazz saxophonist Lionel Hampton learned this lesson the hard way. One night his band played a ballroom in Buffalo, New York, which was packed beyond capacity. Below the stage stood, literally, a solid mass of people. Another sax player in the band caused a sensation by walking on the edge of the stage as if he were on a tightrope while he played a solo. At a dramatic moment, he purposely fell backward toward the people who held up their hands and pushed him back up to the stage. He never stopped playing, and the crowd loved it.

So Hampton wanted to try it. The next time his band played at that ballroom, he was ready to copy his colleague's success. Unfortunately, Hampton failed to notice that the crowd was much smaller than before. He, too, played a great solo for his tightrope walk. But when he dramatically fell toward the audience, the few people nearby stepped aside, and Hampton unceremoniously crashed to the floor. The members of the band could hardly play they were laughing so hard. Fortunately, Hampton wasn't badly hurt. As he painfully climbed back on stage, he knew he had learned his lesson—the hard way.

God has not only given us talents, but creativity as well. If we use the gifts we have without copying others, we will find the results we seek.

Have you ever felt like Hampton, that what worked for others didn't work for you? Resolve to be yourself, to simply be the one-of-a-kind person who God created you to be.

Where there is no vision, the people perish. —PROVERBS 29:18 (KJV)

Today is the birthday of the Russian composer Aleksandr Scriabin, born in Moscow on January 6, 1872. Compositionally, he is best remembered for his piano works and his symphonies, notably his fourth, the *Poem of Ecstasy.* Scriabin is also remembered for his innovative interest in the mysterious relationship between certain musical notes and the color spectrum.

Throughout history, both musicians and artists had sensed an illusive bond between visual color and aural pitch, but no one had quite understood this association. Scriabin determined not only to conquer the problem, but also to use all the senses in his compositions. For his last symphony, he invented a special color keyboard, projecting colors onto a screen synchronized to the music. He envisioned works using music, dance, drama, poetry, colors, and even various perfumes.

Unfortunately, a premature death put an end to his aspirations, but he left us with a portrayal of a man with a vision. Practically every day of his last decade was spent pursuing his theory. He let nothing get in his way. Although his work remained unfinished, it fascinates musicians, artists, and even scientists today.

There is nothing better than understanding God's call for your life and then actually living out that calling. Discovering what God has planned for you can be difficult and take time, but you're never too young to seek His will and start living for Him.

To help celebrate Scriabin's birthday, get out a set of paints, put on your favorite music, and paint what the music inspires. Thank God for giving each of us a mission in life, and ask Him to help you discover His mission for your life.

*And the things you have heard me say in the presence of many wit-
nesses entrust to reliable men who will also be qualified to teach others.*

2 TIMOTHY 2:2

William Bradbury (1816–1868) was just another young singer in
Boston's Bowdoin Street Church Choir. He must have seemed indistin-
guishable from the dozens of other choristers, yet something in him was
stirred every time he participated in his weekly rehearsal. He had a tremendous
mentor, the famous musician Dr. Lowell Mason, who composed such hymns as
My Faith Looks up to Thee and *Nearer, My God, to Thee.*

Working under Lowell Mason was an inspiration for young Bradbury. He
knew that Mason had founded the Boston Academy of Music and had given free
lessons to hundreds of young musicians like himself. Mason personally encouraged Bradbury to continue in his music, and the young man determined to
someday do the same for other needy musicians if he ever had the opportunity.

After years of study and practice, Bradbury was given the position of organist
at New York Baptist Tabernacle in 1841. In his busy lifetime, he composed or
arranged hundreds of hymns, many of which are still sung today. He compiled
fifty-nine songbooks for publication and founded the Bradbury Piano Company.
Furthermore, Bradbury personally befriended and encouraged many other hymn
writers, including Fanny Crosby, Thomas Hastings, and George Frederick Root.

His favorite ministry was always to children. After forming a number of very
successful children's choirs, he organized the Juvenile Music Festivals, which were
known throughout the city. Like his mentor Lowell Mason, Bradbury gave hundreds of free music classes to children and composed hymns specifically for children's Sunday School. Perhaps his greatest legacy was his most childlike: he was
the composer of the very well-known "Jesus Loves Me This I Know." William
Bradbury died on this date, January 7, in 1868.

*Have you ever had a mentor? Someone who inspired you to give of
yourself? Not all of us have the privilege of learning from a great musician, but
we can try to inspire others. Whom could you encourage this week?*

I have hidden your word in my heart that I might not sin against you. —PSALM 119:11

January 8 is the birthday of Hans von Bulow (1830–1894), one of the greatest conductors of the nineteenth century. For decades, this innovative musician championed the works of Liszt, Wagner, Brahms, and a host of other composers.

One of his strong beliefs in his musical life was his emphasis on the memorization of music. He told other conductors, "You should have the score in your head, not just your head in the score!" At times he even insisted on the still-unheard of practice of making the members of the orchestra also memorize their music! He felt that a musician could hardly be expected to put his heart into the performance if he was still at the stage of reading the notes as they went along.

Perhaps such strict insistence on memorization is debatable, but Hans von Bulow understood the importance of using our memory. Jesus told us that, "Out of the overflow of the heart the mouth speaks" (Matthew 12:34). Whatever we habitually put into our hearts and minds will come out, for good or evil.

One thing all Christians should hide in their hearts—or memorize—is the Word of God. In the same way that a soloist will memorize the notes of a concerto in order to be free for its interpretation, we need to memorize God's Word so we think of it often and share it with others. To paraphrase von Bulow, "You need to have your head in the Book and the Book in your head!"

Have you ever memorized a series of verses from the Bible? Today could be the beginning! Start with the opening verse on this page. Write it down and look at it several times throughout the day. Perhaps you and a friend could memorize Scriptures weekly and hold each other accountable.

For the revelation awaits an appointed time; it speaks of the end and will not prove false. Though it linger, wait for it; it will certainly come and will not delay. –HABAKKUK 2:3

Patience is a virtue that few of us possess. When a musician has worked for many hours and prepared for an opportunity to appear—and then it doesn't occur right away—the waiting can be very difficult. Yet often the door is just about to open when we are tempted to quit.

In the late 1960s, two young men in England began to write songs together. After months of diligent work, they composed their first musical, *The Likes of Us.* The response to their creation was so meager that it was never even performed. Continuing to write songs, they could find no one interested. Finally, they were ready to throw in the towel.

If only someone could have told these two—seventeen-year-old Andrew Lloyd Webber and twenty-one-year-old Tim Rice—what was right around the corner. But at that moment, they couldn't see what we know now. Nevertheless, a day came when the head of a small London school needed an appropriate selection for an end-of-term concert. The schoolmaster had known Webber for some time and asked him to compose a "religious work" for the occasion.

Looking into a Bible, Webber and Rice chose the ageless story of Joseph and his brothers. Within two months they had created a new musical, entitled *Joseph and the Amazing Technicolor Dreamcoat.* This was the first of a long string of musicals that would make them internationally famous. If they had given up even a week earlier, the world would be missing some marvelous music.

How is your "patience quotient?" Are you ready to wait years, maybe decades, for the fulfillment of your vision? Don't give up; God has His timetable for your life and knows best when we are ready to be used for His glory.

There is lots of great music available by Andrew Lloyd Webber. Try to attend a performance of Joseph and the Amazing Technicolor Dreamcoat. *If that's not possible, find a CD containing some of his music, then sit back and enjoy, thanking God for Webber's patience and persistence.*

Don't let anyone look down on you because you are young, but set an example for the believers in speech, in life, in love, in faith and in purity. —1 TIMOTHY 4:12

Are there limitations to what God can do through you? Sometimes we may feel that we are too young to be used by the Lord, or too old, or too poor, or too uneducated, or too . . . anything. Kirk Franklin, one of today's greatest gospel singers and composers, proves that you are never too young to do great things for God.

Born in Fort Worth, Texas, Franklin was abandoned by his teenage parents at the age of only three. Fortunately, he was adopted by his sixty-four-year-old aunt, a godly woman who encouraged his musical gifts almost immediately. When he was four, he began piano lessons, and within a few years he was performing on a gospel music circuit.

His aunt often spent her Saturday mornings collecting cans to pay for Franklin's music lessons. But even she could hardly believe how rapidly his ministry developed. When he was seven, young Kirk was offered his first recording contract, but his aunt declined it, believing he was too young. Nevertheless, he was appointed minister of music at Mount Saint Rose Baptist Church when he was only eleven years old.

Could this young man lead others in worship? Of course he could! Did he ever have doubts and insecurities about his age? Doubtless he did, but he refused to let it stop his ministry. Indeed, while still in his teens, Franklin created an entirely new gospel sound and started a new group called "The Family." Their debut album became the first in gospel music to sell one million copies. Was Kirk Franklin too young to be used by the Lord? No one thinks so now!

Take courage. You are never too young to serve the Lord. Though you may not record a gold record, there are many ways you can serve. Think about your interests and talents, then ask your pastor how you can use them to serve the church this week.

"Whoever can be trusted with very little can also be trusted with much." –LUKE 16:10

How astonishing it is to trace the roots of a star and find just how far some have had to climb. The country music celebrity Porter Wagoner has sold millions of recordings, but his beginnings are as humble as one could find. By the age of ten, poverty had forced him to leave school and work on his father's farm. Furthermore, he was so bashful that he would never play his guitar or sing for anyone. This shyness was so severe that neither he nor anyone who knew him could ever imagine him having a career in music.

As a teenager, Wagoner worked in a butcher shop in West Plains, Missouri. His only contact with music was a private time of singing to himself in the back room. That could have been his only audience ever, except that his boss accidentally heard him singing one night. This enterprising butcher wanted more publicity for his shop, so he gave Wagoner a raise to sing commercials on the local radio station.

From the butcher shop, the young musician's rise was slow but steady. A much larger radio station in Springfield, Missouri, heard one of Wagoner's commercials and was impressed. Soon he was bewildered to be offered a job at the big station for seventy dollars a week. Next he was given a position on a new television show called *The Ozark Jubilee*. From there he was noticed by RCA and signed a recording contract. Moving to Nashville, Wagoner recorded his first hit, "Company's Company," and he has been a major force in country music ever since.

At each step in his career, the bashful Wagoner could have balked and let his fears keep him from seizing the new opportunity. Imagine his nervousness when he appeared for the first time on the radio, or on television. Yet he never gave in to his fear. Instead, step by step, he overcame his shyness, and has become known for his relaxed stage presence in live performances.

God wants you to overcome your fears, and He wants to help you do that. What fears can you give to God today?

What are your greatest fears? Write them down on a piece of paper, then pray about each of them—one by one—asking God to help you overcome those fears.

He who works his land will have abundant food, but the one who chases fantasies will have his fill of poverty. –PROVERBS 28:19

When we hear a song being played on the radio or performed live, it usually sounds so polished and "finished" that it's hard to imagine the work that went into it. Nor do we hear the many bits and pieces of the unfinished work that were tried but rejected by the composer. Yet like the work of a sculptor, often a piece of music has to be cut out of a much larger creation before it is truly complete.

A modern example is Bob Dylan's well-known song "Like a Rolling Stone." Dylan recalled that, "The chorus came to me first, and I'd sorta hum that over and over." Then came the long work on all the different verses. As he attempted one idea and then another, frustration set in.

Nevertheless, he determined to forge ahead. Dylan wrote and wrote, until he had a song "about twenty pages long, and out of it I took 'Like a Rolling Stone' and made it a single." By the time anyone else heard this hit, many parts of it literally lay on the floor like the leftover stones of a great statue. Yet each sketch and unused idea was important to the work's creation, and the song could not have been finished without the extra effort.

We all face projects in which we are tempted to give "second best." It is so easy to say, "That's good enough," when a little more effort could make all the difference. When we take the time to give it our all, the end result will be worthy to present to our Master.

What is the last big project you completed? Was it "outstanding," "good," "fair," or "poor"? If you gave it less than your best, what extra effort can you add the next time around?

Remind the people . . . to be ready to do whatever is good.

–TITUS 3:1

The person whose birthday we celebrate today was not really a musician, yet his name (or at least, his initial) is on hundreds of concert programs every day. You may hear Mozart's Concerto for Flute and Harp (K. 299) or Mozart's Piano Fantasia in C Minor (K. 475)—or *anything* by Mozart in a concert—and wonder what those "K" numbers after the titles mean.

The "K" next to Mozart's titles stands for the name "Kochel," and it was on this date in 1800 that Ludwig von Kochel was born. Most composers give an opus number to each piece they compose, but unfortunately Mozart did not. Therefore, sooner or later someone had to accept the task of laboriously researching each Mozart manuscript to put them all in chronological order. The person who accomplished this tedious chore was Kochel, and his work has since aided thousands of musicians.

Kochel was not a musician by profession. He was a botanist and a mineralogist who happened to love Mozart's music. Being quite familiar with the principles of scientific classification, Kochel was horrified by the disorder and confusion that surrounded the works of his favorite composer. Rather than simply disdain the sloppiness of musicians, he took it upon himself to remedy the situation.

So many situations around us are in need of a "Kochel," a person who will take the initiative to work toward a solution. Rather than waiting in inactivity until someone begs for our help, let us always be aware of the needs around us. We cannot meet every need we see—Kochel could not have cataloged every composer's music—but we can ask God where He would have us help, and then take the steps to get involved.

Look around your home, your job, or your church. Ask God to show you something specific you can do to help. Prayerfully set a time for its completion, and do it with all your might!

For where you have envy and selfish ambition, there you find disorder and every evil practice. —JAMES 3:16

It is a rare moment in history when a performer appears who is so remarkably talented that he astounds audiences and fellow musicians alike. Such a wonder was Louis Armstrong, who revolutionized the world of jazz. He played the trumpet like no one before him, routinely hitting notes higher than many thought possible.

In fact, he was such an incredible player that when he first became well known, other trumpet players insisted that he played with a "trick horn," which somehow enabled him to play such an extended range. They could not believe that Armstrong could make a typical trumpet produce the amazing sounds that had made his reputation. Many players were so envious of his playing that they publicly challenged him—to their own misfortune.

During one show, another trumpeter asked to borrow Armstrong's horn for a solo. Armstrong was happy to comply, and his colleague received some quiet applause for his playing. Then Armstrong took his horn back and soon had the audience standing on top of the tables cheering.

At another show, Armstrong knew that "trick horn" rumors were in the air, so before his most difficult solo he invited a well-known trumpeter to examine his horn. The skeptical musician played Armstrong's trumpet, then his own. Again, he played scales on one trumpet then the other. This was *no* trick horn. In Armstrong's next solo he hit over two hundred high C's (they actually counted!), and he ended the piece with a prolonged high F!

The difference was not in the trumpet, but in the man behind the trumpet. He had a tremendous inborn talent, and he had spent most of his life improving that talent. We may at times be tempted to envy those around us and mentally invent excuses why they may succeed where we do not. Yet if we concentrate on serving Christ instead of working for man's praises, we will develop gratefulness for the gifts we have and spend more time developing our own God-given skills.

Think of someone whose talent or ability you envy. Rather than fostering a dislike of that person (which is what often happens when we envy), ask him what it has taken for him to get where he is. How much time does he practice? How many years has he been playing? Are you willing to devote that kind of effort to developing your God-given skills?

The Lord is close to the brokenhearted and saves those who are crushed in spirit. –PSALM 34:18

Ballet is one of the most popular of all art forms in Russia, and on January 15, 1890, the great Tchaikovsky premiered one of his finest—the incomparable *Sleeping Beauty.* The work had been commissioned by the Imperial Opera, and for its first performance, the Czar himself was to be there. Tchaikovsky was often quite critical of his own music, but he was enthusiastic about this score and could hardly wait to hear the Czar's response.

"Very nice" was the mechanical answer. The rather lackluster applause didn't help much either. Tchaikovsky was crushed, and he left the theater in shame. Fortunately, there would be future triumphs for this composer. Commissions, concert tours, and some of his finest music was still to come, but he learned a hard lesson about trying to please the "powers that be."

How should we deal with hurtful, disappointing situations? To begin with, we need to examine our motives. Are we working for the praise of men? It is not only uncertain, but when it does come it is usually worthless. If we are doing our work for the Lord, we cannot be disappointed.

Nevertheless, we are human, and circumstances do arise that leave us feeling humiliated. When that happens, the best thing to do is to draw near to God. There is no hurt He does not understand. No wound He will not heal. When we keep our focus on Him, He will give us the strength to keep going.

When was the last time that you were hurt due to a disappointment?
Offer that pain to God, and ask Him to give you comfort as well as wisdom.

Trust in the Lord with all your heart and lean not on your own understanding; in all your ways acknowledge him, and he will make your paths straight. —PROVERBS. 3:5, 6

On January 16, 1768, a young boy named Mozart finished his Symphony in D (K. 45). This feat would have been amazing for most boys, but this boy had already composed several symphonies. Many have considered Mozart's short but industrious life (thirty-five years) to contain more genius than that of any other musician in history. Mozart's compositional output was astonishing: symphonies, operas, chamber music, concerti, masses, and songs seemed to come effortlessly from his pen. His secret was a combination of matchless intelligence, musical creativity, and an imperturbable faith in God.

Friedrich Kerst, one of the editors of Mozart's published letters, testifies that "Mozart was of a deeply religious nature. . . . Mozart stood toward God in a relationship of a child full of trust in his father." In a typical letter, the composer writes that, "God is ever before my eyes. I realize His omnipotence and I fear His anger; but I also recognize His love, His compassion, and His tenderness towards His creatures. He will never forsake His own. If it is according to His will, so let it be according to mine. Thus all will be well and I must needs be happy and contented."

With such a trusting attitude, his talent was unhindered by the doubts and uncertainty that have plagued many artists. Mozart's faith left him free to use the talent given him, and it flowed from him in a never-ending stream of inspiration.

Attend a concert that will feature at least one piece composed by Mozart. (If you cannot make it to a concert, check out a recording from the library.) As you listen to the music, think about his complete devotion to God. In what area of your life are you lacking faith? Ask God to help you trust Him completely.

For you know that we dealt with each of you as a father deals with his own children, encouraging, comforting and urging you to live lives worthy of God, who calls you into his kingdom and glory.

−1 THESSALONIANS 2:11, 12

Today is the birthday of composer of Francois Joseph Gossec, born in Belgium in 1734. Much of his long life was spent in Paris, as one of the first composition professors at the Paris Conservatory. His influence on dozens of French composers is very evident. In fact, he was the first in France to compose symphonies.

Yet Gossec did not begin his life as a musical prodigy, nor was he born into a cultured or well-educated family. Young Gossec was a cowherd, and might have spent his entire life with cows if someone hadn't noticed an innate musical talent and sent him to the Antwerp Cathedral. He was accepted as a chorister there and given musical training. At seventeen, he traveled to Paris, where he was mentored by the great French composer, Jean Philippe Rameau. Under Rameau's encouragement, operas, symphonies, and chamber music began to flow from Gossec's pen.

The concert halls of Paris are a long way from Gossec's cow pastures, and he would never have arrived there without the reassurance and support of specific people. We have all had such people in our own lives: the teacher who gave us extra time, the relative who supported us when no one else would, the friend who encouraged us when we were discouraged.

As we ponder the turning points in our past and remember those special people who made them possible, we should ask ourselves: "Whom have I encouraged? Who would place me in the top five people of his or her life?" If we can't think of anyone, perhaps it is time to find someone who could use a helping hand.

Think of one person who has made a difference in your life. Write that person a note of thanks, then ask God to show you someone whom you could encourage.

Make the most of every opportunity. Let your conversation be always full of grace, seasoned with salt, so that you may know how to answer everyone. –COLOSSIANS 4:5, 6

On January 18, 1835, a son was born to a French soldier who had come to Russia with Napoleon's invasion, been wounded, and remained behind. The baby was Cesar Cui, and he would have both a musical and a military life, actually rising to the rank of general in the Russian army. Cui was also to become one of Russia's finest composers of his day, and was a member of the famous group of Russian composers known as "The Five."

One notable fact about The Five—which included Cui, Rimsky-Korsakof, Borodin, Balakiref, and Mussorgsky—is that none was a professional musician. Each of them had full-time occupations and composed his music "on the side." Yet their compositions were quite remarkable, and their musical work has always been taken very seriously.

Cui, for example, was not only a great musician, but he also became one of his army's top experts on the subject of fortification. He was well known and admired in musical circles, and even his fellow generals appreciated his talent as a musician.

In the same way, each of us has a ministry even if we are not in full-time church work. God does not expect all the work of the Gospel to be done by professional preachers and missionaries. We need to take our "on the side" ministry seriously and exercise it with every possible occasion.

Next Sunday morning, count the number of people it takes to make your worship service happen. Include everyone, from the ushers at the door to the people serving in the nursery to the ladies making coffee for the fellowship time after the service. Out of all those people, how many are paid, full-time church staff? Ask God where He might want you to serve in your church.

Teach us to number our days aright, that we may gain a heart of wisdom. —PSALM 90:12

America does not have the monopoly on popular Christian bands, as evidenced by the Newsboys from Australia. In the 1990s, their success skyrocketed with their theatrical performances—wearing quite an assortment of extravagant outfits—and with their distinctively Australian accents. The Newsboys are so effective in giving performances that they've probably set world records for endurance: In 1995 they gave almost 250 concerts, sometimes three in a single day.

As you might imagine, such grueling schedules can be very tough on the performers. Their drummer, Peter Furler, once explained that, "When you do this for months in a row, you don't want to talk to anyone. You get burned out." So the Newsboys have limited their appearances, but not to the detriment of their successes. Furler notes, "We definitely could do more, and I hope we can find that balance as the band continues to grow."

Yet there is a price to pay for such common sense decisions. Cutting back usually means cutting out some "good things." For instance, in their former frenzied schedule, the Newsboys used to perform in dozens of antidrug concerts for high school audiences. But when they adjusted their schedule to find a better balance in their ministry, these concerts had to go. Furler says that some of the fans complained. "Man, you won't come to our high school anymore. You guys are selling out." But as Furler wisely concludes, "If we had kept doing that much longer, I guarantee you there wouldn't be a Newsboys today."

We simply *cannot* do everything, even all the "good things" we would like to do. Our job is to prayerfully discern what God wants us to do, to follow through on those things, and to be content with our decision. That means sometimes we have to say "no," and people may not understand. If we don't learn to say no, however, burnout is inevitable, and then nothing gets done at all.

Make a list in order of what is important to you. Now make a list of everything you do in a day and how much time you spend on each activity. How does your time compare to your priorities? Ask God to help you make changes where needed.

Teach me to do your will, for you are my God; may your good Spirit lead me on level ground. —PSALM 143:10

For decades Count Basie has been a household name. Even those who are unfamiliar with his special brand of swing have heard of "The Count." Yet in his early days, he—along with thousands of other young musicians—struggled to find recognition. He had many lessons to learn, and one of them was to never "jump at the first offer."

The American Record Company had heard Count Basie's band and decided to offer the Count a fine recording contract. John Hammond was sent to negotiate the deal, but he found that he wasn't the only one pursuing the Count Basie. When he met with the Count in Saint Louis, Missouri, Basie began, "A friend of yours was here to see me, John." Hammond's heart sank as he discovered that Count Basie had actually signed with a competitor.

In an effort to help, Hammond said, "Let me see what you signed." As he looked over Basie's new contract, he knew that this young musician had just been swindled. The contract demanded twelve new recordings a year for three years, only paying Basie $750 per annum with no royalties. Not only was this fee below the Musicians' Union minimum scale, but it would also mean no income from the massive record sales of such classics as "Jumping at the Woodside" and "One O'Clock Jump."

Fortunately, Count Basie's successful career eventually rewarded him well, but this first lesson with recording contracts was a difficult one. How often do we fail to receive the blessings God has planned for us because we don't take the time to talk to Him about a decision before we make it? Sometimes we settle for second best when God was just about to open a new and greater door for us.

Do you have any important decisions to make soon? Before you do, do your homework. Talk to your parents or pastor about it, and above all, talk to God about it, asking what He would have you do.

"For everyone who exalts himself will be humbled, and he who humbles himself will be exalted." —LUKE 14:11

In 1795, Franz Joseph Haydn was asked to help solve a conflict concerning the music for the wedding of the Prince of Wales. Three noted musicians—Dr. Parsons, conductor of the King's Band, and the two organists of the Royal Chapel—all insisted that they should have the honor of conducting the royal wedding music. On January 21 of that year, Haydn dined with the three contenders.

None of them wanted to back down. The peace-loving Haydn writes, "When forced to express my opinion, I said: 'The younger organist should play the organ, the other conduct the singers, while Dr. Parsons should conduct the instrumental performers.' This did not suit them, so I left the blockheads and went home."

How often have the notorious egos of performers lead to arguments and conflicts? Handel even watched as two rival sopranos began a slapping, kicking, scraping fight—on stage in the middle of his opera! James asks, "What causes fights and quarrels among you? Don't they come from your desires that battle within you?" (James 4:1).

Wanting praise and recognition that places us above our friends can hurt our spiritual growth as well as hurt those around us. A mark of spiritual maturity is the power to let go of this ego drive, to offer to take the last chair, and to be a servant to others.

To remind yourself to have a humble, servant's heart, cut out a heart shape from a piece of paper. Think of each person in your family and write on the heart one way you can serve each of them. Pray that God will give you a servant's heart today.

But one thing I do: Forgetting what is behind and straining toward what is ahead, I press on toward the goal to win the prize for which God has called me heavenward in Christ Jesus. —PHILIPPIANS 3:13, 14

Songwriter and performer Michael W. Smith is an artist who has learned to keep going against the odds. It was only after pulling himself out of the drug culture that he turned his diverse musical talents to serving Christ. He became a very creative songwriter for such singers as Sandi Patty, Larnelle Harris, Kathy Troccoli, and Amy Grant. Indeed, Smith is one of the first CCM composers since Bill Gaither whose songs have appeared in many mainline hymnbooks.

The perseverance that made all of this possible was learned at an early age. Like thousands of other boys, Smith played on a baseball team, this one coached by his father. He remembers one season for an unusual reason: the team had lost the first fifteen games in a row!

But his father refused to let them become discouraged. Smith recalls that "my dad would always say after every time we lost that we would get 'em next time, boys!" And sure enough, his positive attitude finally paid off. Game number sixteen, the last of the season, was won by Smith's team. He remembers that they were so elated that, "we thought we'd won the World Series."

After a number of defeats or setbacks, it's all too common to become discouraged. You can find yourself thinking, "I just don't have what it takes." But we must never give in to such negative thoughts. At one time Michael W. Smith was a mixed-up druggie, seemingly without a future. Now he is one of the true leaders in contemporary Christian music. He turned away from previous defeats and won. By God's grace, we can too.

Is there an area in your life that has repeatedly given you difficulty? Ask God for grace and perseverance, and try again. It may be that the very next try will finally reward you with victory.

In Christ we who are many form one body, and each member belongs to all the others. –ROMANS 12:5

Many composers have been stereotyped as "absent-minded professors," and many have well deserved it. One who would certainly qualify is Muzio Clementi, who was born January 23, 1752. Young piano students know of his popular sonatinas, but few know of his hilariously peculiar behavior.

Once Clementi and a cellist friend named Crosdill were invited for a summer visit with the earl of Pembroke. After they had all been bathing, Crosdill, as a joke, hid Clementi's shirt. The composer came in and dressed perfectly, including his waistcoat, without even noticing that he wore no shirt. Entering the beautiful house, the shirtless Clementi met the other guests, not observing their incredulity, and was happy to oblige when a lady asked him to perform. While playing the piano, he became hot and unconsciously began to unbutton the entire length of his coat. As the lady quickly moved to the other end of the room, the earl—in convulsed laughter—finally let Clementi in on the joke.

Music history is filled with hundreds of such anecdotes, and we are usually quite amused by them. We might not be, however, if the absent-minded composer were our parent, or best friend, or sibling. Suddenly the smiles vanish, and our shame or embarrassment begins to take over.

How tolerant are we toward people who are different? How do we feel toward people in our church who aren't just like us? Do we think that heaven will be filled with Christians who have personalities just like our own? As we stop and think of people who irritate us, we need to ask God to fill us with His love for them.

Is there an eccentric person in your life? Take a moment to pray God's blessing upon him or her. Then give that person a call or write a short note of encouragement.

Then, because so many people were coming and going that they did not even have a chance to eat, he said to them, "Come with me by yourselves to a quiet place and get some rest." –MARK 6:31

When singer/guitarist/songwriter Margaret Becker moved to Nashville in 1985, she had almost nothing for the world to see. She did have incredible talent and an equally incredible faith. Within a decade she was one of the biggest names in the contemporary Christian music world. Becker had recorded eight solo albums, which included fifteen number one singles, and had been awarded three Dove Awards and five SESAC's (Society of European Stage Authors and Composers) Songwriter of the Year Awards.

With so many successes behind her, she was expected by all to continue cranking out album after album, complete with extended concert tours. The conventional wisdom of the Nashville music business insists that an artist produce a new album every twelve to eighteen months to sustain momentum. In 1995, however, she felt that God was calling her to a different setting.

"I became a hermit," Becker later explained. "I took a house on the ocean in winter. I decided to sit there until I felt aired, and I was quiet enough to hear where my life had been and where it was going. It was a four-week retreat that turned into almost three months."

This period of waiting on God continued. It was actually three years before she made her next album. The wait was certainly worth it. After taking the time to clearly discern the direction God was giving her, she then produced some of her best work to date. The resulting album, entitled *Falling Forward*, has made a great impact for Christ.

We all need to have our "batteries recharged" from time to time. With all the noise and busyness of our lives today, it can be difficult to hear the voice of the Lord. When was the last time you set aside some quiet time to be with God?

Need some special time with God? Find a quiet place—no TV, no radio, no computer—set a timer for fifteen minutes, and just listen to the quiet. Then thank God for His presence in the peace.

Obey your leaders and submit to their authority. They keep watch over you as men who must give an account. Obey them so that their work will be a joy, not a burden, for that would be of no advantage to you.

—HEBREWS 13:17

Wilhelm Furtwangler, one of Germany's finest conductors, was born on this date in 1886. A musician through and through, he got himself into trouble during World War II. Furtwangler naïvely thought he could divorce himself from Nazi politics—even as conductor of the Berlin Philharmonic. He was respected for his serious musicianship, however, because he was one of the few conductors of his day who did not believe in being a tyrant.

In fact, Furtwangler was so intuitive in his music that orchestra members were often baffled. He knew what he wanted out of his players, but his verbal skills were not up to his musical genius. A typical quote from a Furtwangler rehearsal was, "Gentlemen, this phrase must be—it must—it must—you know what I mean—please try it again—please."

Often, members of an orchestra complain that the conductor is a dictator with an ego problem. However, Furtwangler's strange methods and obscure baton technique left his musicians longing for clearer leadership. A musician who was new to the orchestra once asked a colleague, "How do you know when to come in with such a mysterious downbeat?" He was answered, "When we lose patience."

All great leaders have their own leadership style, and their followers either adjust to it or no longer follow. If we find ourselves under the authority of someone who is either too lenient or is a dictator, we have to learn to adjust. We also need to remember that God is the Supreme Authority and we must ultimately answer to Him.

Plan to attend a concert soon. Take note of the conductor and his leadership style. What would the music sound like if the orchestral members didn't follow his lead? What does life look like for a person who doesn't follow God's lead? Thank Him for leading your life.

Let us hold unswervingly to the hope we profess, for he who promised is faithful. –HEBREWS 10:23

The date January 26 will always bring a tear to fans of a cellist. It is the birthday of Jacqueline du Pre, one of the most talented cellists of the twentieth century, whose brilliant career was cut short at the age of twenty-six by multiple sclerosis. Jackie was born in 1945 to a musical family in Oxford. At four years old she insisted on having a full-size cello, and she quickly managed to play the huge instrument.

Her first concert was at age seven, and while still in her teens, she performed concerti with orchestras all over Europe. Critics everywhere agreed that du Pre was a phenomenal talent. Throughout the 1960s, she was called Britain's finest musician, and her recordings and concerts inspired rave reviews. In the seventies, however, the onset of her disease slowly brought her playing to a tragic end. After a long and courageous struggle, Jacqueline du Pre died in October 1987.

A thousand questions flood our minds: "How could God allow this to happen?" "What did the young girl do to deserve such a painful, untimely end?" "Why didn't God heal her?" "Doesn't God care?!"

Many things we will simply not understand in this world. When we face such trying times, though, we must remember that God is just, God is good, and God is worthy of our trust. "Now we see but a poor reflection as in a mirror" (1 Corinthians 13:12), but we must believe that someday all our questions will be answered.

Do you know someone who has recently experienced the death of a family member or close friend? Take a moment to write that person a loving note with an appropriate Scripture, such as Psalm 23.

> *The Lord sends poverty and wealth; he humbles and he exalts.*
>
> —1 SAMUEL 2:7

If anyone has known the extremes outlined in the above Scripture, it would be the songwriter and performer Merle Travis. His life began in extreme poverty in Rosewood, Kentucky. His father worked in the coal mines under atrocious conditions, and it seemed that his son's life would also be bound to the mines.

But in the little free time that the boy had, he started playing around with a homemade guitar and an old banjo. At Pentecostal church meetings he picked up tips from local folk musicians and was soon an accomplished guitarist. During the Depression, he formed a band and then began to play on radio programs. Later he was signed by Capitol Records, for which he wrote a number of hit country songs. Travis had eluded the mines forever.

Then Capitol asked him to write some folkstyle ballads. Travis tried his best, but these efforts yielded only frustration. None of the new songs seemed to fit his voice and personality, so he went back to his old style. But a few years later another singer—a disc jockey who had been educated at the Cincinnati Conservatory of Music—took one of Travis' folk ballads and made it famous. In 1955, "Tennessee" Ernie Ford recorded "Sixteen Tons." It became the number one single for months across America.

What was the inspiration of Travis' clever composition? The coal mines of his youth. "Sixteen Tons" did more than make Travis and Ford national stars; it focused the country's attention on the miserable plight of coal miners. Soon officials investigated mining conditions and mistreatment, which led to many important improvements. This was the result of a songwriter who did not forget his humble beginnings and the misfortunes of those he left behind.

Just as Travis' painful past was eventually used to help others, so God can work through our hurts or disappointments to help others. Our part is to be open to His leading, to not forget what He's done in our lives, and to be willing to share our experiences.

Ask someone you know, a grandparent or older person in your church, what life was like during the Great Depression. Praise God for all the blessings you have today.

And whatever you do, whether in word or deed, do it all in the name of the Lord Jesus, giving thanks to God the Father through him.

−COLOSSIANS 3:17

On Sunday, January 28, 1725, the first performance was given of Johann Sebastian Bach's Cantata no. 92, "Ich hab in Gottes Herz und Sinn" ("I have into God's Heart and Being"). The text is one Bach must have cherished, affirming the love between God and himself.

A melody that is heard in five movements of this sacred work was originally a French secular song that Bach "redeemed" for his use in worshiping the Lord. Bach "borrowed" such music quite often, for like Luther before him, he questioned, "Why should the Devil have all the good music?" Indeed, hundreds of composers through the centuries have practiced the art of "redeeming" secular music for use in the church.

Bach made no real distinction between sacred and secular music, believing that all should glorify God. In such "secular" works as his *Little Organ Book,* he wrote: "To God alone the praise be given for what's herein for man's use written." His *Little Clavier Book,* like so many of his compositions, was inscribed, "In the Name of Jesus."

In our society, we are conditioned to think of some actions as sacred, while others are seen as secular. But everything we do, no matter how trivial, should be done to the glory of God. As we have been redeemed, so our actions should be redeemed to reflect the changed life the Lord has given us.

Who is your favorite contemporary Christian musician? How has he or she "redeemed" secular music today? Ask God to help you redeem the areas of your life that remain secular.

Here there is no Greek or Jew, circumcised or uncircumcised, bar-barian, Scythian, slave or free, but Christ is all, and is in all.

–COLOSSIANS 3:11

The great American contralto Marian Anderson was born in Philadelphia, Pennsylvania, in 1902. When the well-known conductor Toscanini heard her sing, he exclaimed, "The voice that comes once in a hundred years."

Most of Anderson's career was spent on the concert stage, but her greatest claim to fame occurred in 1955: she became the first black singer to ever perform at the Metropolitan Opera in New York. She sang beautifully in the role of Ulrica in Verdi's opera *The Masked Ball.* Nevertheless, many "old-school" opera lovers complained to the Met about such casting, and it was still many years before all opera singers were given equal access to American stages—without regard for the color of their skin.

What a disgrace that such prejudice still exists! The evil of discrimination is certainly not new; even Christ had to endure it ("Nazareth! Can anything good come from there?" John 1:46). Scripture tells us of the prejudice against Samaritans, but we see Jesus breaking down that barrier time and again. He ministered to the woman at the well (John 4:7-26), commended the good Samaritan in His parable (Luke 10:30-37), and healed Samaritans in need (Luke 17:11-19). Clearly, God wants us to love everyone just as He does.

As much as we like to think it isn't, prejudice is still alive and well today. We all have some prejudice that we need to ask God to remove from our hearts. "God does not show favoritism" (Romans 2:11). Neither should we.

Think of your circle of closest friends. Does it include someone of another race or culture? If not, ask God to introduce you to someone of a different race with whom you can start a friendship.

"For who is greater, the one who is at the table or the one who serves? Is it not the one who is at the table? But I am among you as one who serves." –LUKE 22:27

Today's birthday of the French composer Francis Poulenc (1899–1963) brings up a centuries-old question: Is the performer the servant of the composer and his music, or is the composer the servant of the performer (that is, providing him the music he needs)? Let us consider this through the life of Poulenc.

By his death in 1963, he had established himself as one of his country's greatest composers. His brilliant choral music, concertos, chamber music, songs, and works for the piano have firmly established his reputation. Poulenc's deep faith worked with his clever originality to create some of the twentieth century's finest sacred compositions—especially his "Gloria" for soprano solo, chorus, and orchestra.

Yet this renowned composer owed much to an outstanding performer, the Spanish pianist Ricardo Vines. All but forgotten now, Vines was famous in his day for premiering the works of modern composers such as Debussy and Ravel. Poulenc would later admit freely, "I owe him everything. It is really to Vines that I owe my first flights in music and everything I know about the piano."

In the early decades of the twentieth century, the musical public knew Vines and ignored Poulenc. Today, they have forgotten Vines and have learned to appreciate Poulenc's innovations. But both were ultimately servants of each other. The composer—often inspired by a great performer's skill—composes music so that performers will have something to play. And the performers play the music so that they bring out the genius of the composer.

Life is full of relationships in which people end up serving each other. God designed it that way. Whom does God want you to serve today?

Plan and serve an entire meal for your family. How did it feel to be the one serving instead of the one being served? Ask God to show you other ways to serve those around you.

Honor one another above yourselves. –ROMANS 12:10

The world of contemporary Christian music is a place of spiritual ministry. But it can also be a place of pressured competition, as many hundreds of artists all try to send their songs into the realm of megahits. The temptation of self-promotion—even at the cost of putting someone else down—can be very real and difficult to resist.

Yet the true servants do resist this urge and receive the blessing of God as a result. Songwriter/performer Wes King certainly has had his share of success, in Dove awards, best-selling albums, and sold-out concerts. But his humility shines through all he accomplishes.

Known for his sensitive storytelling lyrics and powerful voice, King is also a very accomplished guitarist in a field where almost every artist plays that instrument. Rather than playing a simple accompaniment, he uses the guitar to intricately enhance the melody. Yet when asked about his remarkable guitar skills, he modestly chooses to remove himself from the "greats." "I get embarrassed by any comparisons to the skillfully elite, because players like that are a light-year or two beyond me," he insists. "They are in another category altogether."

His fans would certainly disagree with this assessment, but no one could overlook King's admirable humility. In a world filled with ego-driven desires and selfish rivalries, how refreshing is a truly humble brother in the Lord! It is no wonder that God has been able to use Wes King in a very powerful ministry.

How do you feel about "honoring others above yourself"? Does it bring out fears and insecurities? Ask God to help you find a way today to build someone up with encouragement.

> John answered, "The man with two tunics should share with him who has none, and the one who has food should do the same." —LUKE 3:11

Clarinetist Benny Goodman is one of the most famous musicians of the twentieth century. His virtuoso technique and smooth, almost liquid, sound combined to make him an expert in many musical fields. Most know about his work in jazz and swing music, yet he was so versatile he could play the *Ebony Concerto* by Igor Stravinsky—a difficult work now in the classical repertoire.

Goodman had such high standards of excellence that for many musicians, he seemed very difficult to work with. Yet he could be extremely generous when he found a deserving young musician in need. A good example concerns the great saxophonist Lester Young, often known as "The Prez."

Long before Young became well-known, his superb playing was heard by John Hammond, a friend of Bennie Goodman. Hammond wanted Goodman to hear this talented youth, so he arranged for a late-night jam session in New York. It included many of the finest players of the day, including Count Basie, but the session's main point was to showcase Lester Young.

After hearing only a few notes, Goodman was enormously impressed. He pulled out his clarinet and joined in the music making himself. Later in the evening, Lester Young set down his sax and played a clarinet solo. The only one he had was an old battered metal clarinet, but his talent still shown through the inferior instrument. Afterward, Bennie Goodman handed his own excellent clarinet to Young: "Here, take mine," he smiled, and insisted that he keep the gift permanently.

Just as Goodman saw the potential in Young and was willing to give him a great gift to help him fulfill his potential, so God sees our potential and offers us a gift—a priceless gift—called salvation. All we need to do is accept it.

Have you accepted God's gift of salvation? If you have, thank Him for it again today. If you haven't, talk to a pastor or Christian friend about what it means to become a follower of Christ.

Bear with each other and forgive whatever grievances you may have against one another. Forgive as the Lord forgave you. –COLOSSIANS 3:13

Instead of "Groundhog Day," today might be called "National Violin Day," since it is the birthday of two of the greatest violinists the world has ever known. On this day in 1875, Fritz Kreisler was born in Austria, and in 1901, Jascha Heifetz was born in Russia. Both were celebrated performers, but Kreisler also had a claim as a musicologist (one who studies music)—at least, for a while—and then, as a composer.

This requires further explanation. You see, for years Fritz Kreisler supplied his publisher with manuscript after manuscript of pieces by the masters, which he had "discovered." Dozens of works were published in his "Classical Manuscripts" series, which became famous under such names as Boccherini's *Allegretto*, Couperin's *La Precieuse*, Bach's *Grave*, and Vivaldi's *Violin Concerto in C*.

In 1935, Kreisler created a huge controversy when he announced that all these pieces and many others were actually his own compositions. He saw nothing but humor in the situation, but not everyone else took it so lightly. In fact, hundreds of his former fans never forgave Kreisler, and some badgered him about it until his death in 1962.

While it is easy to see the wrong in Kreisler's foolish deception, such a lifelong withholding of forgiveness by his fellow musicians brings up an important question: How easy is it for us to forgive? Are there some actions that we consider impossible to forgive? We must remember Christ's words, "If you do not forgive men their sins, your Father will not forgive your sins" (Matthew 6:15).

Has anyone ever done something to you that you have decided to never forgive? Find a chalkboard and write on it what it is you're having trouble forgiving. Ask God to help you forgive the person who hurt you. Wash the chalkboard clean as you forgive, and forget, the hurt.

"As I was with Moses, so I will be with you; I will never leave you nor forsake you." –JOSHUA 1:5

English scholars will tell you that Avalon is a legendary island paradise to which King Arthur sailed at the end of his life. Young people will tell you that Avalon is a fantastic group of four Christian singers. The precision of the group's tight vocals has contributed to its many hits. When one member feels that it is time to leave such a celebrated group, it can be very difficult to find a suitable replacement.

When this happened to Avalon, the new singer selected was Cherie Paliotta. She knew that she had a tough act to follow. The departing member of the group was Nikki Hassman, an excellent singer whose voice was known by many fans. Could Cherie measure up to this challenge?

Cherie felt that God had called her to Avalon. She remembers, "I'd been praying that the Lord would open a door for me." Then three different friends independently recommended her to Avalon. "It was definitely divine appointment," was her response to their choice.

The result? "It was a big change for me when I came into Avalon. There were days when I didn't think I could get up there and remember one more lyric. But God came through for me in those moments and gave me the courage to anchor onto Him and move forward." A lot of hard work plus the blessing of God made the new singer a perfect fit. At the next Dove Awards, Avalon was voted New Artist of the Year.

When you are in a new position and start to feel insecure, remember the Lord who put you there. He is able to sustain you, and if you commit yourself fully to Him, He can make your plans succeed.

Listen to a song performed by Avalon. Notice particularly how well their voices blend. Is there someone you know who is the "new kid on the block" as Cherie Paliotta was to Avalon? How can you help that person blend in to your community? Ask God for His help.

And as for you, brothers, never tire of doing what is right.

—2 THESSALONIANS 3:13

For many years, all the conductors of the major American orchestras had been born in Europe. This was the case for Erich Leinsdorf, born in Austria this day in 1912. He was educated at the Vienna Conservatory and was Toscanini's assistant in Salzburg. But he became a household name conducting in America, especially with the Metropolitan Opera Company and the Boston Symphony Orchestra.

Every great conductor brings his own style to the podium. For Leinsdorf, this meant precision, attention to detail, and painstaking care in the playing of every note. Such a systematic approach is very demanding on the players, but Leinsdorf's method always resulted in an indisputable creation of technical perfection. Instead of complaining, his players found themselves wanting to work extra hard for him.

There's an old saying among musicians that states, "There are no good and bad orchestras, only good and bad conductors." While it usually brings a smile, there is certainly an element of truth in this saying. A master conductor brings out the best in an orchestra, sometimes even to the members' surprise. And sadly, the reverse is true as well. Even the best orchestras can sound wretched when being led by an incompetent conductor.

How do we affect those around us? Do we bring out the best in people? Even when we are not aware of it, our actions, attitudes, and words affect those around us—for good or for ill. God is the Master Conductor and brings out the best in everyone. We need to imitate His example.

How can we bring out the best in those around us? Say at least one kind or encouraging word to every person you see today. Praise God for His willingness to bring out the best in each of us.

Whatever you do, work at it with all your heart, as working for the Lord, not for men. –COLOSSIANS 3:23

Stephen Clapp is the dean of the Juilliard School in New York City, which contains one of the finest music departments in the world. His faculty includes dozens of world-class performers who work with the highest caliber of aspiring students. But in his own career as a virtuoso violinist, he has been able to apply many biblical principles to the world of music.

Clapp asks: "Who is your audience? Do you think they're counting wrong notes? I can remember once, early in my career, being very conscious that a trustee of my college was listening, and I wanted desperately to impress her. I got so tight that the notes themselves, much less subtleties and nuances, just didn't come across."

Such an experience illustrates the importance of our musical focus. He continues: "If your music is a grateful act of worship to your Lord, and you think about communicating this God-given gift of beautiful music to listeners who are hungry for a lift, you'll be freed from the perfectionistic obsession which results in stiffness. If you focus on somebody out there, or yourself and all the details, it won't sing. It won't fly."

He concludes: "If God is the Observer before whom you live your life in all its activities, you will experience joy, and the freedom to play as well as you can. Maybe a little bit better."

Take a manual camera, or an automatic one with a telephoto lens, and look through the lens, focusing on different objects both near and far. What happens to the other objects in the picture when you change your focus? Ask the Lord to help you stay focused on Him.

"See that you do not look down on one of these little ones. For I tell you that their angels in heaven always see the face of my Father in heaven."
—MATTHEW 18:10

We often do not realize the critical part we may play in someone's life. Sometimes this causes us to miss opportunities for ministry. For instance, if we knew that the student, neighbor, or coworker next to us would grow up to be "the next Billy Graham," we would be very motivated to share our faith with him. But we don't know that, and in the meantime he may seem rather unimportant and ordinary.

This can be illustrated in the life of singer/songwriter Susan Ashton. Today she is a top CCM success, with sold-out concerts, top-selling albums, and Dove Awards to her credit. Her voice is so extraordinary that she is often sought by the top mainstream artists as well, such as when she toured with singer Garth Brooks.

But of course, Ashton was not always a star. As a Texas girl of eleven, she started smoking and drinking hard liquor. She could have gone the way of the world, except for a youth group that she somewhat unwillingly attended with her sister. Ashton tells that "we ended up liking it, thanks to a couple of kids who followed up our visit." A few months later, she accepted Christ and changed her lifestyle to reflect her new beliefs. The rest is history.

"Thanks to a couple of kids who followed up our visit." Those kids did not know that they were ministering to Susan Ashton, future star. They simply saw her as a child of God who needed His love. When you next hear an Ashton song or see her in a packed concert, consider the vital role that those kids played in a ministry that has touched thousands for the Lord.

Next Sunday, make a visit to your church's nursery. Say a prayer for every baby you see, asking God to place people in each one's life who will help him or her grow to know His love.

Do not forget to entertain strangers, for by so doing some people have entertained angels without knowing it. —HEBREWS 13:2

If you unexpectedly met someone very important, perhaps someone who could really help you, how would you act toward that person? It would be a natural response to fall all over him with smiles, compliments, and polite offers of help. If that is the case, why not show such kindness to everyone you meet? Would not God bless such efforts?

Two of Nashville's top songwriters, DeWayne Blackwell and Earl "Bud" Lee, decided one day to purchase a new pair of boots. The young salesman who waited on them had no idea who they were, but he gave them such care and expert attention that both were sincerely impressed. He carefully brought out pair after pair of boots and explained each one down to the last detail. Bud Lee later remembered his cheerful attitude: "We really liked this guy. He was polite and did everything he could to make sure we got a good deal."

During their lively conversation, the sales clerk found out that his customers were songwriters. His face glowed as he began to share his own aspirations to become a top singer. He was newly married and had come to Nashville to try to get into the music business. After finding that the young man had a solid singing background and was working hard, they agreed to hear him.

The boot salesman's name was Garth Brooks, and that was his first big break. He was initially hired by the songwriters to sing on their demo tapes, but the talent of Brooks now had an outlet to be heard. Within a few months, he had a contract with Capitol Records and was on his way to being a superstar. Only three years after leaving his job as a boot salesman, Garth Brooks made over fifty million dollars as one of America's favorite singers. It all began with a sincere attitude of polite service to two strangers. Today is Garth Brooks' birthday.

Think about how you act when you are with someone you want to impress. Now show that same kindness and friendliness toward the first stranger you meet this week. Ask God to help you practice this attitude until it becomes a part of your character.

"Now I know that you fear God, because you have not withheld from me your son, your only son." –GENESIS 22:12

Very few of us have ever had to undergo such a difficult test as Abraham—being willing to sacrifice his only son. Yet tests do come for us, and often they involve laying down something that means a great deal to us. The hardest tests are called "death of a vision," deliberately setting aside—at least for a season—something that you know God has given you.

Singer/songwriter Layton Howerton has made some tough choices to follow the Lord in his life. Born with musical gifts, he also felt that God wanted him to become a pastor. When his musical career began to blossom, the pastoral call was put aside. But finally, Howerton surrendered to God and left Nashville for a church in Wyoming. He remembers, "I left my music behind. I suddenly had such a powerful assurance that pastoral ministry was His will for my life that music just didn't even matter anymore."

Yet the Lord wasn't finished with Howerton. While he was faithfully pastoring, a friend told his wife, "You tell Layton that he may think he's done with that music, but God is going to use it in a way that Layton never dreamed of to reach people." He was correct. Howerton wrote songs to go along with his sermons, and eventually these songs found their way to an executive at Sparrow Records. His first album, appropriately entitled *Boxing God*, beautifully describes his long journey in following Christ.

Layton Howerton was willing to lay down his musical career, but God soon brought it back from the dead. He declares, "When I finally surrendered, I wound up realizing that it wasn't a sacrifice at all; it was simply obedience. Now I tell people, 'You wanna see things happen? Don't just behave. Be obedient.' "

What would be difficult for you to give up at this time? Ask God if there is anything that is between you and His perfect will for your life. Write down whatever you think that might be, place it in a box, wrap it as a gift, and offer it back to the Lord.

You, therefore, have no excuse, you who pass judgment on someone else, for at whatever point you judge the other, you are condemning yourself, because you who pass judgment do the same things. –ROMANS 2:1

Today is the birthday of the serialist composer Alban Berg, born in Vienna, Austria, in 1885. A pupil of Arnold Schoenberg, Berg's music is very complex and difficult to comprehend quickly. During his lifetime, he became quite accustomed to musical rejection.

In one performance in 1935, the Viennese audience—reinforced by Nazi troublemakers—began shouting over the music, "Long live Tchaikovsky!" On hearing this, Berg observed wryly, "Poor boys. Their grandfathers behaved just the same when Tchaikovsky's Fifth Symphony was played in this hall forty years ago. Only then they shouted for some Schubert!"

From the beginning of music history until today, composers have been rejected when trying anything new or modern. Such compositions as Beethoven's string quartets were considered abominable when they were written, but are now recognized as genius and are performed everywhere. In our own day, symphony orchestras can lose hundreds of needed subscriptions if they perform too much modern music. Most of us seem to dislike or resist change.

Christ Himself was rejected by many people because they could not tolerate the changes He was proclaiming. We do not have to be old in years to be "set in our ways." We each need to examine our hearts and our openness to change. We need to use wisdom in areas new to us, or we may find ourselves rejecting something that God has indeed inspired.

Ask yourself a tough question: Of the many people you know, is there anyone you may have unjustly judged? Ask God to show you how to turn away from judging and to accept others as He accepts us.

Accept one another, then, just as Christ accepted you, in order to bring praise to God. –ROMANS 15:7

Who is wiser? Is it the man who insists that he is smarter than someone else, or is it the man who humbly allows others to degrade him—while inwardly knowing the truth of his own worth? Let us see who is the wiser man in today's story of jazz great Eubie Blake.

When jazz was in its infancy, it was unusual for many players to know how to read music. Those who could do so were dubbed "Professor," and sometimes treated with suspicion. There were, of course, many exceptions, such as the brilliant African-American musician Eubie Blake, who could read music and compose with ease.

Yet those early days contained so much prejudice and bigotry that some white owners of jazz clubs could not bring themselves to believe that a black man could be well educated or intelligent. Blake remembers: "In those days, Negro musicians weren't even supposed to read music." It was as if the owners felt threatened if a black musician could perform this task as well as white musicians.

Blake could have made a scene to display his reading abilities, which would have unfortunately caused his band's dismissal. Instead, he chose a humbler idea, seating his band members in front of the music stands and playing fabulously. "We had to pretend we couldn't read," he later explained, "then they'd marvel at the way we could play shows, thinking we'd learned the parts by ear." Since the owners assumed that Blake's band couldn't read, they were actually credited with the much greater feat of memorizing all the music of entire shows! As this enormously enhanced the band's reputation and success, Blake and his friends must have smiled to themselves.

Blake's humble approach ended up bringing him greater rewards than if he had chosen to make a scene. God notices when we act humbly and love and serve others. And though we may not see rewards for such service here on earth, we will be rewarded in eternity.

News of hate crimes or prejudice are, unfortunately, on the rise today. Take a look at the headlines in your paper, find a story of a person who has been a victim of that type of crime, and pray for that person for the upcoming week.

Therefore let us stop passing judgment on one another. Instead, make up your mind not to put any stumbling block or obstacle in your brother's way. –ROMANS 14:13

On this day in 1697, Georg Handel died—but not George Frederic Handel, one of history's greatest composers. It was his father, a "surgeon-barber" at the court of Weissenfels, in Saxony. His claim to fame was to leave a perfect example of how *not* to be a father to a talented young musician.

Georg Handel Senior disliked anything musical—he considered music-loving a sign of weakness!—and discouraged his son whenever possible. No one even knows how the young Handel taught himself to play the organ and clavier. His sympathetic mother helped him smuggle a spinet into the attic, covering the strings with strips of cloth so that Dad wouldn't hear any practicing.

At the age of seven, George Junior happened to perform for the duke (his father's boss), and so pleased his audience that his father was all but ordered to find a music teacher. At eleven he played so well for the electoral highnesses in Berlin that they offered to send him to Italy for further study. His outraged father canceled these plans.

Why such opposition? Georg Senior had long since decided that his son was to be a lawyer. He had pushed so long and hard for it that even five years after his death, George Junior entered the University of Halle as a law student, putting off his musical studies. Handel's father was so blinded by his expectations that he could not see his son's incredible talent that should have been obvious—and was to everyone else.

Have you ever stopped to consider how our expectations of those around us might be holding them back? We can't make other people into who we want them to be. We need to accept them as God created them, and encourage whatever work He may be doing in their lives.

Has anyone ever put a stumbling block in your path? Ask God to help you stick to His plan for your life, even when it seems others are against it.

Give thanks in all circumstances, for this is God's will for you in Christ Jesus. −1 THESSALONIANS 5:18

Great hymns have been cherished for decades, but do you know who holds the "world record" for writing more hymns than anyone else? Her name was Frances Jane Crosby (1820–1915), better known as "Fanny," and her grand total was more than 8,000! She actually did not begin to write hymns until the age of forty-four, but she lived ninety-five years and often wrote as many as eight hymns each day.

Attending a revival meeting in 1850, Crosby was profoundly moved by an Isaac Watts hymn, "Alas, and Did My Savior Bleed?" After committing herself to the Lord, she was inspired to write hymns with a similar mission: to bring people to Christ. In 1864, she met the Sunday School hymn writer William Bradbury, who was impressed with her talents and greatly encouraged her work. Crosby was soon under contract with the publisher Biglow and Main to submit three hymns each week for publication.

All of these accomplishments would be outstanding for any hymn writer, but it is even more remarkable when one knows that Fanny Crosby was blind. As a baby of six weeks old, she was permanently blinded by an incompetent country doctor's improper treatment, and yet she had no bitterness in her heart. Indeed, her positive attitude is an inspiration to all of us.

A minister once said to her, "I think it is a great pity that the Master did not give you sight when He showered so many other gifts upon you." But she exclaimed, "Do you know that if at birth I had been able to make one petition, it would have been that I should have been born blind?" When the astonished preacher asked, "Why?" she responded, "Because when I get to heaven, the first face that shall ever gladden my sight will be that of my Savior!"

Make a list of all the blessings in your life. Ask God to forgive any feelings of ingratitude you've had, and allow Him to fill your heart with cheerful thankfulness.

Everyone who competes in the games goes into strict training. They do it to get a crown that will not last; but we do it to get a crown that will last forever. –1 CORINTHIANS 9:25

It was on this day in 1883 that Richard Wagner (1813–1883) breathed his last. By the end of his life, the composer was known throughout the world for his musical accomplishments. When he premiered his massive four-opera cycle, *The Ring of the Nibelung,* in 1876, even his critics were awed by the composer's achievement.

But the name Wagner had not always been a household word. For three solid decades (until his music finally gained acceptance), the composer experienced more rejection than any other musician in written history.

Wagner's first opera was rejected, and his second was soon withdrawn. He was hired as a conductor at Konigsburg, and the company immediately went out of business. After being fired from another conducting job in Riga, he went to Paris, where, after another opera failed, he actually spent time in debtor's prison. By this time, his marriage was in ruins, debts continued to mount, and he was often sick, needing expensive medical treatments. Wagner's next few operas, all of which are in the repertoire today, were total flops.

Following such a series of disasters, one might have wondered if he had the right stuff to make a successful composer. But Wagner refused to acknowledge the word "impossible." In the midst of poverty and rejection, Wagner continued to write music that would someday shake the musical world.

Even those who do not enjoy his operas or respect his idiosyncratic character must have a profound regard for such unstoppable perseverance. Wagner's example causes us to ask ourselves, "How much opposition would it take to stop me from doing God's will in my life?" When we seek to do His will, we may not receive "crowns" of praise or glory here on earth, but we will receive a crown that will last forever.

When a musician is preparing for an important performance, he goes into "training," concentrating on practicing particular skills and music. Make up a training schedule for your Christian life, including time for prayer, worship, and service, and put it into practice today.

The Lord God said, "It is not good for the man to be alone. I will make a helper suitable for him." –GENESIS 2:18

Since this is Valentine's Day, it is time for a musical love story. Shakespeare wrote, "If music be the food of love, play on!" Perhaps he knew the ridiculous situations that often occur when musicians fall in love—as the following true story illustrates.

The composer Richard Strauss was also a talented conductor, especially of opera. In one rehearsal with the singer Pauline de Ahna, a disagreement developed over some minor musical point, and the singer threw a monstrous tantrum. She screamed at the conductor, ran off the stage and into her dressing room, and slammed the door. Needless to say, the orchestra members were stunned.

Strauss was not to be beaten so easily. He stopped the rehearsal, bolted after the singer, and—without knocking—charged into her room. As the astonished musicians waited, they heard hysterical shrieks from the struggle inside. The argument became louder and louder, then fell to a sudden silence.

The orchestra members gasped, wondering which of the two combatants might have killed the other. As Strauss quietly opened the door, the orchestra manager came forward nervously and said, "The orchestra is so horrified by the incredibly shocking behavior of Fraulein Pauline de Ahna that they feel they owe it to their honored conductor to refuse in the future to play in any opera in which she might have a part."

Strauss smiled at his orchestra's support, and then stammered, "That hurts me very much, for I have just become engaged to Fraulein de Ahna."

As you listen to the radio today, notice how many songs you hear about love. Thank God for His unending, unconditional love for us.

Let the wise listen and add to their learning. –PROVERBS 1:5

Nearly everyone knows that a Steinway piano is a very remarkable instrument. This reputation for excellence goes back to Heinrich Engelhard Steinway, who was born February 15, 1797. Although Steinway was German-born, he moved to America and made some of the first American instruments to rival those of European quality.

Of course, Steinway did not invent the piano, or any part of it. His talent was in improving what others had already done. His company was one of the first to master the important step of using an iron frame inside the piano. In 1874, the Steinway company became the first to perfect the sostenuto pedal (the third, or "middle" pedal on most good pianos). From the company's beginnings, the Steinway people have always found ways to improve upon the status quo.

There is nothing we do that could not be improved. When Scripture urges musicians to "play skillfully" (Psalm 33:3), it assumes that no one is born with such an ability. God gives us our talent, but it is our job to practice and develop our skill. The same is true in other areas of life as well. God gives us the ability, but it is up to us to work on improving ourselves for Him.

To improve your skill on whatever instrument you play, set aside an extra fifteen minutes to a half hour each day this week for additional practice. Praise God for the beauty of music and the talent He has given you.

He who ignores discipline despises himself, but whoever heeds correction gains understanding. –PROVERBS 15:32

The premiere of Jules Massenet's opera *Werther* took place on this date in 1892. The success of this opera—as well as Massenet's *Manon, Thais,* and many others—made the composer an influential figure in French music of his day. Singers all over Europe wanted to sing in Massenet's operas, which meant that he worked with both the "greats" and the inept.

One particular tenor exasperated Massenet because of his poor intonation. What made matters worse was that the singer had no idea he had this problem. After a performance in which the tenor was again unaware that he had sung flat all evening, he went backstage, hoping to receive congratulations from Massenet. "I hope you were pleased, chér Maître?" asked the tenor. "Delighted, delighted," answered the composer dryly, "but how could you sing with that dreadful orchestra? They accompanied you a half tone sharp all evening!"

Do we find ourselves "out of tune" with our friends or family? Is it possible that we are blind to character faults that are hurting others and perhaps even ourselves? The only way we can overcome the "blind spots" that sabotage our relationships is to allow someone we love and trust to gently point out those areas where we fall flat. Though none of us likes to hear what our weaknesses are, we need to be aware of them before we can change them. How does God want you to change?

Think of someone who you really trust; someone you know who loves you and will always be honest with you. Pray about meeting with this person for a heart-to-heart talk. It may be that God will use this friend to reveal something within you that, when changed, will help you to be more effective for the Lord.

Now you are the body of Christ, and each one of you is a part of it. –1 CORINTHIANS 12:27

Today is the birthday of the baroque composer Arcangelo Corelli (1653–1713), born in Fusignano, Italy. He wrote many wonderful pieces, including twelve concerto grossi and forty-eight trio sonatas. Probably his most famous composition is his Concerto Grosso Op. 6, no. 8, known as the "Christmas Concerto," which is played in hundreds of concert halls and churches every December.

Have you ever heard of him? Many people haven't. In fact, if a list were made of history's greatest composers, Corelli would not make it in the top three. Perhaps not even the top twenty. And yet his impact on the musical world has lasted for centuries. Corelli's musical influence has had a dramatic effect on hundreds of composers, even when some of the masters might never have heard of him!

How did he influence so many people without being rich and famous? It so happened that this composer made a key contribution to the art of writing for orchestra when that genre was just getting started. His innovation: he insisted that all the string players in his orchestra bow in the same way, a practice long since taken for granted. But in his day, this novel approach to performing produced (according to a contemporary account) "an amazing effect, even to the eye, as well as the ear."

No big deal? It may have seemed so then, but this practice revolutionized orchestral performance practice, making it possible for Mozart, Beethoven, and hundreds of other composers to create their masterpieces. Not everyone can be a Mozart or a Beethoven. Not everyone has those special talents. But everyone can make his contribution, and use the gifts he does possess.

Do you ever feel like a small, unnoticed part that doesn't make much difference? If so, try this. Unplug the phone line from your computer. (It's probably way in the back where it goes unnoticed.) Now try to get on-line, look something up on the Internet, e-mail a friend. What happens? Thank God for giving each of us a job to do, no matter how small it may seem.

Let the word of Christ dwell in you richly as you teach and admonish one another with all wisdom, and as you sing psalms, hymns and spiritual songs with gratitude in your hearts to God. —COLOSSIANS 3:16

Everyone knows Martin Luther (1483–1546) as the great leader of the Protestant Reformation. But few today realize what a major influence the musician Luther had on the history of Christian music. Not only did he compose hymns such as the well-known "A Mighty Fortress Is Our God," but he also helped to create an entirely new genre of music.

For centuries before Luther, even the most devout people in church understood little of what was being said or sung in the Latin masses they attended. One of Luther's basic beliefs involved the "priesthood of all believers," which meant that he wanted every man, woman, and child to be directly involved in the worship service.

His influence in this area eventually included the replacement of Latin singing with vernacular hymns and chorales, which were often set to the tune of local folk songs. When people around him objected, he said, "Why should the devil have all the good music?" In the same way that he insisted every word of the Scripture readings and sermons should be understood by all, Martin Luther insisted that the music of his churches should reach all people—whether educated or illiterate.

The result was a musical revolution. Thousands of great hymns through the centuries have their roots in the Lutheran traditions—all due to a man who did not put limits on what God could do through music. Martin Luther believed "that next to the Word of God, music deserves the highest praise." He once wrote that "I have always loved music. Whoever has skill in this art is of a good temperament and fitted for all things. We must teach music in schools. A schoolmaster aught to have skill in music or I would reject him. Neither should we ordain young men as preachers unless they have been well exercised in music."

Turn on your radio. Starting at one end of the FM band, slowly move through each of the stations, noticing how many different types of music you hear. Do you think God can use any type of music? Thank Him for the variety of music we can listen to.

Peacemakers who sow in peace raise a harvest of righteousness.

–JAMES 3:18

If there was ever a great diplomat among famous musicians, it was Luigi Boccherini, born this day in 1743. This Italian cellist and composer wrote chamber music—nearly fifty string trios and more than one hundred each of quartets and quintets!

For much of Boccherini's career, he was employed by royalty, so he became a gifted diplomat. His "people skills" were as sharp as his musical talents. This peace-loving musician sometimes worked with rival monarchs. He had to learn to choose his words carefully so he didn't stir up more trouble between them.

Two of his greatest admirers were the king of Spain and the emperor of Austria. Both were musicians who often played with Boccherini. The emperor insisted on asking Boccherini to decide which of the two rulers was the better musician. Boccherini was too wise to start a quarrel. He diplomatically replied, "Sire, Charles IV plays like a king, but your Imperial Highness plays like an emperor."

When we see friends getting into arguments, we do no one a favor by taking sides and adding to the quarrel. Jesus said, "Blessed are the peacemakers" (Matthew 5:9), and people who can resolve conflicts are some of the most valuable people on the planet. Instead of joining a disagreement or taking sides—which is all too easy to do—try to be a Boccherini and be the one who brings peace.

Do you know two friends who are at odds with one another? It may be that God could use you to be a peacemaker. Pray about this, and if nothing else, pray that the Lord would help your friends to reconcile.

But the Lord said to me, "Do not say, 'I am only a child.' You must go to everyone I send you to and say whatever I command you."

—JEREMIAH 1:7

Sibling rivalry is as old as the very first family and occurs in a wide variety of forms. Often the older child feels threatened by younger ones and is the one who stirs up trouble. But in today's story, a younger child was intimidated by the talent of the older to the point of not realizing her own gifts.

Chasing Furies is the name of a unique Christian band. Not only is its musical style unorthodox, but it also has the uncommon distinction of being a band made up of two sisters and their big brother. The brother is an exceptional guitarist and songwriter, and it was all too easy for his sisters to feel as if they were "in Joshua's shadow."

Sarah, two years younger, privately began songwriting, but initially lacked confidence. She remembers, "Josh had always been the writer of the family, and I had always just sung backup for him. When I started writing, I felt silly. I had just learned to play guitar so I could write songs, and here Josh is this phenomenal guitarist."

Finally Sarah asked her younger sister, Rachel, to sing with her at a local coffeehouse. The response to Sarah's compositions was remarkable, and her confidence was boosted. They then asked their brother Joshua to join them—and the new band was born! Now the three work together, sharing both the singing and the songwriting, and their ministry has inspired thousands of young people for Christ.

When we start comparing ourselves to others, it's very easy to begin to feel insecure. (Ever notice how we always compare ourselves to those we think are more talented than we are, rather than to those who may just be starting out?) But God wants us to take whatever talents He has given us and use them as best we can. Whatever our talents are, we can and should use them for His glory.

Do you know what talents God has given you? If not, ask those who know you well—parents, siblings, close friends—what special abilities they see in you. Thank God for giving you the talents He has, and ask Him how you can use them to serve Him.

And let us consider how we may spur one another on toward love and good deeds. –HEBREWS 10:24

On February 21, 1893, a man was born in Spain who would revolutionize the way the world was to view the guitar. It is difficult to really understand Andrés Segovia's influence. Today, the guitar is second only to the piano in popularity among amateur musicians, with approximately twenty million in the United States alone. Yet in 1893, the guitar was not even considered a legitimate concert instrument; it was associated with taverns, gypsies, and vagabonds.

Young Andrés saw that this neglected instrument had tremendous concert potential, and he became a virtuoso such as no guitarist had ever been. For decades he toured around the world, proving to all who would listen that the guitar could play great music. Segovia made arrangements of Bach, Beethoven, Mozart, and countless other masters. He taught scores of guitar students and inspired hundreds of composers to create a solid repertoire for the guitar. A true pathfinder, he was still performing in his eighties.

Despite his popularity, he had to overcome resistance every step of the way. His family and friends were horrified by his interest in such a "barroom instrument" and pleaded with him to play the piano or cello. Without any credible teachers available, Segovia had to teach himself. For years, critics looked down upon his instrument. Opposition to his work was great, but he did live long enough to see his life's work pay off.

Of course, God does not call each of us to do such groundbreaking work. But to different degrees, He does call each of us out of our "comfort zones" from time to time. If He didn't, we would never grow! If God is asking you to stretch in some way right now, hang in there. He'll give you what you need to see it through. And if you know someone else who is being stretched, keep that person in your prayers and offer all the encouragement you can.

To see what it feels like to be out of your comfort zone, try playing an instrument you've never played before. How difficult is it? Would you continue to play it if you had no one to give you instruction or encouragement? Thank God for the people in your life who encourage you.

A word aptly spoken is like apples of gold in settings of silver.

−PROVERBS 25:11

On this day in 1903, the composer Hugo Wolf died in Vienna, Austria. His creative life was sadly marred toward the end, as he grew more and more unbalanced and was finally committed to an asylum. Yet when at his best, Wolf was one of the nineteenth century's greatest songwriters. There was one story that Wolf often told of an incident that encouraged him throughout his musical career.

When Wolf was a young man, the most famous composer alive was Richard Wagner. Like many young composers, Wolf idolized Wagner and wanted to meet him more than anything in the world. But he might as well try to meet with the queen of England. Wagner was so well-known that he was always protected by a large group of close friends. How could a young unknown ever hope to meet him?

Nevertheless, Wolf was determined. He shadowed Wagner for some time and finally got into a place where the great composer was staying. Wolf was eventually able to convince a servant to take a message to the master: "Herr Wagner, a young artist who has waited upon you for a long time wishes to speak to you." Wagner met the young man and brought him into his reception room.

At first, Wagner answered guardedly to his unknown devotee. As he realized that this was no ordinary musician, however, but a composer of great promise, Wagner warmed to young Wolf. He ended the conversation with words of comfort: "I wish you, dear friend, much happiness in your career. Go on working hard and, if I come back to Vienna, show me your compositions." Wolf never forgot that moment. He later wrote, "I left the master profoundly moved and impressed."

When is the last time you encouraged someone you know? Single someone out today and sincerely give that person "a word aptly spoken."

Therefore . . . pray for each other so that you may be healed. The prayer of a righteous man is powerful and effective. –JAMES 5:16

Performing a difficult and exposed solo in an orchestra concert is always a challenge. Even more stress is added when the solo is so famous that the audience would recognize even the smallest mistake. How would you like to try this—while you were feeling very ill?

That was the dreadful situation confronting Scott Fearing one evening. Fearing's full-time job is playing French horn with the National Symphony, but his summers are spent performing and teaching at the Christian Performing Artists' Fellowship's MasterWorks Festival. One of the MasterWork's concerts included Tchaikovsky's Symphony no. 5, and Fearing was to play the long delicate solo in the second movement.

The night of the concert arrived, and to his dismay, he was horribly sick to his stomach. What to do? In his pitiful condition, it seemed that his personal prayers weren't helping much. At intermission, just before the piece was to begin, he staggered to his friend, John Kasica the tympanist, and asked for prayer. Kasica immediately agreed, and Fearing quickly got to his chair.

Fearing was somewhat astonished when he then heard a powerful voice from across the stage. His friend boldly prayed out loud while the rest of the orchestra was setting up. The audience may have wondered what was happening, but the result was miraculous. Fearing was completely healed and played a flawless performance of the famous solo.

What do you do when a friend asks you to pray? It is so easy to put it off. Why not pray immediately, if at all possible? The next time someone asks you for prayer, pray then and there. You never know what God might do!

"Whoever wants to become great among you must be your servant."

–MATTHEW 20:26

On this date in 1842, Arrigo Boito was born in Padua, Italy. If you haven't heard of him, it is because he was not so much a star, but a star-maker. He was an opera composer, chiefly known for his version of the Faust legend, which he entitled *Mefistofele.* But his greatest contribution to music was not in writing the music to operas, it was for writing the words. Boito was an excellent librettist.

Without his work, we would never have seen the creation of two of the greatest operas of all time, Giuseppe Verdi's *Othello* and *Falstaff.* For fifteen years after Verdi's last opera, *Aida,* he had practically given up as a composer. But his friend Boito came to him with a libretto that awoke the flame of Verdi's talent, and soon *Othello* was composed. Again Verdi decided to quit, but Boito brought another libretto that couldn't be refused. The comic opera *Falstaff* was the result.

Of course, when you hear of these two operas, you hear only the name Verdi. Yet without the skill and encouragement of his friend Boito, neither of those operas would exist. Boito was the enabler; he didn't stand in the spotlight, but he made it all possible.

When it is within our power to enable the success of someone, how do we respond? Is there a part of us that holds back because we envy the notice he will receive? How do we feel when we do a good deal of work but someone else gets all the credit? Though it may not feel like it, often the best thing we can do is to serve someone else and enable him to do his best. After all, isn't that what Christ did for us?

Write the name of a person who you know could use a helping hand right now. Ask God to help you be a Boito to that person, and pray for him or her this week.

Two are better than one, because they have a good return for their work: If one falls down, his friend can help him up. But pity the man who falls and has no one to help him up! —ECCLESIASTES 4:9-10

Being one of the Beatles may have seemed like an awesome job to millions of their fans. Yet in the midst of their success, they each had challenges to overcome. One of their constant challenges was to continually come out with new songs that were just as good as their old ones. It's what their fans expected.

One day George Harrison brought to rehearsal a song he had been creating that he called "While My Guitar Gently Weeps." Unfortunately, when he played the piece, the others were unimpressed. Finally, Harrison turned away feeling depressed and rejected.

Still convinced that his song had merit, he pondered what to do. The next day he was driving with his friend, the famed guitarist Eric Clapton, and Harrison had an inspiration. "Why don't you come and play on this track?" Clapton declined at first, "Oh, I couldn't do that, the others wouldn't like it."

Harrison became more determined, and he convinced Clapton to give it a try. The two of them marched into the next rehearsal and began the new song. Impressed by the confidence of this new team, the others listened with respect and interest. The five of them later recorded the song, and as Harrison remembers, "The song came together nicely." Today is Harrison's birthday.

Often, even the most intimidating project can become manageable if we just have someone who will do it with us. As the opening Scripture points out, "Two are better than one."

Do you have a challenge in front of you? Is it possible that someone could help you in overcoming that challenge? Ask God for a friend who can help you today.

He who listens to a life-giving rebuke will be at home among the wise. —PROVERBS 15:31

If anyone in the music business had to learn from the "school of hard knocks" it would be Johnny Cash. From his birth on February 26, 1932, his childhood was spent in utter poverty, and as soon as he was old enough, he left home to join the air force. While stationed in Germany, he learned to play guitar and was soon writing his own material. After Cash was discharged and back in America, he and some friends formed a band and began the difficult task of breaking into the music business.

Finally it looked as if their big break was before them. Cash had arranged for an audition before Sam Phillips of Sun Records. This was a man who could surely launch their careers, and their hopes were high. But Phillips was unimpressed by the raw talent before him. He flatly turned them down, telling them to sharpen their talents or give it up.

Stab! Such a stunning defeat must have hurt terribly. But Cash took Phillips' rebuke seriously and worked to produce better material. After an intense time of practicing and rehearsing, Cash felt bold enough to set up another audition with Sun Records. The second time, Phillips was impressed with the marked improvements. Knowing that he had musicians who would put in the work needed, he signed the band for Sun. Soon they were touring, recording, and producing hits that would someday make Cash famous.

Nevertheless, this tremendous potential was sidetracked and almost destroyed when the stress of Cash's success led him into a series of drug addictions. Fortunately his life was turned around when he married June Carter and became a steadfast Christian who was a regular with the Billy Graham crusades. When his producer once pointed out to Cash that his sacred album *The Gospel Road* did not sell as well as his famous pair *Johnny Cash at Folsom Prison* and *Johnny Cash at San Quentin,* the singer jokingly complained, "My record company would rather I be in prison than in church."

How do you respond when faced with a failure? Do you give up, or do you resolve to work harder? Listen to a song by Johnny Cash, and thank God for helping us learn from our mistakes and keep trying.

"According to your faith will it be done to you." –MATTHEW 9:29

Today is the birthday of the celebrated tenor Enrico Caruso, born in Naples in 1873. In his forty-eight years, he became the greatest vocal legend the world had even seen. Amazingly, much of his talent has been preserved for us, as he was one of the first serious singers to make creditable gramophone records.

There are many interesting stories about this notable tenor. One of the best-known is about his beginnings in the new era of recording. In 1902, a British record producer heard Caruso sing an opera, and he immediately went backstage with a contract. They agreed that Caruso's fee would be one hundred pounds sterling for singing ten songs.

The delighted producer cabled his company in London for confirmation, but was astonished at their reply: "Fee exorbitant, forbid you to record." This man was so convinced that Caruso would be a hit, that he decided to sign him *anyway*, at his own expense. Those ten records soon yielded a profit of fifteen thousand pounds. In fact, over the next twenty years, Caruso's records would earn him almost one million pounds!

There are times as Christians when we may believe God wants us to do something, even when others are against it. When we face such a situation, we need to pray fervently, study the Word for guidance, and ask advice from many different people. Ultimately, the decision is an individual one, and then we must be ready to deal with the consequences.

It can be painfully difficult to "step out in faith," especially if a decision makes life difficult for us or someone else. There comes a time for all of us, however, when we must take a stand for the Lord and what we believe He is calling us to do. In those times, we must remind ourselves that even if it seems that we are all alone with our step of faith, the Lord has promised to never leave us or forsake us.

Read the popular poem "Footsteps," and thank the Lord that He is truly with us every step of the way. If you know someone else who is facing a difficult time in taking a stand for the Lord, offer that person a copy of "Footsteps" along with your prayers.

A generous man will prosper; he who refreshes others will himself be refreshed. –PROVERBS 11:25

Many times when we hear success stories, we don't hear about all the many people who helped the successful one along the way. Sometimes these helpers are parents, or friends, or even strangers. But without their assistance, the success story would never have been possible.

Jazz great Bennie Carter had such a helper, at just the time when Carter needed help the most. Long before he was well known, Carter had a band that played regularly in New York at the Club Harlem. But the club was about to go out of business, and Carter's band would soon be on the street.

One of Bennie Carter's fans was a wealthy gentleman named George Rich. When he heard about the problem, Rich determined to help. "They can't do this to you," he told Carter. "You've got to have a place for your band. Come over to the house tonight after the gig." That night Rich told Carter that he intended to buy the club, which he soon did. Years later, Carter remembered, "His only purpose for buying the club was to keep my band together, and I shall never forget him for it."

All around us are people with needs. Of course, we are not able to meet them all, and very few of us have the money to be a rich benefactor. But we can all help someone who is in a time of need.

We can help others with our time and talents as well as with our money. In your prayer time today, ask God to send you on a mission of mercy to someone in need.

He who works his land will have abundant food, but he who chases fantasies lacks judgment. –PROVERBS 12:11

March 1 is the birthday of the conductor and pianist Dimitri Mitropoulos, born in 1896, in Athens, Greece. He moved to the United States in 1936, and for a decade conducted the Minneapolis Symphony before becoming conductor of the New York Philharmonic. Loved by both his players and his audiences, he guest conducted all over the world until November 2, 1960, when he died while rehearsing the La Scala Orchestra in Mahler's Third Symphony.

Mitropoulos was an excellent musician who had an extraordinary memory, and he had strong opinions on the subject of being prepared. He once said, "If I were a lion tamer, I would not enter a cage of lions reading a book entitled *How to Tame Lions.* In the same way I would not enter a rehearsal not completely prepared."

Some people seem to think that "having faith" means we are not to bother with preparing ourselves for the future. But being prepared is a key part of diligence, which the Bible commands again and again. If I were a member of an orchestra, I would certainly want my conductor to be adequately prepared before a rehearsal. If I were a member of an audience, I would certainly want all the musicians to be prepared for a performance. How selfish to not be prepared when it is expected of us.

Do we have a reputation of being well prepared and diligent?

Choose a specific book to read that will help you become better at something you like to do. Set a date to begin the book and a date for its completion.

Enable your servants to speak your word with great boldness.

—ACTS 4:29

Licciardello. How could someone with such an unpronounceable last name ever be a CCM star? Typical entertainment figures usually have simple, short names that are easy to remember. If they don't already have one by birth, a stage name is invented for this purpose. Carman Domenic Licciardello had an uncomplicated idea on this subject: he is known all over the world simply as Carman.

Carman became a Christian while attending a concert by Andrae Crouch and The Disciples, where, as he asserts, "I got saved to the bone!" His many recordings, videos, and books are extremely popular. In fact, in 1994, one of his performances set a CCM record, with a crowd of 71,132 fans—the largest in contemporary Christian music.

Yet the praises from (and record sales to) the masses have never tempted Carman to compromise his mission. To him, being a Christian musician means being a bold evangelist. His lyrics, especially his dramatic brand of spiritual warfare, are very deliberately "in your face," with albums entitled *Revival in the Land, Comin' on Strong, The Standard,* and *Radically Saved.*

Far from the "Christianity lite" approach of some singers, Carman's concerts (which are always free) preach the Gospel and ask people to come forward to receive Christ. Does such boldness work? In a recent concert tour, over 21,000 people signed commitment cards as new Christians. Carman's fearless approach has created an entirely new form of evangelism and has made a tremendous impact on the lives of thousands.

The great German writer Goethe once commented, "Boldness is genius." While we typically need to be sensitive and discerning as we present the Gospel, there are times when bold is best.

How do you feel about sharing your faith? Most of us are rather fearful and need the Lord's grace to succeed in this critical area. Ask God to give you an opportunity today to share your faith and to give you the necessary boldness to seize the opportunity.

But in your hearts set apart Christ as Lord. Always be prepared to give an answer to everyone who asks you to give the reason for the hope that you have. But do this with gentleness and respect. —1 PETER 3:15

Jerome Hines is one of the twentieth century's finest opera singers. He has performed more than forty consecutive seasons at the Metropolitan Opera in New York, and his powerful bass voice was in demand throughout the world. But as a devoted Christian, his favorite singing was usually in a ministry setting. Often Hines could be found singing at the Met and at a Salvation Army mission in New York's poorest districts on the same evening.

Being a strong witness for Christ in the world of opera gave him a number of challenges. Once he was contracted to sing in a major performance of Debussy's beautiful *Pelleas et Mellisande.* When they began rehearsals, he was horrified to find that the opera director had decided to "modernize" the performance with a long sexual scene.

What was Hines to do? He was under contract to sing this opera with them, but he wanted no part of this ungodly interpretation. After an evening in prayer, the next morning he asked if he could speak to the entire assembly. Overcoming his fears, he explained that he "didn't want to make trouble for the company, but as a Christian man [he] just couldn't take part in this production." Hines asked if perhaps he could find a qualified substitute—at his own expense, which would have been considerable.

God blessed his courageous act. To Hines' surprise, the director omitted the objectionable scene. Hines' courageous stand for his biblical convictions—in front of his professional colleagues—affected what hundreds of opera lovers saw when they came to that production.

What about you? Of course, you may say, "Well, that was the famous Jerome Hines. I'm nobody special. If I did that, no one would care." The Lord wants us to stand up for our convictions, and He will give us the power, the grace, and the courage to do so.

When was the last time you had to stand up for what you believe in? It may come today. Are you prepared? Decide now that you will stand for Christ in any situation.

"How much more will your Father in heaven give good gifts to those who ask him!" —MATTHEW 7:11

A devastating earthquake terrified the citizens of Venice on this day in 1678. The composer Antonio Vivaldi was born during the upheaval, and the midwife immediately baptized the child for fear they would all perish. But Vivaldi would live until 1741, composing some of the finest music of his day. From his pen came over four hundred concertos, including *The Four Seasons*.

"The red priest" (nicknamed for both his vocation and the color of his hair) amused his acquaintances by his impulsive, unpredictable, and eccentric nature. Once, in the middle of saying a mass, a theme for a fugue suddenly came to him. To the shock of his congregation, Vivaldi rushed from the altar, scribbled down the melody, and then returned to finish his service. Called before the Inquisition for this offense, they took pity on the red priest and simply forbade him to say any more masses.

From where did this melodic idea suddenly come? From where does any "bolt of lightning" idea come? Some might look to their intelligence, or their subconscience, or even some mystical oracle. For the Christian, we know that "every good and perfect gift is from above, coming down from the Father of the heavenly lights" (James 1:17). He is also the "Father of inspiration," and therefore all the glory for our good ideas should go to Him alone.

When we need inspiration, motivation, or a great idea, we have a direct link with the Creator of the creatively wonderful universe. If we make our needs known to God, in His time and in His special way, He will answer. Of course, we may want to write the idea down quickly—depending upon what we happen to be doing at the time!

Do you need a great idea for something on which you are working? Ask God for it, and when it comes, give Him all the glory.

But you know that Timothy has proved himself, because as a son with his father he has served with me in the work of the gospel.

—PHILIPPIANS 2:22

Today is the birthday of Brazil's musical son Heitor Villa-Lobos, born in 1887, in Rio de Janeiro. Largely self-taught, his unconventional education led him to compose many exotic and innovative pieces, especially those entitled *Bachiana Brasileira* (alluding to Bach and his country). He once explained, "I learned music from a bird in the jungles of Brazil, not from academies."

The hundreds of compositions he produced might have been lost to us if not for the great pianist Artur Rubinstein. While on a South American concert tour in 1919, Rubinstein happened to hear a fascinating melody in a motion picture show. Finding that it was written by a local composer, he sought out Villa-Lobos. Becoming convinced of his remarkable talent, Rubinstein persuaded the Brazilian government to give the young composer a stipend. It was the big break for a formerly unknown composer, soon to be world renowned.

Villa-Lobos may not have ever been known if it weren't for Rubinstein, but Rubinstein would not have had anything to discover if Villa-Lobos had not been faithful in using his talent and gift, even when it appeared no one would notice. Villa-Lobos—like Timothy—proved himself long before he was discovered and got his "big break." In what areas would God have you work on proving yourself today?

Do you know someone who has been a Rubinstein to others? Perhaps there is someone in your church or community who has done a lot to help others. Tell that person thank you, either in person or by writing a note, for all he has done for others. Then ask God to show you how you can be a Rubinstein to someone else.

Let us not give up meeting together, as some are in the habit of doing, but let us encourage one another—and all the more as you see the Day approaching. –HEBREWS 10:25

God created us to be unique, and we are all in different places in our Christian walk. Some of us are very new to it, while others have been growing in the Lord for many years. Yet none of us can make it alone. We each need the encouragement of Christians around us.

Tom Sperl plays the double bass in the Cleveland Symphony Orchestra. Like most professional musicians, he began playing at an early age, and his musicianship was directly related to his life in Christ. "The age of nine was very important to me," he recalls, "since in that year I fell in love with Jesus and in love with the bass!"

Yet few of his experiences as a young musician included much Christian fellowship. As a result, his growth as a believer was slow and unsteady. Little fellowship was found in music school or in his first orchestral jobs. Then Sperl was invited to join the prestigious Cleveland Orchestra. Would the lack of fellowship and encouragement be sadly repeated?

Finally, his first somewhat nervous day on the job arrived. In the break of his first rehearsal, a violist named Stanley Konopka turned around to the basses and boldly announced, "I heard that you're a believer!" That was the beginning of many Christian friendships in the orchestra. Sperl, Konopka, and the other Christians there encourage one another regularly in their witness, their service, and their growth in Christ.

God wants Christians to stay together, to continually encourage one another. Whom can you encourage today?

Have you ever seen a hot coal set apart from a grill full of hot coals? What happens to it? How long does it stay hot? What about the charcoal still in the grill? Christians are a lot like that charcoal. We need to be surrounded by others who are on fire for the Lord or we run the risk of dying out. Thank God for the Christians who surround you.

"Rid yourselves of all the offenses you have committed, and get a new heart and a new spirit." —EZEKIEL 18:31

The great French composer Maurice Ravel was born this day in 1875, at Cibourne on the Basque coast. Renowned for such masterpieces as *Bolero,* the *Mother Goose Suite, La Valse,* and *Daphnis and Chloe,* he also orchestrated and popularized the piano works of fellow composers, such as Mussorgsky's *Pictures at an Exhibition.*

Indeed, Ravel is known and remembered as a master orchestrator, as well as for being a composer. Although he was a brilliant pianist and composer for the piano, it seems that the orchestra was his favorite "instrument" for his best creations. His boldness in using wild orchestral effects has thrilled audiences worldwide.

Such a talent did not come without effort. He once told a friend that he would like to write about orchestration, illustrating with examples of failures from his own works. Ravel worked diligently to become the best in French orchestration, revising, experimenting, ever-learning from mistakes in order to produce a flawless score.

The difference between those who succeed and those who do not is seldom reflected by the number of mistakes they might have made. The difference comes from how well they learned from their mistakes. Some, fearful of committing errors, seldom attempt anything. Others repeat the same errors over and over. But those who grow and are fruitful are those who admit their mistakes, resolve to change, and move on.

Even as "all have sinned" (Romans 3:23), so too, everyone makes mistakes. But if we can learn from them, renounce them, and avoid them in the future, even our greatest errors can have purpose.

What mistakes have you made lately? What circumstances, thoughts, or feelings caused them? How can they now be corrected? Ask God to show you what can be learned from your errors, and how He can bring good from them.

Now there lived in that city a man poor but wise, and he saved the city by his wisdom. But nobody remembered that poor man.

—ECCLESIASTES 9:15

On March 8, 1902, one of the greatest twentieth-century British composers was born. His name was William Walton. He wrote for nearly every genre, and his masterpieces include the dramatic cantata *Belshazzar's Feast;* concertos for violin, viola, and cello; the opera *Troilus and Cressida;* two excellent symphonies; and many other works for orchestra, including his notable *Facade* for reciter and chamber ensemble. His film scores to Laurence Olivier's great Shakespeare trilogy, *Henry V, Hamlet,* and *Richard III,* are superb.

Yet Walton suffered the fate of many composers throughout history: he was acutely underappreciated in his lifetime. He once made the gloomy observation, "I seriously advise all sensitive composers to die at the age of thirty-seven." This sentiment was similarly expressed by another twentieth-century composer, Arthur Honneger. He wrote, "It is clear that the first specification for a composer is to be dead."

Why is this? Sadly, this situation has been the plight of dozens of composers, now considered "masters" yet neglected in their own time. Certainly it is often difficult for audiences to understand the many innovations that composers often display in their music. But what is it about us that seems to keep us from appreciating someone until he is gone?

Rather than losing ourselves in philosophical speculation, let's ask a more practical question: Do we truly appreciate the people God has placed around us? Our family, our friends, our peers—if one died today we would surely be grieved and say warm things at the funeral. Why not show them sincere appreciation *today* instead?

Choose someone you often see and give that person a warm message of encouragement—today!

The wicked man flees though no one pursues, but the righteous are as bold as a lion. —PROVERBS 28:1

In the city of West Chester, Pennsylvania, one of America's finest composers was born on this date in 1910. His name was Samuel Barber, and his orchestral works, songs, and chamber music are now performed throughout the world. The celebrated Barber Adagio for Strings (a movement from a string quartet and later adapted for orchestra) was played for the ceremony at John F. Kennedy's funeral.

Barber came from a musical family and began piano at an early age. At twenty-five he won the coveted American Prix de Rome, enabling him to study in Europe. While he was there, he yearned to fulfill a lifelong dream to meet the famed conductor Arturo Toscanini, who was living at Lake Maggiore. The timid, young, and unknown Barber was very intimidated at the thought of trying to meet such a master; he had been told that the only possible way to see him was to first impress the maestro's formidable wife. With great trepidation, the young man finally rang their doorbell, bashfully asking the servant for Mrs. Toscanini.

Barber was in for a wonderful surprise. Mrs. Toscanini was not in, but, would he care to see the maestro? The two of them spent the afternoon together, talking about nearly every aspect of music, complete with singing together through the entire score of Monteverdi's *Orfeo*. The meeting developed into a warm friendship, and Toscanini became very influential in Barber's expanding career, premiering his works whenever possible.

Often we find ourselves—like the terrified Barber on Toscanini's doorstep—anxiously facing a frightful task. Rather than give in to our fears, we need to ask for God's strength and courage, and do what He has asked us to do. In this way, we give God the opportunity to bring us through with His grace. We may even, like Barber, be pleasantly surprised by the outcome.

Is there something you need or want to do, but are afraid to do? The Bible is filled with encouragement along the lines of "Do not fear." Look up a few of these Scriptures, and ask the Lord for a special gift of courage.

"Open wide your mouth and I will fill it." —PSALM 81:10

Littlehampton is a quiet seaside town on the southern coast of England—not a very likely place for a Christian band to have its start. The Arun Community Church had a burden for the lost young people in its area and began a monthly outreach service called Cutting Edge. The musicians involved were exceptionally talented, and after a few years of leading worship sessions and making demo tapes, they emerged in 1996 as a band called Delirious.

Their background was very evangelistic. Describing their church's outreach services, drummer Stewart Smith explained, "It wasn't about rules anymore. It was about 'this is how God has changed my life.'" Because of this emphasis, the group doesn't want to limit its ministry to entertainment. "We want to push music outside the boundaries of the church," affirms lead singer Martin Smith. "We are a band who plays for the church and the street."

Perhaps their greatest characteristic is their boldness, their far-reaching vision. "We really feel like we can make history," Smith maintains. "Maybe that's kind of naïve, but if we don't believe that, how can we expect anyone else to?" One of their choruses confidently proclaims, "I'm gonna be a history maker in the land. . . . I'm gonna be a speaker of truth to all mankind."

Does this seem impossible? Is it any more ridiculous than sending out twelve barefoot men to conquer the Roman Empire for Christ? Christians are called to humility, but we are also called to believe God for great things. If our world is to be changed for the Lord, we must first believe that it can be, and then that He can use us to make a difference.

When is the last time you boldly asked God for something big? Can the Lord use you to reach your city, your state, even your country? Ask the Lord to fill you with vision, courage, and revelation. He is looking for followers who will believe Him for great things.

Follow my example, as I follow the example of Christ.

–1 CORINTHIANS 11:1

God created each of us the way He did for a reason. We are all unique individuals with diverse backgrounds, talents, and interests. Because musicians and artists are so creative, they often want to show their uniqueness even more than others. Yet each of us—musicians included—can and should learn from and follow the example of our teachers. That is how we develop and improve the talents God has given us.

Joseph Silverstein, former concertmaster of the Boston Symphony Orchestra, spent his life in the violin world and thoroughly knew every work in the standard repertoire. Yet one day he was astonished by a young violinist who was auditioning for him. Instead of playing Bach, Beethoven, or any of the great masters, this violinist played a piece that Silverstein had never heard.

When asked why he chose such an unknown (and terrible) piece, the young man explained that his teacher insisted upon it, because he didn't want his students imitating anyone else's style. As Silverstein listened aghast, he was told that the young man was even forbidden to listen to any recordings of violin music, for fear that he would copy what he heard instead of being completely original.

Finally, he was dismissed and advised to get some recordings of Jascha Heifetz—one of the greatest violinists of the twentieth century. It was excellent advice. Long before we can be creative and imaginative, we need to learn from those who have gone before us.

The same is true for our Christian walk. We need to learn from the Master before we are ready to be the "original" He created us to be.

With your instrument (or voice) try to imitate one of your favorite performers. Listen to one specific song over and over, then try to play it exactly as it sounds on the recording. Now play the piece with your own style and thank God for giving us teachers and making us each unique.

One who is slack in his work is brother to one who destroys.

—PROVERBS 18:9

The jazz world lost one of its greatest players on this day in 1955. Everyone who heard Charlie Parker (nicknamed "Bird") was stunned by his playing. One of his friends remarked, "The thing about Charlie Parker was that he was such a giant, he was so much better than everybody else. It was not like there was this guy, and that guy. There was everybody else and then there was Charlie Parker!"

Yet for all of his phenomenal talent, Parker had a number of bad habits. One of his worst was his notorious custom of showing up late—if at all!—to his performances. Dozens of times his band members would look everywhere for him, only to find him asleep in the oddest places. He was constantly fined by his manager for such no-shows, but nothing seemed to work.

Once he was playing a series of concerts at Detroit's Paradise Theater. Determined not to miss the next night's show, Parker announced, "I'm going to stay in the theater all night to make sure that I'm here." His band said good night to him and left him alone on the bandstand.

But when they arrived the next day for rehearsal, Parker was nowhere to be found. They rehearsed without him, and then began the show in his absence. Finally, the curtain came down on a disappointing performance, and the band began to pack up their equipment. Hearing a noise from underneath, they discovered that Parker had been asleep under the bandstand throughout the entire rehearsal and performance!

God doesn't want us to go through life half-asleep. He has wonderful blessings waiting for each of us, if we will just keep our eyes open and on Him.

Have you ever overslept for something? Are you known to be reliable and punctual? Think about your daily schedule and note the areas where you could use some improvement.

Examine yourselves to see whether you are in the faith; test yourselves. –2 CORINTHIANS 13:5

This day in 1935 saw the publication of Serge Rachmaninoff's *Rhapsodie on a Theme of Paganini* (version for piano, four hands). The melody is taken from Paganini's violin Caprice no. 24, and Rachmaninoff's *Rhapsodie* has become a very popular work for pianists. Its creator was both a composer and a concert pianist who had an expert's knowledge of his instrument.

An exile from his native Russia since the revolution in 1918, Rachmaninoff nonetheless kept his rather droll sense of humor. His humor showed itself in interesting places, including the middle of an important recital in New York, which he gave with the violinist Fritz Kreisler. When Kreisler had a sudden lapse of memory, he frantically whispered to his pianist, "Where are we?" Without missing a beat or even looking up, Rachmaninoff calmly replied, "At Carnegie Hall."

Fortunately, history doesn't record the violinist's response to Rachmaninoff's comical answer. But the original question—taken more seriously—is actually one of the most significant ones we can ask concerning our spiritual walk.

Every so often, it is wise to ask ourselves, "Where are we?" "Are we where God wants us to be today?" "Where are we going?" "What am I currently doing that will bring me closer to where God wants me to be?" Too many people are so busy *doing,* that they never quite stop to think about such questions. If we are to use our life for Christ, we need to look at where we are once in a while, testing the direction of our walk and seeking the answer to these questions.

How good are you at reading maps? Ask a parent or friend to name a place where he would like to visit, then get out an atlas and plan the best route to take. Thank God for giving us a map for life—the Bible—and praise Him for giving us directions.

"From everyone who has been given much, much will be demanded; and from the one who has been entrusted with much, much more will be asked." —LUKE 12:48

Today might be called "Mendelssohn Day." It is not his birthday, but it is important for two of his greatest works. On this day in 1833, he completed his celebrated Symphony no. 4 (The "Italian" Symphony), and in 1845 on this day, his Violin Concerto was premiered.

Mendelssohn was incredibly talented from birth, not only as a piano prodigy but as a true mental genius as well. A friend once found him writing music, so he started to leave. Mendelssohn invited him to stay, remarking, "I am merely copying out." There was nothing there to copy, and he was obviously composing, yet their conversation never flagged. Soon he finished his Grand Overture in C Major.

Another example of his mental power shows the capacity of his memory. When the young Mendelssohn stepped up to the podium to conduct Bach's *Passion According to Saint Matthew*, he found that the wrong score had been placed on his music stand. He chose to simply conduct the mammoth work by heart, turning pages in his useless score so as not to alarm the unknowing soloists!

Truly, we are all "fearfully and wonderfully made" (Psalm 139:14). Mendelssohn recognized that the Lord had given him a tremendous intellect, and he used his gifts to their fullest capacity for God's glory. He wrote, "I know perfectly well that no musician can make his thoughts or his talents different to what Heaven has made them; but I also know that if Heaven had given him good ones, he must also be able to develop them properly."

Are we using the wonderful abilities God has given each of us? Are we stocking our minds with things that will improve us and make us productive? Or do we waste our time, resources, and talents with things of no lasting value? Since God has already given us all we need, it is our responsibility to fully develop and use our gifts for His glory.

Think of the talents God has given you. Choose one talent you have and list several ways you can develop that talent. Then choose one of those ways and get started.

"Again, the kingdom of heaven is like a merchant looking for fine pearls. When he found one of great value, he went away and sold everything he had and bought it." –MATTHEW 13:45, 46

It was on this date in 1959 that the great band leader Tommy Dorsey died. He always insisted on the highest degrees of excellence in his work, often imposing fines on his musicians if they were merely a few seconds late. This did not make him very popular with many musicians, but those with an equal desire for quality had a great respect for him.

Dorsey was known as a tough guy when it came to auditions. Indeed, his high standards usually caused the players to be nervous, and many wouldn't even try out for his band. But he knew the importance of finding the very best in musicians, and when he found such a player, he rewarded him generously. In fact, his way of attracting the finest musicians was legendary.

A typical example was his approach to saxophonist Willie Smith. When Dorsey heard him play, he knew he had found quality. He gave Smith a ride home one day, and when they arrived at the door, Dorsey opened his checkbook and signed his name to a blank check. "You see," he said as he handed it to an astonished Smith, "where it says 'Pay to the Order of . . .'? Put down whatever amount you want."

Very few of us have the confidence—or for that matter, the bank account!—to make such a bold offer. Nevertheless, we should have just as much desire to produce excellence in our work—God deserves nothing less—and be willing to pay the price.

What's the single most expensive thing you have ever bought? What were you willing to do to be able to buy that item? Thank God for the price He was willing to pay for your salvation and for all you mean to Him.

"I will lead the blind by ways they have not known, along unfamil-iar paths I will guide them; I will turn the darkness into light before them and make the rough places smooth. These are the things I will do; I will not forsake them." —ISAIAH 42:16

So many rags-to-riches tales are stories of flexibility and endurance. Flexibility is needed to try new ideas and adjust when things don't go as expected. Endurance is necessary to keep going when neither ideas nor opportunities seem to appear.

A singer named Leonard Franklin Slye wanted to start a western-style singing group, but he had one problem: he didn't know any other singers. In 1931, he placed an ad in the newspaper and met several other musicians, forming the Rocky Mountaineers. They had little success, and Slye actually failed with three more groups within the next year or so. In 1933, he formed the Pioneer Trio and things got a bit better. They soon added a fourth member and became the Sons of the Pioneers.

Then a most unexpected opportunity appeared on their horizon. One of the group's songs, "Tumbling Tumbleweeds," was used in Gene Autry's first "singing cowboy" movie. Suddenly the Sons of the Pioneers were famous and in much demand. Furthermore, Hollywood realized that America loved the singing cowboy idea and wanted more. Slye received a movie offer of his own and soon became known as the "King of the Cowboys"—Roy Rogers!

Not only did Roy Rogers have a long movie career, but when he wasn't riding his horse Trigger in movies and on television, this wholesome cowboy was also making recordings, including many Christian songs in a country/western style. The movie star Dale Evans became his wife in 1947, and they made a number of religious albums together, including *The Bible Tells Me So* and *In the Sweet By and By*. If you could have told him back in 1931 of all his later successes, he might have laughed. But Roy Rogers never stopped trying different things until some finally worked!

Are there new ideas God wants you to try? When heading in a new direction, we need to be flexible. Read Proverbs 3:5-6 and ask God to lead you and to help you to be flexible.

"Listen to me, you who pursue righteousness and who seek the Lord: Look to the rock from which you were cut and to the quarry from which you were hewn." –ISAIAH 51:1

Singer and songwriter Michael Card has always strived to inspire his audiences to dig into the truths of God's Word. Each of his songs has a biblical base and is as thought-provoking as it is entertaining. Having composed and recorded dozens of powerful songs and performed all over the world, Card has earned a very prominent position in the world of Christian music.

Yet in recent years, this modern troubadour has found a new musical passion: Celtic music. His most recent works often feature Celtic melodies, even including Irish harps and whistles. These new ideas are not gimmicks, but spring from a heartfelt desire to return to his own family roots.

Card told an interviewer, "The first time I went to Ireland, I felt so much a sense of having been called there." Then he added the interesting point, "The call of God has a geographical dimension to it as much as anything else." Beginning with his first trip, Card, whose own family was originally from Celtic Wales, has become more and more captivated by Ireland and the British Isles.

In these fast-paced times, few of us slow down enough to consider our roots. Sometimes they are unknown to us, sometimes they are painful, but they are often filled with fascinating realities that can reveal much about who we are. If we take time to examine our past, we may discover the wisdom we need to set a course for our future.

How much do you know about your heritage, your ancestors and their beliefs? Is there anyone you could talk to about such matters? If so, start working on a family tree, going back as many generations as possible. Praise God for the gift of family.

But he said to me, "My grace is sufficient for you, for my power is made perfect in weakness." Therefore I will boast all the more gladly about my weaknesses, so that Christ's power may rest on me.

–2 CORINTHIANS 12:9

Today is the birthday of Charlotte Elliott, who wrote the celebrated hymn, "Just as I Am." In the last half of the twentieth century, this hymn was the final song in hundreds of Billy Graham crusades, and thousands have given their lives to Christ while hearing its simple message:

> Just as I am, without one plea,
> But that Thy blood was shed for me,
> And that Thou biddist me come to Thee,
> O Lamb of God, I come.

Many people have heard the story of this song, how Elliott, an invalid, felt useless and miserable in her room while the rest of her family was busy preparing a bazaar to raise money for a hospital. In her misery and self-pity, God gave her a tremendous feeling of peace. Then Elliott quietly wrote all the words to this hymn, which has since been used in ministry all over the world.

Yes, many people have heard this story, but few realize the lifetime perseverance of this godly woman. Though Elliott was an invalid, she was determined to use her life to serve Christ. She became an editor of hymnbooks and prayer books, and also composed over one hundred hymns. Each of these accomplishments was a struggle, but she relied on the grace and strength of God.

Charlotte Elliott wrote, "My Heavenly Father knows, and He alone, what it is, day after day, and hour after hour, to fight against bodily feelings of almost overwhelming weakness. . . . He enables me to . . . rise every morning determined on taking this for my motto: 'If any man will come after me, let him deny himself, take up his cross daily, and follow me.' "

Do you know someone with a disability? Write her a note of cheer today. Or if you can, give her a visit soon. If you suffer from a disability, draw your strength from His grace and persevere in His purpose for your life.

He who guards his mouth and his tongue keeps himself from calamity. —PROVERBS 21:23

This day in 1859 saw the premiere of Charles Gounod's notable opera *Faust*. It was not immediately popular, but soon gained in popularity, having over five hundred performances in Paris by 1887. The classic conflict between heaven and hell is dealt with as Faust first gives in to and then defies the temptations of the devil.

Gounod was a deeply religious man and spent much of his life creating and performing sacred music. He was so devout that he spoke of composing his music while "on his knees." He was quite open about his Christian convictions. He once ended a talk given at the public meeting of the Academie des Beaux Arts with the verse John 3:3, which he called "the supreme formula": "Truly I say to you, except a man be born again he can in no case enter into the kingdom of heaven."

Yet with all his devotion, Gounod was still a man with imperfections. Like all of us, he had struggles and areas of his life of which he was not proud. In one known instance, his difficulty controlling his tongue placed him in a very embarrassing situation.

One afternoon in Paris, the pianist Charles Halle gave a piano recital. That evening he happened to meet Gounod at a party. Gounod praised Halle profusely for the pleasure the recital had given him. Imagine Gounod's embarrassment when his wife appeared and—not having heard her husband's previous words—began to apologize to Halle for Gounod missing the concert because of a previous engagement!

When we hear such a story, we both smile and cringe, knowing how we would feel in such a predicament. The Scriptures tell us clearly that we need to "tame the tongue" (James 3:8). How easy it is to let our tongue lead us into similar situations. How much better it is to always speak the simple truth.

Do you remember the last time you lied to someone? Ask God to forgive you, and also ask Him to help you to always be completely truthful.

Do not join those who drink too much wine or gorge themselves on meat, for drunkards and gluttons become poor, and drowsiness clothes them in rags. —PROVERBS 23:20, 21

The great jazz clarinetist Irving Fazola died on this date in 1949. One of his most notable performances was of a series entitled "Journeys into Jazz" at the Academy of Music in Philadelphia. The fans who arrived in the concert hall early that night were somewhat surprised to see this jazz great sitting by himself on stage—quietly putting his clarinet together—long before the concert was to start. They would have been flabbergasted had they known the reason for his rather early appearance.

Earlier that evening, the director of the concert series received a frantic call from the manager of a local restaurant: "Do you know a Mr. Fazola?" Apparently the great clarinetist had eaten so much that he was stuck between the arms of his chair! A number of busboys had tried hard to free him, but they couldn't.

The concert director raced to the restaurant and called an ambulance. While they waited, he questioned Fazola how this could have happened. Fazola answered that he had come in for a few hamburgers. When asked, "How many did you eat?" Fazola replied, "Thirty-six!" The ambulance arrived and six people loaded him into it (chair intact) to drive him to the Academy of Music. Fazola was carefully unloaded in the middle of the stage to wait for the concert.

He played superbly through the first half—though it was noted that he did not rise for his solos as was his usual custom. Fortunately, Fazola was somehow freed from the chair during intermission, and the concert was a great success. As soon as it was over, the clarinetist asked to be taken to a restaurant. What did he order upon his arrival? More hamburgers!

Have you ever eaten so much of something you like that it made you sick? Have you ever tried fasting? Pray about setting aside a time for a short fast, asking the Lord to lead you in this.

You hear, O Lord, the desire of the afflicted; you encourage them and you listen to their cry. –PSALM 10:17

Today in the year 1700 was a very sad birthday for a fifteen-year-old boy in Ohrdruf, Saxony. Because of insufficient funds, the promising youth had been turned out of school less than a week earlier. The boy had been orphaned only a few years earlier and seemed to have no future before him. It looked as though he might simply fade away into the rural German countryside.

Although unrecognized by the school officials, this youth was outstandingly talented and motivated. He soon developed into a fine singer, and he demonstrated a remarkable ability to play the organ, the violin, and many other instruments. Many times he tramped thirty miles to Hamburg to hear the renowned organist Reincken, and he even walked sixty miles to Celle to attend programs of French music. In 1705, this inspired young man walked all the way from Arnstadt to Lubeck—a two hundred-mile trek!—to hear Dietrich Buxtehude, one of the greatest organists of his day.

Today, three centuries later, there are few educated people in all the world who have not heard of Johann Sebastian Bach (1685–1750). For decades, thousands of musicians have learned and respected his work, and millions have appreciated the joy of his compositions. Hundreds of books have been written about Bach and his music. This was the incredible future of the ragamuffin orphan who didn't have enough money to go to school.

Before we are ready to write someone off, thinking he is hopeless or has little potential, we should try to see him as the young Bach. No one would have thought he had such a world-changing future ahead of him. In the same way, we shouldn't be discouraged about our own future. If we become depressed, tempted to think that we have nothing to look forward to, we should put ourselves in Bach's youthful shoes. At the age of fifteen, he hadn't yet discovered his true talents and could not have dreamed of the impact he would someday have. In the same way, who knows how God may use us to His glory?

Listen to a recording of some of Bach's music. As you listen, imagine the young fifteen year old who was out of school and seemingly out of luck. Pray for someone you know who, like Bach, may be feeling discouraged today.

Let us examine our ways and test them, and let us return to the Lord. –LAMENTATIONS 3:40

Today in 1687, Jean-Baptiste Lully, the favorite composer of the French king Louis XIV, died at the age of fifty-five. His death would go down in conducting history; he was the first conductor to die from a work-related accident! It may be difficult to believe, but what started as a minor injury was left unchecked until it became fatal.

A few months earlier, he had been supervising a performance of his *Te Deum*, written to honor the king's recovery from a serious illness. This was before the days of modern conducting technique, and to beat time Lully used to bang his cane against the floor. He accidentally struck his foot, which caused a blister to form.

We may not think of a blister as a major medical problem, but this one refused to heal. Later, his toe had to be amputated, then his foot, and finally his entire leg. On March 22, the conducting mishap took Lully's life.

Like many problems, this one could have been prevented if it had been taken seriously. In the same way, a "small sin" can seem so minor that we think we don't need to worry about or deal with it immediately, if at all. But *all* sin is serious, and if it's continually ignored, it will gain a hold on our life and be even more difficult to get rid of.

Why not deal ruthlessly with our sins *today?* If we keep ourselves free of sin, we can be open to God's leading and can be fully devoted to completing the work He has for us.

Think of one sin that is a particular struggle for you. Maybe no one knows about it except you and God. Set a timer, and spend ten minutes in prayer, asking Him to remove that sin from your life.

Guide me in your truth and teach me, for you are God my Savior, and my hope is in you all day long. —PSALM 25:5

Haydn's music is always full of surprises, and on March 23, 1792, he premiered his "Surprise Symphony" (Symphony no. 94 in G Major). In this famous work, Haydn demonstrates his wry humor. The second movement begins with very quiet music from the strings, followed by even quieter music. Suddenly a fortissimo chord from the whole orchestra rocks the concert and wakes any would-be sleeper in the audience. The composer's comment was simply, "This will make the ladies scream."

But in one critical area of his life, Haydn himself had a dreadful surprise. As a young man, he fell in love with a girl who later stunned him by entering a convent. He impulsively proposed to her older sister, and she agreed to marry him. The two newlyweds turned out to be utterly incompatible. Haydn's new bride had so little regard for his composing genius that she cut up his manuscripts to use for hair-curling papers!

As you might imagine, his hasty marriage caused Haydn dreadful pain throughout his life. Nonetheless, Haydn remained faithful, never considering divorce. He generously supported his wife throughout his life and in his will. He is remembered never to have spoken an unkind word about her. But the devout Haydn must have many times regretted his quick decision.

If only he had taken the time to ask God about it before he made a decision with such lifetime consequences. How often do we forget to pray about big decisions, though? Even the most dedicated believers make such mistakes, forgetting to inquire of the Lord (1 Chronicles 15:13). It's easy to do, but no matter how appealing something may appear to us, we need to pray about every decision, asking for God's direction, guidance, and confirmation.

Do you have any decisions, major or minor, that need to be made soon? Make a list of all the pros and cons of each choice, then take these before the Lord and listen for His guidance.

I have seen a grievous evil under the sun: wealth hoarded to the harm of its owner. –ECCLESIASTES 5:13

War has often brought a tragic end to great musicians. On this day in 1916 the Spanish composer Enrique Granados was killed when a German submarine attacked and sank the SS *Sussex* in broad daylight. The ship was in the English Channel, and there were many survivors—but not the forty-eight-year-old composer.

The reason that Granados was not rescued is both grievous and tragic. Although well-known in Spain, he had just recently received international acclaim as a composer. Imagine his delight when he learned that New York's Metropolitan Opera Company wanted to stage his opera *Goyescas*. The Met had even agreed to bring the composer to New York for the premiere—with all expenses paid.

So Granados traveled first-class to the great city to see his work performed. He was somewhat disappointed with the production itself, but not with Met's generous payment. Yet here was another difficulty. Because of World War I, the world's economy was very unsettled. Granados was afraid to accept either checks or banknotes from the Met. How were they to pay him?

Finally the opera management agreed to the composer's demand: he was to be paid in pure gold. Granados then insisted on carrying this rather heavy currency at all times in a special belt under his clothes. He was wearing this belt on his way home to Spain when the SS *Sussex* was sunk. While most of the travelers were rescued by nearby ships, the weight of Granados' golden payment from the Met instantly pulled him down below the waves.

All good things come from God, including money. If we hoard it, hang on to it tightly, and let it become more important than Him, it will pull us down, just as the gold pulled down Granados. We need to be willing to let go of whatever possessions we have if we are to keep God first in our lives.

Have you ever found yourself in trouble because you wanted more money or things? The next time you start feeling that way, take a trip to a local homeless shelter. Ask the Lord to help you be content with what you have, and praise Him for supplying all that you need.

Whoever heeds correction shows prudence. –PROVERBS 15:5

Perhaps the greatest of all conductors was born today in 1867, in the Italian town of Parma. His name was Arturo Toscanini. In his long career, he presided over La Scala, the Metropolitan Opera, the New York Philharmonic, and his own NBC Radio Orchestra. His demand for complete memorization, the faithful rendering of the composers' ideas, and maintaining a balance of emotion and precision, has made him a living legend.

Almost every musician who worked under Toscanini remembered warm or amusing stories about him. Because he had a very strong personality, few dared to challenge him on musical matters. Once, while rehearsing an orchestra—from memory, of course—he stopped the music and pointed out a wrong note in the cello's part. When the principal cellist objected, showing that they were playing what was on their page, Toscanini called for the score to be brought to him. Sure enough, the conductor's memory had been correct, proving that the wrong note was a mistake on the printed part.

Toscanini worked with thousands of musicians, and was known to give a quick rebuke to even the most famous soloist if he or she wanted to perform the music differently than what was on the composer's score. Often he had to restrain the inflated egos of his opera singers. In a rehearsal of a Puccini aria, when he rebuked one soprano who wanted to sing it her way, she exclaimed, "Maestro, please remember that I am a star!" Toscanini replied, "The place for stars is in heaven."

From time to time, we all need to be brought down a notch. Without an occasional slap on the hand, we begin to think the whole world revolves around us, and we become the star, "only fit for heaven." How well we handle correction shows a great deal about our spiritual maturity.

When we are corrected, we need to learn from the situation and use it to grow into a stronger Christian. In this way, God can work through even the most painful punishment to make us more like Christ.

How good are you at receiving correction? The next time you are facing correction, head outdoors, look at the stars, and remember that everyone needs to be corrected from time to time. Then thank God for the beauty of the heavens!

I tell you, now is the time of God's favor, now is the day of salvation.

—2 CORINTHIANS 6:2

The date March 26 concerns two different and very important events in the life of Ludwig van Beethoven (1770–1827). On March 26, 1778, he gave his first public recital as a pianist. And on this same date in 1827, he died. In the forty-nine years between those two events—despite overwhelming obstacles including complete deafness—he gave the world some of the greatest music ever written.

Beethoven had many devoted friends, yet his life was filled with loneliness and misunderstanding. He remained a bachelor, though not by choice. He proposed to several different women, all of whom admired his genius but clearly realized that his erratic personality would make an intolerable husband.

On his deathbed he reassured his brother of his "great readiness" to make his peace with God. One of his last acts was to receive Communion. Beethoven's friend Anselm Huttenbrenner remained with the composer at his death, which took place during a violent storm. Following a loud clap of thunder, Huttenbrenner wrote, the unconscious Beethoven awoke, "opened his eyes, raised his right hand, his fist clenched, and looked upward for several seconds with a grave, threatening countenance, as if to say, 'I defy you, powers of evil! Away! God is with me!' "

None of us knows how long we're going to live. We have each been given a certain amount of time to glorify God on this earth. How we face our end in the future depends on our relationship with God now. We need to make our peace with God now, and know the joy of His forgiveness and the confidence of our salvation.

Write a letter to God, thanking Him for the gift of salvation.

He who gathers crops in summer is a wise son, but he who sleeps during harvest is a disgraceful son. –PROVERBS 10:5

One of the many Christian rock bands that emerged in the 1990s is known as The Waiting. Like many similar groups, the four band members are talented, creative, and very dedicated to Christ. But one thing that sets this group apart is its willingness to indulge in a great bit of hard work.

When Todd and Brad Olsen were first forming the group, their parents gave them both encouragement and good advice. The encouragement often took the form of buying their sons needed equipment. The good advice they offered was to work hard and to never give a bad performance. The words and actions of these parents have paid many dividends.

The Waiting's first albums marked the group members as serious artists. But for their album, entitled *Unfazed,* they wanted to take their music to the next level of excellence. Instead of writing the usual twenty songs or so (and then selecting the best for recording), they wrote over fifty songs—and under grueling circumstances. Brad Olsen remembered, "It wasn't the four of us in a basement. I was flying to California to write with someone, Clark was in Nashville writing with someone, Todd and Brandon were off doing their things. It was tough, but it was definitely something we needed to do."

As you might expect, the end result was worth the effort, and the album *Unfazed* places The Waiting on a much higher plane than its earlier work. But how many musicians would have paid such a price?

Do you have a reputation for being a hard worker? If so, praise God and keep it up! If not, you can begin changing today. Ask God to give you grace in this area, and then share your new commitment with a trusting friend who will help keep you accountable.

"Who despises the day of small things?" –ZECHARIAH 4:10

On March 28, 1842, a group of musicians gave its first concert together under the baton of Otto Nicolai. He was an excellent performer and the composer of an opera that is still produced today, the *Merry Wives of Windsor.* He called the new ensemble the Vienna Philharmonic.

In 1843, no one could have foreseen that this group would evolve into one of the world's finest musical institutions. Like many other new ideas, it might have passed into oblivion after a few seasons. But its members were enthusiastic and ambitious. Within a year they were taking on such challenges as Beethoven's Ninth Symphony!

Every organization on the planet today, even the largest and most influential, had to start somewhere. Many people want to see a grand idea take form, but they lack the perseverance to keep going in the early days of the plan. At first, it may seem so insignificant that it is difficult to take it seriously. But those who stick with it and have the patience to wait for gradual growth will see great results in the end.

Throughout the Scriptures, God calls ordinary men and women to do extraordinary things. When He called Noah (Genesis 6:14), Abraham (Genesis 12:1-3), Moses (Exodus 3:16-20), Gideon (Judges 6:14), or many others, they didn't have much to start with. Yet they lived to see God fulfill the vision. If God calls you to take part in a long-term project, be patient to see it grow from infancy to fulfillment.

Choose a large company or corporation that interests you—McDonald's, Wal-Mart, IBM. Do some research and find out about its beginning. Praise God for what He is beginning in you.

Though the fig tree does not bud and there are no grapes on the vines, though the olive crop fails and the fields produce no food, though there are no sheep in the pen and no cattle in the stalls, yet I will rejoice in the Lord, I will be joyful in God my Savior. —HABAKKUK 3:17, 18

Anyone can praise God when everything is wonderful. But it is in times of trial and adversity that our faith is truly tested. How we react to calamity—whether with praise or despair—not only shows our level of faith but also affects those around us.

Millions today know the name John Wesley, the great founder of the Methodist church. Countless congregations still sing the many stirring hymns he and his brother Charles composed. But in 1735, the brothers were two unknown missionaries on their way to take the Gospel to the New World. Their journey nearly saw a tragic end. They sailed into a terrible storm, and it seemed to passengers and crew alike that the ship would soon be at the bottom of the Atlantic.

What a scene was before the Wesley brothers. While they struggled with their own fears, they saw the terrified panic of almost everyone on board and heard the other passengers' despairing screams. But soon they noticed another scene. A group of Moravian missionaries traveling to America was calmly praying and singing hymns of praise. The contrast could not have been greater, and that amazing act of faith stayed with the Wesleys for the rest of their lives.

The influence of those missionaries had an impact even for us. John Wesley translated many Moravian hymns into English, and he traveled across Europe to meet the Moravian leader, Count Nickolaus Zinzendorf. The count was also a hymnwriter, and the influence of his people is still heard in Methodist hymnals today. While in America, John Wesley edited the first hymnal that was published in the New World, named simply *A Collection of Psalms and Hymns*. In his lifetime, he and his brother published over fifty more such collections! Today is John Wesley's birthday.

Consider the catastrophe of the Titanic. How do you think you would react in such a situation? How well have you handled adversity in the past? Thank God for bringing you through past trials, and praise Him for His everlasting love.

However, if you suffer as a Christian, do not be ashamed, but praise God that you bear that name. —1 PETER 4:16

The New York Philharmonic premiered Benjamin Britten's *Sinfonia da Requiem* on this date in 1941. The huge work was a major success and was soon performed by the Boston Symphony under Serge Koussevitzky. Afterward, Koussevitzky commissioned Britten to compose a new opera, his renowned *Peter Grimes*—the most successful of all modern British operas.

But this series of events started with a strange rejection. The *Sinfonia da Requiem* was not intended to be premiered in America. It had been commissioned by the Japanese government to help celebrate the 2,600th anniversary of the Japanese Imperial Dynasty. But in 1940, the completed work was rejected because they considered it "too Christian," since it used text from the traditional Catholic requiem mass. The composer was both hurt and baffled, but as events proved, it turned out for the best.

In today's secularized world, any believer can be rejected at times because he is "too Christian." Sometimes this can be subtle, in other cases, the rejection or prejudice can be quite blatant. Should we fight back, take revenge, or exhibit hatred for hatred? Or will we choose to "bless those who curse you, pray for those who mistreat you" (Luke 6:28)?

The apostles were often mistreated because of their faith, but they rejoiced "because they had been counted worthy of suffering disgrace for the Name" (Acts 5:41). This is our example to imitate. When mistreated, we must resist the urge to "repay . . . evil for evil" (Romans 12:17). Instead, we need to believe that God will bring some good out of it for His purposes.

Have you been rejected, ridiculed, or had to sacrifice because of your faith? Take time to offer it up to the Lord, and give thanks to Him for calling you His child.

The Lord is with me; I will not be afraid. What can man do to me?

—PSALM 118:6

Many, many young musicians are trying to "break into" the music business. Of course, some have more talent than others, but even among the very talented there are further divisions. All too many simply sit and wait for the big phone call to come. But some have the courage to venture out, to boldly knock on doors that the Lord may open.

In the mid 1990s, singer/songwriter Nichole Nordeman was as unknown as a thousand other wanna-bes. Unlike some of the others in this group, she was extremely talented, both as a singer and as a songwriter—with lyrics deep and meaningful. But what truly set Nordeman apart was her determination to take the needed risks.

One day she heard about a nationwide songwriting competition that had a $200 entry fee. She could have come up with a dozen objections. "They must have a million other songwriters applying." "I'm bound to lose." "Do I really want to know if my songs are any good?" "Where can I get $200?!" Instead of listening to her fears, Nordeman borrowed the money and entered the competition.

She won first prize, earning her a recording deal with Star Song Records. Within a year of borrowing that $200, Nordeman was reading national rave reviews of her first album, entitled *Wide Eyed*. But who else won from that competition? Answer: the thousands of Nordeman's fans who are deeply blessed by her artistry. Unless she had faced her fears and ventured out, her fans might not have ever heard of her.

Listen to a copy of Nordeman's album Wide Eyed. *As you listen to her music, thank God for helping her face and overcome her fears, and ask Him to help you do the same.*

A cheerful heart is good medicine. —PROVERBS 17:22

April Fools' Day might be a good time to have a laugh from the world of music. Some of the funniest situations occur in orchestra rehearsals, often because they are so very unexpected. Sometimes great musical geniuses are "absent-minded professor" types, and the attempts to communicate their interpretations of the music can be quite funny.

Perhaps the best known example of this was the renowned conductor Eugene Ormandy, who led the Philadelphia Orchestra for many years. His genius has never been doubted, and he was so brilliant at blending orchestral timbres together that people still speak of the "Ormandy sound" he could create. Yet the strangest things would often come from his mouth at rehearsal. Members of the Philadelphia Orchestra have collected dozens of "Ormandy-isms" from which the following were selected:

"I don't want to confuse you anymore than is absolutely necessary."
"Who is sitting in that empty chair?"
"Start three bars before something."
"Let's start at 35 because I don't know where it is."
"I was trying to help you so I was beating wrong."
"Why do you always insist on playing while I'm trying to conduct?"
"I guess you thought I was conducting, but I wasn't."
"Don't play louder, just give it more."
"The tempo remains pianissimo."
"Write it down in your own handwriting."
"It's difficult to remember when you haven't played it before."
"I never say what I mean but I always manage to say something similar."
"During the rests, pray."

Well, at least we can all agree on that last one!

Modern medicine can learn a lot from the Bible. Do you remember the movie Patch Adams, *which is about a doctor who has "discovered" the healing power of laughter? Thank God for the gift of laughter and share these "Ormandy-isms" with someone else today.*

"But they all alike began to make excuses." —LUKE 14:18

Every schoolteacher has heard hundreds of excuses explaining why homework isn't ready. Every boss has heard just as many why an employee is late for work. But what a joy it is to find someone who doesn't look for excuses to get out of responsibilities.

The expression "The show must go on" gives the impression that those in the music world tend to keep going even when difficulties come up before or during a performance. Unfortunately, it seems that not all musicians have heard, or at least believe in, that expression. Excuses for a poor performance abound. "It was my reed." "It was the audience." "It was my headache." If the show is to go on, it must do so with excellence.

You'll find, however, that the "greats" in any field—from music to sports to academics—are not the ones who make excuses. They're the ones who keep going when most of us would quit. Perhaps the most outrageous example of this kind of determination is that of the legendary jazz drummer Buddy Rich, who died this day in 1987. One season when he was touring with Tommy Dorsey's band, the group arrived in Dayton, Ohio. Most of the band went to the hotel to sleep, but Rich was wide awake so he set out to play some handball. During the game he tripped, breaking his left arm in three places.

Rich would not be stopped. Since he had to wear a cast, he had a special sling made to match the band's uniforms. The performances? His own words describe it best: "I played with my right hand and used my foot as a left hand. Solos, too. I never missed a day for the three months the cast stayed on."

Do we show that kind of determination in anything we do? God wants us to consistently do our best and avoid making excuses.

Imagine playing the drums with just one arm, and if you're really daring, throw in a foot. How easy is it to play even one song? The next time you're tempted to give an excuse for not doing something, think of the determination shown by Buddie Rich and ask God to help you do your best.

"Give, and it will be given to you." –LUKE 6:38A

On April 3, 1897, at about 8:30 in the morning, Johannes Brahms (1833–1897) died in his Vienna apartment. In his sixty-three years, Brahms composed some of history's finest masterpieces, conquering every genre of music except opera. His four symphonies rival even those of Beethoven for their beauty, popularity, and frequency of performance. His choral music, especially the *German Requiem,* is cherished by every singer. His fascinating chamber music, exquisite songs, and superb piano music form the basis for thousands of recitals today. When conductor Hans von Bulow included Brahms—along with Bach and Beethoven—in his famous phrase, the musical "three B's," he expressed the agreement of history.

Yet this celebrated composer was an unpretentious man, whose greatest pleasure was to take long walks through the countryside. Even after his music made him quite wealthy, he continued to wear old suits and to brew his own coffee. As he approached fifty, this world-famous musician grew a long bushy beard for the simple reason that he was tired of shaving and wearing ties!

Brahms was generous with his money, supporting many friends and charities, and caring so little about his fortune that he would often stuff bundles of banknotes in a closet and forget them. He constantly sent gifts of money to needy people, including total strangers. He was willing to help fellow musicians as well. He helped the young composer Dvorak find a publisher, and he offered to help support his family.

In letters to his parents, he always asked if there was "enough money." Once Brahms sent his father a large bundle of banknotes wrapped in a score to Handel's oratorio *Saul,* with the amusing note attached: "Father dear, if at any time things go badly with you, music is always the best consolation. Only study my old *Saul* attentively; you will find something there that will be of use to you."

God wants us to give—our talents and time as well as money. In what ways can we give today?

Have you ever given someone an anonymous gift? Leave a batch of cookies or some fresh fruit with an inspiring Scripture on a teacher's desk or a neighbor's porch. You will both be blessed.

For to me, to live is Christ and to die is gain. –PHILIPPIANS 1:21

Few composers in history have written as many masterpieces as Wolfgang Amadeus Mozart. Symphonies, operas, concertos, keyboard works, and chamber music—all were written in his short life of thirty-five years. Like the Apostle Paul, who wrote the above Scripture from a prison cell, Mozart never feared death. Rather, he welcomed it as God's will whenever it might come.

On this day in 1878, Mozart wrote his father a fervent letter of faith, in which he states: "I never lie down in my bed without reflecting that perhaps I—young as I am—may not live to see another day; yet none of all who know me can say that I am socially melancholy or morose. For this blessing I daily thank my Creator and wish it from my heart for all my fellow men."

Mozart realized that life could end at any time, so he made the most of every day, thanking God for the gift of life each day.

When his beloved mother died, it was the young Mozart who consoled both his older sister and his father: "It will greatly assist such happiness as I may have to hear that my dear father and my dear sister have submitted wholly to the will of God, with resignation and fortitude—and have put their whole confidence in Him, in the firm assurance that He orders all things for the best."

This is the testimony of a Christian whose faith in the Lord was unwavering. Mozart's advice is for each of us: "Let us put our trust in God and console ourselves with the thought that all is well, if it is in accordance with the will of the Almighty, as He knows best what is profitable and beneficial to our temporal happiness and our eternal salvation."

Do you know that if you should die, you would go to heaven? If you aren't sure, talk to a pastor or youth counselor about this soon.

"Whoever serves me must follow me; and where I am, my servant also will be. My Father will honor the one who serves me." –JOHN 12:26

The Christian life is a walk; we are not standing still. Sometimes we find that the road we're on changes, and we head in a different direction than we started out.

Singer Kim Hill's debut into Christian music was tremendous, and she soon had three solid albums to her credit. Then in 1994, she tried something new, launching successfully into the country music scene. Her video "Janie's Gone Fishin'" reached number one on Country Music Television (CMT), but she knew that God had more for her to do.

What next? Kim Hill has now become one of America's most sensitive worship leaders and songwriters. After releasing her 1997 album, she acknowledged, "There's definitely been a change in the focus of my life. I realized that this whole thing—the career, the music, and the ministry—isn't about me. It's about Him. He's called me to do more than entertain. He's called me to help people enter into His presence through worship."

Explaining the new focus of her ministry, Hill gives an illustration of our ongoing Christian walk: "I've heard that when a marksman gets a new gun, he rarely hits the bull's-eye on the first try. It's on the second or the third shot that he gets closer to the center." As she leads thousands into praise and worship, it is clear that Kim Hill's persistence in ministry and service to God has yielded high dividends.

Go to a local state park or forest preserve, and set out on a walk along one of the paths. As you follow the path ahead of you, think of what it means to follow Christ. Pray as you walk, asking for His leading in your life.

Though an army besiege me, my heart will not fear; though war break out against me, even then will I be confident. –PSALM 27:3

This was a sad day for country music fans, for on April 6, 1998, Tammy Wynette died. Often called the "Queen of the Country Heartache" for her many tearful songs, her personal experiences with poverty and suffering made the lyrics very real to her audiences. Her father died when she was a baby, and she was passed among various poor relatives with little hope for a future.

Ironically, it was her desperate need that gave her the courage to break through her poverty. Married young, Wynette was pregnant with her third child when her husband left her. Then the new baby had many medical problems, leaving Mom with huge bills to pay. What could she do? She had no training and only one skill: singing.

In order to feed her family, she auditioned to sing for a radio station. Soon, her powerful voice became known locally, and the money she earned helped hold her family together. But it was very tough, for the singing took time away from her young children. She needed to either get a serious contract soon—something that would pay her well yet enable her to spend time with her family—or she would have to abandon singing and find another way to make it.

In 1966, Wynette drove to Nashville and showed up unannounced at CBS Records. She wanted an appointment with Billy Sherrill, the company's top producer, but his secretary was out. Boldly marching into his office, she introduced herself. Sherrill was impressed by her talents as well as by her audacity, and he gave her a contract. Many hits were to follow—notably her famous song, "Stand by Your Man"—and her bills were paid and more. Often one moment of boldness can affect a lifetime.

There are times we need to be bold for God, to be filled with His confidence and strength. When the time comes, will we, like Tammy Wynette, have the courage to be bold?

Can you be bold when the need arises? Study the many Scriptures on this subject, and memorize a few to use in those moments when you need the courage to be bold.

Then the Lord replied: "Write down the revelation and make it plain on tablets so that a herald may run with it." —HABAKKUK 2:2

If you could say anything to the world, what would you say? So many young musicians, struggling to "make it to the top," need to ask themselves: "What will I do when I get there?" "What will I say to the many fans who are now wanting to follow me?" This type of soul-searching was experienced by the members of a Christian band called Switchfoot.

At first they were just three musicians playing together. But their success grew quickly, and now the public is expecting new CDs from them regularly. Their only desire was to have songs that have meaning and purpose. Jon Foreman, guitarist, singer, and songwriter, pondered, "Now that we've been given a voice, what do we want to say? What do three guys from San Diego want to tell the world?"

Tough questions! But Switchfoot prayed and received some answers. Foreman explained, "There were three key themes. First, the inability to find significance in the marrow for pop culture. There is a magnificence to life veiled behind the facades of America. Second is our personal confession of the inability to find wholeness within ourselves. Third is that our only hope for completion is in Christ." In other words, they want to let people know that life is precious and that we can find our fulfillment only in Christ.

Since these musicians have a clear understanding of their core message, the music of Switchfoot has unity and authority. God has used their songs to touch thousands. But the hard questions had to be answered first.

Do you have a "life message" that you could share if the opportunity opened? Pray about it, then write down some ideas for your life message. Ask God what He would have you say to the world.

In humility consider others better than yourselves. –PHILIPPIANS 2:3

Master of the comic opera, Gaetano Donizetti (1797–1848) died on this date in Bergamo, Italy. He was very successful not only because of his operas' irresistible humor, but also as a result of the beauty of his melodies. Donizetti had an amazing gift for lyric melody, and even his instrumental parts sound as if they should be sung instead of played. His principle works—*The Elixir of Love, The Daughter of the Regiment, Don Pasquale,* and *Lucia di Lammermoor*—are in the repertoire of every major opera company today. In his lifetime, he completed almost seventy operas, receiving acclaim from throughout the musical world. In Rome, Donizetti was crowned "King of the Opera," and in Vienna, he was given titles by the emperor himself.

With so many honors and with such worldwide recognition, those near Donizetti may have wondered how he would deal with a loss of fame. Fans easily become fickle. Perhaps a new talented composer would arise and steal Donizetti's fans. Perhaps tastes would change and the public would tire of his music. How would he handle such rejection? Would he become bitter?

When his last opera was written in 1844, and health problems were trying to stifle his spirit, it seemed that such questions would need to be addressed. Yet, instead of feeling discarded, it seems he welcomed a new generation of composers. In a letter of that year, Donizetti writes, "Others have ceded their places to us and we must cede ours to still others. . . . I am more than happy to give mine to people of talent like Verdi."

In such a competitive world as the performing arts, how refreshing to hear such a statement! There are few who would have the honesty, security, and goodness to applaud the talents of younger musicians—those who would soon displace him. How liberating it is to let go of such worries. Donizetti saw the next generation as a blessing rather than a threat. He knew this was God's natural order, and he found peace and happiness in surrendering instead of fighting it. What do we need to surrender to God rather than fight today?

The world sends us a message that is totally opposite of the above Scripture. The next time you are watching TV, notice how many commercials give you the message, in one way or another, that you are number one. Ask God to keep you humble in such a self-promoting world.

There is neither Jew nor Greek, slave nor free, male nor female, for you are all one in Christ Jesus. –GALATIANS 3:28

Most people know of the great Nat "King" Cole's vocal talents. But long before he was a famous singer, he played piano in a jazz trio. It was usually an instrumental-only group, but occasionally he would "break the monotony" by singing a few numbers. Soon, more and more people requested him to sing, and eventually a star singer emerged.

After Cole had achieved tremendous success, he still had to endure the bigotry that so many other black musicians have known. Long into his career, he and his wife bought a home in a Los Angeles suburb. It was a lovely house, and they gave little thought to the fact that it had been an all-white neighborhood.

Sure enough, several of the neighbors began talking, and they began a petition to block "undesirable people" from moving in nearby. As it was passed from house to house for signatures, the petition accidentally came to Cole's attention. He could have reacted with anger, resentment, or revenge. Instead, he chose humor to make a point. He simply walked to a neighbor's house and asked if he could also sign the petition: Cole said that he, too, didn't want any "undesirables" moving in!

It takes a great man or woman not to strike back when attacked. With God's grace, we can show love even to our enemies.

When was the last time you were hurt by someone? Pray for that person now, that the Lord might bless him or her, and bring peace to that relationship.

"We do not know what to do, but our eyes are upon you."

−2 CHRONICLES 20:12b

Making the decisions God wants us to make is something we all want to do. But sometimes we ask, "How can I know God's will for my life?" Singer/songwriter Michelle Tumes experienced a dramatic answer when she asked a similar question.

Born in Adelaide, Australia, and trained as a classical pianist, Tumes might have seemed an unlikely candidate for being a popular singer in America. Yet even at an early age, her talent for writing songs was impressive. Indeed, it had so impressed those around her that her eleven-year-old sister gave forty dollars she had earned on a newspaper route to pay for a demo tape of one of Tumes' songs.

This demo tape helped Tumes "get discovered," and she soon signed a songwriting contract and moved to America. But many things in her life were still uncertain. She wrote some songs for other artists, yet her own future was unsure and she needed to make some important decisions that would affect her entire life.

"One day I was trying to decide if I should go home or stay in America," she recalls. "I was really at an impasse. I just prayed, 'God, if you want this to happen, let me know, because I don't know what to do.' About three minutes after that prayer, I got a call from Sparrow Records asking if they could meet with me the next day. I had never even contacted them. Someone had given them one of my tapes without my even knowing it."

God heard her prayer of desperation and sent her a clear answer.

Is making decisions hard for you? List as many ways you can think of that people use to make decisions: tossing a coin, making lists of pros and cons, seeking out a fortune-teller, etc. Thank God for allowing us to come to Him whenever we need to make a decision.

"For the battle is not yours, but God's." –2 CHRONICLES 20:15b

Douglas Yeo, the bass trombonist for the Boston Symphony Orchestra, is a devout Christian with a burden for the souls around him. When he found that outrageous immoralities were being introduced in his local schools, he and his wife began a campaign to have them stopped. Organizing with fellow Christians, the Yeos worked tirelessly to collect enough names on a petition to have the issues voted upon by the public.

Immediately he was attacked and ridiculed as a "prude" by the local media. But with much perseverance, they eventually accumulated the two thousand names required to bring the issues to the ballet box. Thousands of Christians around the country prayed as the day for the vote drew near. It finally came, and . . . he lost. The vote was 54 percent to 46 percent against him.

Deeply disappointed, Yeo trudged to orchestra rehearsal the next day, still crying out, "Why, God?!" They began rehearsing the Berg Violin Concerto, a dissonant piece that changes dramatically in its second movement as the composer introduces a lovely chorale by J. S. Bach, "Es ist genug." God gave Yeo a tremendous peace as he pondered the comforting words of this chorale:

> It is enough. Lord, if it please You, unyoke me now at last! My Jesus comes: now good night, O world! I travel to my heavenly home; I travel surely and in peace.

Yeo concludes: "Winning isn't the only thing. Our victory is in the Lord, His timing known to Him alone. I may suffer loss, but when I needed it, His encouragement picked me up to fight another day."

We may not win every battle we face while on earth, but with Christ, we know we have the ultimate victory.

Is there a battle you need to fight for the Lord? Ask God for His direction, decide what one step you can take today in that fight, then praise Him for giving us the ultimate victory.

The end of a matter is better than its beginning. –ECCLESIASTES 7:8

If you want to hear some interesting stories, find a group of musicians and ask each one how he or she first began in music. The variety of answers will amaze you. Some began very early while others were late bloomers. Some tried a number of different instruments while others have always stayed with the same one.

The motives behind musicians' beginnings are also fascinating. Some had wonderful parents supporting their every effort. Others grew up feeling unnoticed by their parents and practiced diligently on their instrument in order to gain attention. Some persevered in music even when their friends ridiculed them. Still others would have never continued if not for the encouragement of their friends.

One of jazz's top saxophonists, Phil Woods, had a not-too-inspiring beginning. He describes his lack of enthusiasm for his first lesson: "My uncle died and left me my alto and I went for my lesson. I didn't want to, but they said, 'The man died. The least you can do is take a lesson.' " So he trudged off to his lesson, and became one of the greatest players of his day.

When King Solomon said, "The end of a matter is better than its beginning," he might have been talking about musicians. Not many of the renowned players today began with great fanfare. They were just kids taking lessons, often against their will. So stick with it. We never know how far God might want us to go with the talent He has given us.

Go to the library or a record store and look for recordings of young artists. Learn how they began, and let it inspire you to persevere with your God-given talents.

That is why, for Christ's sake, I delight in weaknesses, in insults, in hardships, in persecutions, in difficulties. For when I am weak, then I am strong. —2 CORINTHIANS 12:10

John Fischer is a deep-thinking songwriter who has become a prophet to the entire Christian music industry. His many albums include *Have You Seen Jesus My Lord?*, *Still Life*, and *New Covenant*. Fischer has also written nine books and numerous articles that challenge Christian musicians to stay focused on high-quality ministry and to avoid the trappings of the "star" business.

Much of his wisdom was learned through humility. A concert he remembers well was performed for a small audience in a huge, cold cathedral. To create a more intimate atmosphere, Fischer came down off the platform and sang directly in front of the pews. All went well while he accompanied himself on the guitar. But when he needed to play the piano, he again had to mount the seven-step platform, and the piano was in the very back behind a low wooden wall.

Seated far from his audience, he played his first song on the piano. In this awkward arrangement, Fischer got halfway through the song when his mind went blank: he couldn't find a needed chord. He tried the song again and again but without success. Completely despairing, he was about to give up when a person in the audience stood up, then another. The audience quietly moved forward to stand and sit around the piano.

Fischer recalls: "I am suddenly surrounded by warm human bodies as if I were in someone's living room. Everything is now changed. I sing the song without a flaw. I throw away whatever plan I had and sing whatever comes to mind. It is a warm, spontaneous evening and a concert better than I could have ever planned. It was humbling, but out of my weakness and humiliation God poured out his presence. I call it 'The Night the Audience Came Up.' "

God can—and does—work in mighty ways through people who perform "perfectly," and God deserves nothing less than our best efforts. But God can—and does more often—work through humbling experiences as well, and that is often when we learn the most.

Have you ever been to a concert that had a disaster? During the next performance you attend, take time to pray for those on the stage. You may never meet them, but your prayers can have a powerful effect.

A fool finds no pleasure in understanding but delights in airing his own opinions. —PROVERBS 18:2

Today, the music of Peter Ilyich Tchaikovsky is everywhere: the *1812 Overture,* the *Nutcracker Suite, Swan Lake,* the six great symphonies—all and more are in the standard repertoire. But as a young composer, Tchaikovsky was very sensitive to criticism. When his opera *Eugene Onegin* was premiered in 1879, he was particularly concerned to hear the opinion of two specific people. At that time, the leading Russian musicians were the Rubinstein brothers: Anton, founder of the Saint Petersburg Conservatory; and Nikolai, founder of the Moscow Conservatory.

What would these distinguished experts say? Surely, if anyone could discern the quality of Tchaikovsky's music, these were the best judges in all of Russia. They were proficient performers and composers and were consulted in every musical situations in the country. Their authoritative verdict of Tchaikovsky's new opera? Nikolai loved it, and Anton hated it!

The verdict of history would finally side with Nikolai, for Tchaikovsky's *Eugene Onegin* has long since become a very successful opera. But at the time, the young composer must have been filled with the insecurity that comes from conflicting opinions. And ironically, we all know of the great compositions by Tchaikovsky but those of the Rubinstein brothers have mostly been forgotten.

Today, so much attention is given to the opinions of so-called experts that we forget that everyone is quite fallible. The greatest musical works throughout history have been condemned by many authorities, and inferior pieces have received undue praise. Time, the better judge, will ultimately overrule all such expert opinion.

In the same way, each of us has an opinion and a right to express it. But we need to remember that opinions shouldn't be taken too seriously, for they are just that: opinions. The wise judge, no matter how expert, always admits that he may be in error. God is the ultimate judge—and the only perfect one. Let us remember that it's His opinion that really matters.

We all tend to take ourselves too seriously. Take a moment to pray and ask God to help you to see yourself and your opinions in His perspective.

Instruct a wise man and he will be wiser still; teach a righteous man and he will add to his learning. –PROVERBS 9:9

Listening to a new CD, we may forget how the recording industry has changed over the years. From the earliest acoustical recordings on waxlike discs, to the electrical methods, to the old 78s, to 45s and LPs, to the array of contemporary gadgets of today, recording has constantly improved. Anyone who has ever heard a recording from the early twentieth century will quickly admit to the quality we have today.

Yet all of the improvements we take for granted came from a determination to make things better than the status quo. Engineers have constantly experimented with recording techniques in order to discover better possibilities—to "add to their learning," as the above Scripture states. Of course, not all experiments work the first time, as we can see from the following example.

Bessie Smith, the "Empress of the Blues," was asked to record for Columbia in 1925. This state-of-the-art studio had just converted to the new electrical recording technique, and the engineers were still doing a lot of experimentation. For the session with Bessie Smith and a band of six musicians, the chief engineer thought that the studio was too big for the new carbon microphone.

An idea was suggested: a huge, conical tent of thick cloth was constructed and suspended from the ceiling. This giant "teepee" was large enough to cover the singer, her band, the engineers, and their equipment. The result was unfortunately lost to history. After the second take of "Yellow Dog Blues," the entire tent collapsed on all of them! It would later be called "the wildest scramble ever seen in a recording studio." So much for that idea!

God applauds our efforts—even the ones that fail—for it is through trying that we learn and grow.

Incidentally, Bessie Smith was born on this date in 1894.

How quick are you to try a new idea? Identify one area of your life that needs improving, and list as many different ideas as you can to help yourself make progress. Though many may fail, thank God that He will reward your efforts and help you find at least one way to improve.

*Therefore, my dear brothers, stand firm. Let nothing move you.
Always give yourselves fully to the work of the Lord, because you know
that your labor in the Lord is not in vain.* —1 CORINTHIANS 15:58

America's most popular hit song in 1959 was a ballad named "The Battle of New Orleans." Its own producers expected few sales from the record, but as soon as it was released it was an instant hit. Sung by Johnny Horton, the song gives a folksy version of Andrew Jackson's defeat of the British troops during the War of 1812.

One of the reasons its producers did not anticipate the song's potential was its humble origins. The song did not originate in the powerful recording studios of Nashville but in the backwoods of the Arkansas Ozarks. Its composer was not a well-known artist but a poor schoolteacher named Jimmy Driftwood. In fact, when publisher Don Warden first heard of the songwriting teacher, he had a very difficult time locating him—Driftwood did not even have a telephone! When he was finally found, Warden asked him to tape a few of his songs, but he was again stymied—Driftwood replied that he had no possible access to a tape recorder.

Eventually these obstacles were overcome and the song sold millions of records. But the motive behind the creation of the song is what merits our attention. When Jimmy Driftwood wrote "The Battle of New Orleans," it was not to sell records, or to make money, or to become a star (yet all these things came to him as a result of the song's success). He was an excellent, enthusiastic teacher who was searching for ways to interest his students in American history. Driftwood had tried all kinds of pictures, reports, and visual aids to no avail, but he found that his sixth-graders loved his history lessons when they were put to song!

We often find ourselves working hard for a very small and ungrateful "audience." Yet if we will do our work excellently, as unto the Lord, He will crown our efforts with greater blessing than we might have imagined.

Go to the library and find a recording of the song "The Battle of New Orleans." As you listen to it, pray that God will give you grace to do your work for His glory alone and to give you patience as you wait to be rewarded, in this life or the next.

Who may ascend the hill of the Lord? Who may stand in his holy place? He who has clean hands and a pure heart. —PSALM 24:3, 4A

In the world of contemporary Christian music, there are a number of groups that involve brothers and sisters from the same family. One family musical group is unique, however: it is a father/son act. Aaron Jeoffrey is the name of a very talented duo, Jeoffrey Benward and his son Aaron Benward. Their recordings are exceptional, and their concerts display both musical excellence and a heart for ministry.

One of the keys to their success is actually the whole reason they began working together. Jeoffrey had been working in Christian music for years, and when his son Aaron first brought up the idea of working together, Dad was hesitant. He knew of the many pitfalls in the music business and didn't want to see his son dealing with them. But he soon found that Aaron's vision came from a desire to serve God—not to grab a recording deal.

Aaron describes their vision: "Our goal is to show a positive parent/child relationship and hopefully to be role models for fathers and their sons, or parents and their children. Every social problem that we have today can be traced back to a dysfunctional family life. We want to address these problems, not only through our songs but by simply being who we are."

Do you think God can bless such a motive? Obviously. The Lord is looking for Christians who want to use their talents, not to gain fame and fortune, but to reach others.

Can you think of a time when you had a struggle with motives? Sometimes we do the right thing, but for the wrong reasons. Pray that God will purify your heart and make you sensitive to doing what is right—and for the right reasons.

Be very careful, then, how you live—not as unwise but as wise, making the most of every opportunity, because the days are evil.

It is quite a paradox that Igor Stravinsky (1882–1971) is best known as the composer of *Firebird, Petrushka,* and the *Rite of Spring,* the latter subtitled "Pictures of Pagan Russia." These early ballets explore secular and even pagan subjects that offer no clue to the personal religious faith he possessed later in life. All three of these works were written when Stravinsky was in his thirties and had long since abandoned the Russian Orthodox faith of his upbringing. Yet in the mid 1920s at the age of forty-four, Stravinsky experienced a permanent conversion to Christianity.

In the church of his childhood, Stravinsky had been required to read the Bible. Reaching his teens, he began criticizing and rebelling against the church, and he parted ways with Orthodoxy for nearly three decades. Yet years later he would explain, "For some years before my conversion, a mood of acceptance had been cultivated in me by a reading of the Gospels and by other religious literature."

Stravinsky dedicated his next major composition, the *Symphony of Psalms,* "to the glory of God." When asked where his inspiration came from for his innovative compositions, he was almost blunt in his modesty: "Only God can create. I make music from music." Concerning his genius, he wrote, "I regard my talents as God-given, and I have always prayed to Him for strength to use them." Like many geniuses, Stravinsky had his share of eccentricities. For instance, he often balanced an extra pair of glasses on top of his head in case he lost the pair he was wearing.

Here was a man whom the world acknowledged as a tremendous genius, and he possessed a sincere faith in Christ. Stravinsky lived a full, long life enriched by a wide circle of friends, all of whom respected his Christian beliefs. Because he combined his outspoken faith and his musical excellence, he was a witness that the world could not ignore. Stravinsky's life proves that the world will listen to our Christianity if we will first earn its respect by doing our work with excellence.

Is there someone whom you would like tell about Christ? Since actions speak louder than words, find a way to serve that person, and then he or she will hear you with respect.

As iron sharpens iron, so one man sharpens another.

–PROVERBS 27:17

Whenever we come up against a competitor, we have two choices. We can choose to attack, to cut down the other, to spread gossip, and to try to get ahead. Or we can choose the way of two Christian rock bands whose names are Disciple and Nailed.

Both of these bands formed in Knoxville, Tennessee. Before long, they were the two Christian bands in that city, both releasing successful albums and having number one hits. Their many fans were divided over which band was the best. But the competitive aspects never divided the bands' members, who have all become good friends.

Nailed guitarist Scottie Hoaglan describes his "competition," the members of Disciple: "They are great guys and we love them. We've known each other for all these years, and we know how true and genuine they are. They inspire us to be a better band." Both bands loan each other equipment when needed, and each has been in situations where their van broke down and the other band lent them theirs.

Disciple's Kevin Young explains: "There are going to be people who like Nailed better than Disciple and vice versa, but it doesn't matter to either of us because we are both into it for Jesus." He concludes, "We need Nailed around pushing us to be better. It's kind of like Sammy Sosa and Mark McGuire. Without Sosa, I don't think McGuire would have hit seventy home runs like he did. Each guy pushed the other to try harder. That same dynamic exists between Disciple and Nailed, and I think it makes a world of difference."

We need other Christians to keep us sharp—just as the Scripture says. And together, we can make a world of difference.

Do you have a friend who "sharpens" you, who inspires you to try harder? If so, praise God for such a friend. If not, ask the Lord to bring someone like this into your life.

Like a madman shooting firebrands or deadly arrows is a man who deceives his neighbor and says, "I was only joking!" –PROVERBS 26:18, 19

A small lie can grow to huge proportions if left unchecked. In 1959, a writer for *Down Beat* magazine named Don DeMichael sent his editors an article about the legendary blues singer Blind Orange Adams. DeMichael was very knowledgeable about jazz and blues history, so the editors published his article in the next issue.

DeMichael was astonished to see it and quickly called his boss. "That was a joke," he explained. "I thought you'd get a laugh and take it out of my copy. It's a pun on Blind Lemon Jefferson! Jefferson, Adams—get it?!" Fortunately, his editors had a sense of humor and laughed off the incident.

But once published, the legend grew rapidly. Soon there were references to Blind Orange Adams performing all over the country. Mail began to come in for him, so the good-natured DeMichael rented a postal box for him. Later, the Blind Orange Adams Appreciation Society was founded. Once a letter from a top New York record label was sent, stating that it wanted to make recordings of the great artist!

DeMichael tried to hold the jest a little longer. He arranged to make a recording of some friends, which he would produce himself. But the record company executives insisted on meeting Blind Orange Adams themselves, so the joke was over. DeMichael finally had to write another article, this time about a terrible car crash involving Blind Orange Adams.

God wants Christians to be joyful, to have fun, and to enjoy life. After all, He gave us our sense of humor! There is a difference, though, between having a good laugh and having a laugh at another's expense or letting a lie get out of control. The closer we are to God, the easier it is to recognize that difference.

Do you remember the animated movie Aladdin*? How did Aladdin's lie (pretending to be who he wasn't) get him into trouble? How did his lie affect his relationships with others? What finally got him out of trouble? Ask God for the grace to be truthful in all that you do.*

It was he who gave some to be apostles, some to be prophets, some to be evangelists, and some to be pastors and teachers. –EPHESIANS 4:11

So many people are trying to break into the music business that it seems odd to find three very successful artists who are trying to not let their music careers interfere with their "true calling." The CCM group known as Phillips, Craig & Dean consists of three excellent singers whose albums and live concerts continually keep them in demand. Indeed, they could do much more in the CCM world if they desired, but they are careful not to give it too much emphasis.

The reason? All three of these men are pastors! From three different churches, from three different parts of the country, Randy Phillips, Shawn Craig, and Dan Dean preach sermons by day and give concerts by night. Far from being a distraction to their music, they believe that their pastoral duties—especially counseling—keep them close to people, which makes their music very real. "As pastors," Craig explains, "we come in contact with people faced with great tragedies." Such emotions show through in their impassioned songwriting.

Obviously, having two full-time professions—and, of course, families!—makes for very busy lives. Why don't these men simply give up their pastorates and enjoy being CCM stars? Because of their commitment to the local church. Their music is important but could never overshadow their church work. "The greatest challenge we have is balancing the two," states Phillips, "because we feel strongly that our future and our place is in the local church."

What a testimony to the importance of our church life! How many of us value the blessing of our church to the point of altering our careers around it? God has a place for each of us in the church. Perhaps we should reconsider the place of the church in our plan of priorities.

As the above Scripture states, God has given each of us a gift to use in serving the church. Do you know what your spiritual gifts are? If not, talk with your pastor about discovering your spiritual gifts and how you can use them in your church.

Come near to God and he will come near to you. –JAMES 4:8

The Czech composer Antonin Dvorak (1841–1904) finished his Symphony no. 7 on this date in 1885. The great Christian took today's opening verse of Scripture very seriously. Throughout his life, he drew near to God and maintained a reputation of character, high morals, and great faith. His faith and his life mirrored one another; both were simple, unpretentious, and steadfast. This composer of such masterpieces as the *New World Symphony* worshiped in the same devout manner whether in a great cathedral or in a country church.

Dvorak's relationship to God appears to have been consistently reverent and personal. His principle biographer, Otakar Sourek, notes that an unchanging feature of Dvorak's nature was his "sincere piety." The composer loved to read the Bible and owned copies in English as well as modern and ancient Czech. Dvorak's letters are full of spiritual observations, and his manuscripts regularly began with the marking "With God" and ended with the benediction, "God be thanked."

He spoke of his musical genius as "the gift of God" or as "God's voice." When writing about his colossal Mass in D Major, Dvorak characteristically proclaimed, "Faith, hope, and love to God Almighty and thanks for the great gift of being enabled to bring this work in the praise of the Highest and in the honour of art to a happy conclusion." Then Dvorak added, "Do not wonder that I am so religious. An artist who is not could not produce anything like this. Have we not examples enough in Beethoven, Bach, Raphael, and many others?"

He viewed his extraordinary composing skills as being inspired by God, claiming that he would "simply do what God tells me to do." Dvorak attended the Bohemian Catholic Church, but the faith he expressed in his life and his music was nonsectarian. The same Dvorak who wrote a *Latin* Requiem also depicted his beliefs in his *Hussite* Overture, glorifying the ministry of Czech reformer John Hus. He was from first to last a simple man of peace.

What many lessons can be learned from such a devout soul? Dvorak's trusting faith was based on a very personal relationship with his Savior Jesus Christ. We need—daily—to draw near to Him.

As you go through your day today, remind yourself each time you start something new that it is done "With God" and as you finish each task, say to yourself, "God be thanked." Note what a difference it makes in your day.

Rejoice in the Lord always. I will say it again: Rejoice!

–PHILIPPIANS 4:4

On April 23, 1586, Martin Rinkart, the creator of the great hymn "Now Thank We All Our God," was born in Eilenburg, Saxony. The hymn's powerful words have inspired countless believers for hundreds of years:

Now thank we all our God, with hearts and hands and voices,
Who wondrous things hath done, in whom his world rejoices;
Who, from our mothers' arms, has blessed us on our way
With countless gifts of love, and still is ours today.

This testimony of praise came from a life filled with disappointment and tragedy. Rinkart's beginnings forecast great promise. The brilliant man became a foundation scholar, a chorister, a theologian, and a bishop by the age of thirty-one. Surely he could expect a comfortable life of study and quiet.

Yet the bulk of his ministry was during the horrors of the Thirty Years War. Because his small city of Eilenburg was walled, it attracted thousands of refugees seeking protection. The result was famine and disease. During most of the Pestilence of 1637, Rinkart was the only minister in the city and personally conducted funeral services for over half of the eight thousand people who died—sometimes as many as fifty services in a single day. One of these funerals was for his own wife.

Yet Martin Rinkart somehow kept a heart of praise alive. He was constantly aware of God's "countless gifts of love" and encouraged his people to praise the Lord "with hearts and hands and voices." When the war was finally over and the Peace of Westphalia concluded, what song was sung at the great celebration? Rinkart's masterpiece of praise, "Now Thank We All Our God."

We are all faced with difficult times. God didn't promise that life would be easy. He did promise to love us and to be with us, though, and for that we can continually thank Him.

What are your favorite songs of praise? Make a list of them, and start each day for the next week praising the Lord in song.

The Lord is my shepherd, I shall not be in want. —PSALM 23:1

Everyone gets nervous from time to time. Violinist Christopher Wu learned a valuable lesson in finding God's peace in the middle of a "fear attack." It happened on the day he was to audition for the Pittsburgh Symphony Orchestra.

"While I was warming up, I could barely play two notes together. I was truly scared and started to pray." Still, he could not calm himself. "Things got worse when I got on stage and my violin bow started to shake uncontrollably. I tried everything to get my nerves under control." But nothing worked. What to do?! This audition was terribly important.

He had brought two things with him. The first was a picture of his father, a wonderful Christian man who had died when Wu was fourteen. The other was a small piece of paper on which he had written two passages from the Bible, Psalm 23 and the fourth chapter of Philippians. He remembers, "As I stared at the picture and the two verses, my bow stopped shaking and God took over and gave me a peace that was beyond words."

The audition went beautifully and Wu was given the job the next day. But even before he had known that, he was praising God. "As I drove home from the audition, I was so thankful—not for anything related to the Pittsburgh Symphony Orchestra—but for God's grace. He is in control; He loves us and knows what is best for us."

Do you remember the last time you were really nervous? Look up the two Bible passages mentioned above, and find others on this subject. Keep your favorite verses in your wallet or pocket.

Instead, you ought to say, "If it is the Lord's will, we will live and do this or that." –JAMES 4:15

How easy it is to take things for granted! God has given us so much—our lives, our family, our friends, our talents, our possessions—and we seldom stop to thank Him. Yet everything we have is by His grace, and each day is a new gift to us from the Lord.

The land of Italy has produced many of the greatest composers of opera. One of these, Giacomo Puccini, was from a long line of Italian musicians. Like Bach, he was the very best in his family's musical traditions, and gave us such masterpieces as *Madame Butterfly, La Boheme, Manon Lescaut, Suor Angelica,* and *Gianni Schicchi.*

In 1924, Puccini was sixty-five and at the height of his fame. The Italian public was clamoring for another Puccini opera. He frantically worked on *Turandot,* but he never finished the score. Puccini was undergoing treatment for cancer of the larynx when he suddenly died of a heart attack. The last two scenes remained uncompleted.

The opera was later "completed" by Franco Alfano, and this version is now a great favorite around the world. But on April 25, 1926, the great conductor Toscanini gave a very dramatic production of Puccini's *Turandot.* Coming to the last two scenes, he laid down his baton and announced to the audience, "Here death stopped Puccini's hand." The lights dimmed and the audience silently exited—hushed by the drama of the moment.

We never know when God is going to call us, or someone we love, to be with Him in heaven. Rather than allowing the uncertainty of death to make us afraid, let us be motivated by it to live each day to its fullest and to Christ's glory.

Read James 4:13-17. Begin every new day God gives you with a prayer of thanks for the gift of life. Then thank a member of your family for being a part of your life.

"Apart from me you can do nothing." –JOHN 15:5

When we turn on the radio or the CD player, we hear the finished product only—never a "work in progress." We are so accustomed to hearing the final version of a composer's work that we can easily forget the many hours (or days, or weeks, or months) of work which went into the music. Working through the creative process is a task for all those in the creative arts, whether writing a symphony or a folk song.

Singer/songwriter Sarah Masen has known many long hours of this process and testifies to its anguish. "I'm so afraid sometimes when I sit down and write," she admits, "that nothing will be there, that nothing will happen, that the well will be dry. It feels like stepping into a void."

In describing this void, Masen depicts the very nature of composition: "There's a mystery that happens in the creative process, but I don't know how to make that mystery happen. It always seems to happen when I'm not looking. It hits me when I'm not aware. We're all involved somehow in Jacob's wrestling with God, in looking for truth, in praying for it, in trying to figure out what all of this beauty is for."

Finally, Sarah Masen concludes that for the process to be blessed, both prayer and her own efforts must be involved. "As I seek to pray my way through confusion and create my way through self-doubt, I've found that my efforts to do something—and this is true not just of songwriting but of all of life—I've found that my efforts to do something are always met by God, but almost never in the way that I thought."

God does come to meet us and help us along our journey in life, but we need to take steps toward Him first. For truly, without Him we can do nothing.

Sit down and create a work of art that represents to you what it means to be near to God. Thank Him for His gift of creativity.

And we know that in all things God works for the good of those who love him, who have been called according to his purpose.

—ROMANS 8:28

On April 27, 1749, George Frederic Handel's *Music for Royal Fireworks* was performed in Green Park, London, to celebrate the peace treaty of Aix-la-Chapelle. By this time, Handel was a famous composer, well-known throughout Europe. A few decades earlier, this German-born musician moved to England with one great specialty: composing Italian opera.

For a while all was well, and he produced some excellent operas. But soon the fickle public got tired of them. Although Handel toiled furiously, composing one opera after another, nothing seemed to work. The audiences deserted Handel, one calamity followed another, and financial disaster was imminent. The composer's health failed, and he must have surely wondered why God had so abandoned him to such a hopeless position.

However, Handel's music career was not over, only his opera career. In hindsight, we can see that God was arranging things so that Handel would compose in a new form, the oratorio. Taking stories from the Bible such as Esther, Saul, and Israel in Egypt, Handel began to create one masterpiece after another—and the audiences began to respond. It was in this new medium that he wrote his greatest music, including the classic *Messiah.* Thanks to this complete change of direction, his health, popularity, and fortune returned in greater measure than he had ever known.

When we are in the middle of trying or difficult times, it is difficult to have any hope for the future. But God has promised to never abandon us, and He often uses circumstances to get our attention and to take us in new direction. Instead of fighting Him and clinging to "what worked before," we need to look to God and see where He is leading us. Maybe He has an entirely unique course for us, through which He can bless us and greatly use us for His glory.

Listen to a recording of the Messiah. *Thank God for taking Handel through his "dead end" and inspiring him to head in a new direction, and ask Him to give you such inspiration the next time you feel discouraged.*

Even when I am old and gray, do not forsake me, O God, till I declare your power to the next generation, your might to all who are to come. —PSALM 71:18

James Cleveland (1932–1991) was known as the "King of Gospel Music" and the "Crown Prince of Gospel." His influence has been felt by virtually every gospel singer since 1960. In his lifetime, he recorded fifty-four albums, including such best-sellers as *Jesus Is the Best Thing, Lord Help Me, I Stood on the Banks,* and *Peace, Be Still.*

His was not the smooth sound of a typical soloist, but his rough, "Louis Armstrong" voice nonetheless kept his audiences' attention. His many compositions were performed by such stars as Mahalia Jackson and Billy Preston, as well as by many mass choirs. Yet Cleveland still found time to pastor churches—such as Detroit's Prayer Tabernacle, and the Cornerstone Institutional Baptist Church in Los Angeles.

But his greatest accomplishment was not created by his voice or his many compositions. Cleveland had a dream of helping young musicians in the world of gospel music. When he was young, he got his first taste of the gospel style while at Chicago's Pilgrim Baptist Church where Tommy Dorcey was the music director. Inspired by Dorcey's genius, Cleveland now wanted to pass on that inspiration to the next generation.

In 1968, he gathered a select group of talented musicians in Philadelphia in hopes of making his dream a reality. The result was the Gospel Music Workshop of America, which has been the training ground for hundreds of budding artists. With over 30,000 members and 150 chapters, the GMWA has encouraged far more young musicians since Cleveland's death than he would have ever been able to meet in his life.

We never know what God may choose to accomplish through our lives—and we may never know while we are still living! We need to live for God the best we can each day and leave the rest to Him.

Remember a time when you were inspired by a teacher or pastor, and share this memory with a sibling or friend.

But now, this is what the Lord says—he who created you, O Jacob, he who formed you, O Israel: "Fear not, for I have redeemed you; I have summoned you by name; you are mine." —ISAIAH 43:1

When you have a very difficult task before you, it can feel overwhelming. But if you can find even one person who believes in you and can encourage you, it can make a world of difference. Jazz trumpeter Clark Terry remembers a great example of this principle, when his encourager was the legendary Duke Ellington.

Terry was playing in Ellington's band when they were to record a new album. The Duke came to him beforehand and said, "Clark, I want you to play Buddy Bolden for me on this album." The trumpeter had to confess that he didn't know who Buddy Bolden was. This was all Ellington needed to explode with inspiration.

"Aw, he was so fantastic! He was fabulous! He was always sought after. He had the biggest, fattest trumpet sound in town. He bent notes to the nth degree. He used to tune up in New Orleans and break glasses in Algiers! He was great with diminisheds. When he played a diminished, he bent those notes, man, like you've never heard them before!"

Terry's eyes were wide open. He later remembered, "By this time Duke had me psyched out! He finished by saying, 'As a matter of fact, you are Buddy Bolden!' So I thought I was Buddy Bolden." Clark Terry played on this album as he had never played before. When the sessions were over, Duke Ellington—whose birthday is today—went over to the trumpeter, put his arms around his shoulders and announced, "That was Buddy Bolden!"

As Christians, we always have someone who believes in us and is there with constant encouragement—God is our biggest fan! Let Him put His arms around your shoulders today.

Who are you in this story, Clark Terry or Duke Ellington? Many of us have had people who believed in us. But whether or not you've ever had a "Duke" to encourage you, you can be an encourager. Find someone today, and give that person the message that he can "be Buddy Bolden."

"I was eyes to the blind and feet to the lame. I was a father to the needy; I took up the case of the stranger." —JOB 29:15, 16

The popular singer Willie Nelson was born this day in 1933. Raised on a poor farm in Texas, it would have been difficult for him to imagine the success he would one day find. Yet he was helped by many people on his way, and two in particular were supportive at times when he needed them the most.

The first helper was a fellow songwriter, Hank Cochran. After hearing a few songs by the struggling young Nelson, Cochran asked him to audition for his small company, Pamper Music. Nelson answered, "I'll come if someone can give me some money for gas." Cochran gave him the money and later urged his boss to hire Nelson as another songwriter. His boss explained that if Nelson were hired, then there would not be enough money to give Cochran his anticipated raise. Cochran considered this, but replied, "I'm getting by now; let's do it!" Willie Nelson was given his first contract.

Sometime after this came Nelson's second big break, at the hands of country singing star Faron Young. Nelson had just written a song entitled "Hello Walls," and was unsuccessfully trying to sell it. When he heard it, Young was impressed. He wouldn't buy it then, but he promised to record it sometime. But Nelson needed money immediately, so Young gave him a $400 loan.

Faron Young kept his promise to record "Hello Walls," and it turned out to be his biggest hit. Suddenly Willie Nelson was in demand, and large royalty checks began rolling in. As soon as the first one arrived, Nelson went to Young with the $400. Young laughed and replied, "You don't owe me a thing. If anybody owes anybody here, it's me that owes you!"

We are surrounded by people whom God loves and wants us to help. All we need to do to be "eyes to the blind" is to open our own eyes. Who can we help today?

In what ways have you helped the needy? Offer to volunteer at a homeless shelter or soup kitchen, even if it's for just one day, and thank God that you are able to help others.

Slaves, obey your earthly masters in everything; and do it, not only when their eye is on you and to win their favor, but with sincerity of heart and reverence for the Lord. —COLOSSIANS 3:22

In the twenty years he has played with the National Symphony Orchestra, trombonist Jim Kraft has worked with hundreds of musicians. Many of these are fellow believers, for Kraft is a founding director of the Christian Performing Artists' Fellowship. But regardless of who he is performing with, he has learned how to show them the love of Jesus Christ.

Showing Christ's love can be challenging at times, especially with many of the conductors who step to the podium. Most are, of course, world-class musicians, but one in particular was so terrible that Kraft could not check his negative attitude. He remembers, "I recognized that this was not a particularly godly approach to my job, but this fellow was beyond hope. In my readings and quiet time, however, the Holy Spirit gently tapped on my shoulder to suggest that it was I who needed to change."

Kraft wrestled with God about this. He wanted to do the right thing, but it seemed that this incompetent and arrogant conductor was getting in his way. Yet as he prayed, the Lord spoke to him: "I'm trying to mold you into a useful vessel for my kingdom, and YOU are the one who is in the way. How about you just give it a try?" He knew what God wanted—for him to look up to the podium and see the image of his Lord.

"That took some kind of strong willpower for me," Kraft confesses. "I had to squelch ninety-five percent of my thoughts and allow myself to see the image of Christ in the man up-front. The experience was electrifying. The performance was filled with such joy that I was in tears at the end."

Is there an authority figure in your life who you don't respect or do not like? The next time you see him or her, think of this story and try to see the Lord in that person.

"For I am the Lord, your God, who takes hold of your right hand and says to you, Do not fear; I will help you." –ISAIAH 41:13

Imagine how nervous the members of a young jazz band from Kansas might feel as the date for their New York City debut approaches. Now imagine getting a postcard from a rival band in New York with the intimidating message: "We're going to send you hicks back to the sticks!" Talk about discouraging!

That is exactly what happened in 1942 to bassist Gene Ramey, while playing in Jay McShann's band. They had the opportunity to perform at New York's Savoy Ballroom, and they boldly accepted. The band arrived exhausted, having driven several hundred miles with as many as six men in one car. Their equipment and uniforms were very shoddy, especially by big-city standards. But these men were determined to give it everything they had.

Ramey remembers the critical opening. "From the time we hit that first note until the time we got off the bandstand, we didn't let up." Their determination paid off, and the band was an instant success. Two days later they were given the chance to play fifteen minutes on a live radio show. After hearing the band, the radio director called·out, "Let them go ahead; don't stop them!" They played a full hour, and dozens of listeners called in to demand, "Who is that great band playing?"

Suppose you had received that postcard. Would you have given in to its threatening message? Or would you have chosen to believe today's opening Scripture instead?

Find someone to encourage today. Write that person a postcard that will give him a smile. Perhaps you could include today's Scripture as well.

"For everyone who exalts himself will be humbled, and he who humbles himself will be exalted." –LUKE 18:14b

On this day in 1919, one of America's greatest storytellers was born. The folk singer Pete Seeger has spent his long life telling the stories of others rather than of himself. Indeed, he is so selfless by nature that when he published his well-known book *How to Play the Five-String Banjo,* he refused to copyright it, "because the banjo belongs to everyone."

The composer of such standards as "Where Have All the Flowers Gone?" "If I Had a Hammer," and "Turn, Turn, Turn" never put himself forward. But he did so much for the poor that he sometimes faced persecution. During the political witch-hunts of the 1950s, Seeger was often under suspicion. His courageous stands on environmental issues caused him to actually be banned from appearing on the 1962 television show *Hootenanny,* prompting thousands of folk music fans to boycott the program. Later, Seeger was given his own television show, but he used it less to advertise his talents than to showcase a new generation of folk musicians, such as Joan Baez, Bob Dylan, and Buffy Saint Marie.

Of course, the above Scripture proved true, and this unpretentious folk singer has now been highly exalted. Seeger has recently been given America's highest cultural awards, the Kennedy Center Honors and the National Medal of Art. But the honors haven't change the man. In 1995, he told an interviewer, "I'm seventy-five years old and I've lost most of my voice, but I can still pick a banjo, and my main purpose is to get a crowd singing."

Interestingly enough, Pete Seeger doesn't find all the fame worth having. Asked if the recent honors have changed anything, he jokingly responded, "It's caused more trouble than I would have ever dreamed. Now I'm drowned in mail and phone calls. 'Where can I find this and what about that and will you sign this and support that,' they say. I should have realized that my protection wouldn't last forever."

As Christians, we know that God wants us to be humble and to serve others. We also know that, like Pete Seeger, we will someday receive a reward. Remember that our ultimate reward is to spend eternity with Jesus Christ.

Have you ever heard any of the three well-known Pete Seeger songs mentioned above? If not, find a recording of at least one and listen. The song "Turn, Turn, Turn" is based upon the Scripture Ecclesiastes 3:1-8.

Sing to him a new song; play skillfully, and shout for joy.

—PSALM 33:3

Unless you are a trained musician, or an "early music" lover, you may not have heard of the great Renaissance composer Josquin des Prez (c. 1440–1551). He was one of the greatest musicians of his day, and his music still strikes us as very beautiful centuries later. Martin Luther gave Josquin this profound tribute: "He is the master of the notes, which must do as he wills; other composers must do as the notes will."

Whether you have heard his many compositions or not, each time you listen to a favorite song or a great symphony, you owe him a tremendous musical debt. Why is this? Because Josquin added two critical elements to the world's musical vocabulary, which have been essential to composers ever since.

1. Josquin was the first composer to use, master, and show the infinite possibilities of imitation. From simple rounds to complex fugues, Western music could not have developed without this musical tool. It may seem obvious today, but it was quite an innovation during the Renaissance.

2. He was one of the first great masters of emotion in music. Like Beethoven a few centuries later, Josquin openly sought to move his audience. This is especially true in his hundred or so motets, based on many dramatic Bible stories. The emotional element is also found in his twenty masses, in which he skillfully uses word painting and imitation to inspire his listeners with the ancient Latin text.

Who knows? Perhaps God will lead you to develop something new that will still be used centuries later, even after your name may be forgotten!

Find a recording of Josquin des Prez's music at your library or CD store. It is especially beautiful to hear as you are going to sleep. Can you imagine what the music of heaven will be like?

Therefore encourage one another and build each other up, just as in fact you are doing. –1 THESSALONIANS 5:11

On this date in 1862, a son was born to the eminent conductor Leopold Damrosch. The child was named Walter and was soon trained to follow in his father's footsteps. In fact, the son would one day surpass his father, taking over his post with the New York Symphony and the Oratorio Society. He conducted with many other orchestras and opera companies, but his major contribution to America was an innovative use of the newfangled radio.

Walter Damrosch became musical adviser to the National Broadcasting Company in 1927. He soon began an hour-long music appreciation program that would reach across the country as no show ever had. Every Friday, millions of listeners—including thousands of school children in their classrooms—were given a weekly taste of great music. Many years later, countless impressionable students would still remember Damrosch's cordial salutation, "My dear children. . . ."

These innovative radio shows were broadcast during the Great Depression. Life was hard, luxuries nonexistent, and concert tickets unaffordable. Into this bleak picture, Damrosch's weekly program was a ray of sunshine for thousands of music lovers. At least one time each week they knew they would be provided with the joy of beautiful music—for many, the anticipation of this exhilarating hour was something to look forward to during the long, hard week.

God wants us to encourage other people. It is such an easy thing to bring joy to others. Many need just an encouraging word, a compliment, even a smile. If we would start our morning with a resolve to bring a good word to even five people each day—what a difference we could make over a lifetime!

Choose five people to encourage today. Write notes, give compliments, offer smiles, and see how you are encouraged as well.

My son, do not forget my teaching, but keep my commands in your heart, for they will prolong your life many years and bring you prosperity.

—PROVERBS 3:1

The "Queen of Soul," Aretha Franklin burst upon the music scene in the 1960s and soon became America's leading female vocalist. Her tremendous talents (including a five-octave vocal range) have made her one of the most celebrated singers of all time. She has won more Grammy Awards (seventeen) than any other woman, she was the first black woman to appear on the cover of *Time* magazine, and she was the first female performer inducted into the Rock and Roll Hall of Fame. Franklin's voice has even been designated a "natural resource" by her home state of Michigan.

What is less known about this star is that her inspiration finds its source in a wonderful father, a Baptist minister and pastor of the New Bethel Baptist Church in Detroit, Michigan. It was in his church where she first met Jesus, and in his church choir where she began to sing. Her aunt was the great gospel singer Clara Ward, and at the age of nine, Franklin was instructed in gospel singing by James Cleveland. At twelve she became a soloist in her father's traveling gospel revue.

Long after Aretha Franklin was a household name, tragedy struck her beloved father. Learning that he had been shot by burglars and was in a coma, she stopped everything, taking a full year off from recording and performing, and moving back to her hometown. After his death in 1984, she honored him by recording a new gospel album in her father's church. She called the album *One Lord, One Faith, One Baptism.*

Doubtless, the unconditional love from her father has helped Franklin remain an unpretentious woman with a love of simple pleasures. The "Queen of Soul" may be worth more than twenty million dollars, but her lifestyle is not that different from her friends at church. "When I'm home," she proclaims, "I cook, wash, and iron as good as the next lady, and I sew with the best of them."

Unfortunately, not everyone has as good an earthly father as Franklin did. But the Good News is that we do all have a Heavenly Father who loves and adores us more than we can understand.

Write a short letter of encouragement and gratitude to your parents today. Make sure to tell them that you love them.

Remove the dross from the silver, and out comes material for the silversmith; remove the wicked from the king's presence, and his throne will be established through righteousness. –PROVERBS 25:4, 5

The main idea from the above Scripture can be applied to many different areas of our life. In the same way that dross (the scum) must be removed from silver, sin must be rooted out of our hearts. As the wicked must be removed from the king's presence, evil influences must be removed from around us. A musical application might be: in order to have an excellent performance, all wrong and out-of-tune notes must first be removed.

Since today is the birthday of Johannes Brahms, an amusing example of this idea from his life might be appropriate. It seems that the great composer loved a good cup of black coffee, which he brewed himself when at home. He seldom found coffee to his liking when he visited inns, because the local cooks usually mixed it with chicory, a money-saving practice Brahms loathed.

One day while tramping through the Vienna woods, he had a great desire for coffee. Stopping at a nearby inn, he called for the owner. "My dear old lady," he asked graciously, "have you any chicory?" When she replied that she did, he seemed delighted. "It's not possible! May I see it?"

The lady rummaged through her cupboard and brought the composer two packages of chicory. Holding them in his hands, he asked, "Is this all that you have?" As soon as she said yes, he put both packages in his pockets and declared, "Well, now you can go back and make me some black coffee!"

What do you use as "filler" in your life that keeps you from focusing fully on God? For many people, it's the TV. Try going for twenty-four hours without watching any TV, and instead use the time you would have spent being a couch potato doing something nice for a member of your family or a friend.

Those who are wise will shine like the brightness of the heavens, and those who lead many to righteousness, like the stars for ever and ever. –DANIEL 12:3

Each of us is called to spread the Gospel, but we are called to be wise in our witness as well as to be sensitive to the leading of the Holy Spirit. Sometimes we should be subdued, sometimes bold. There are times when a courageous stand must be immediately taken, and there are times when a more gradual approach with the Gospel is appropriate.

The Christian band Plumb discovered that having the overt label of "Christian band" can sometimes be a hindrance to evangelism. For instance, once they were performing in a secular setting in Myrtle Beach, South Carolina. A woman who owned a nearby bar was touched by the group's music, and to show her appreciation she insisted: "You can have all the free beer you want."

Lead singer Tiffany Arbuckle thanked her and said, "You know what? We'll be fine with just water." They performed a number of their songs, and at the concert's conclusion, the woman reappeared, ready to both talk and pray. She said, "Thanks for not telling me you guys were Christians. Thanks for letting me *see* that you were. It wasn't that you turned down the alcohol that made me start thinking. There's just peace and joy in your life, and I want that."

Arbuckle knows the exhilaration of being used to spread the Gospel. She told *CCM Magazine,* "There's no greater joy, there's no paycheck or amount of units sold or people's opinions or covers of magazines that could ever replace that moment of looking in her face and knowing that God used me."

On a clear night, stand outside and look at the brightness of the stars. Pray for someone you know who is not a believer, and ask God to help you be a shining star for Christ in that person's life.

For you, O Lord, have delivered my soul from death, my eyes from tears, my feet from stumbling. —PSALM 116:8

It is amazing what depth of misery and suffering some people have climbed out of into happiness and accomplishment. The famous country music singer/songwriter Hank Snow, born this day in 1914, is a prime example. In the 1950s he became such a popular entertainer—with fans and friends alike—that few ever knew of his horrific upbringing.

Clarence Snow (his real name) was born in Nova Scotia, Canada. His parents bitterly divorced when he was only eight years old, and family life was destroyed. His two sisters were sent to an orphanage, while he was to live with grandparents. Sadly, they were both neglectful and abusive.

After three years of wretchedness, Snow's mother remarried and brought her son to her new home. Here it was even worse. His stepfather beat him every day. Finally, at the age of only twelve, he left home to become a cabin boy at sea. Could anything come of such a mistreated young boy?

Of course, we now know the "end of the story." The singer Hank Snow was able to put all his troubled childhood behind him and to achieve more than he could imagine. It is appropriate that his first national hit in 1950 was entitled "I'm Moving' On," as that is exactly what he did with his life. His perseverance is an inspiration to all those who have struggled and gives them hope for the future.

What troubles and scars can God help you to overcome?

Look up Jeremiah 29:11 and write it down. Now give that verse to someone you know who, like Snow, is facing an unhappy life. Reassure that person that no matter how hard our beginnings, God has a future planned for us.

"Nazareth! Can anything good come from there?" Nathanael asked. "Come and see," said Philip. –JOHN 1:46

The Carter family has been aptly called "The First Family of Country Music." These three singers initiated an expression of rural life that would grow to the multibillion-dollar industry of today. Of course, there was country music before their first recording in 1927, but not on the national scale to which their songs would rise. However, when they were first discovered by recording executive Ralph Peer, they did not look very impressive.

Sara Carter, her husband A. P. (or "Doc"), and his sister-in-law Maybelle were poor country folk from southwestern Virginia. They were very talented—not only vocally but instrumentally as well, with Maybelle's extraordinary guitar finger-picking—but their clothes were homespun at best. The Carters heard that Peer would be in nearby Bristol, Tennessee, and these God-fearing musicians were ready for any opportunity their Lord might open.

After driving twenty-five miles on dust-covered roads, these hillbillies must have been a sight to behold! Maybelle—who was born this day in 1901—was seven months pregnant, plus Sara and A. P. brought their two ragamuffin children. As they entered the makeshift studio to record for the Victor Talking Machine, Peer thought he had simply met another poor country band with no future.

His doubts were soon blown away. The Carters' strong talents immediately set them apart, and Peer spent his day recording their first six songs and obtaining the publishing rights. Within a few months, their classic song "Wildwood Flower," would take the entire country by storm. They may have looked unimpressive, but the Carters were the first great trailblazers for the thousands of country music performers who would follow their humble beginnings.

If you think that the world doesn't pay attention to outward appearances, consider dressing in old clothes that are out-of-date and don't fit well. How would you be treated in a department store or different stores at the mall? Look up 1 Samuel 16:7 and thank God that He looks at our hearts.

"He who has ears, let him hear." —MATTHEW 11:15

On the night of May 11, 1809, Napoleon's cannons pulverized the city of Vienna, which surrendered the following day. One of the many worried residents of that city was Ludwig van Beethoven. During the bombing, he was in his brother Caspar's cellar, covering his head with pillows, so as not to further damage his already impaired hearing.

The defining tragedy of his life, and the one which diminished his performing career, was his growing deafness. The pain and humiliation he experienced drove him almost to suicide. In 1802, he poured out his heart in a letter to his brothers, saying deafness meant he "must live as an exile."

Beethoven wrote, "It was impossible to say to others: 'Speak louder; shout! For I am deaf.' . . . How great was the humiliation when one who stood beside me heard the distant sound of a shepherd's pipe, and I heard nothing; or heard the shepherd sing, and I heard nothing. Such experiences brought me to the verge of despair."

It was this miserable affliction, and not bitterness toward others, that intensified the eruption of emotion that characterizes Beethoven's life and music. In his famous *Heiligenstadt Testament,* the deaf composer gave voice to his deepest longings: "Almighty God, you look down into my innermost soul, you see into my heart and you know that it is filled with love for humanity and a desire to do good." Even long after his hearing failed he continued to work, composing masterpieces that still inspire us today.

Cover your ears as tightly as you can. Imagine never being able to hear: no joy of music, no hearing people talk to you, so many difficulties in communication. Praise God for the senses you have!

There is a friend who sticks closer than a brother. –PROVERBS 18:24B

Living under the communist regime in Russia made life very difficult for composer Dmitry Shostakovich (1906–1975). Although his early
works brought him the title "Composer-laureate of the Soviet State," this offi-
cial favor did not last. His innovative music began to irritate the communist officials and he was branded an "enemy of the people."

Stalin himself wrote an article denouncing Shostakovich, which he entitled
"Muddle Instead of Music." When he tried to organize a performance, the news-
papers announced, "Today there will be a concert by the enemy of the people
Shostakovich." Rocks were often thrown through the windows of his home.

Through the tense years of Soviet persecution, the support of his friends
meant everything to the composer. One in particular, the great cellist Mstislav
Rostropovich, had a keen understanding of his friend's pain. Shostakovich would
frequently telephone him with the words, "Come quickly, hurry."

Their apartments were many miles apart, yet Rostropovich never failed to
come. At the door, the composer always greeted him, "Sit down, and now we can
be silent." Rostropovich remembers, "I would sit for half an hour, without a
word. It was most relaxing, just sitting. Then Shostakovich would get up and say,
'Thank you. Goodbye, Slava.' It was very special, sitting like that with him."

We all long for such a friend, one who is so close he would come and just sit.
What a joy it is to know that we have that Friend—in Jesus!

*Visit someone this week, just for the purpose of blessing him. (You don't
have to be silent the entire time!)*

"You shall speak to him and put words in his mouth; I will help both of you speak and will teach you what to do. He will speak to the people for you, and it will be as if he were your mouth and as if you were God to him."

–EXODUS 4:15, 16

In the above Scripture, God puts together a winning team, Moses and his brother, Aaron. God would later have many such teams, such as Joshua and Caleb, David and Jonathan, Ruth and Naomi, Elijah and Elisha, Paul and Timothy. Often a task seems too overwhelming for one person to handle, and the Lord brings another nearby to help shoulder the load.

On this day in 1842, a son was born to an Irish bandmaster living in London. The boy showed tremendous musical talent and would be very well trained. By eight he could play several instruments well, and by twelve he was appointed chorister to the Chapel Royal. The following year, his first composition was published, and at the age of fourteen he won a Mendelssohn scholarship enabling him to study abroad. This young man was soon working with some of Europe's greatest musicians, including Liszt, Moscheles, and Grieg.

Yet this prodigy had still not found his niche. He had composed some choral and orchestral music, but nothing that would stand the test of time. Then one day, this young man—whose name was Arthur Sullivan—made the acquaintance of a writer named William Schwenk Gilbert.

You guessed it! These two very different men would team up to create all the "Gilbert and Sullivan" operettas, still performed over a century later: *Trial by Jury, HMS Pinafore, The Pirates of Penzance, The Mikado, The Gondoliers,* and many others. Without the other, neither one may have reached his full potential. Working together made all the difference.

Do you have a huge task ahead? If so, look around. God may just have someone waiting nearby to help you shoulder the load.

Write down as many famous duos as you can think of, both from the Bible and popular culture (Joshua and Caleb, Simon and Garfunkle, etc.). Thank God for giving us friends and other people to help us through life.

Young men, in the same way be submissive to those who are older. All of you, clothe yourselves with humility toward one another, because, "God opposes the proud but gives grace to the humble." –1 PETER 5:5

In the background of every movie is a musical soundtrack. As you might imagine, to produce an excellent soundtrack takes a huge amount of work, talent, and time. J. A. C. Redford is a Christian composer in Hollywood who has written the music for a number of top movies and television shows. In order to do this with excellence, he must use the wisdom he has found in God's Word.

A good example might be his attitude toward a movie's director or producer. Both are his authorities, and he must submit to their judgments. Yet many of these are musical judgments, and while Redford is a highly trained musician, the director may have no musical training or talent.

Redford remembers, "I once wrote a theme I thought particularly beautiful. Upon hearing it, the producer complained, 'I can't hum it.' " Redford could have chosen to explode at the man's musical ignorance. Instead, he chose the submissive route. "What could make it more hummable for you?" They discussed various ideas, and Redford agreed, "I could do that. Is there anything else?" "Yes, your theme keeps going down," the producer said. "I want it to go up. In fact, I want it to go up, up, up!"

This might have been the last straw, but Redford's humility was up to the task. "Okay, let me work on it." He labored all day, and then presented reams of new material his boss liked. "Great!" exclaimed the producer. "Can we combine the first part of number one with the middle part of number two, then go back to number one to finish it?" Redford stifled a scream, said, "Sure," and went back to work. He recalls the final result: "The strange thing is, it turned out to be a really good theme."

We never know how God may work through other people or circumstances to bring out the best in us. As hard as it is at times, we must all submit to those in authority, remembering that the ultimate authority is God.

What is your favorite movie soundtrack? Do you usually like music wild and exciting, or thoughtful and gorgeous? Thank God for the unique way He has made you.

Let the wise listen and add to their learning, and let the discerning get guidance. –PROVERBS 1:5

Most of us have had the embarrassing experience of accidentally showing our ignorance in public. Perhaps we're called to answer in a classroom, and our guess is so wrong that everyone laughs. As painful as this can be, it might be encouraging to find that even great musicians have been just as ignorant at times.

Louis Armstrong had such a natural gift with the trumpet that high C's seemed to be easy for him. Yet when he was young, he had very little musical education. He was taught to read the notes on a page, but that was about it. As the following story shows, he was not taught details, such as *PP* meaning "pianissimo" (play very softly).

Fletcher Henderson gave young Armstrong a job in a big New York band. At the first rehearsal the newcomer was playing just as many notes as the other brass players and was beginning to gain confidence. Then they played an arrangement in which at one point the entire band was to play FF ("fortissimo" or very loud) and then diminuendo to PP. The band meticulously followed the music as marked, but Armstrong continued to howl on his trumpet at full volume.

Henderson stopped the band, saying, "Louis, you are not following the arrangement." Confused, Armstrong answered, "I'm reading everything on this sheet." Henderson asked, "But Louis, what about that *PP*?" Imagine the band's roaring laugh when young Armstrong innocently replied, "Oh, I thought that meant 'pound plenty'!"

God wants us to be wise in His ways and to continually add to our learning about Him. He also wants us to be wise in other subjects, however, and to make the most of His gift of intelligence.

So that you might avoid such an embarrassing moment, "add to your learning" each day. Have you read a biography of a great musician? Find one in your library or bookstore and read it this week.

I desire to do your will, O my God; your law is within my heart.

–PSALM 40:8

For many popular performers on a stage surrounded by thousands of fans, it is difficult to keep one's heart pure. Yet there are artists who truly believe that their music is a gift from God to be used for His glory. Gospel singer Larnelle Harris is one of these artists. Despite best-selling albums, awards, and honors, he has been successful at keeping ministry the first priority.

"I've never been a good traveler," admits Harris, "and I do not feel a need for any of the trappings of success and recognition." He explains that when looking for new material to sing, "My prayer is, 'Lord, put something in my heart and teach me how to give it away,' That's what I've always needed, and still need today."

Harris has a simple criterium to judge a song. "I'm basically a word person," he reveals. "I always ask, 'What does a song say?' 'What does it mean?' And I do my best to tell the truth of the Bible. I write and look for songs that are very distinct and clear that it's the Lord I'm singing about."

Such desires come from a trusting heart. Larnelle Harris confesses, "I'm continually amazed every day that Jesus still loves me. We've fouled up every good thing He's put before us. I really don't know why He loves us . . . but He does! And it really is an unbelievable love."

Need to know just what God's will is? Look up the following verses about His will, then choose one to memorize this week: Matthew 28:16-20; Philippians 2:3; 1 Thessalonians 5:18; Hebrews 3:13.

Even in laughter the heart may ache, and joy may end in grief.

–PROVERBS 14:13

Today is the birthday of the French composer Erik Satie (1866–1925), certainly one of the strangest musicians in history. His *Three Gymnopedies* is frequently played by pianists, but most of his compositions have never been in the standard repertoire. His titles are especially unusual: the *Bureaucratic* Sonata, Flabby Preludes for a Dog, and Three Pieces in the Shape of a Pear. This last work was to answer a critic who complained that Satie's music had no form!

Satie seemed to have been as much a comic as a composer. He is known to have written the longest piece in history, a piano work of 180 notes with instructions to repeat them 840 times. (Finally receiving its premiere in 1963, five pianists played it in relays for many long hours.) Another of his compositions calls for a typewriter, a siren, and a revolver. Satie once wrote that he allowed himself "to be inspired" only from 10:27 to 11:47 A.M., and from 3:12 to 4:07 P.M.

If you are now thinking, "This guy was a nut," so did most of his colleagues. Unfortunately, many of his jokes were at the expense of others. Satie fell to mocking the music of many great composers, instead of using his musical genius creatively. Later in life he became more and more cynical. At the age of fifty-nine, he died in utter poverty.

What can we learn from the strange life of Erik Satie? For one thing, though laughter can be good for our souls, we need to make sure that our jokes are not at another's expense. A second point is that we should resolve to use our God-given talents for good, never for ridiculing others. God wants us to use them for His glory. Let's make certain we do!

Look up more information about Satie on the Internet or in the library. Find a recording of his music and form opinions of your own.

Trouble and distress have come upon me, but your commands are my delight. —PSALM 119:143

Shaded Red is a Christian band that has a tremendous testimony of sticking with it when things get rough. It is sometimes known as "the band that had the wreck." For in January 1998, their tour van hit a patch of black ice and crashed. The drummer Chris Yoeman was killed, and guitarist Jon Roberts was severely injured.

Such a tragedy is often followed by a time of despair. Roberts' pelvis was crushed, and his recovery and therapy would take many months. He remembers, "After the accident I wasn't able to play my guitar for about three months. I had no heart for music. I was trying to decide if Shaded Red should go on. I felt enormously pained and guilty. I felt like a failure. Going through my head was, 'God, are you there? Do you love me?' "

But God was there, and inspired Roberts to fight his way step by step out of bed and back into ministry. He used the bedridden time for songwriting. Five months after the wreck, with Roberts not completely recovered, Shaded Red hit the road again. It was still difficult. "Every chord, every song was more of a struggle," says Roberts. "Just getting into the van was horrible."

The band persevered, released a top album, *Red Revolution,* and has allowed God to bring good out of the tragedy. "It has given us added depth," claims Jamey Roberts, brother of Jon and another member of the band. "When we talk about the hope we have in Christ, that God's bigger than your problems, that God can do the impossible, that's not something we just say. That's something we know."

God has used such tragedies to inspire us to never give up. For even more inspiration, read more about this group through its Internet site.

Blessed is the man who trusts in the Lord, whose confidence is in him. He will be like a tree planted by the water that sends out its roots by the stream. It does not fear when heat comes; its leaves are always green. It has no worries in a year of drought and never fails to bear fruit. —JEREMIAH 17:7, 8

The quality of being fruitful was well illustrated in the remarkable life of Wolfgang Amadeus Mozart (1756–1791). Like the Apostle Paul, Mozart had to learn "the secret of being content in any and every situation, whether well fed or hungry, whether living in plenty or in want" (Philippians 4:12). His was an unusual life. Instead of going from "rags to riches," he went from "riches to rags"!

Young Mozart began as an extraordinary prodigy, quickly winning the acclaim of the world. By the time he was six, he was touring Europe and performing before delighted courts and nobility. Indeed, history records that on May 19, 1764, the eight-year-old genius performed splendidly for King George III and Queen Charlotte of England.

By his death at the age of thirty-five, he was barely staving off poverty. What happened? Many things—including some of Mozart's own mistakes—but primarily a fickle audience that became indifferent once the child prodigy, such a novelty, became a man.

When the pressures of money mismanagement were overpowering him, Mozart would tear headlong into a brilliant new composition. When he saw other composers winning over the public and denouncing his works, he would start over, coming up with new ideas and approaches that would put him back in the spotlight.

Whenever he got a commission, he quickly fulfilled the request. Though he often lived without such an incentive, he continued to create masterpieces, such as his last great symphonies, composed without commission or even the prospect of an upcoming performance. Mozart had the wonderful virtue of refusing to allow circumstances to affect his musical output.

Take a walk and note the many different kinds of leaves there are (if it's winter, check out the evergreens). Thank God for their continued fruitfulness and ask for His help to remain fruitful even when things get tough.

Then God said, "Take your son, your only son, Isaac, whom you love, and go to the region of Moriah. Sacrifice him there as a burnt offering on one of the mountains I will tell you about." –GENESIS 22:2

We all know the story from which the above Scripture is taken. God tested Abraham by commanding he give up his only son, but at the last moment God saved Isaac. How difficult for us to imagine the anguish Abraham must have felt when he first heard God's command! Yet we must ask, "What would we have done in his place?"

A somewhat parallel situation happened to flutist Pam Adams, who plays with the Fort Worth Symphony. Her church was in the process of raising funds for a new building, and each family was asked to pray about what they could give toward the project. In the following Sunday service, a large basket would be set in the front of the church for the families' contributions.

Adams took the call to prayer seriously. But in each quiet time that week she felt God was nudging her, "Put your flute in the basket Sunday." She was totally dismayed. Aside from her family, her flute was everything to her—it was her principal talent, her source of income, her whole life. It was an extremely expensive instrument that she could not afford to replace. Yet she could not escape the conviction that the Lord had truly spoken to her.

Next Sunday, she played a special offering of music for the congregation. As dozens of others placed envelopes in the basket, Adams carefully laid her flute there and walked away. She had no idea how she could now continue in her career. Yet that very evening her pastor called with some astonishing news. A member of the congregation had found out about the donated flute and offered to pay the church its market value so that the owner might have it back. Whenever she now plays this "redeemed" flute, Pam Adams always remembers how God blessed her act of obedience.

Make a list of the three things you possess that would be the most difficult to give up. Then offer the list to the Lord, and ask God to help you be willing to relinquish everything for Him.

"Act with courage, and may the Lord be with those who do well."

—2 CHRONICLES 19:11b

Imagine this terrifying scene. You are taken at gunpoint, thrown into a car by gangsters, and taken to the headquarters of Public Enemy Number One. What would you do? Pray, no doubt, harder than you've ever prayed before! Does this scenario sound inconceivable to you?

In 1925, the great jazz pianist Thomas "Fats" Waller (1904–1943) was playing at a hotel in Chicago. He noticed that his audience contained several tough-looking men dressed in fine clothes, but he gave it no mind. Consider his horror when, during a break backstage, one of these men stuck a revolver in his stomach and ordered him into a waiting car!

The terrified musician was driven through the Chicago streets to a seedy part of town. The gangsters would tell him nothing, and Waller must have felt that this was the end for him. Finally, the car stopped at a saloon guarded by several huge men. Waller was forced out of the car and quickly inside. He soon found that he was in the secret headquarters of Al Capone, known as "Scarface," the prince of gangsters.

The reason for the abduction? It was Capone's birthday, and his thugs wanted a top pianist for his party! A frightened Waller began to play as best he could, but when he found that Scarface and his cronies were some of his biggest fans, his performance improved. Fats Waller was forced to stay for three days and nights, but the ordeal wasn't quite so unrewarding after all: Capone stuffed hundred-dollar bills into the pianist's pocket after every request, and when they let him go free, he had thousands of dollars for the birthday performance. (It's Waller's birthday today.)

Chances are that most of us will not be abducted by gangsters. When we do face frightening situations, however, we can take confidence, knowing that the Lord is with us.

To get an even better idea of the danger Fats Waller was in, look up some information on Capone. Praise God for how He has protected you in countless ways in your life.

Be patient with everyone. —1 THESSALONIANS 5:14b

On this day in 1874, the great opera composer Guiseppe Verdi premiered his magnificent *Requiem*. Someone once explained the Verdi *Requiem* as "a bunch of opera singers let loose in a cathedral!" Such a comment hardly does justice to this great work, which is a sincere expression of Verdi's faith. The gorgeous quartet writing of "Domine Jesu Christe," the prayerful duet in the "Agnus Dei," the final resolution of the "Libera Me"; these and many other moments give us glimpses of Verdi's inner self.

The beginnings of Verdi's musical appreciation had their troublesome moments. Raised in the Catholic faith, Verdi was serving as a seven-year-old altar boy when he first heard a church organ. The beautiful harmony so touched the youth that he stood mesmerized and forgot his duties. When the priest asked for the water, the boy didn't hear him. A second request received the same response.

After a third unsuccessful demand, the exasperated priest gave his neglectful altar boy a stout push. The boy rolled down three steps of the altar and was picked up unconscious and carried away. Fortunately, there was no permanent damage. Indeed, when the young Verdi awoke, his first words were to beg his father to be able to study music. He had found his great love.

Before we condemn the insensitive priest of this story, we need to ask ourselves, "Are we, too, impatient or annoyed with people who don't respond to us?" Let us ask for the Lord's patience today.

Have you ever played an organ? Look at an organ up close, noticing the many intricate parts that go into producing its sound. Think of the years of practice—and patience—it takes to learn to play such an instrument. Then ask God for patience in your life, especially in your relationships.

I planted the seed, Apollos watered it, but God made it grow. So neither he who plants nor he who waters is anything, but only God, who makes things grow. –1 CORINTHIANS 3:6, 7

As Paul points out in the above Scripture, God uses all of us in different ways to spread the Gospel. At one time the Lord may use you to lead a person to accept Christ. At another time He may arrange for you to disciple a young Christian so that she may grow in the Lord. What is important is to be faithful, no matter which task God has placed before you.

One of the frustrations for touring Christian musicians is that they seldom are able to stay in the same place for very long. Like traveling missionaries, they "plant the seed" but must allow others to water it. The Christian band known as Third Day has been used to plant thousands of seeds for Christ. Drummer David Carr says, "This is how we meet people's needs, whether their need is to know Christ or to be led to Christ or to be challenged or to be just loved and encouraged."

The group members are well aware of the restraints of such a ministry. Bassist Tai Anderson notes, "There have been times when any one of us would be in a conversation with someone and actually feel like God was using us; we're making some progress, we're talking about something real. But you've got twenty people tugging at your elbow and wanting an autograph and wanting their picture with you. It makes it really hard to have a conversation. So maybe that's no longer our role in the whole scheme of things. Maybe our role is to be more of an example and to encourage people from the stage."

Their guitarist Mark Lee confirms the need to work with other believers: "A lot of it comes down to youth pastors using our music to reach out to unchurched kids and people inviting their friends who aren't Christians to a concert. It's really out of our hands, out of our control. We just have to remain faithful to God that He is going to use us."

The next time you are at a Christian concert, or a musical performance at church, try something new. Pray that God will use the music to touch the hearts of those listening—and to bring them closer to Christ.

Do not repay evil with evil or insult with insult, but with blessing, because to this you were called so that you may inherit a blessing.

—1 PETER 3:9

Like coaches of a football team, jazz bandleaders are always searching for new talent to add to their roster. Unfortunately, this may take the form of luring a musician out of another band by offering him more money. When Benny Goodman's band made a tempting offer to trumpet player Cootie Williams to leave Duke Ellington's band, his colleagues worried that he might defect.

Williams manfully decided to talk it over directly with "the Duke." His boss's generous answer astonished him. Not only did Ellington not resent letting the top trumpeter depart to further his career, he wanted to help. "Let me handle everything," he offered. "Let me see how much I can get for you. You deserve to make some money."

True to his word, the Duke arranged the details wonderfully to Williams' advantage. The deal was signed; he even assured Williams that he could have his old job back if he ever wanted it. The trumpeter prospered with Benny Goodman's band, but when the contract was up in 1941, he felt duty bound to return to Ellington.

Rather than selfishly coveting this top player for his band, the Duke was still looking out for Williams' best interest. He told him, "You're too big for the job. You're bigger than you think you are. Go on your own." This encouragement gave Williams the confidence to take Ellington's advice. Within two years, Cootie Williams' new band had made a quarter of a million dollars. He never forgot the generous actions of the great Duke Ellington, who died on this date in 1974.

In this story, both men—Cootie Williams and Duke Ellington—acted with honor, integrity, and respect for the other. If these gracious attitudes seem to be missing from society today, ask God to help you be a "Cootie Williams" or a "Duke Ellington." When we repay evil with good, we just might be surprised by the good that comes back to us!

Put yourself in Duke Ellington's shoes. How would you have felt when your player wanted to leave for another band? Betrayed? Deserted? Ask God to help you be generous to the next person who does you wrong.

When a man's ways are pleasing to the Lord, he makes even his enemies live at peace with him. –PROVERBS 16:7

When a great musician plays a concerto with an orchestra, he is determined to give everything he has to make a superb performance. When he is also a Christian, like classical guitarist Christopher Parkening, he is all the more committed to strive for the highest standards of biblical excellence. Parkening has played upwards of ninety concerts a year for several decades and knows the concerto literature as well as any guitarist alive.

But of course, some concerts are naturally better than others, no matter how much one tries to give his best. One performance in particular was a trial for Parkening, because he did not do as well as usual on several difficult passages. He missed an especially long guitar run, and he felt bad about it afterward.

When the concert was over, he met a friend who had been present. She was very encouraging and insisted that it had been a fabulous performance. But Parkening knew every missed note and regretted the inevitable review that would be in the next day's newspaper. Nevertheless, his friend's optimism was comforting to hear.

Finally his friend suggested they pray that God would cause the critic to only remember the great parts of the concert. Parkening had seen amazing answers to prayer in his life, but this idea sounded a bit radical to him. Imagine his astonishment the next morning when the title of the review was: "Parkening gives flawless performance!"

God certainly wants us to do our best at whatever we do, but, as we've seen from this story of Christopher Parkening, it's the state of our heart that matters most.

Have you ever heard classical guitar? Listen to a recording from your library or CD store, especially one by your brother in the Lord, Christopher Parkening.

Buy the truth and do not sell it; get wisdom, discipline and under-standing. —PROVERBS 23:23

One of the hardest tasks in the world is to follow in the shadow of a great man or woman. Whether it is an outstanding world leader stepping down from office or a younger sibling following in the footsteps of a "successful" older one, it is not easy. People generally expect an imitation of the original. So, the "new kid on the block" is often frustrated and feels restricted in being himself.

In the world of country music, a prime example of this problem is Hank Williams, Jr., born this day in 1949. Everyone loved his father so much that when the son began his music career, everyone wanted him to be a chip off the old block. For some years he did exactly that. Country hit followed country hit in the tradition of his father.

But Hank Williams, Jr., could not live indefinitely with this false expectation. He knew that he was getting rich by putting on an image that was not really true, and he couldn't live with himself any longer. In the late 1970s, he told his producers that he was branching out in a new musical style that was his own. They were incredulous. After all, they insisted, he was making plenty of money doing the old style.

Nevertheless, he began the transformation—which was a painful one. His old fans (were they really his?) were outraged. At one concert, an audience of two thousand began to jeer, and Williams ended that show with only two hundred people remaining. Yet the number of his fans would grow. Hank Williams, Jr., was now performing with integrity, and people began to respond. Within a decade of the change, twenty-five new hits could truly be called his own. It was well worth the tough transition to be true to his audience—and to himself.

God calls us to be true to ourselves and who He made us to be. He wants nothing more, and nothing less.

Have you ever felt that you weren't "being yourself" around certain people? Let your confidence be in knowing God's plan for you, and pray for His help to always be yourself.

"And if you spend yourselves in behalf of the hungry and satisfy the needs of the oppressed, then your light will rise in the darkness, and your night will become like the noonday." —ISAIAH 58:10

Imagine the scene: the great conductor and composer Gustav Mahler (1860–1911) is conducting Wagner's massive opera *Das Rhinegold* in Vienna. The performance is virtually flawless until the last scene, when Mahler gives the cue to the tympanist for the dramatic drum roll. To his horror, the conductor looks up to find that the tympanist is not there!

After the performance, a furious Mahler is told that the missing musician lived a long way from the opera house. *Das Rhinegold* was so long that he had to leave the stage early or miss the last train out to the suburbs. Bristling with rage, the conductor sent a midnight telegram ordering the missing musician to a meeting early the next morning.

When the tympanist sheepishly entered Mahler's office, he was met with a torrent of abuse. The conductor's anger finally spent, he then demanded an explanation. The man quietly apologized and revealed that his salary was only sixty-three guilders a month (a very small amount). He explained that he had a wife and child and could not afford to live in central Vienna near the opera house. So his family moved far away and he had take the train to rehearsals and concerts.

Instantly Mahler's attitude changed. Now it was his turn to apologize, and he did so profusely. He had not realized the musician's situation. The conductor immediately raised the orchestra's salaries—knowing that this would mean cutting back on costumes and scenery. As soon as Mahler realized that those in his care were in need, he did all within his power to help them.

God wants us to help the poor and those who have needs. Let us have a change of heart, just as Mahler did, and open our eyes to the needs of those around us.

Often the reason we don't help the poor or those in need is simply that we don't ever see them. Take a drive through a less-fortunate area of town, and try to put yourself in the shoes of the people who live there. Then ask God to show you a way to help.

The plans of the diligent lead to profit as surely as haste leads to poverty. —PROVERBS 21:5

Warren Pettit is a music professor at Greenville College in southern Illinois who has pioneered the creation of a degree program in contemporary Christian music. This innovative approach integrates the professional music industry with a Christian worldview perspective. As the academic year wears on and the students begin to complain about their workload, he and his colleagues must emphasize the importance of the hard work of musical excellence.

Pettit himself remembers an important "life lesson" he learned on this subject. As a young piano student, he was eager to perform Beethoven's Piano Sonata no. 8 in C Minor, better known as the "Pathetique." At his piano lesson, he hastily played through the first page, though the music is marked "grave" (very slow).

After reaching the bottom of the page in record time, his wizened old piano teacher suggested that he write out by hand, note for note, the entire first page before continuing with the rest of the piece. What quickly became apparent to Pettit was the tremendous amount of physical work required to put pen to paper and write out the notes of a single page of manuscript. When he then considered the thousands of pages written by Beethoven, Bach, and many others, their work ethic and genius became very real.

The true value of this exercise, however, was revealed at his next lesson. Pettit remembers paying much greater attention to each note, tempo marking, and articulation, because he now "owned the page." Suddenly, the music seemed more intimate and accessible, as though there were a familiar bond between the composer and himself. He concludes: "It is this sense of ownership, achieved only through hard work and attention to detail, that is so rewarding. If we are going to really connect with a page of music or the lives of those around us, then we must daily commit to the effort of ownership."

God wants us to know just as thoroughly and to own every word of His book. Have you read your Bible today?

Copy by hand a page of music you are working on or a favorite passage of Scripture. Afterwards, note the different way you feel about what you've written.

Not many of you should presume to be teachers, my brothers, because you know that we who teach will be judged more strictly.

−JAMES 3:1

In today's world, thousands of people are trying to get ahead, to be out in front, to be in charge. But the Bible's portrait of true leadership is that of servanthood. The biblical leader is the one who puts his own interests aside and focuses on helping others. A good example of such a leader was the Russian composer Mily Balakirev, who died on this day in 1910.

If you have never heard of him, you will learn that there is good reason for it. Balakirev was born in 1837 with a tremendous musical talent. He was already composing for orchestra in his teens, and by the age of twenty-five, he had personally founded the Free School of Music. The greatest Russian composer at that time, Mikhail Glinka, predicted that Balakirev would become his musical heir.

This young composer had higher aims than his own personal career. He felt that the musical world of Europe had bypassed the culture of his beloved Russia, and that all too often Russian musicians were simply imitating the music of the West. Balakirev knew the great heritage that was being neglected, and he begged his people to "look to Russian folk tunes for inspiration. Look to the East, but don't look to the West and Germany; Russia can find her own musical identity."

Balakirev worked tirelessly to produce concerts of fellow composers. His leadership skills brought together the great musicians Rimsky-Korsakov, Mussorgsky, Cui, and Borodin—together forming a group still known as "The Five." They each looked to Balakirev as their leader, yet through his efforts they all became more famous than he. His dedication created a growing musical heritage that would later produce such masters as Tchaikovsky, Stravinsky, and Shostakovich.

In the same way, God may work great things through us, though we may never get any of the "glory." That's true leadership.

Being a leader is not easy. Do you know a leader who exemplifies servanthood? Send that person a short e-mail or letter of appreciation and encouragement.

Blessed is the man who does not walk in the counsel of the wicked or stand in the way of sinners or sit in the seat of mockers. —PSALM 1:1

Richard Wagner's music always evokes a definite response. Most people either love it or hate it. Mark Twain once wrote that "Wagner's music isn't as bad as it sounds."

Wagner is most well known for his operas based on Norse mythology. He did use other themes as well, however. Once he announced that he wanted to compose a heroic opera on the life of Martin Luther. And at the age of thirty-six, Wagner wrote, "I had been inspired by a study of the Gospels" to write a huge work entitled "Jesus of Nazareth." He worked months on the libretto, a dramatic harmony of the Gospel accounts, and left unfinished extensive sketches that include dozens of other New Testament verses.

What happened to this remarkable idea? Unfortunately, Wagner was discouraged by those around him. His principle influence at the time, the pessimistic philosopher Bakunin, "insisted that I must at all costs make Jesus appear as a weak character." With no support or encouragement, Wagner eventually abandoned what could have been a major work.

Suppose Wagner's main influences had been godly men and women. What an incredible difference it could have made! The Scriptures are so clear, that "bad company corrupts good character" (1 Corinthians 15:33), that we should continually think about who we're spending time with. Are our friends people who encourage us and help us grow closer to God? Or are they people who are going to pull us down?

Think about those around you. You may have more influence on them than you realize. Determine, with God's help, that you will be a positive and never a negative influence on your friends.

Children, obey your parents in the Lord, for this is right. "Honor your father and mother"—which is the first commandment with a promise— "that it may go well with you and that you may enjoy long life on the earth."

—EPHESIANS 6:1–3

John Kasica, who holds the distinguished percussion chair of the Saint Louis Symphony Orchestra, is a devout Christian with a passion for worshiping the Lord. He has the distinction of having played percussion concertos with more major orchestras than any other percussionist. Kasica and his wife, Paula, a flutist, share the Gospel in their many duo concerts.

A percussionist lives in a unique musical world, having to give his attention to dozens of different instruments. Most every day Kasica plays tympani, xylophone, bells, marimba, cymbals, vibraphone, and a huge array of drums. But, unknown to most of his colleagues, he also plays another instrument: the accordian.

When Kasica was young, all he wanted to do was play drums. His parents were not thrilled with this idea and insisted he study the accordian. The youth was mortified by this unpopular instrument, but submitted to his parents' wishes. Only after many lessons on the accordian—during some of which he cried the entire time—did his parents also allow the drum lessons he loved.

Were the accordian lessons a waste? Years later, when Kasica was a percussion student at the Juilliard School in New York, he learned the answer. For he put himself through music school by playing accordian at dozens of receptions, bar mitzvahs, and weddings. As a child he never could have foreseen how God would someday bless his obedience, enabling him to reach his dreams.

It is often difficult for us to appreciate all that our parents have done on our behalf. Write a note of thanks to your parents, and tell them how much you love them.

Sing the glory of his name; make his praise glorious! —PSALM 66:2

Today is the birthday of one of the greatest names in gospel music, Andrae Crouch. His father, a "bootleggin' street preacher," started a church in Los Angeles, and the youth choir became Andrae's musical laboratory. His life was soon a combination of writing and performing gospel songs.

For some years he worked with a touring band, Andrae Crouch and the Disciples, but he had an extensive solo career as well as being a pastor himself. Yet he will always be known for his exceptional vocal style. Anyone who has ever heard him sing "To God Be the Glory," is immediately struck by the power and the sincerity of his voice.

Perhaps the reason Crouch has had such an impact on the gospel music world is that he had an ability to appeal to both white and black audiences. Many artists remain in either "black gospel" or "white gospel," unable to make the crossover. More than any other musician, he has brought those two worlds of gospel music together, reaching out without a musical bias whatsoever.

Another thing that has made Crouch so successful is his awareness of his audience. Like a good pastor, he wants to truly know his flock, refusing to become locked into the "ivory tower" of the recording industry. Andrae Crouch once explained, "I have one question when I write a new song: 'Does it reach you?' I feel the feedback from an audience if the song is working. I know what is real. That's what I get from being raised in the church, before those congregations."

Go to a library, CD store, or Christian bookstore near you to find some of Andrae Crouch's songs. Take time to pray for Pastor Crouch, his church, and his music ministry.

Pay attention and listen to the sayings of the wise.

—PROVERBS 22:17a

A large part of being a musician is listening—that is, listening to others and listening to yourself when you are playing or singing. In an ensemble it is essential to constantly listen to the other musicians, to know exactly how your part fits in and relates to the other parts. Any musician who neglects this and simply expects all other musicians to follow him will not go very far—as seen in the following amusing story.

Six great jazz musicians—Eddie Tone, Mel Davis, Carl Janelli, Ray Cohen, Buddy Morrow, and Bobby Shankin—were once in the same band, and were to back up a number of different vocalists. When the leader, Eddie Tone, saw a certain name on the list, he audibly groaned. This specific singer (who will remain nameless) had a horrible reputation for never listening to her accompaniment.

To test this, the players decided to play a little trick on her. Just before the singer came in to rehearse, they all switched instruments! Each holding an instrument he couldn't play, they began the first piece. The cacophony of noise was so bad that the singer actually noticed. Not knowing exactly what was wrong but wanting to sound authoritative, she shouted, "No, no, it's too slow!"

Tone ventured, "I know how to fix this. Buddy, you play the trombone, Mel the trumpet, Carl, you play sax, Bobby play drums, Ray, you play piano, and I'll play the bass." The confused singer made no objection to this odd remedy, and soon each musician was playing his correct instrument. They started the piece once more, and it was note perfect. Nevertheless, none of them was very surprised when the singer stopped them again with, "No, no, it's still too slow!"

God wants us to be good listeners. He wants us to listen to Him, and He wants us to listen to each other, just as He listens to us.

Are you a good listener? Make it a point today to ask people about themselves and simply sit back and listen. Then thank God for being the best Listener of all.

As you know, we consider blessed those who have persevered.

—JAMES 5:11a

Georges Bizet's masterpiece *Carmen* is one of the pinnacles of the opera world. Brahms exclaimed, "I would go to the ends of the earth to embrace the composer of *Carmen.*" Tchaikovsky considered it such a perfect work that he very nearly memorized every note. It is the "C" of the "ABC" of opera (the "A" being Verdi's *Aida,* and the "B" is Puccini's *La Boheme).*

But it might have never been written if its composer had not persevered against failure. Bizet endured so many fiascos in his musical career that it is truly amazing he did not quit. It was not a question of talent. A child prodigy on the piano, he entered the Paris Conservatory when only nine. Bizet wrote an excellent symphony at the age of seventeen and won the coveted Prix de Rome in 1857.

His successes soon came to an abrupt end. Throughout the decade of the 1860s, he wrote one opera flop after another. In 1872 Bizet thought he had finally created a hit with *Djamileh,* but the title role was poorly cast and the first performance was a disaster. He composed some beautiful incidental music for Daudet's play *L'Arlesienne* (later arranged into an orchestral suite), but the theatrical production was a failure.

Yet Bizet would not be stopped. He began working on *Carmen,* and he wrote a friend of "the absolute certainty of having found my path." Unfortunately, his Paris audiences were not ready for the innovations of this opera and gave it a disappointingly cool reception. Not long after the premiere, Bizet suffered a heart attack and died on June 3, 1875, at the age of thirty-six. Paris would soon awaken to *Carmen's* charms. Within a few months after Bizet's death, it was proclaimed a masterpiece and was soon was playing in every opera house in Europe.

God promises in Scripture that those who persevere will be blessed. Like Bizet, we may not realize that blessing while we are still alive, but we do know that God is faithful and will keep His promises for eternity.

Do you have a dream, something big you would really love to do someday? Write down a list of all the obstacles you can think of that would hinder you. Now prayerfully offer this list to God, and ask Him to help you overcoming each obstacle one by one.

He said to them, "Go into all the world and preach the good news to all creation." —MARK 16:15

Roslyn Langlois has been called to lead the life of a double agent, or even a triple agent. She is a concert pianist who has performed extensively, both in recital and with orchestras. She is also a Christian wife and mother, who believes strongly in putting her family first. Finally, she has worked in full-time ministry for years, in Youth with a Mission and the Christian Performing Artists' Fellowship.

Obviously, anyone with so many roles must be careful to keep her priorities straight. For instance, during the days when she had little ones at home, she had to carefully weigh the implications for her family of each music and ministry possibility. Therefore, when she was approached at that time of life with a request to travel in music ministry, she automatically began to refuse.

Langlois had been asked to perform with an Australian children's choir that had been invited into China toward the end of its "cultural revolution." As she tried to dismiss the idea, the thought immediately occurred: "Not so fast with your conclusions!" As she prayed about it, she believed that this thought "was from the Lord Himself, to whom my husband and I together had given the total right to say where we would go, with whom, when, etc., in our married life. He is the Lord in REAL terms!"

As if to confirm this decision, grandparents and close friends immediately came forth to help with the children, enabling both Roslyn and her husband, John, to make the historic trip into China. The trip was a resounding success both musically and in terms of ministry opportunities. Her willingness to let God be the Lord over all times of her life was a great faith builder, as she remembers, "this experience of the Lordship of Christ Jesus reinforced for us the fact that His wisdom and love are beyond all that we can imagine!"

If God called you to stop what you were doing and go to a foreign country for Him, what would you do? Spend a few moments looking at a globe or map, and ask God if He might send you somewhere unexpected for His glory.

Train a child in the way he should go, and when he is old he will not turn from it. —PROVERBS 22:6

The above Scripture is commonly interpreted as training children about the Lord, or about living a godly, moral life. It certainly does mean these things, but it also can show how parents' training and example can send a child in any number of different directions. For instance, a love for music.

The composer Carl Marie von Weber, who died today in 1826, was raised in a very musical environment. His father was a Kapellmeister who wanted his children to become great musicians. One of his cousins had married Wolfgang Amadeus Mozart, and a stepbrother had studied with Franz Joseph Haydn.

With his father's loving encouragement, Weber's musical abilities flourished. He studied with Michael Haydn (younger brother of the famous Haydn) and composed his first opera at the age of fourteen. Weber became a noted conductor, guitarist, and pianist. In 1806, an unfortunate accident ruined his beautiful singing voice. His father tinkered with lithography (a printing process), left out a glass of nitric acid, and it was mistakenly drunk by the thirsty composer.

Weber's greatest musical triumph was his opera, *Der Freischutz*. As Germany's greatest opera conductor, his influence spread to many other composers, from Beethoven to Wagner. As we can see, his father's desire to see his son love music was fulfilled. He had indeed, trained up his child in the way he wanted him to go, and his son never departed from it.

How do the personalities, tastes, and dreams of your parents compare with yours? Are they similar or different? Ask your parents about their favorite things when they were your age.

Humble yourselves before the Lord, and he will lift you up.

—JAMES 4:10

For many thousands of young musicians, the violin will always be associated with the name Suzuki. Yet Shinichi Suzuki did not begin playing the instrument until he was eighteen years old. He never tried to become a renowned virtuoso, but his efforts have brought the joy of music into countless households around the world.

One of his many students was a boy named Koli Toyoda. When in his early teens, this Japanese boy became a Christian. Suzuki was impressed with the boy's devotion, and one day told him to "go to church and play before Christ." The lad did as directed, playing the magnificent Bach *Chaconne* for Violin Solo.

Koli returned, saying, "I played the *Chaconne* in church." Suzuki asked, "Good. How was it?" "There was no one present," the boy said, "I felt very good." His teacher answered, "Good. Wherever and whenever you play, always think that Christ is listening to you."

That same lad went on to study in Europe and became the first Japanese musician to be named to a principal chair in a major European orchestra: concertmaster of the Berlin Philharmonic. He and his teacher corresponded for many years, and each letter from Japan contained gems of greatly appreciated wisdom. Suzuki's main advice, often repeated, was, "never lose your humility, for pride obscures the power to perceive truth and greatness. Please, by all means, don't forget this."

God wants us to remain humble as well. He helps us to do great things and wants us to always do our best for Him, but we need to remain humble and to remember that all our abilities come from Him.

The Bible is filled with examples of people who lived a life of humility. Moses was called "more humble than anyone else on the face of the earth" (Numbers 12:3). Read chapter twelve from the Book of Numbers to learn more about Moses' humility.

"For the worker deserves his wages." —LUKE 10:7b

Our world is filled with huge companies, universities, and organizations. Have you ever stopped to wonder, "How did they begin?" Often the largest establishments in the world began with only a few people and very little money—but with a great idea. Sometimes, things can begin from a simple kindness.

For many years, especially during the 1930s and '40s, the pinnacle of American jazz was New York City's 52nd Street. Jazz clubs were lined up and down the street, and some of the country's finest players got their start on this road. Yet this was not a dream of the city planners. This national center of jazz can trace its origin to an afternoon in 1930.

Following the stock market crash and the ensuing Depression, thousands of musicians were out of work. Pianist Willie Smith was one of them. He would drift into restaurants, taverns, nightclubs, anywhere that had a piano, and offer to play for tips—which he seldom got.

One of his favorite places to visit was owned by a man named Joe Helbock. He liked music and particularly enjoyed the style played on his old piano by Willie Smith. So one day, Helbock told Smith, "Why don't you stop by every day around five, and I'll give you a little salary for your trouble." He did, and soon other establishments were hiring musicians to play regularly. Within a few years "The Cradle of Swing" was known all over the country.

Smith could have quit working and given up. Instead, he kept at it, and eventually his work was rewarded. God honors our work—sometimes with a little money, sometimes with a lot. Our job is to keep at the work He's given us, regardless of what it is.

How can your talents bless someone today? Perhaps you could perform for your family or friends. (Who knows? Maybe they'll even give you a tip!)

"Open their eyes and turn them from darkness to light, and from the power of Satan to God, so that they may receive forgiveness of sins and a place among those who are sanctified by faith in me." —ACTS 26:18

Reggae is a form of music seldom associated with Christianity. Yet there are those who are using reggae to boldly bring the light of Jesus Christ to many held in darkness. One of the greatest champions of this evangelistic effort is a Christian band known as Temple Yard.

"We see ourselves as penetrating the darkness that's generally associated with reggae music," explains the group's lead singer, Erik Sundin. "We don't step back from any of the truth of the Gospel at all. I tell you, it's a blessing to me personally to be able to do altar calls and give the message of Christ. Anytime we have an opportunity, we do an altar call."

Temple Yard has been used to bring thousands to Christ. "We basically feel that our mission field is the world," declares guitarist Johnny Guerrero. "We want to bring the message of hope to as many people as possible. Marky Rage, a band member born in Barbados, says that Temple Yard's ministry 'provides a spiritual alternative for those who are in desperate need of true peace and are searching for answers to their life's questions.' "

What about those Christians who might think that reggae music could never be used for the Lord? Erik Sundin shares his heart's conviction, to which he has dedicated his life: "I believe God has created music for His glory and for His uses, for His tools. And I believe that when I take reggae music and we use it for God, it's glorifying Him as it was supposed to be originally."

What is your favorite type of music? Try composing a Christian song in that genre today.

You have heard these things; look at them all. Will you not admit them? "From now on I will tell you of new things, of hidden things unknown to you." —ISAIAH 48:6

On this date in 1915, a man was born who would revolutionize the recording industry. Not a famous performer, he made his many contributions in a "behind-the-scenes" manner. Although an excellent guitarist, he is known not for playing the guitar but for reinventing it. His name is Les Paul, often called the "father of the solid-body electric guitar."

Thousands of musicians play Gibson's outstanding Les Paul guitars. These are immensely popular, yet many guitarists who play Les Paul guitars don't even realize that Les Paul is also a real person. He doesn't mind being known for his guitar, joking, "They think I am one."

Another area of his expertise was to invent recording equipment. His creative thinking came up with the electronic reverb, overdubbing, sound-on-sound recording, and the multitrack tape recorder. These ideas came to him at odd times, as when he thought of sound-on-sound in the 1940s. He and his wife Mary were in the backyard. "Mary was hanging up laundry and I'm looking at the tape machine and she says, 'What are you thinking up now?' I said, 'Oh, I have an idea here and it's crazy.'"

The idea for multitrack recording goes back to the 1920s, long before the tape recorder itself. On his mother's piano roll, he noticed that "the piano keys go down when there is a hole in the paper. I thought, 'If I punch a hole somewhere else in that paper a key's gonna go down,' and it did. Now when a real roll came on—say it was Fats Waller playing something—there were lots of places for me to play along with him. So I'd punch out extra holes. . . . I could make him play fifths, I could make him play thirds. . . . I was having a field day with this thing!"

God is the Master of all creativity—just look at His Creation! Our creativity and "new thoughts" come from Him. Let's thank Him for that today.

Try exploring a different creative field than you're used to. If you prefer music, explore painting or sculpting, or writing poetry. You never know what hidden creativity God may reveal!

There they were, overwhelmed with dread, where there was nothing to dread. —PSALM 53:5a

Courage is not the absence of fear. Courageous people still have fears, but they have learned to face those fears, never letting them get in the way. Yet there are still so many who have allowed fear to dominate their lives. Life would have much more joy if we could all determine to never listen to our fears.

Frederick Delius (1862–1934) was an unusual composer who preferred the company of poets and painters to that of musicians. Born in England, he spent most of his life in France, Norway, or Florida. He was capable of writing beautiful music—such as his Florida Suite or the exquisite "On Hearing the First Cuckoo in Spring"—but his output was relatively small. Delius was very reclusive, and late in life he became blind and paralyzed. He died on this date in 1934.

When World War I broke out, Delius and his wife were living in France. He was then working on a composition to be performed in London, so they decided to leave for England. As soon as they arrived, they visited the conductor Henry Wood, who was "deeply distressed with Delius' tired and tragic appearance."

To the conductor's astonishment, Delius began to unbutton his coat and shirt. One by one he pulled out the pages of a new orchestra score, entitled "Once Upon a Time." Mrs. Delius told of their journey, "I was so afraid they might search him and commandeer it." It seems that they were told that the Germans were looking for someone who was supposedly carrying coded war secrets.

Delius lived his life with fear and dread that were often unfounded. God doesn't want us to be "overwhelmed with dread," but because of our human nature, we often are. When we feel afraid, we need to remember that God is our strength, and with Him, we truly have nothing to dread.

When was the last time you were afraid of something that never happened? Choose a brave Bible character (David, Ruth, Nehemiah, Paul, etc.) and write down several ways that person showed courage. In which one of those ways can you show courage today?

Blessed is he who has regard for the weak; the Lord delivers him in times of trouble. —PSALM 41:1

Today is the birthday of the composer Richard Strauss (1864–1949). His great tone poems—*Don Quixote, Till Eulenspiegel, Don Juan, Death and Transfiguration, A Hero's Life*—are as much in orchestral repertoire today as Brahms symphonies, but each was condemned at its premiere.

One review proclaimed, "The possibilities of cacophony seem to be exhausted." Another said, "*Don Quixote* is no music; it may possibly be something else—a big, huge, monumental, colossal joke." All of Europe heard with amusement the incident concerning the king of England. The band of the Grenadier Guard one day played an arrangement of Strauss' music. The following memorandum from George V was soon received: "His Majesty does not know what the band has just played, but it is never to be played again!"

Like so many masterpieces, Strauss' works are filled with innovations that were quite ahead of their time. But the composer continued to produce, and eventually the audiences caught up with him. In the meantime, he supported himself by conducting. It is in this role that he performed one of his greatest, unsung deeds to help struggling composers.

At the turn of the century, while he was conductor of the Berlin Philharmonic, Strauss used his influence to begin the practice of paying composers a royalty fee whenever their works were performed. This unheard of idea saved many composers from starvation. It spread from concert halls to opera houses around the world. Today there are "performing right societies" that see that composers are paid when their music is played in concert, in recordings, on radio, or television. Composers and songwriters everywhere owe a great deal of thanks to the composer/conductor Richard Strauss.

God is pleased when those who are stronger are willing to help the weak. In fact, that's the plan of salvation in a nutshell! God knew that we humans are far too weak to save ourselves, so He sent His Son to be our salvation. Thank God today for His "regard for the weak"!

Turn on your radio. Whether you know the song you hear or not, its composer is being paid by the radio station for the use of his song. Take a moment to pray God's blessing upon your favorite composer or songwriter.

"But when you are invited, take the lowest place, so that when your host comes, he will say to you, 'Friend, move up to a better place.' Then you will be honored in the presence of all your fellow guests." —LUKE 14:10

When Jesus gave the above instructions, He gave us a biblical principle that can be applied to many different situations. "The lowest seat," could be the thankless task, the position of service, or the place in the background. One place where it can be clearly seen is in the seating in an orchestra.

When clarinetist Harry Hill took a job teaching at a college in South Carolina, he soon checked into playing in the nearby Asheville Symphony Orchestra. The conductor was impressed with Hill's résumé, but as there were no positions available, all he could offer him was the lowly job of assistant second clarinet.

"Not exactly what I had in mind," Hill remembers, "but the season was a week away and I trusted that this was a door opened by God. I walked through." He duly sat in the lowest chair for the first rehearsal, but the second rehearsal presented a new opportunity. The principal clarinetist couldn't be there, and Hill was asked to fill in. The orchestra now had a chance to hear what he could do, and the new clarinetist caught everyone's notice.

Nevertheless, the first year was humbling. He often substituted as principal for rehearsals, but in the concerts he always had to sit in the last chair. "This may sound like a form of ancient torture, but I saw it as God's blessing. The next season I was moved to a coprincipal position, and one year later became the principal clarinetist, where I have served for twelve years. God truly made the last first in this situation. Praise Him!"

Not everyone can be the first chair, or the quarterback, or the boss, but everyone can serve. Find a way to serve someone today, a friend or member of your family.

"I know your deeds. See, I have placed before you an open door that no one can shut." —REVELATION 3:8a

The jazz world lost a great musician on this day in 1986—clarinetist Benny Goodman. One of the finest performers America ever produced, he made recordings that will be studied by young players for many decades. He had so much influence in the musical world that he was able to help many unknown musicians get started on their careers.

One of these unknowns was a guitarist named Charlie Christian who lived in Oklahoma. Through a mutual friend, Christian was brought to the attention of Goodman's colleague John Hammond. Hammond was determined for Goodman to hear Christian play, but he explained to Christian that he would have but one chance to impress Goodman.

First, Hammond convinced Goodman to fly this guitarist from Oklahoma to Los Angeles for an audition. Unfortunately, when Christian arrived with his guitar and amplifier, Goodman was extremely busy. He hardly had time to hear more than a few notes before he had to continue with his own work. Christian was crestfallen, but Hammond had another idea.

That night the Goodman Quintet was opening at the Victor Hugo Restaurant. The industrious Hammond arranged for the guitarist to be in the kitchen before the show. When the time came for the band to play, Christian walked boldly from the kitchen door to the stage. Goodman didn't want to make a scene before the audience, so he graciously allowed him to play along. It was Charlie Christian's one chance and he seized it. He played so well that when the first song was over, the audience gave him an ovation and Goodman gave him a job.

Sometimes God places before us an open door—just as Hammond did for Christian. We need to be bold, as Christian was, and walk through that door of opportunity and right out onto the stage!

Have you ever had such a "one time" opportunity? How did you do? Thankfully, even if it didn't go well God can give us new opportunities. Look up the passage that says that God's love is "new every morning" (Lamentations 3:22, 23).

If we confess our sins, he is faithful and just and will forgive us our sins and purify us from all unrighteousness. —1 JOHN 1:9

Today is the birthday of one of the greatest vocalists in the CCM world, soprano Sandi Patty. She is best known in Christian circles, but her powerful voice impresses all who hear it—as evidenced on July 4, 1986. After she sang the "Star-Spangled Banner" on national TV, the phone lines at ABC News were jammed for hours with people asking about this amazing singer.

Patty has learned that life as a celebrity has crushing burdens and pressures. At one point in her many tours, she gave in to temptation and had an affair. Later, this and other problems destroyed her marriage. It looked as though her ministry might be finished as well. But Patty took three courageous steps:

1. She repented and owned up to her sin. After her divorce and remarriage, Patty gave an open confession before her church and a long interview in *Christianity Today* magazine, admitting that the affair was "nobody's fault but my own."

2. She has now made herself accountable before other Christians from her church. By this honest action, Patty shows that none of us is free from temptations and that we need each other to keep on the right path.

3. She believed God for forgiveness—and kept going. Throughout the painful struggle she endured, "it was hard to believe that God still loved me." But down deep, she knew the truth of the above Scripture. She had confessed, repented, and then allowed the forgiveness of God to come into her soul.

Her ministry now has a new depth of character. Sandi Patty has experienced the profound richness of God's grace. She told *CCM Magazine,* "I am in awe. God still loves me! God still loves me!"

Have you ever done something that you think God could never forgive? Peter denied the Lord, and Paul helped murder Christians—yet God forgave them and used them for His glory. Memorize the above Scripture and say it to yourself every morning.

As they approached the village to which they were going, Jesus acted as if he were going farther. But they urged him strongly, "Stay with us, for it is nearly evening; the day is almost over." So he went in to stay with them.

—LUKE 24:28, 29

Henry Francis Lyte (1793–1847) was one of the nineteenth century's great hymnwriters. He wrote the words to many hymns that are still in use today, such as "Praise, My Soul," "The King of Heaven and Jesus," and "I My Cross Have Taken." But his best known hymn comes from a story that influenced most of his adult life.

Born in Scotland and educated at Trinity College in Dublin, Lyte won the coveted English Poetry Award three times. Entering into full-time ministry, he was particularly applauded for his care of the elderly in his church. After tending another clergyman until his death, he became newly inspired in his faith. He wrote that "I began to study my Bible and preach in another manner than I had previously done."

Two years later, Lyte was again at the bedside of a dying friend who kept repeating the phrase, "abide with me." After his death, Lyte penned the words that are now known to thousands:

Abide with me—fast falls the eventide;
The darkness deepens—Lord, with me abide;
When other helpers fail and comforts flee,
Help of the helpless, O abide with me.

Lyte kept his poem to himself for many years. But in September of 1847, his poor health necessitated a move to southern France. Calling his friends together, he preached his last service and afterward gave a close relative a copy of "Abide with Me." He later sailed to Europe and died that November in Nice, France, but Henry Francis Lyte's legacy lives on in his hymns.

Do you have a favorite hymn? Try writing one yourself, on a theme that inspires you.

"I consider my life worth nothing to me, if only I may finish the race and complete the task the Lord Jesus has given me." —ACTS 20:24

Every music-lover knows of George Frederic Handel (1685–1759), and of his *Messiah, Water Music,* and many other pieces. But how many know the price he paid to create these masterpieces? Time after time, disasters threatened to stop Handel's progress, yet this composer always found a way to keep going.

Many times he must have been tempted to "throw in the towel." For years he watched as other London composers, obviously with less talent, received accolades and applause. His lack of early success must have irritated him immensely. But through all these frustrating years, Handel did not give up.

Furthermore, Handel endured one financial failure after another. Various causes left him facing total bankruptcy more than once. He was constantly dealing with unreliable patrons, unpredictable audiences, and the competition of untalented (but more popularly favored) British composers. In 1741, with deteriorating health, Handel felt that the debtors prison was unavoidable. Yet this was at the very time when he composed his great oratorio, *Messiah.*

How did Handel keep going? Perhaps one reason he was able to bounce back from so much adversity was his sense of humor. Once before an important concert, some of Handel's friends were concerned about the sparse audience. Knowing that the acoustics of empty concert halls often sound superior to full ones, he smiled and replied, "Never mind, the music will sound the better."

It was Handel's faith in God and his positive character that gave us so much music that is still loved more than two centuries later. A friend remembered that in church Handel was often seen, "on his knees, expressing by his looks and gesticulations the utmost fervor of devotion."

If you are going through a difficult time, take courage. The last page of your story has not yet unfolded. Like Handel, through your faith in God—and perhaps, the power of humor—find the strength to bounce back and complete whatever task it is that God has given you.

God knew that it would be difficult for us on this earth, so He placed dozens of passages about perseverance in the Scriptures. Use a concordance to look up some of these verses, or study a topical Bible on this important subject.

Sing to the Lord with thanksgiving; make music to our God on the harp. —PSALM 147:7

Conductor John Nelson has been producing musical miracles for many years. But one event in 1994 truly showed God's hand in saving a situation when all seemed lost. Nelson had just conducted a successful concert of music by the Polish composer Henryk Gorecki. Now he was to record Gorecki's moving *Miserere* (fifty-four minutes of difficult unaccompanied choral music) in only two recording sessions.

Nelson remembers, "The first session was as much a disaster as the concert had been a success. That left us with one session. A miracle was needed, otherwise the entire project would have fallen apart with heavy financial responsibilities. Our backs were against the wall." Needless to say, that called for a time of very serious prayer.

Before the final recording session, his wife Anita had an inspiration. "Bless Anita for giving me a God-given thought: clear the church where we were recording and have the composer Gorecki sit as the lone person to whom we would sing. Wouldn't we die to sing for Brahms, or Bach? Well, here we had the chance to sing for the composer of this magnificent work."

It worked! "The inspiration and energy this gave us caused us to literally sail through the session. We all erupted into applause at the conclusion, amazed at what we had accomplished." Afterward, Nelson also pointed out that such an experience illustrated how all music should be played—not just for its musical creator, the composer—but for the glory of its ultimate Creator, the Lord God.

Henryk Gorecki is one of the greatest Christian composers of classical music today. See what you can find about him on the Internet or in an encyclopedia, then find a recording and listen to some of his music.

The desires of the diligent are fully satisfied. —PROVERBS 13:4b

The brilliant inventor Thomas Edison once described his work as "10 percent inspiration, 90 percent perspiration." Whatever the actual percentage may be, the point is obvious. No matter how inspired an idea, to bring it to completion will always take a lot of hard work.

One morning in 1965, a songwriter woke up with a lovely melody going through his mind. Lying on his bed, he decided to put some nonsense words to the melody so that he wouldn't forget it. The first words to the tune were, "Scrambled Egg."

For less diligent composers, such an incident might have stopped at breakfast. But Paul McCartney (who was born this day in 1942) had not become one of the world's favorite songwriters without labor. He immediately went to work on the new melody.

First he wanted to make certain that the tune wasn't taken from another source. He played it for everyone who would listen, but they all declared it original. Hours were spent finding the right text for the melody, carefully deciding on the right harmony, and working out the background organization. The song was finally recorded with only a guitar accompaniment and a string quartet arrangement by George Martin. The result? "Scrambled Egg" became "Yesterday," one of the all-time greatest sellers. Fifteen years later, Paul McCartney would still say, "I really reckon 'Yesterday' is probably my best song."

McCartney had a desire to write great music. But that desire alone wasn't enough. He had to be diligent and work hard in order to satisfy that desire. When God gives us an inspiration—or a desire—He will see that the desire is satisfied as long as we are diligent in our work for Him.

Have you ever had a melody just "come into your head?" Take a moment to make up a short song of praise to the Lord.

David, wearing a linen ephod, danced before the Lord with all his might. —2 SAMUEL 6:14

There are people who think that being a Christian means wearing a long face and not having any fun. Yet King David (among others!) celebrated in jubilant praise before the Lord. A duo of two brothers known as Dawkins & Dawkins also knows how to praise God with their music.

Dawkins & Dawkins bring a wonderful, refreshing message with its rhythm-and-blues sound: "It's fun being saved," declares Erik Dawkins. "And we want all young people to know that it's not square to be saved. We have fun praising God, and that's what our music brings about."

The sons of a Pentecostal minister, the two brothers have a long history of performing at revivals where their father preached. Dawkins & Dawkins believe in being accessible to their audience and even put their e-mail address on their album covers. "That's the kind of group we want to go down in history as being," Erik explains. "One that young people can say, 'Yeah, I talked to them. They actually wrote me back.'"

What is the ultimate message they bring to their audience? Anson Dawkins answers, "God sent His Son, Jesus, to die for everyone. He loves us in spite of what we've done. He is able to deliver. He is able to set free, if we will just allow Him to." It doesn't sound too square, does it?

When people see you, which message do you think you convey: "It's fun being saved," or "It's square being saved"? Have a smile for those you meet, and ask God to fill you with His joy, that your life would help others to see that being a Christian can be fun.

. . . the authority the Lord gave me for building you up, not for tearing you down. —2 CORINTHIANS 13:10B

Have you ever considered what you would do in a high position of authority? Suppose you were the dean of an important music school or the president of a major record company. If you had such power and influence, how would you use it?

A good model is the great country guitarist Chet Atkins, who was born this date in 1924. After making dozens of excellent recordings, he became one of Nashville's most important musicians. He had a lot of power at RCA studios that could make or break careers. Fortunately, he used this power to help others. Indeed, much of his time was spent trying to find talented unknowns whom he could turn into stars.

For instance, in the early 1960s, Atkins was seeking a young talent with a background in both country and folk music, so the artist could release songs for RCA in each area. After hearing many possibilities, he found Bobby Bare, a poor young man who had recently moved to Nashville. Now what Atkins needed for Bare was a great new song for him to record.

Earlier that year, he noted how Billy Grammar had recorded "I Want to Go Home" with only moderate success. Atkins judged that this song would be perfect for Billy Bare. To make certain the disc jockeys would notice this as a new act, he arranged to have the song retitled "Detroit City." It was a huge hit, winning a Grammy Award and launching Bare's career. Chet Atkins had found the singer, the song, and the title—using his power to help someone achieve his dreams.

While we may not all have the power to make and break careers, God has given everyone of us the power and authority to build others up—or tear them down—with our words. How will you use that power today?

The Bible instructs us to pray for our leaders—and not just political leaders, but all those in positions of responsibility. Pray for someone you know of who is a leader in the music world.

Trust in the Lord forever, for the Lord, the Lord, is the Rock eternal.
—ISAIAH 26:4

Four young women—Shelley Breen, Denise Jones, Heather Floyd, and Terry Jones—form the female vocal group known as Point of Grace. They met as students at Ouachita Baptist University and have been making music ever since. Whether recording number one hits, leading thousands in worship, or authoring devotional books, these excellent vocalists have found a powerful niche in Christian music ministry.

Point of Grace's music is positive and upbeat, with an emphasis on the hope offered in Christ's love. These women serve as godly role models to their many young female fans—who buy "Girls Rule" T-shirts at their concerts. Their singing is filled with emotional zeal for the Lord. Shelley Breen explains, "I do believe that the Last Days are coming, and I have a real sense of urgency to tell people that God loves them."

The vivacious and hopeful image of Point of Grace does not hide the fact that these women deal with real life issues. Denise Jones told *CCM Magazine* of a friend battling deep depression, and admits, "I've doubted God more than once this year, asking, 'Why aren't you healing her faster?' "

Each of us asks God such questions at times. Yet even when we cannot fully understand, God is still there. Jones has been brought closer to the Lord even in her doubts: "If I never questioned this year what was going on with my friend, I may not have realized that God was showing me who He is, that He's big enough to handle my questions, and that He's faithful."

All of us have times of doubting. One of the best things to do in such times is to talk to a trusted friend. The next time you have a period of doubt, talk to your pastor or a friend who will understand—or be that listener for one of your friends.

Then those who feared the Lord talked with each other.

—MALACHI 3:16a

Four young men—Andy Chrisman, Mark Harris, Marty Magehee, and Kirk Sullivan—form the male vocal group known as 4HIM. After seven albums, twenty number-one hit songs, and six Dove Awards, one might think that this group had arrived. Yet in 1997, they went through a corporate "year of questioning."

"It's not that we hated each other or that we wanted to disband," explained Mark Harris to *CCM Magazine.* "But we asked ourselves, 'Is there more for us to do? Is this something God wants us to continue?' Because we don't want to continue this just because it's a living." They felt that God didn't want them to give up, but things just weren't working.

To show these men the answers they needed, God used a quartet of women. When 4HIM toured together with the female group Point of Grace, the men saw how the women dealt with problems by discussing them freely with one another. Harris noted, "These are four women; they communicate. We'd just as soon go back to the hotel room and turn on ESPN and let it blow over."

"Over the years, we let a lot of that happen," admits Andy Chrisman. "Pretty soon we had a huge pile in the corner that was too big to blow over." When they realized that they had years of unresolved relationship problems and began to openly deal with the issues, God's grace and healing were soon apparent. The renewal in 4HIM that followed has brought them closer together and closer to Christ. The questions are now answered, and Kirk Sullivan affirms, "We're probably closer now as a group than we have ever been."

When we have an argument or conflict with another person, God doesn't want us to pile it in a corner and hope that the garbage man will pick it up and carry it away. While He also doesn't want us to go to the other person yelling and screaming, He does want us to talk with each other and work out the conflict. Disagreements are never pleasant, but by working through them, people really can end up being closer than ever.

Being in a public music ministry has many pressures. Pray for the members of 4HIM and Point of Grace today, that God will continue to use them for His glory.

For by the grace given me I say to every one of you: Do not think of yourself more highly than you ought, but rather think of yourself with sober judgment, in accordance with the measure of faith God has given you.

—ROMANS 12:3

If there were ever a great master who had a wonderfully humble spirit, it was Johannes Brahms (1833–1897). The composer's friend George Henschel wrote that Brahms, "coveted neither fame nor applause. He was of a very simple, kind, childlike disposition. He loved children, whom—poor or rich—to make happy, was to himself a source of pure happiness." Even when Brahms had achieved both fame and wealth—at his death he left an estate valued at more than $100,000, a large fortune in the nineteenth century—this intrinsic humility and simplicity never left his character.

One example of this humility was the way he praised other composers. He publicly lauded the music of Mendelssohn, Schumann, Beethoven, and many others. Once a friend began a dinner toast to the "world's greatest composer." Before he could finish, Brahms jumped to his feet, glass in hand, and shouted, "Quite right! Here's to Mozart's health!"

He could also admit when he was wrong. In 1890, he was invited to hear the young Gustav Mahler conduct the Budapest Opera Company in Mozart's *Don Giovanni.* The exhausted composer tried to make his excuses, having heard many young conductors ruin a good opera. But his host was undaunted, insisting that there was a couch in the box, which Brahms could use if needed.

As soon as he arrived, Brahms threw himself on the couch and prepared for a long evening. During the overture his friends noticed that he sat up with approval. Brahms' enthusiasm rose as the opera progressed. When the first act ended, he ran backstage to embrace the conductor who had produced the finest *Don Giovanni* Brahms had ever heard. Mahler remembered long after, "He immediately became my fiercest partisan and benefactor."

Finding the right balance of humility and self-confidence isn't easy, but with God's help, we—like Brahams—can find that balance.

Brahms is one of the most frequently performed composers, in concert and on the radio. Tune in to a classical music station today and see if you don't hear some of his fabulous music.

Blessed is the man who perseveres under trial, because when he has stood the test, he will receive the crown of life that God has promised to those who love him. —JAMES 1:12

Mark Lowry is a very funny man. He is a Christian comedian whose humor has brought a great deal of laughter and joy to thousands. But he has many other talents as well, including a fine singing voice. For years he sang with the Bill Gaither Vocal Band, and he has some excellent advice for up-and-coming singers. His words are often humorous, yet they contain much wisdom—especially about perseverance. Here is a shortened version of his "Five P's."

1. PITCH—If you can't sing on pitch, learn to type.

2. POCKET—Sing with the music. Ride the rhythm. Don't get too far ahead or too far behind the beat.

3. PRESENCE—This is "magnetism" on stage. The person with presence is self-assured and has a plan. He is prepared.

4. PASSION—Whatever vocation you choose in life, it should be something you're passionate about.

5. PERSEVERANCE—Don't quit. Laugh at your critics. Don't quit. Sing. Don't quit. Run from negative people. Don't quit. Shoot for the stars . . . you may hit the moon! But whatever you do . . . don't ever . . . ever . . . quit.

Then he adds: "Keep it in perspective: Right before you go on stage . . . take a few deep breaths . . . forget about yourself . . . give it to God . . . then go out and do your best. This is not a competition. You have already won the prize . . . Jesus Christ."

To add some humor to your life, read a joke book today (there are a number of Christian joke books available). Then share a laugh or two with a friend.

To the man who pleases him, God gives wisdom, knowledge and happiness. —ECCLESIASTES 2:26a

On this day in 1767, perhaps the most prolific composer in all history died. Georg Philipp Telemann composed some forty operas, two hundred concertos, six hundred orchestral pieces, and over one thousand works for the church. He played a number of different instruments and was so talented at the organ that many churches fought to hire him. One in particular tried everything to persuade him, but he turned the job down. Instead, they hired their next choice: Johann Sebastian Bach!

Telemann had a congenial personality, and he was good friends with many great musicians, including Handel and Bach. In fact, he was the godfather to Bach's son Carl Philipp Emanuel Bach. Such a responsibility was taken quite seriously by Telemann and Bach, both of whom were deeply committed Christians.

Telemann's music reflects his cheerful disposition. It is elegant and polished, yet it gives the appearance of being composed naturally and without stress. Whereas most composers have to toil for hours over a composition, Handel noted that his friend Telemann "could write a motet for eight voices as easily as one could write a letter."

How could this be? One reason was a vast amount of God-given talent. But another factor must surely have been Telemann's positive attitude toward his gifts. He said that "Music ought not to be an effort," and never complained about his long hours of composing. His outlook was humble and unpretentious: "A good composer should be able to set public notices to music." And if he had, we would all love it.

When we are doing work that pleases God, as Telemann did, God will reward us with wisdom, knowledge, and happiness just as the Scripture promises. That doesn't mean that every job we do will be easy, but work well done will be rewarded.

Do you find yourself complaining about your workload? Make a list of all you need to do today, and offer it to the Lord for His wisdom, knowledge, and happiness.

"But a Samaritan, as he traveled, came where the man was; and when he saw him, he took pity on him." —LUKE 10:33

The traveler in the parable of the Good Samaritan was in about as bad a situation as can be imagined. Robbed, beaten, and utterly stranded, he was left far from home. Except for not being beaten, many early jazz groups found themselves in similar situations when their tour promoters skipped town with the funds. It happened to many, including such greats as trumpeter Buck Clayton.

In the mid-1930s, Clayton's band was on tour when they were stranded in Tracy, California, by a crooked promoter. The eight musicians knew no one in the area and were completely destitute. Several days without a bite of food left them in despair.

It so happened that Tracy was the hometown of Jimmy Maxwell, a young trumpeter. Walking downtown one day he noticed several strangers. Being a jazz fan, he thought he recognized their leader and ventured to ask, "Are you Buck Clayton?"

The astonished Clayton answered, "Yeah." Maxwell blurted out, "What are you doing here?" "I'm here with my band and the promoters ran out," was the dispirited answer. Maxwell immediately took them to his home. His mother gave them a very appreciated dinner and the band stayed with the Maxwells until they were able to arrange a way to get home. The visit inspired young Maxwell to become a professional musician himself, and he would one day perform with many bands, including Benny Goodman's.

Can you be a "Good Samaritan" right where you live? Visit a neighbor and ask how you can be of help.

"It is written: 'Worship the Lord your God, and serve him only.' "

—MATTHEW 4:10b

On June 27, 1972, gospel music lost one of its true legends when Mahalia Jackson died. Her rich, deep contralto voice held audiences around the world spellbound, and her recordings sold millions. Yet she came from the humblest of beginnings. She and her five siblings were born in a shack on Water Street, next to the Mississippi River in New Orleans.

Her father was a storefront preacher, and Jackson joined his choir when only five years old. As a teenager, she had to take jobs as a laundress or a maid, but the love of music was always part of her life. "When the old people weren't home and I'd be scrubbin' the floor, I'd put on a Bessie Smith record to make the work go faster."

When only sixteen, she moved to Chicago and joined the Greater Salem Baptist Church Choir, but her extraordinary voice soon singled her out as a soloist, and she made her first recording in 1934. In one church, she was handed a microphone, but answered, "Don't need a microphone. Just open the windows and the doors and let the sound pour out." Jackson's faith shone through her singing: "Time is important to me because I want to sing long enough to leave a message. I'm used to singing in churches where nobody would dare stop me until the Lord arrives!"

Elements of blues and jazz are found in her musical style, but she insisted on singing only gospel music. "I am a sanctified woman," she declared, and turned down opportunities to sing secular music that could have made her millions. Mahalia Jackson explained, "The blues are fine for listenin'. But I could never sing them. I was saved. Remember David in the Bible? 'Sing joyfully unto the Lord with a loud voice.' I took his advice."

Not everyone is called to sing only gospel music, but each of us needs to know our calling and focus on it. Make a list of some of the activities you are currently involved with, and ask God to give you focus to find His priorities for your life.

"But he knows the way that I take; when he has tested me, I will come forth as gold." —JOB 23:10

Cole Porter (1891–1964) was one of America's best-loved songwriters. Born in Peru, Indiana, he loved music from a very early age and was writing songs when only ten years old. Sent to France during World War I, he stayed in Paris, where he studied music at the Schola Cantorum. It was there he met and married Linda Lee Thomas, and their happy marriage lasted until her death in 1954.

From 1928 to 1937, Porter enjoyed spectacular success on Broadway. His many hit shows of those years include *Anything Goes, The New Yorkers, Fifty Million Frenchmen, Jubilee,* and *Let's Do It, Let's Fall in Love.* His songs were in constant demand, and he also began to score Hollywood musicals, such as *Rosalie* and *Born to Dance.*

Then tragedy struck. In 1937 he had a devastating horseback accident, which nearly resulted in having both legs amputated. Porter spent most of his remaining decades in pain and suffered through more than thirty operations. It seemed to everyone that America would lose one of its principle creators of entertainment.

Porter's answer to his catastrophic situation? In the midst of physical pain, he threw himself back into his work. He continued to score hits on Broadway, including his biggest: *Kiss Me, Kate.* This hilarious tale of ham actors trying to produce Shakespeare's *The Taming of the Shrew* ran for more than one thousand performances, and it's still popular today. Cole Porter found that the remedy for his affliction was to keep giving to others.

When we are tested and face challenging situations, God wants us to come out shining as gold. Some of the greatest music, literature, and art has come as a result of the creator's suffering. When we face challenging situations, we can choose to let them get the best of us, or we can rise to the occasion and keep doing our best for God. Which way will you choose?

Do you know someone who is sick or bedridden and needs encouragement? Do something creative for him: drop by a gift you make yourself, or write a poem or a song.

The tongue of the wise commends knowledge, but the mouth of the fool gushes folly. —PROVERBS 15:2

Have you ever met someone who simply won't listen? Even when the truth is clearly presented before him, he stubbornly hangs on to his opinion. Perhaps the best thing we can learn from such people is to never imitate this annoying practice.

One of the greatest violinists of the nineteenth century was Joseph Joachim (1831–1907). He spent much of his time encouraging composers, and many of the great Romantic concertos were premiered at his hands. His many friends included Franz Liszt, Robert and Clara Schumann, and especially Johannes Brahms.

Perhaps the great length of his career contributed to the following outlandish story. Joachim had just finished a concert late in his life when he was approached by an admirer. "Allow me, sir, to congratulate you on your performance which I thought very fine. But also to remind you that I had the privilege many years ago of hearing your father, the great Joachim."

The violinist smiled and explained that it must have been himself, for his father had never played violin and had been a wool merchant. Hearing that information from Joachim himself should have definitively ended the matter. But the man insisted that he knew better. He walked away and was heard mumbling, "It's all wrong. It was his father I heard!"

How tempting it can be to not listen to others and talk about things we think we know. As the above proverb points out, sometimes it is better to just keep our mouths shut!

Because of Joseph Joachim's encouragement of composers around him, many of our best-loved pieces of violin music were composed. Encourage a friend or family member to do something creative today.

And so after waiting patiently, Abraham received what was promised.

—HEBREWS 6:15

Patience is a virtue that few of us constantly practice but all of us need. Like Abraham, we must be willing to wait patiently and without despairing. For someone trying to break into the country music business, patience is essential. As one very talented guitarist/songwriter found out, some things are worth waiting for.

Ed Bruce had spent most of his life in country music but had little to show for it. Now in his mid-thirties, he had recorded a few songs and opened concerts for some big stars, but he had failed to write a real hit. In a mood of discouragement, he sketched out an autobiographical song he called "Mama, Don't Let Your Babies Grow Up to Be Guitar Players."

His wife suggested changing "Guitar Players" to "Cowboys" and the song was soon finished. He convinced United Artists to record him singing the new song, but it still only made it to a disappointing number fifteen on the charts. Again, Ed Bruce had failed to make it to the top. Would he ever?

He had to wait two more years for his break, but he never stopped trying. Finally, the stars Waylon Jennings and Willie Nelson decided to record "Mama, Don't Let Your Babies Grow Up to Be Cowboys." This time it topped the charts, becoming the number-one country song in 1978. Finally, his patience had been rewarded. Ed Bruce found himself with an MCA recording contract and an NBC weekly television show. It was worth the wait.

Many times when it feels we are waiting on God or that He is not answering our prayers, it is actually because He is preparing something big for us. The next time it feels as if you are waiting and waiting and waiting, watch out. God may be just around the corner with a big surprise!

What is your "P.Q." or "Patience Quotient?" One way to raise it is to talk to someone older who has reaped the rewards of patience. Write a letter or e-mail to someone you admire, asking that person how long it took for his dreams to come true.

O Lord my God, I take refuge in you; save and deliver me from all who pursue me. —PSALM 7:1

This is the birthday of Thomas A. Dorcey (1899–1993), often called "the father of gospel music." His long life spanned most of the twentieth century, and he wrote more than eight hundred gospel songs. The persecution he faced was almost prophetic, in that it foreshadowed the struggles of many future musicians in this field. He began his music career as a noted ragtime and blues musician, accompanying famous singers of his day, such as "Ma" Rainey and Bessie Smith.

While attending a meeting of the National Baptist Convention and hearing the songs of Charles Tindley, he was deeply moved. After a struggle between whether to work in secular music or gospel, Dorcey finally chose the latter. Many churches shunned his jazzy blues music, and his beginnings were discouraging. At one point he, "borrowed five dollars and sent out five hundred copies of my song 'If You See My Savior,' to churches throughout the country. . . . It was three years before I got a single order. I felt like going back to the blues."

Dorcey never let the persecution stop him. By 1929 he had devoted himself exclusively to gospel music, and three years later he organized the Gospel Singers Convention in Chicago, Illinois. The next two decades were spent touring the United States with talented Christian singers who propagated his spirited gospel music songs, eventually leading to acceptance and imitation. He inspired such great musicians as Mahalia Jackson, Clara Ward, and James Cleveland.

Thomas Dorcey was one of the first of a long line of modern Christian musicians whose music was condemned as "the devil's music" by much of the church. Blending sacred text with what some churchmen considered the "secular style" of blues and jazz was considered radical, and he was often persecuted for it. His answer has inspired many musicians of later generations: "When I realized how hard some folks were fighting the gospel idea, I was determined to carry the banner."

Have you ever felt persecuted because of your beliefs? Decide now to show mercy to those around you, even if you disagree with them.

With long life will I satisfy him and show him my salvation.

—PSALM 91:16

A great innovator was born today in 1714, the opera composer Christopher Willibald Gluck. He had a brilliant mind, but was less of a court musician than a man of the people. One of his contemporaries said, "Anyone meeting Gluck would never have taken him for a prominent person or a creative genius. He called things by their name, and therefore, twenty times a day offended the sensitive ears of the Parisians used to flattery."

For years Gluck composed the conventional Italian operas, which hardly contained a plot: they were simply used as a vehicle for the vocal gymnastics of opera stars. But he became less and less satisfied with such limitations. Finally Gluck composed *Orfeo ed Euridice,* full of emotion and drama. This opera was completely radical, adding many new instruments and removing the traditional harpsichord. This work of 1762 and his later works revolutionized opera and prepared the way for the music dramas of Wagner.

Gluck lived a long life, but in his seventies he developed health problems. After a severe stroke, he was put to bed for rest but was visited by many friends. In one visit, several singers were discussing a certain piece of Gluck's sacred music. A dispute ensued about the manner in which the part of Christ should be sung. Finally, the composer intervened. "Well, my friends, as you cannot decide how we should make the Savior sing, I'll go to Him and ascertain from His holy countenance what to do." He died in this quiet certainty of salvation on November 15, 1787.

The Lord wants all of His followers to be certain of their salvation through Christ. The world and the devil would create many doubts around us. But God's Word—which will never pass away—is clear that Christians can be assured of eternal life.

Read the first twelve verses of I John, chapter 5. Praise God for giving us the assurance of salvation we need to dispel our doubts.

I have learned to be content whatever the circumstances.

—PHILIPPIANS 4:11b

Today is the birthday of Leos Janacek (1854–1928), known as the greatest composer from the country of Moravia. He was born in a small mountain village, and like most of his neighbors he might have stayed there his entire life. But his talents propelled him to higher education. At eleven he was sent to study in a monastery in Brno, capital of Moravia. Later he studied in the Prague Conservatory, and finally at the Leipzig and Vienna Conservatories.

Janacek was exposed to the finest music on the continent, yet he preferred to explore the folk music of his own land. Throughout Europe in the late nineteenth and early twentieth centuries, there was a rebirth of national styles. While Vaughan Williams examined English folk music, Bartok collected Hungarian tunes, and Grieg compiled Norway's heritage, Janacek brought elements of ancient Moravian melodies into his music.

In one way, Janacek had a very different experience than the other great composers of his day. He worked most of his life in extreme obscurity. After his European education, he returned to Brno, composing industriously but without the world's notice. It was not until his sixty-second year that his opera *Jenufa* was performed at the opera house in Prague.

At last, the music world began to discover this creative composer. Performance followed performance of his works, and for his last twelve years his name was the talk of Europe. How did this long-earned success affect his life and work? Not at all. Like Paul, Janacek had worked in obscurity and now in the spotlight, but his steadfastness was consistent until his death. Like Paul and Janacek, we too need to learn to be content whatever our situation.

A country's folk music reveals much about its culture and tradition. Find some folk music of your ancestors' culture and see if any of it expresses faith in God.

The wisdom of the prudent is to give thought to their ways.

—PROVERBS 14:8

January 13, 1944, should have been a happy day for the great Russian composer Igor Stravinsky. Born outside Saint Petersburg, he had spent much of his adult life in Europe and was now delighted to become an American citizen. In gratitude and with simple patriotism, he composed a new orchestration of the "Star-Spangled Banner," and dedicated it "to the American people." Its premiere took place on July 4, in Cambridge, Massachusetts.

Unfortunately, someone discovered an old state law that declared it illegal to tamper with the national anthem. The police commissioner was notified, and police officers went to the concert two nights later, when the program was to be repeated. The police warned the baffled composer of Chapter 246, Section 9 of Massachusetts law: "Let him change it just once," the police said, "and we'll grab him." Stravinsky sadly withdrew his patriotic gesture, and the orchestration was not heard.

The composer had sincerely and reverently made this arrangement, saying, "I gave it the character of a real church hymn." Instead of satisfying the admirable urge to show his gratitude to the country that had taken him in, he was rudely rebuked. The law, which had been made to guard against disrespectfully mocking our anthem, was instead used to quench the very patriotism it was created to inspire.

Often we can hurt others without even realizing it. Unless we take the time to see the whole picture in a given situation, we can easily make a thoughtless decision or comment that can have painful results. May God give us sensitive hearts and discerning wisdom to minister effectively to those around us, even to hear what is often left unspoken.

Do you know someone who has recently been hurt by others? Ask the Lord to show you how you can be a "healer" in that person's life.

"Whoever acknowledges me before men, I will also acknowledge him before my Father in heaven." —MATTHEW 10:32

The Christian rock band Petra, named for the Greek word for "rock," has outlasted all the others. Founded by guitarist Bob Hartman in 1972, it was still together at the end of the century. The group has not only recorded more than twenty albums, but has also created its own Bible studies, devotional books, and retreat materials. Petra has won every award possible in its genre and has sold more products than any other Christian band (over six million units).

Doubtless, a key factor in Petra's endurance is its commitment to ministry. Hartman explains the group's calling: "We began with a sense that God had called us to use our talents to reach our peers for Christ. It was not glamorous. It was not financially rewarding. But we knew we were supposed to do it because we felt a calling."

Over the years, the musicians have changed, but the vision has not. "We felt pressure to change. We were told by a particular distributor of secular and Christian records that they could do a lot more with us if we were less 'gospel' and more 'inspirational,' as they put it. What that translates to is: 'Take the Jesus out. We can deal with God. We can deal with good times and good feelings and family and all that, but take the Jesus out. We can't deal with Jesus.' "

That is one thing that will never happen with Petra. Hartman is emphatic. "That's what scares me. And that's what makes me sick. Take the Jesus out? No stinkin' way! Jesus stays in because He is everything. If I can't talk about Jesus, if I can't express what Christ's done for me, there's no sense in doing this. There's no reason. Jesus is everything."

Have you ever felt pressure to hide your faith? We need to pray for each other, that we will always stand up for Christ. Take a moment to pray for Bob Hartman and Petra, that they will be strengthened to continue their bold stance for Jesus.

"What do you think? If a man owns a hundred sheep, and one of them wanders away, will he not leave the ninety-nine on the hills and go to look for the one that wandered off? And if he finds it, I tell you the truth, he is happier about that one sheep than about the ninety-nine that did not wander off."

—MATTHEW 18:12, 13

How amazing to realize to what lengths the King of the universe will go in order to save one soul! Like the shepherd in Christ's parable, He will leave everything to search for that one lost sheep. Often the Lord uses circumstances beyond our control in order to bring us the Good News.

When violinist Lee Joiner was fourteen, he spent a summer at the Aspen Music Festival. There he met John Wakefield, a Christian musician in college who welcomed him. They spent much time together, and his friend made a strong impact on him that summer. They went to church together, but Joiner's spiritual life did not continue after he returned home.

The following year Joiner again went to Aspen. Since they had become good friends, he asked to room again with John Wakefield. The worker checked the list for a "Wakefield" and assigned Joiner a room with, not his Christian friend John Wakefield, but a total stranger, David Wakefield (who was not a believer). Was this disappointment part of God's plan?

Joiner was later accepted at the Juilliard School, and he discovered that his new friend David Wakefield was also accepted. They arranged to room together. But since their last meeting, David Wakefield had become a strong Christian. His witness was profound, and Joiner soon gave his life to Christ. Today they are both professional musicians using their talents for the Lord. God had arranged everything in His love and wisdom.

Whom do you know who is a "lost soul"? Pray for that person today, that God would use you to bring that person to Christ.

A man's pride brings him low, but a man of lowly spirit gains honor. —PROVERBS 29:23

On this date in 1940, a child was born in Liverpool, England, who would one day become one of the most popular musicians of the century. The boy was named Richard Starkey, but he would later be known around the world as Ringo Starr, the drummer for the Beatles. He met John Lennon, Paul McCartney, and George Harrison in Hamburg, Germany, where he had been playing with a group called Rory Storm and the Hurricanes.

After replacing Pete Best as the Beatles' drummer, Ringo found his place in the hearts of millions. Despite the fact that—unlike the other three Beatles—he seldom sang or wrote any songs, Ringo developed a friendly, amusing stage personality. For instance, when asked about classical music, Ringo replied, "I love Beethoven, especially his poems."

When Ringo first joined the Beatles, he had a humiliating experience that he has never forgotten. The other three musicians had scheduled their first recording session for September 11, 1962. Apparently no one had told George Martin, the group's producer, about the new drummer. The excited young Ringo showed up at the studio, and Martin bluntly stated that his services would not be needed; he had already hired a studio drummer to make the recording.

What should Ringo do? He could rant and rave and insist on getting his way, or even walk out on the group. Instead, he humbled himself and asked if there was any help he could provide. Very much in the background, he played maracas and tambourine for "Love Me Do" and "P.S., I Love You," the two sides of the Beatles' first single. His humility was noticed and appreciated: never again would the Beatles record without Ringo Starr on the drums.

Though others may not notice our humility, God always does. Let's strive to honor Him with our humility in all we do.

Put yourself in Ringo's shoes when he arrived at the recording studio. What would you have done? Determine now to keep a cool spirit in such situations and to take the humble approach as he did.

"And when you stand praying, if you hold anything against anyone, forgive him, so that your Father in heaven may forgive you your sins."

—MARK 11:25

On this date in 1791 Oxford University bestowed an honorary doctorate on Franz Joseph Haydn. At that time he was the most famous composer alive. When the imperial authorities wanted a new national anthem for Austria, it was natural to ask Haydn. He wrote what is considered by many to be the best national anthem ever composed, "Gott erhault Franz den Kaiser."

It was first sung at the National Theater in Vienna on the emperor's birthday, February 12, 1797. Francis II himself attended with great pomp, and the new anthem was sung that day at theaters throughout Austria. This has always been a popular melody; Haydn also used the theme in the second movement of his String Quartet in C Major, Op. 76, no. 3, giving this work the nickname "The Emperor." The melody has also been used for the well-known hymn "Glorious Things of Thee Are Spoken."

The anthem served its country well until 1938, when the ruthless Hitler abducted the beautiful melody. Hitler changed the words to fit his warped ideology and Haydn's song now became the German national anthem, flaunted by thousands of goose-stepping Nazis. Due to this terrible association, many of the Allied war survivors want no part of Haydn's anthem—the memories it now stirs are too disturbing.

What a painful situation when something good you have done is suddenly turned around and used for evil. A slander against you is one of the hardest wrongs to forgive. Yet being in this very position can prove the authenticity of our faith. There are many things that we, in our natural selves, could never forgive. But as we ask God to fill us with His love and forgiveness, then we become able to pardon others as He has pardoned us.

Are you holding a grudge against someone? First, ask God to fill you with His love and forgiveness toward that person. Then, go to that person as soon as possible for reconciliation.

Praise the Lord. Sing to the Lord a new song, his praise in the assembly of the saints. —PSALM 149:1

One of America's finest hymnwriters, Philip Paul Bliss, was born in a Pennsylvania log cabin on this date in 1838. His family was devout but poor, and his schooling stopped at age eleven, when he had to find work. For most of his teen years, he toiled in sawmills, lumber camps, on farms, or anywhere he could find work.

When Bliss was twelve, he was taken to a revival meeting in the little town of Elk Run, Pennsylvania, where he gave his life to Christ. The young man had an outstanding voice, and when he wasn't singing during his farm work, he was singing in dozens of country churches. Soon he began writing his own hymns, and in 1864 Bliss moved to Chicago to work for the Root and Cady publishing house.

Most hymnwriters either compose the music or write the text, but Bliss did both with equal skill. He gave us the words and music to "Hallelujah, What a Savior," "Jesus Loves Even Me," and "Wonderful Words of Life," plus the music to the celebrated "It Is Well with My Soul." Bliss edited and published many songbooks, and insisted on donating all royalties (almost thirty thousand dollars) to an evangelistic ministry with whom he worked.

But from first to last, Bliss was a singer for the Lord—and he encouraged everyone to sing! In an article for *The Musical Visitor,* he pointed out: "There is a deal of mighty fine talking, a few earnest prayers, but very little hearty singing. Why is it that so few ministers sing? Wouldn't it improve their voices, and hearts, too?" To summarize his admonitions, Bliss said, "I believe that every Christian family should be a praise-giving family, and if possible, 'psalm singers.' "

Not all of us are from "praise-giving families" but we can each be a "praise-giving Christian." Go somewhere alone today and sing a song of praise to your Savior.

"Whenever I bring clouds over the earth and the rainbow appears in the clouds, I will remember my covenant between me and you and all living creatures of every kind. Never again will the waters become a flood to destroy all life." —GENESIS 9:14, 15

World War II was a growing up time for America. Not only did it send young men to the farthest reaches of the world, but it also brought together thousands of soldiers from every part of the country. One of the strongest bonds that held them together was music. The titles of hit songs became the names of regiments, and the music from home gave many tired soldiers the inspiration to keep going.

One of the most popular songs was written by Zeke Clements, a cowboy singer and regular at Nashville's Grand Ole Opry. (Clements has another interesting claim to fame: he was the voice of "Bashful" in Walt Disney's film *Snow White.)* A dedicated Christian, he was especially comforted by his Bible as his country continued through the dark war years.

One night he had a dream, which he used to create a stirring song. "It was from a Bible passage," Clements later explained. "It said that God put a rainbow in the sky, and the world would not again be destroyed by water. The next time it would be destroyed by fire. I felt that it was possible that this war would consume the world with fire as the Bible had predicted."

In a short time, he wrote the song "Smoke on the Water," and it was recorded by Red Foley in 1944. It was a huge hit, not only at home but with the troops oversees as well. The title became a password among many units on the front lines, and the song's inspirational message kept many from despairing. For years after the war, veterans sent mail to Clements thanking him for the song that heartened them to keep going.

Music has been used for centuries to inspire soldiers in battle. Read in 2 Chronicles 20:21, 22 how God used music in Israel's battles.

And if you call out for insight and cry aloud for understanding . . .
—PROVERBS 2:3

Today is a sad day for American music, for on this date in 1937 George Gershwin died during surgery for a brain tumor. He was only thirty-eight. He was one the few musicians to successfully write popular songs and serious compositions. His compositions run the gamut from the famous *Rhapsody in Blue* and the *Concerto in F* for piano and orchestra to trendy songs like "Swanee" and "I Got Rhythm."

Gershwin's friends included Hollywood stars and Broadway producers. But he also mixed with a number of serious classical composers whose expertise and training intimidated Gershwin, who was largely self-taught. Painfully aware of his technical shortcomings, he was always trying to study with other composers, which led to several amusing incidents.

While he lived in Hollywood, Gershwin became a friend and tennis partner of the atonal composer Arnold Schoenberg. (He had fled the Nazis in Germany and found work in Los Angeles.) Gershwin begged the older man for composition lessons, but received the following answer, "I would only make you a bad Schoenberg, and you're such a good Gershwin already."

At another time, Gershwin asked the impressionistic composer Maurice Ravel for lessons. Ravel smiled and asked, "How much do you earn a year from your compositions?" Gershwin replied, "About $100,000." Ravel's eyes widened, "In that case, you give me lessons!" Similar conversations occurred with Stravinsky and several others. Gershwin never found his teacher, but he never stopped trying.

God wants us to be the individuals He created us to be, but He also wants us to learn and grow from those around us. Thank Him today for the teachers He has placed in your life.

Finding a great teacher—whether for music or any other subject—is a wonderful discovery. Take a moment today to write a short note of thanks to one of the best teachers you have ever had. It will be a tremendous encouragement to him or her.

Let your gentleness be evident to all. The Lord is near.

—PHILIPPIANS 4:5

On July 12, 1900, at the World Exposition in Paris, the beautiful Requiem by Gabriel Faure (1845–1924) was performed for the first time with full orchestra. Unlike the bombastic hellfire requiems by so many other composers, Faure's is quiet, calm, and comforting. "It is as gentle as I am myself," the composer admitted. "Someone has called it a lullaby of death."

Faure spent most of his life in Paris, in the midst of ongoing controversies between very opinionated composers. Yet his gentleness gave him the position of peacemaker. Another musician remembered that "his language, always moderate, is like well-bred discourse. He never raises his voice too high. He works in quiet colors. He is most discreet. He leaves much to be inferred. And his reserve is something quite as eloquent as louder outbursts."

One might wonder how such a quiet composer's music could have ever received the attention it did, and continues to do. Possibly because Faure chose to invest his life so much in the lives of others. After teaching for years at the Paris Conservatoire, he served as its director from 1905 to 1920. His guiding influence was felt by many of Europe's greatest young talents, including Boulanger, Ravel, Florent, and Enesco.

Paul commands us to "let our gentleness be evident to all"(Philippians 4:5), and our Lord says of Himself, "I am gentle and humble in heart" (Matthew 11:29). The life of Faure shows that the way to a successful life is not through competition and rivalry, but by quietly putting others first.

Think of someone you know who has a spirit of gentleness. Tell that person how much you appreciate this quality in him, and ask God to help you develop this virtue.

Sons are a heritage from the Lord, children a reward from him.

—PSALM 127:3

Singer/songwriter Cheri Keaggy has been given many gifts: a beautiful voice, songwriting abilities, a great CCM career complete with successful albums, 100 concerts each year, tours, and all the trimmings of celebrity. Yet the gifts she values far more are her husband and children. The issue of priorities is a critical factor in her busy life.

This concept struck her clearly after watching a news program that flashed photos of famous actors who were celebrating their birthdays. She recalls, "Most of them were fairly old and were best known in their younger years. I remember thinking about how fast time flies and how important it is for us to focus on the things that really, truly matter in life."

For Keaggy, that means focusing on her own family's needs. "Spending time with my family is going to be more important than mopping my kitchen floor, so my floor might go longer than it should without being mopped. But that's okay because I don't think God cares very much about linoleum. He cares about the pitter-patter of little feet that run across the linoleum."

This realization puts even the greatest career into perspective. Keaggy concludes, "What really matters in the end is, 'How did I love my family? How did I raise my children?' All the bigger things. That's the struggle for me, to learn how to prioritize and determine what matters most."

Remember: "The main thing is to keep the main thing the main thing!" Prayerfully write down your top five priorities for this year. Offer them to the Lord and ask Him to help you in keeping these "the main thing."

"What good will it be for a man if he gains the whole world, yet forfeits his soul? Or what can a man give in exchange for his soul?"

—MATTHEW 16:26

Steven Hendrickson is the principal trumpeter of the National Symphony in Washington, D.C. Furthermore, he is a devoted Christian and leads the brass quintet Gabriel's Brass, a chamber music group of the Christian Performing Artists' Fellowship. Yet his road to Christ was hindered by a detour into worldly philosophy.

While at college, he fell away from his faith and embraced the philosophy of Friedrich Nietzsche, a self-styled "anti-Christ" and Christian-hater. Hendrickson remembers, "My faith in God disappeared and reappeared in me. I could become great!" He got married and gained much career success. His philosophy seemed to have given him the whole world—or did it?

"I was still following the philosophy of 'self first,' but it gradually dawned on me that I was bored and unfulfilled. I had reached some of my goals, yet there was no enjoyment. I became bitter and hard to deal with. Then one night I began reading the Bible and decided to experiment. Immediately I noticed a change. I felt peace and joy.

"The experience showed the Bible to be right on every point. Nietzsche's philosophy may having sounded good before, but it didn't work. Jesus Christ came into my life, and He's never left me. For this I am deeply grateful, and I want to radiate His light, show His love, and be His advocate in our musical profession."

Do you know someone who is living a worldly "self-first" philosophy? Perhaps you should share Steven Hendrickson's testimony with that person, praying for God to open his eyes to the truth.

"Blessed are the peacemakers, for they will be called sons of God."
—MATTHEW 5:9

Composers are usually quite opinionated, especially about the music that they either love or hate. Perhaps this is understandable since they spend many hours editing and polishing their own works until they reach the highest standards for excellence. Whatever the reason, it is always a danger to sit between two composers at a dinner table. Unless, that is, you are a peacemaker.

The great Russian violinist Adolf Brodsky and his wife, Anna, once gave such a dinner, to which both Brahms and Tchaikovsky, among others, were invited. Unfortunately, these two masters had a profound dislike for each other's music. Their personalities were completely different—Brahms was rustic and uncultured while Tchaikovsky was elegant and courteous. They had never met until this dinner, and their first meeting was almost a disaster.

When Tchaikovsky arrived, he learned that Brahms was already there and playing his music with Adolf Brodsky. The two composers were introduced but the atmosphere remained cold and formal. Tchaikovsky was noticeably uncomfortable listening to Brahms' piece, and everyone nearby was dreading the comments that might follow it. But just at the work's conclusion, the door opened to admit two late arrivals, the composer Grieg (1843–1907) and his wife, "bringing, as they always did, a kind of sunshine with them," remembered Anna Brodsky.

Fortunately, Grieg's music was loved by both of the other composers, and his presence brought a cheerful ambience into the home. When dinner was served, Nina Grieg found herself seated between Brahms and Tchaikovsky and admitted, "I cannot sit between these two; it makes me feel so nervous." Her husband came to the rescue. "But I have the courage," he laughed, changing seats with her. Soon, all three composers were in high spirits. Anna Brodsky later claimed, "It was more of a children's party than a gathering of great composers." Today is Grieg's birthday.

God blesses those—like Grieg—who act as peacemakers in this troubled world. Strive today to bring even just a little bit of peace to your troubled world.

Do you have strong opinions as to what music you like and dislike? Be careful not to take yourself so seriously that you might hurt or offend others. Jesus' way is the way of the peacemaker.

"For I know the plans I have for you," declares the Lord, "plans to prosper you and not to harm you, plans to give you hope and a future."

—JEREMIAH 29:11

Is it possible that music could actually save your life? It may seem far-fetched, but that was exactly what happened to the great jazz pianist and composer Dave Brubeck. During his lifetime, this versatile musician became renowned in his field, as well as branching out to compose several effective works of "sacred jazz music." These include "The Voice of the Holy Spirit," "The Gates of Justice," "To Hope," "A Celebration," and his very popular "The Light in the Wilderness," which contains a wonderfully jazzy "Sermon on the Mount."

But it almost didn't happen, because during World War II Rifleman Brubeck was sent to Europe to fight. Like thousands of other soldiers, after D day he was assigned to General Patton's army as a replacement. At this time, the army was engaged in heavy fighting. The future looked grim for Brubeck.

As he arrived at the front, so did a Red Cross troupe sent to relieve the battle-weary soldiers. They had brought a piano, and someone shouted, "Can anyone here play the piano?" Brubeck volunteered, played awhile, and was heard by nearby Colonel Pearlman. This officer was concerned for the morale of his regiment and had decided to put together a band for the soldiers' entertainment. He had the clout to pull Brubeck from the front line, and he assigned him to be the band's pianist.

Brubeck's musical abilities probably saved his life. Immediately after this, his old outfit was sent into the hottest part of the fighting. He remembers, "Some guys I never heard from again were in on that, where I would have been that day." Instead, he served by bringing the troops music and laughter. Dave Brubeck still had many adventures, including an outdoor show during which German planes strafed the stage—but it was God's plan that he make it back home.

Did you know that Dave Brubeck composed "sacred jazz" music? Try to find one of the pieces mentioned above in your library or CD store. Praise God for placing His servants in all different types of music!

They read from the Book of the Law of God, making it clear and giving the meaning so that the people could understand what was being read. —NEHEMIAH 8:8

Issac Watts, the "Father of English Hymnody," was born this day in 1674. His family belonged to the devout Christians known as Dissenters (this included all Baptists, Presbyterians, and Congregationalists). The state-affiliated Church of England did not accept their beliefs, and they were severely harassed. His father was twice imprisoned for his faith. Isaac was fifteen when the Toleration Act was finally passed, granting Dissenters legal freedom to worship.

Isaac Watts became a great scholar and preacher, and yet he was never removed from the common man in his church. In writing his many hymns, he always tried to make the Bible clearly understandable to his flock. One set of hymns he called the "Psalms of David Imitated in the Language of the New Testament." Watts said he wanted "to make David speak like a Christian of the eighteenth century"—that is, like a man of his day.

Watts became a pastor at the Mark Lane Independent Chapel and developed into one of the finest preachers of his day. His greatest gift, however, was undeniably hymnwriting. During his life he created more than six hundred hymns, creating such masterpieces as "When I Survey the Wondrous Cross," "Alas and Did My Savior Bleed," "Joy to the World," "Jesus Shall Reign," "Am I a Soldier of the Cross," and "There Is a Land of Pure Delight."

Watts also composed an entire book of hymns especially for youth, entitled *Divine Songs Attempted in Easy Language for the Use of Children.* In it were charming lessons of the "little busy bee," "the perfume of the rose," and "the industry of the ant." Concerning his songs for children, he wrote, "I have endeavored to sink the language to the level of a child's understanding." This genius scholar spent countless hours working to simplify his language so that even the youngest child could appreciate the lessons from the Word of God.

We need to be sure that we fully understand what we read in the Bible. Compare three different Bible translations of a favorite passage of Scripture, and write down what you learn.

"You did not choose me, but I chose you and appointed you to go and bear fruit—fruit that will last." —JOHN 15:16

When studying the life of Johann Sebastian Bach (1685–1750), it is difficult to keep straight all the churches in which he worked. In 1723, he had been living in the city of Cothen, but wanted to get a position in Leipzig. He sent his prospective employer an example of his compositional powers: his Cantata no. 22, "Jesus nahm zu sich die Zwolfe" ("Jesus Called to Him the Twelve"). As you may expect, Bach got the job. On this date of that year, he composed his beautiful motet, "Jesu Meine Freunde" ("Jesus, My Friend").

As a young man Bach knew God's call on his life. He explained it this way: "To create well-regulated church music to the glory of God." Most of his adult life was spent in this service. Bach has now become a kind of "patron saint" for church musicians to emulate. His incredible talent could have made him a world-renowned performer or composer. Instead, he chose to spend his days in relative obscurity, in the confidence that he was God's man doing God's work.

Not every Christian is called to full-time ministry work, but we each have an important call on our life. Being redeemed by Christ is more than just salvation from damnation in the next life. God's plan is also to use us right now for His great glory. For us to maximize the time He has given us here, we need to know the nature of God's call on our life. There is nothing so fulfilling as knowing that you are performing the very mission for which God has chosen you.

What is it that God has appointed you to do? If you already know, do it with all your might. If you do not yet know, make this a significant area of prayer, that the Lord may prepare, direct, and enlighten you on this essential subject.

"And if anyone gives even a cup of cold water to one of these little ones because he is my disciple, I tell you the truth, he will certainly not lose his reward." —MATTHEW 10:42

Musicians are constantly striving toward excellence, and the result of such hard work usually means moving higher and higher in musical circles. But not always. Young musicians should remind themselves to focus on excellence and not the pursuit of greater celebrity or fame.

Greg Luscombe, principal trombonist of the Memphis Symphony Orchestra, learned this lesson from one of his high school instructors. This man had won many competitions and honors, and had offers from several colleges, yet he continued to work in a high school. Luscombe, along with many others, wondered about this—until he one day read an interview of the man in a local paper.

The interviewer asked the question that many had pondered: "With all the success that you have had, have you ever considered working for a college or a major university?" The result was profound. "For a while I considered this and even applied for a few positions, but then I realized that I was already in the big time."

Luscombe concludes: "That comment has helped me to realize the importance of what we do as teachers at all levels. Being planted in the big time for God's kingdom may not be what the world thinks is the big time. I believe that God will plant us in places where we can be of the best service to Him. In other words, where we can be in the BIG TIME for His people."

How do you feel about the place you are currently planted? Remember that even sharing a cup of cold water is noticed by God. Praise Him that being in His plan is always being in the BIG TIME.

He appointed the priests to their duties and encouraged them in the service of the Lord's temple. —2 CHRONICLES 35:2

The "he" referred to in the above Scripture was the good king Josiah. When he appointed the priests (and temple musicians) for their work, he began by encouraging them. Perhaps he knew that such a life is not easy, and that all musicians need encouragement.

This date in 1924 saw the premiere of Serenade, Op. 24, by Arnold Schoenberg (1874–1951), a composer who had long since learned the importance of being encouraged. His atonal music was so ahead of its time that for decades it found little appreciation. One musician concluded, "A Schoenberg concert can empty a concert hall faster than a bomb scare."

Nevertheless, there were always a few courageous enthusiasts, and their encouragement was like water in the desert to Schoenberg. At the premiere of his Chamber Symphony in 1907, most in the audience were loudly booing. But the composer/conductor Gustav Mahler thought he heard genius in the innovative music. He reproached a young man near him who continued to boo. "Young man, aren't you ashamed?" He was answered with scorn, "No, not at all, and I assure you for your next symphony I will do just the same."

Mahler would not be silenced. When the performance was over, he publically championed Schoenberg, predicting that "from the direction he had taken, extraordinary things could be expected." History proved Mahler right and the critics wrong. Schoenberg founded the Second Viennese School of composition and his "twelve-tone rows" were soon found in the works of hundreds of young composers.

Though the world may boo at us, if we are doing what God has designed and called us to do, we will receive applause from the Lord.

Have you ever heard any of Schoenberg's music? To many, it still sounds very strange. Get a recording from the CD store or library and decide for yourself.

"Go, stand in the temple courts," he said, "and tell the people the full message of this new life." —ACTS 5:20

Three young musicians attending Kentucky Christian College in the 1980s were approached by a fourth who had written a song. Together, they recorded the song, "My God," and decided to form a new band. When the already popular band dcTalk performed at their college, a tape recording of "My God" was given to one of the members of dcTalk, who passed it to his recording label. The executives were duly impressed, and the new band, Audio Adrenaline, was soon in heavy demand.

Explaining the group's mission to *CCM Magazine*, guitarist Bob Herdman is very clear. "When we first started the band, the goal was ministry first, music second. We put on a killer show, so when I say that music is second, it's not that we don't take it seriously. But we take ministry much more seriously. Our number-one goal is to spread the Gospel."

Bassist Will McGinniss continues the explanation. "Our heart's passion is for people to know that we're Christian guys, and that our message is sincerely about God." Their albums have such names as *Some Kind of Zombie, Don't Censor Me,* and *Bloom,* and their music is heard frequently on both Christian and secular radio stations.

These musicians realize that for many kids in their audiences, this may be their only exposure to the Gospel. "We're really feeling that responsibility," says singer Mark Stuart. "I really want people to be moved by the music. Second, we feel powerfully motivated to give them something eternal to take home with them."

You may or may not be a fan of Christian rock bands, but we can all pray that many young people are reached for Christ by their ministry. Pray today for your favorite Christian musician.

Elisha said, "Go around and ask all your neighbors for empty jars. Don't ask for just a few. Then go inside and shut the door behind you and your sons. Pour oil into all the jars, and as each is filled, put it to one side."

—2 KINGS 4:3, 4

A great blessing is usually preceeded by a great preparation. In the story above, the poor widow is told to prepare for her blessing by getting as many jars as she can find. The more she prepares, that is, the more jars she can find, the greater the blessing will be.

For a young musician, most of the preparation comes in the hours of practice, not on the spotlighted stage. One young man who experienced this principle was the great jazz pianist Al Haig, born this date in 1924. Like thousands of other young players, Haig longed for a chance to perform in the big time. But he did more than just long—he practiced hour after hour, readying himself if the chance ever came.

One of his first professional jobs was with the Tiny Grimes Quartet in a small club in New York. Imagine Haig's astonishment when two of jazz's most renowned figures—Dizzy Gillespie and Charlie Parker—entered the club! He later remembered, "They both sprang up on the bandstand and were auditioning me. Nobody said anything. I was only about twenty-two. They just said, 'I Got Rhythm' and started to play."

As confused as Haig must have been, he began playing, and the years of preparation were soon apparent. "When they stopped, Dizzy asked me if I would be interested in joining a group with him and Charlie. I said, 'Yes, oh yes, absolutely!' " The long hours of diligent practicing had paid off.

Are you putting in long hours right now? If so, take heart. God sees your diligence, and it will be rewarded.

Read the entire story of Elijah and the poor widow: 2 Kings 4:1-7. Find a way this week to be more prepared with your talents.

When the time drew near for David to die, he gave a charge to Solomon his son. "I am about to go the way of all the earth," he said. "So be strong, show yourself a man." —1 KINGS 2:1, 2

Fathers throughout history have given such charges to their sons and daughters, hoping to inspire them to take up their mantle. It is interesting to see how many great composers had parents who were also musicians. For instance, today is the birthday of Domenico Scarlatti (1685–1757), the great harpsichord composer. His father was a renowned composer of Italian opera.

Beethoven's father was a singer in the Electoral Chapel in Bonn. His grandfather also was a singer. Bizet's dad was a vocal teacher, and Offenbach's was the cantor at the Cologne Synagogue. Stravinsky's father was a leading bass singer at the Saint Petersburg opera.

The list of composers with piano-playing mothers includes such masters as Grieg, Britten, de Falla, Honneger, Mussorgski, Scriabin, and Rachmoninoff. Two notables whose fathers played piano are Rimsky-Korsakov and Liszt, the latter becoming the greatest pianist in his century! Those with a violinist for a father include Mozart, Smetana, von Weber, and Vivaldi. Composers who grew up listening to their dads playing the cello include Schubert, Dohnanyi, and Villa-Lobos. Brahms' father played the double bass in the municipal theater in Hamburg, and Richard Strauss' father played horn in the Munich Orchestra.

Some composers had a mom and a dad who played music. Both Chopin and Rossini had mothers who were excellent singers, but Chopin's father played the flute and Rossini's father the horn. Both of Bartok's and Shostakovich's parents were pianists, and Walton's parents were both singing teachers. Puccini came from three generations of musicians—and how about Bach?! Practically his entire family tree was musical. Over fifty musicians bearing that name are remembered by musicologists today.

Do you have musical parents? If you do, thank them for their musical influence on your life. If you don't, think of another area in which they have encouraged or inspired you, and tell them thanks for that.

"See I am doing a new thing! Now it springs up; do you not perceive it?" —ISAIAH 43:19a

Yesterday we learned that many of the greatest composers through-out history have had very musical parents. But that doesn't mean that God can't start a new thing: great musicians from very nonmusical parents. For instance, today is the birthday of the renowned Jewish composer Ernest Bloch (1880–1959), the son of a clockmaker. Many of the masters—including Mendelssohn, Verdi, Paganini, Franck, and dozens of others—were the first in their families to enter the field of music.

Whether you know nothing about music or become a professional musician, you can someday give the gift of great music to your children. And they to their children, and on and on. Who knows? Perhaps musicologists someday will be studying the many renowned musicians who bear your last name. Or perhaps you will simply encourage your children to love music and use it to praise the name of the Lord. Either way, it's wonderful!

The composer/pianist Felix Mendelssohn had an interesting experience that shows that great musicians have children who do not follow in their footsteps. Visiting Italy in 1831, he was invited to the home of the military commandant at Milan. This commander's wife was Dorothea von Ertmann, a close friend of Beethoven, to whom he dedicated his Piano Sonata, Op. 101.

The couple asked Mendelssohn to play the piano for their many guests, and he happily obliged. A minor official from the Austrian army was quietly sitting in the corner, and during a break in the music he quietly approached the piano. "Won't you play something of my dear father?" he asked timidly. Confused, Mendelssohn asked, "Who was your father?" "Ach! Mozart!" answered the offi-cial, Carl Thomas Mozart. Mendelssohn later recalled, "I did play Mozart for him, for the rest of the evening!"

Whatever our family background, we know that music is a gift created by God. What musical legacy do you wish to someday pass to your children?

Therefore, judge nothing before the appointed time.

—1 CORINTHIANS 4:5a

The music world can be a very competitive place, with many hopefuls each trying to achieve one of the very few top openings. For a Christian in the music world, keeping one's heart free from a competitive spirit can be very difficult. It helps to remember that the Lord is the only true Judge, and that the judgments of men are of little worth. Although the two composers in the following stories are not named, their experiences dramatically demonstrate the folly of being overly concerned about human judging.

A contemporary composer was present when the Cleveland Symphony Orchestra performed one of his pieces. The orchestra did not do very well on the difficult work, but the audience still cheered with approval. A week later, the orchestra played the same piece in a different city and played it flawlessly. The crowd booed the performance. What was the composer to conclude?

Another young composer sent in a new piece to an annual competition. To keep the judges from seeing the composers' names, the compositions were numbered rather than signed. Unfortunately, the young composer's work did not even make it through the first round and was rejected. This was a large national contest, which attracted hundreds of composers, so he was not too discouraged by the rejection. But he resolved to try another piece next year.

The following year was a very busy one for that young man. When the deadline for the new competition came, he found that his new piece was not ready. Having nothing better to send, he decided to simply send the same composition as last year. This time the judges gave the work first prize in the entire country! As excited as he was to receive the award, he always remembered the absurdity of the competitive world.

Though we consistently hear the judgments of the world, we need to remember that God is the only Judge whose opinion counts.

Have you ever been in a competition? When you are, remember to simply do your best and leave the results in the Lord's hands.

A simple man believes anything, but a prudent man gives thought to his steps. —PROVERBS 14:15

Like any other portion of society, the music business has its share of swindlers. Experienced players have learned to be wary, but many young musicians have been naïvely taken in. An example of this occurred to country fiddler Ernie Rouse during the Great Depression.

The Rouse Brothers was a hillbilly band from Florida, pounding out an existence playing county fairs. In nearly every performance, Ernie Rouse played a fast fiddle piece he had written but never named. The crowds loved it, but Rouse just called it "a little bit crazy."

The group's manager, Lloyd Smith, had an idea about the tune. He persuaded the director of the Seaboard Railroad Company that he had the perfect piece of music for the dedication of the new Miami-to-New York rail service. Smith even claimed that the song had been named after the new train, "The Orange Blossom Special." His fast talking arranged for the band to perform it at the train's opening ceremony in 1936.

Ernie Rouse couldn't wait to play his composition for all the festivities—but he later discovered that Smith had copyrighted the song in his own name! It took many months of legal battles for Rouse to get the credit and royalties he deserved. He learned his lesson in prudence, and "The Orange Blossom Special" became a classic for every bluegrass group in the country.

God doesn't want us to be "of this world," but He doesn't want us to be taken by it either! He gave us our brains and intellect, and He wants us to use them.

Before we make major decisions, we need to seek for His guidance. Read these two passages from King David's life—when he forgot and when he remembered to seek the Lord: 1 Chronicles 13:5-14; and 15:11-15.

"Honor your father and your mother, as the Lord your God has commanded you, so that you may live long and that it may go well with you in the land the Lord your God is giving you." —DEUTERONOMY 5:16

There aren't many popular singers who are offered a recording contract at the age of fourteen. But this is exactly what happened to Jaci Velasquez, who had been singing in her father's church for many years. "I was doing what I loved doing, singing in churches with my mom and dad," she told *CCM Magazine.* I loved singing for the Lord, and I loved singing in church about the one I loved the most: Jesus."

Soon she was touring and recording, living a life much busier than most high school students. In 1997, Velasquez won the Dove Award for New Artist of the Year, and already had several number-one hits to her credit. How did one so young handle the new pressures? The answer for this young girl was her family.

She is very close to her father, as well as to her big brothers, whom she adores. But it is her mother, who homeschools and travels with her on tour, who keeps Velasquez together. "My mom's my best friend. She's about the only person who really knows everything about me. I mean, when I got my first kiss, I told her about it."

Jaci Velasquez has learned the joy of honoring her mother. "If I'm trying to get to my dressing room so I can get ready, and I notice someone who wants an autograph, I may be tempted to duck. My mom calls me on it. 'Jaci,' she says, 'do you remember when you used to sit there at an autograph table when you were opening for 4HIM, and you just had five people in your line? You were so embarrassed. Now you have these people who want to be a part of your life, and you're trying to duck.' I can't do that because it's those people who make up my ministry."

Look up the word honor *in a dictionary. Then make a list of the ways you can honor your parents today, and thank them for all they've done for you.*

If you look for it as for silver and search for it as for hidden treasure . . . —PROVERBS 2:4

Two sad things happened on this date in 1741. The first was that the great Italian composer Antonio Vivaldi (1678–1741) died in Vienna, Austria. The son of a prominent violinist, he entered the priesthood in his twenties but spent most of his life in music. His flaming red hair gave him the nickname "il prete rosso" ("the red priest"), which he retained even after he became famous throughout Europe for his talents.

Vivaldi worked as the director of music at Venice's Conservatory of the Pieta for thirty-five years. This organization was a large, well-endowed orphanage for girls, and one of its principle programs was music education. The result was that these talented teenagers kept their music director quite busy. Vivaldi composed with lightning speed, and once said that he was able to write a new piece faster than the copyist could reproduce the individual parts!

He is best remembered for his instrumental concertos (over four hundred!), which were usually performed by his best students at the frequent church festival services. The most famous of these compositions are the four violin concertos, collectively known as *The Four Seasons.* Each "season" is a complete three-movement work, the whole being written around a four-section poem: "Spring has returned again . . . the satisfaction of a fruitful harvest . . ." Vivaldi also wrote a great deal of choral music, including his beautiful *Gloria.*

The second tragedy of July 28, 1741, is that Vivaldi's great compositions died with him, and were virtually forgotten for almost two centuries! Count Giacomo Durazzo took all the hundreds of scores from the Venice Conservatory and locked them away. His will even stipulated that none should be published or performed, and his heirs obeyed these strange demands. It was not until the 1920s that these masterpieces were released to the world.

Can you imagine all the wonderful Vivaldi scores sitting unused for decades? The Bible tells us to search for wisdom "as for hidden treasure" (Proverbs 2:4). Read a chapter from the Book of Proverbs today, and ask God to give you a heart of wisdom.

Lazy hands make a man poor, but diligent hands bring wealth.

—PROVERBS 10:4

The Bible is filled with dozens of commands concerning the importance of hard work. One of the most frustrating times in a composer's life is when he desires to work on a piece but finds himself in a state similar to "writer's block." Nothing seems to work, and he can't break out of it. At such times, only the most determined musicians persevere to achieve the ultimate result.

Such was the position of Justin Hayward, the singer, guitarist, and songwriter for the Moody Blues. Except that he had the added pressure of needing to finish quickly. That very next day the studio was rented and waiting to record his new song. He had been working with two different songs with very different tempos, but neither had come to the final solution.

Finally, after hours of struggle, the answer presented itself. Hayward later explained, "I just put the two songs together and strung the lyrics together to make it work—and it worked! The two had always been in the same key and the same tuning, but because of the different tempos I never thought of putting them together." The new composition, "Question," became a key feature on the groups best-selling album, *Question of Balance*.

Hayward could have given up, and no one would have ever heard the song. Instead, a hit was created. Its very uniqueness left it as a special memory for the hard-working songwriter: "This would have to be the number-one favorite, because it is so very different."

One wonders how many songs, even great songs, are never heard because they are never finished. Is it difficult to keep going when "writer's block" sets in? Of course it is! Many people quit at this point. But God wants us to keep at it, and it will always be worth it to break through for the final creation.

What is an area in which you have difficulty following through to the end? Chores around the house? Homework? Ask God to help you be a "finisher," and not a "quitter."

Jesus said, "My kingdom is not of this world." —JOHN 18:36A

The Metropolitan Opera Company is one of the pinnacles of the opera world and, of course, uses only the greatest singers. When the Met was preparing for its centennial celebration to be televised internationally, it wanted to showcase the very finest singers in the world. Therefore, when soprano Myra Merritt was asked to sing in a duet from Mozart's *Don Giovanni,* she was both thrilled and terrified.

Merritt had performed many times at the Met, but a televised special before millions seemed unnerving. She remembers, "I prayed about it and decided that 'I can do all things through him who strengthens me'—though I agreed to do so in fear and trembling."

After many rehearsals, the performance day arrived. "During the day, I girded myself with the Word and prayer, and I began to feel less anxious. However, as the day progressed, I was besieged with battles of fear." Arriving backstage at the Met, Merritt soon found that the other singers were at least as nervous as she.

Standing in the wings, she prayed a final prayer, then heard the Lord say to her, "My Kingdom is not of this world." "Suddenly, I had a very different perspective. As I shifted my focus from the celebration to God and His Kingdom, I began to rest in His peace." Merritt sang with joy and confidence and was afterward deluged with compliments. "The comment that I heard so often was, 'You seemed so calm.' I really was."

The next time you are nervous about something you must do, remember the words of the Lord, "My Kingdom is not of this world." Strive to find God's perspective—and sing a song of praise to Him!

Each of you must bring a gift in proportion to the way the Lord your God has blessed you. —DEUTERONOMY 16:17

The greatest pianist of the nineteenth century, Franz Liszt (1811–1886), died on this date. He was a very complex man, full of both virtues and faults. Certainly one of his greatest virtues, for which he was universally known during his lifetime, was his legendary generosity.

As a young man, Liszt's earnings helped to pay his father's debts and to support his mother. At the height of his career, with potential millions right at his fingertips, he renounced giving concerts for money. For example, he once raised huge sums in Russia, and then gave every cent to charity. Hearing that a Beethoven memorial was being planned, he immediately volunteered to help and paid for most of it himself. Another time, his concerts raised a small fortune for a "pension for destitute musicians."

Throughout his life Liszt supported the music and careers of many other composers, often at his own expense. As the private teacher of a generation of pianists, Liszt refused to be paid for his invaluable lessons. An immense amount of time was freely invested into his pupils, which included Von Bulow, Weingartner, Albenez, Bizet, Moszkowski, Joachim, Rosenthal, Smetana, and Saint-Saens, among others. Without his encouragement to countless musicians, perhaps many of the great romantic compositions would not be in the repertoire today.

Finally, in order to give all of his life to the Lord's service, Liszt entered the Order of St. Francis in 1865. By that time he had sacrificed so many of his worldly goods that when he entered the order, he possessed nothing but "his cassock, a little linen, and seven handkerchiefs."

Liszt acknowledged that all talents were a gift from God, and he used them (and the proceeds they amassed) for the benefit of others. Very few of us have the talents or resources of Franz Liszt, but each of us has something we can give. It may be that today God will bring someone's need before you or prompt you to give in a certain way to God's work. What will be your response?

Count today the number of people who help you in some way—teachers, parents, friends, etc. Next, count the people you help. Are the numbers matching up? God wants us to give according to what we've been given. Ask Him to show you someone you can help today.

"Rise in the presence of the aged, show respect for the elderly and revere your God. I am the Lord." —LEVITICUS 19:32

Steve Green's recordings have sold more than three million to date, and every year he performs for many thousands of fans. Furthermore, he has won numerous honors, including six Dove Awards. Obviously, Green is no unknown; he is one of the world's best-known Christian artists.

Yet of the many people who enjoy his music as he sings of His Father in heaven, perhaps few know of the special bond he has with his earthly father. Steve Green's parents were missionaries with a call to Argentina. During his teen years in that country, the son grew rebellious, and the relationship with his parents became strained. His father continued to minister love to his son—even when it may have seemed a useless gesture—and over time they were finally reconciled.

Today Steve Green is in full-time ministry and his parents have retired from their missionary work. Was all that love and ministry to his rebellious son worth the effort? The result is seen in every song Steve Green sings. Furthermore, his gratitude toward his parents has found a devoted and practical expression. After his father was diagnosed with Parkinson's disease, Steve and his wife, Marijean, arranged to move his parents from Arizona to a house next door to them in Tennessee. In this way they are able to minister back to his parents in a time of their need.

When people get older, it is all too common for our busy society to "put them out to pasture." But the Scriptures call us to respect the elderly, as well as to honor their wisdom. For most of their lives, they gave of themselves. Should we not give back to them?

What is your attitude toward the elderly? Can you make time for them in your busy schedule? Think of a way that you can be a blessing to one of the Lord's "senior citizens" and make arrangements to do so.

"I know your deeds, your hard work and your perseverance."

—REVELATION 2:2a

In 1961, Hank Cochran (whose birthday is today) was known as one of the best songwriters in Nashville. He had a part in the discovery of both Willie Nelson and Patsy Cline, yet he knew that a songwriter is only as good as his next hit. He freely admitted, "When you start to think about where the inspiration comes from for writing a song, the only real answer is the 'Man Upstairs.'

"One minute you don't have an idea in the world, and then the next, bam, it just hits you. Suddenly you are writing lyrics that just seem to fall out of the air. This is the way it had always been for me, and I knew it was the same for most of the other writers I worked with. Something would happen, it would trigger an idea, and then what had been so hard for so many weeks would be so easy."

At one point he needed inspiration quickly. Patsy Cline was about to record and she wanted another hit from Cochran. Working many hours at the studio found absolutely no success. After one long day with other songwriters, "Around five or six o'clock, everyone started to drift toward home. I decided to stay, hoping that the solitude would help me come up with some new ideas."

Again, hours without a breakthrough. Finally, "I pulled open the desk drawer that was right in front of me. The first thing I saw was a picture. Just like that, the idea came to me. I picked up a pad and wrote, 'I've got your picture, the one you gave to me,' and from that point it all fell together." Hank Cochran quickly wrote the song called, "She's Got You," and it soon became Patsy Cline's biggest hit. Enough "hard work and perseverance," and the inspiration was finally supplied.

Open a desk drawer and pull out an object. Can you now think of an idea for a song? Use your God-given creativity and persevere until you do.

You may say to yourself, "My power and the strength of my hands have produced this wealth for me." But remember the Lord your God, for it is he who gives you the ability to produce wealth, and so confirms his covenant, which he swore to your forefathers, as it is today.

—DEUTERONOMY 8:17, 18

Everything we have is a gift from God. Yet it is all too easy for young musicians to forget this, especially after spending years working, practicing, and honing their skills to the highest degree. Violinist Lisa-Beth Lambert was reminded of this valuable lesson in a time of transition between college and career.

She had graduated with honors from the Curtis Institute of Music, performed with the Philadelphia Orchestra, and played violin concertos with other orchestras. Life was going well for Lambert, and it seemed as if a wonderful career were right at her fingertips. But more importantly, she was a dedicated Christian who had long since entrusted her life and talents to God.

Then one day she stumbled on some stairs, badly straining a ligament in the first finger of her left hand. Suddenly she could not play at all and spent two full months with a cast on her hand. Would her big chances now disappear? Instead of worrying, Lambert used the time she would have been practicing to seek the Lord and to have fellowship with her friends.

The finger healed perfectly, and the following year was one of tremendous blessing. Among other things, Lambert was accepted into the Marlboro Music Festival and given a position with the National Symphony Orchestra. Looking back, Lisa-Beth Lambert sees this critical time as a reminder from Lord: "It all comes from God. He can take our talents away in an instant and we should never take them for granted. Instead, we can use our lives for His great glory!"

Have you ever had a bad physical accident? What would be the most difficult type of injury for you? Spend some time today with an "imaginary handicap," such as not using your right arm. Praise God for the abilities He has given you.

A generous man will himself be blessed, for he shares his food with the poor. —PROVERBS 22:9

Today is an important day in jazz history, because on August 4, 1901, the great trumpeter Louis Armstrong was born. He rose from poverty and obscurity to revolutionize the role of the jazz trumpet. He played with such power that the best of his fellow trumpeters were in awe.

Armstrong was also a master of the one-liner. His simple humor was evident in every interview. One newspaper man asked him to define jazz. Armstrong pondered a moment and answered, "Jazz is what I play for a living." He had an even better answer when asked about folk music. "Man, all music is folk music. You ain't never heard no horse sing a song, have you?"

The musical wonder was never ashamed of his humble roots. One Christmas season his wife, Lucille, went on tour with him, and she decided to put up a small Christmas tree with lights in their hotel room. Her husband was so touched by it that he couldn't sleep that night; he kept gazing at the tree like a little boy. Armstrong confessed, "You know, that's the first tree I ever had." He was about forty years old.

If any one particular virtue was associated with Armstrong, it was generosity. A friend remembers, "He was a saint. He was the softest touch in the world. When I went into his dressing room at Basin Street, or someplace like that, it would be full of broken down musicians or show-biz types looking for a buck. It finally got so that Joe Glaser, who managed 'Pops' most of his life, put a twenty-dollar lid on each handout. Even so, I think he helped support hundreds of people. It was one of his greatest pleasures."

God has blessed us with much. He blesses us even more when we share those blessings with others. May generosity be (or become) one of your greatest pleasures.

"One of his greatest pleasures." What a marvelous attitude toward giving! What can you give to bless someone else today?

In everything set them an example by doing what is good.

—TITUS 2:7

Most of us know the Russian composer Sergei Rachmaninoff (1873–1943) through his beautiful piano music. Much of it is very difficult to play, partly because the composer who wrote it and first played it had huge hands. He could stretch for chords that most pianists cannot reach (Rachmaninoff is listed in the *Guinness Book of World Records* as the musician with the largest hands).

Of course, his success as a musician was not founded on large hands, but on working hard with his God-given talent. As a youth studying at the Saint Petersburg Conservatory, he was known for setting the example for the other students. If three problems were assigned, he would complete five. If he had to learn a composition within one week, he would learn it in a day so that he could polish it all week.

In one of the many competitions in the Conservatory, Rachmaninoff and the other students performed for Russia's finest musicians, including the great composer Tchaikovsky. The highest mark ever given was a five, which could, in extraordinary circumstances, be augmented with a "plus" sign. Rachmaninoff had worked extremely hard for this and was delighted to receive the top score of five.

That was not to be all. The judges asked him to play again, and he performed one of his "Songs Without Words." As he finished, the young pianist noticed Tchaikovsky writing in the examination journal. The old composer was so moved by the performance that he wrote four "plus" signs to the score of five, making Rachmaninoff's achievement the highest in the Conservatory's history!

God wants us to continually do our best and—like Rachmaninoff—to go the extra mile. He set a perfect example for us in Christ and wants us to learn from that example to do what is good.

Sergei Rachmaninoff was not just an example to his fellow students, but serves as an example to us as well. Choose one task you must do today, and give it an extra effort.

I remembered my songs in the night. —PSALM 77:6a

For many old-time jazz lovers, the words "cornet" and "Beiderbecke" were synonymous. Bix Beiderbecke played with a sweetness that was greatly admired, even when the country was in love with the trumpet of Louis Armstrong. He had taught himself the cornet by simply playing along with records, but he created a personal style that has never been duplicated.

Many amusing stories are told about Beiderbecke's "trick tooth." It seems that when he was a boy, he had knocked out one of his front teeth. A dentist had made him a removable false tooth, slotted on the sides. This tooth often fell out, even in the middle of a performance. Sometimes announcements were made for the musicians and audience alike to get down on the floor to search for the fake tooth. But no one seemed to mind, because, as Beiderbecke admitted with a hole in his smile, "No tooth, no music!"

Beiderbecke was known for his generosity, especially toward friends who needed a break. When he hired musicians for his band, he always took more than he needed, disregarding his budget. Once he needed a clarinetist for a job and asked Pee Wee Russell, who later recalled, "He had hired me for the date but rather than hurt anyone's feelings he also hired Jimmy Dorsey and Benny Goodman and Tommy Dorsey and everybody."

His cornet and his personality were both loved by thousands. In his last year he stayed in an apartment in Queens with a bass player named George Kraslow. Beiderbecke had an odd habit of practicing his instrument in the middle of the night. The neighbors were often awakened at three or four in the morning, but never complained. They even told his roommate, "Please don't mention we said anything as we don't want him reprimanded and would hate for him to stop." Bix Beiderbecke died on this date in 1931.

To experience "songs in the night," take a CD/tape player outside, and—softly—play some of your favorite music as you watch the moon and stars. Thank God for the music He has given us.

Boldly and without hindrance he preached the kingdom of God and taught about the Lord Jesus Christ. —ACTS 28:31

Many of us may have a secret desire to "be a Billy Graham," preaching to millions. But are we ready to be a credible witness right where we live? Are we praying for opportunities to share God's love, and are we prepared when they come?

Mezzo-soprano Linn Maxwell Keller has sung in opera houses all over the world. As an outspoken Christian, she spends her summers as the opera director in the Christian Performing Artists' Fellowship's MasterWorks Festival. But her greatest vocal love is not opera, but oratorio. She points out that many of the great oratorios—such as Handel's *Messiah*—give her the opportunity to sing about the Lord from the concert stage.

Being a witness for Christ in the performing arts world is a challenge for any believer. Keller prays before each concert that God would open the door for some type of ministry. When she was on tour singing Bach's St. John Passion with conductor Helmut Rilling, the Lord gave a her a wonderful opportunity.

In one of the cities the tour was visiting, National Public Radio called and asked to interview one of the soloists. Keller was chosen for this national interview, and the host asked her what she loved about singing Bach. What an opening! She started by telling about her favorite aria in the St. John Passion, entitled "Es Ist Vollbracht" ("It is Enough"). Keller stated, "This aria expresses Christ's finished work on the cross," and then continued to give her testimony of the love of Jesus Christ.

Read 2 Timothy 4:2. Pray for—and then expect—an opportunity today to share your faith.

All your commands are trustworthy; help me, for men persecute me without cause. —PSALM 119:86

The emergence of CCM (contemporary Christian music) occurred in the 1960s, a very turbulent decade in American history. At the same time that antiwar protests took place and mindbending drugs became widely used, God sent a revival among thousands of young people. What were these ex-druggies and flower children to sing within their newfound Christianity?

Developments in secular rock music had progressed so quickly that the distance between it and most church hymns was almost as wide as what missionaries encounter in foreign cultures. So a new genre of Christian music arose, and its first champion was Larry Norman, often called the "Father of Contemporary Christian Music."

He understands the music of his generation, since Norman says he himself "walked out of church when I was nine years old. I didn't like the hymns and couldn't stand singing the hymns anymore." Norman began writing his own songs and formed a rock band, People. His first album, *Upon This Rock,* is considered by many to be the first complete album of Christian rock music. *Time* magazine once called Norman the "Poet Laureate of the Jesus Movement."

Norman sincerely loves God and desires to serve Him through his music. Yet his Christian rock has often been misunderstood, censured, and denounced by many church leaders. He still has many critics within the body of Christ, yet he continues to have a profound influence on CCM artists. Some of Larry Norman's many songs are "UFO," "One Way," "I Love You," "Moses," "I Wish We'd All Been Ready," "666," and "I Am a Servant."

Find the words to a hymn and compare these to the lyrics of a Christian rock song. Whichever you prefer, always use music to glorify God, and be careful not to criticize what you don't like.

All kinds of animals, birds, reptiles and creatures of the sea are being tamed and have been tamed by man. —JAMES 3:7

Today's musical tale might come under the category "Believe It or Not." In 1829, a man named Curtis from Cincinnati, Ohio, had the peculiar idea to make a grand organ whose sounds all came from cats. That's right—cats. He built an "instrument" that housed forty-eight cats with a wide vocal range, from tiny kittens to old toms. They were each placed in separate compartments and screeched their appropriate pitches when a lever pressed down on their tails!

The enterprising Curtis rehearsed his felines for days until he was satisfied, then he plastered the town with the following poster:

CURTIS CAT HARMONICON
GRAND VOCAL AND INSTRUMENTAL CONCERT
FORTY-EIGHT CATS!

The hall was packed with people (as curious as you) to find out about this strange new instrument. Unfortunately, the audience seemed to have little appreciation for great music, for as soon as the first piece began—"Auld Lang Syne"— they howled with laughter. The newspaper account continues the story:

"The cats were excited to fury at the uproarious audience and the severe pounding to their tails. They forgot all lessons, paid no attention to time, tune, rhythm, or reason, but squealed, mewed, yelled, spat, and phizzed in the madness of pain and terror, drowning the sound of the organ in the unearthly tornado of caterwauling.

Frustrated by the fiasco of his new production, Curtis freed his cats into the auditorium. They darted in every direction, adding to the confusion. There was a cry of 'Fire!' A fire engine raced to the theater and shot water through the upper window, drenching the berserk feline musicians as well as the audience. It was a performance never to be forgotten!"

If you are ever part of a "performance fiasco," remember this story and smile. God has a wonderful sense of humor! Tell about the Curtis Cat Harmonicon to any musicians or cat lovers you see today.

Each of you should look not only to your own interests, but also to the interests of others. —PHILIPPIANS 2:4

Today is the birthday of the Russian composer Alexander Glazunov (1865–1936). In many ways, he connected the Russian music of the nineteenth century with that of the twentieth. As a youth he studied with the great Rimsky-Korsakov, but as a man he became the director of the Saint Petersburg Conservatory, whose students included Stravinsky, Prokofiev, and Shostakovich.

Glazunuv did not agree with the communistic philosophy of Lenin, whose revolution took over Russia in 1918. Yet this musician was determined to keep the conservatory going for the sake of the many fine young musicians in his country. Courageously he lobbied the new antimusical government for funds and support, but it was always an uphill battle.

Finally in 1924, the communists thought they would win the director over to their side with honors and money. A large concert and banquet was held for Glazunov in Moscow in which the People's Commissar of Education gave a speech. He announced that the government had decided to support Glazunov—who was now a very poor man—and give him excellent facilities for his composing.

All eyes turned to the composer, who slowly rose to thank the commissar. He wore a threadbare suit that was too big for him, for he had lost a great deal of weight in the last few years. He said that he needed nothing and did not want to be treated any differently than any other musician. But if the government really wanted to help, well, his conservatory was freezing as they could not even afford firewood. Alexander Glazunov's unselfish answer caused a national scandal—which could have ended his life—but the conservatory did obtain a supply of firewood.

How easy—and tempting—it would have been for Glazunov to accept the honors for himself and better his own position. Instead, he chose to put his fellow musicians' needs above his own. God sees and will reward such acts of courage and generosity.

Imagine yourself in Glazunov's shoes listening to that speech. Could you have refused such a bribe? Read what Isaiah 33:15, 16 has to say about bribery and determine to always turn away from temptation.

Come, let us sing for joy to the Lord; let us shout aloud to the Rock of our salvation. —PSALM 95:1

Lowell Mason (1792–1872) did more than any other person for the sacred music of the nineteenth century. Born in Medfield, Massachusetts, he was a choir leader by the age of sixteen. For several years he worked as a banker in Savannah, Georgia, but his musical talent was such that Mason was soon conducting a number of choirs and offered a salary of two thousands dollars to conduct in Boston—a considerable amount of money in those days.

Mason was an innovator in music education and cofounded the Boston Academy of Music. Within a few years, he was also teaching in the Boston public schools. Two of his most significant publications were *The Child's Introduction to Sacred Music* and *The Juvenile Psalmist*.

He had such a heart for children that he began dozens of free music classes in Boston, which hundreds of children attended. Later Mason organized large music conventions that taught thousands of music teachers around the country. His genius was such that he became the first individual in America to be awarded a doctor of music degree granted by an American college (the New York University).

His greatest legacy to us was in hymns. Lowell Mason composed or arranged the music for dozens of the hymns we still sing today. Much of the great texts of Isaac Watts and Charles Wesley are best known to us in the musical setting Mason created. Among his many masterpieces are "My Faith Looks Up to Thee," "Come, Sinners, to the Gospel Feast," "A Charge to Keep I Have," "And Let Our Bodies Part," "Be Present at Our Table, Lord," and "Nearer, My God, to Thee." He joined the heavenly choirs of praise on August 11, 1872.

Read Revelation 5:6-14. Close your eyes and imagine singing praise surrounded by all the believers in the world's history.

Sow your seed in the morning, and at evening let not your hands be idle, for you do not know which will succeed, whether this or that, or whether both will do equally well. —ECCLESIASTES 11:6

The above Scripture is good advice, as modern today as it was in King Solomon's time. It is another way of saying, "try everything!" This is especially applicable to the life of a songwriter, for not even the most experienced ones can predict what the public will like from year to year.

One of the best country songwriters was not a Nashville product, but came from the West and instituted the "Bakersfield Sound." Buck Owens was born in Texas on August 12, 1929, and grew up in Depression-burdened Arizona. In his twenties he played guitar in a band but wanted to break into the music business as a singer. He was told by producers, "Owens, we got plenty of singers. What we need are songs."

Owens then determined with equal fervor to write winning songs, and in 1957, he finally landed a record contract. One of his songs, which he felt would be a great hit, was called "My Heart Skips a Beat." It was an upbeat, happy tune that seemed irresistible. Now all he needed was a song for the flip side of the record.

He quickly tossed off another piece, "Together Again," then almost threw it in the trash can. It didn't seem to Owens to have much potential. But he reluctantly consented to it being put on the "B" side of "My Heart Skips a Beat." The result? Both songs were on the country charts for over six months in 1964, and "Together Again" turned out to be the more popular of the two. In 1976, the same song, which was almost rejected, launched the career of Emmylou Harris. Buck Owens liked her version even more than his own.

Do you have a problem you wish were solved? Ask God's help, then write down every possible idea you can think of, even if some of them seem crazy. Remember: the best way to get a great idea is to get a dozen ideas—one of them will probably be great!

It is better to heed a wise man's rebuke than to listen to the song of fools. —ECCLESIASTES 7:5

Sir Edward Elgar (1857–1934) is known as the greatest composer from England in over two hundred years. He was showered with many honors, commissioned to write the music for Edward VIII's coronation, and later knighted for his contributions to the music of England. Elgar was made a baron, and given the appointment of master of the king's music. It was on this day in 1900 that he completed his monumental Christian oratorio, *The Dream of Gerontius.*

Even after he was world famous, Elgar kept both his modesty and his sense of humor. Once, he passed a street musician in London playing the "Salut d'Amour," one of his early works. This so delighted the composer that he gave the violinist the large gift of half a crown, asking him, "Do you know what you're playing?" "Yes, it's 'Salut d'Amour' by Elgar," the grateful musician replied. His benefactor smiled and said, "Take this; it's more than Elgar ever made out of it."

One of Elgar's many fine qualities was his loyalty to his friends. His *Enigma Variations* were composed as compliments to his closest companions, many of whom were lifelong colleagues. Several of Elgar's musical friends felt the freedom to give him suggestions concerning his music. Rather than resent such criticisms, he patiently listened and often gratefully incorporated their ideas.

Lady Alice, his wife, was not a trained musician. Elgar especially listened with appreciation to her comments. Once he played her a new work, which she seemed to like . . . except for the ending. However, she said nothing negative. The next morning, the composer found a note pinned to the music: "All of it is beautiful and just right, except this ending. Don't you think, dear Edward, that this end is just a little? . . ." Sir Edward Elgar worked on the ending until both of them were satisfied.

God often speaks to us through the wisdom of others. Are we listening?

How well do you handle criticism? Rather than waiting for helpful comments that might never come, why not ask a friend's opinion of something on which you are working and see if it doesn't improve.

Humility and the fear of the Lord bring wealth and honor and life.

—PROVERBS 22:4

Today is the birthday of Connie Smith, one of the greatest female country singers. But unlike many popular singers, she had no burning drive to be on the stage. Indeed, she was so humble and unassuming that it took a lot of encouragement to make her a star.

In the early 1960s, Smith was a wife and mother living in Ohio. She loved to sing, but had little time for it. When she won a local talent contest, she had no idea that the audience included Bill Anderson, one of Nashville's best songwriters. He was immediately struck by her beautiful voice and arranged to meet her.

After the little performance, Anderson told the housewife that she should sing in Nashville. Smith demurred, not believing that she had what it takes. After he left, she went home and promptly forgot about it. But Anderson called again, and arranged for her to sing on Ernest Tubb's post-Opry radio show. Smith accepted, but when it was over she drove back to Ohio, thinking that this would be her one-time career event.

Anderson recognized the remarkable talent of Connie Smith and got her a contract with RCA. He wrote all her first songs, and one of them, "Once a Day," became a blockbuster hit. Suddenly the housewife was a national star. Other songs would soon follow, yet Smith was always rather surprised and embarrassed by her fame. After a few years, she chose to slow down her singing career and devote more time to her family. She refused to let the glamour of stardom change her into something she wasn't.

The Lord doesn't want us to be so "humble" that we ignore or don't use the talents He gave us, but neither does He want success to go to our heads. Pray today that you will have a healthy humility as you use the talents He has given you.

Imagine yourself suddenly a national star. Do you think it would go to your head, that it would change you? Write down the definition of humility, and remember to practice it today.

Your wife will be like a fruitful vine within your house; your sons will be like olive shoots around your table. —PSALM 128:3

The great gospel-singing Winans family had ten olive shoots around a very large table. All of the ten children are in various aspects of music ministry, but the best known are the brother/sister duo of CeCe and BeBe Winans. These two have recorded a number of excellent CDs, and now they are also releasing successful solo albums.

CeCe Winans was the seventh child from this musical family. She now has a busy vocal career, but she insists that her main priority is her own family. Juggling all her responsibilities is still a challenge. "It can be very overwhelming at times," she admits, "especially when you don't feel like you're giving what you need to give or you just feel like, 'I'm failing at everything.'

"The answer is to go back and seek God a little while longer. He gives you the strength and the courage to let you know that everything is going to be okay. You know when you've made that mistake; but when you know He's with you, it's a lot easier."

How does a wife and mother keep a growing music ministry alive? "It's a lot," CeCe Winans concedes, "but it's pretty simple to me. It's keeping God first and really keeping your priorities straight. It's real important keeping Him first and making sure your family knows that they're right there; they're number one after Him. Everything else falls in line."

What are your priorities for this day? Spend time in prayer, putting God first and asking for guidance as you plan your day.

Sing praises to the Lord, enthroned in Zion; proclaim among the nations what he has done. —PSALM 9:11

BeBe (or Benjamin) is another one of the talented Winans family. Music ministry is truly his great passion. "I could go through each song and tell you what I felt and what I was going through. I'm in love with Jesus, and I love Him because He loves me like no other. He has a way about Him that I'm attracted to."

BeBe and his sister CeCe have had tremendous success in their ministry, yet they have also known the pain of censure from fellow Christians. Their upbeat sound has not always fit into some people's ideas of "church music," but it is deeply loved by many unbelievers. BeBe says with a smile, "God has people everywhere, and I'm honored that my music can be misunderstood in and service both Christian and non-Christian markets."

"From the beginning," he explains, "people would say the same things about me and CeCe. That we weren't Christians, that if we were Christians we would sing things this certain way and our lyrics would say things in a certain way. If you're willing to be misunderstood, and you're willing to be talked about, God can really use you. But if you care about what people think or say about you, you can only be used to a certain degree. I made a decision that I was going to be true to me and to God, and He's the One I want to please."

Yet God has always given the Winans duo the encouragement they need to keep going. For example, BeBe was at a restaurant in Chicago and a waitress recognized him. She told him, "Because of you and your sister, you are looking at a woman who is no longer on cocaine, and is now a mother to her child. I just wanted to thank you."

Each of us has fallen into the trap of worrying about what other people think of us. What does God think of you? Read Jeremiah 31:3.

"Who of you by worrying can add a single hour to his life?"

—MATTHEW 6:27

"Do not worry" is surely one of the most difficult challenges for many of us. How often have we worried about some situation out of our control, only to find afterward that we had nothing to worry about. Pianist Derek Smith, born this day in 1931, learned this lesson the hard way: in an accompanist's nightmare.

Coming home late from a piano job, he found that his manager had just booked him to accompany the famous tenor Luciano Pavarotti on the nationally broadcast television show "Good Morning America." Unfortunately, no one knew what music he would be playing, and the live show was the next morning!

Smith was an excellent pianist, but he had never played for Pavarotti and had no idea how difficult the piano part might be. Would there be adequate rehearsal time? What if he had to sight-read a string of complicated opera scores? It isn't likely that he found much sleep that night.

Arriving at 5:00 A.M. sharp at the television studio, Smith discovered that no one knew about the music. A very long hour later the great tenor arrived, but he was surrounded by clamoring people. Smith was unable to ask about the accompaniment until a few moments before airtime. Finally, Pavarotti's manager pulled the music from his briefcase. Imagine Derek Smith's uproarious relief when he saw the title page: "We Wish You a Merry Christmas."

Take a few minutes to make a list of your current "worries."
Prayerfully give these to the Lord, then throw the list away as a sign that you have now given them up.

After three days they found him in the temple courts, sitting among the teachers, listening to them and asking them questions. Everyone who heard him was amazed at his understanding and his answers. —LUKE 2:46, 47

Sometimes it is very tough to be young, especially if the adults nearby don't take you seriously. Even Jesus Himself, as a young boy in the temple, found that His answers astonished the older men who hardly believed someone so young could also be so wise. At times the only way for a young person to get a chance is for someone to stand up for him.

That is exactly what the young conductor Artur Nikisch (1855–1922) discovered at the beginning of his career. He was scheduled to conduct the Leipzig Gewandhaus Orchestra in a performance of Wagner's opera *Tannhauser.* This had been arranged by the musical impresario Angelo Neumann, who truly believed in the twenty-three-year-old conductor's talents.

But the day before the first rehearsal, Neumann received a telegram from the members of the orchestra: "Orchestra refuses to play under Nikisch. Too young!" They had never even met Nikisch, yet they had already condemned him. Nevertheless, his advocate Neumann had a plan. He called all the orchestra together and said that he would listen to their complaints only after they had rehearsed the overture with the young conductor.

Nikisch knew that he had only one chance to convince the doubting orchestra of his abilities. Mounting the podium with confidence, he conducted the overture so superbly that the players began cheering at its conclusion. In this turning point of his life, having one person who believed in him made all the difference. He had been given his chance to shine, and Artur Nikisch soon was known as one of Europe's greatest conductors.

What is something really important to you? How would you explain it to your elders? Write several paragraphs sharing your thoughts on this matter.

"But seek first his kingdom and his righteousness, and all these things will be given to you as well." —MATTHEW 6:33

Today was a turning point in the life of Claudio Monteverdi (1567–1643). For the first half of his adult life, the great composer had primarily worked in the household of the wealthy Vincenzo I, duke of Mantua. Under his patronage, it seemed Monteverdi had everything a musician could want—honor, riches, and influence. He composed his great opera in 1607, *L'Orfeo,* which is the earliest opera to still be in the ongoing repertoire.

The celebrated life of a court musician began to wear on the thoughtful composer however. He had to accompany his boss everywhere, whether seeking a cure for gout in Flanders or to fight a war in Hungary. When Monteverdi's wife died, he suffered a nervous breakdown, which took several years to recover from. Vincenzo I died and his successor fired the composer. Then a fire destroyed the manuscripts to twelve of his operas, and finally his only daughter died. Not unlike Job, his wonderful life had come apart.

In the midst of his distress, Monteverdi composed his beautiful *Vespers,* frequently performed today. It must have been a time of soul-searching for the forty-four-year-old composer, who loved God and tired of all the worldliness around him. He decided to devote his life and his music to the Lord. On August 19, 1613, he became the "Maestro du Capella" at St. Mark's Church in Venice.

Monteverdi was much happier working for the church than he had been at court. In 1632 he felt called to enter holy orders. But he continued to write beautiful music and is today often considered the first great composer of the Baroque period of music. His works are sensitive, dramatic, and innovative; he was the first to employ orchestras as large as forty players. His progressive ideas in music would one day prompt an innovator from the twentieth century, Igor Stravinsky, to comment on Monteverdi's music: "Amazingly modern and, if one can say such a thing, near me in spirit."

Not all musicians are called to write church music exclusively, but all of us are called to put God first in our lives. Listen to the Monteverdi Vespers, *and use it to inspire your devotion to Christ.*

Now it is required that those who have been given a trust must prove faithful. —1 CORINTHIANS 4:2

In the year 1724, this date in the Lutheran calendar was the eleventh Sunday after Trinity. This occasion was the first performance of Johann Sebastian Bach's Cantata no. 113, "Herr Jesus Christ, du hochstes Gut" ("Lord Jesus Christ, Thou Highest Good"). He composed over two hundred of these cantatas, generally for use in Sunday church services.

Hearing this Bach cantata, or studying its intricate composition, one would certainly think that the composer of such a beautiful masterpiece must have spent many weeks or months toiling over the work. The care that obviously went into it, the subtle word painting over specific texts, and the balance between each movement all speak of meticulous scrutiny that could not have been rushed.

Yet Bach produced hundreds of such pieces, often at the hectic pace of one per week, while performing a number of other demanding tasks. Knowing the time pressure, plus the fact that the composition would probably not be performed again for years (if at all), many composers would simply have filled the required pages with minimal effort. But Bach treated each work with the care of a master on his most renowned showpiece, knowing that he was preparing a work for a greater Master. He knew that God had "given him a trust" in his great musical talent, and he determined to be faithful.

There are many times in our lives when a minimum effort would be noticed by no one and a maximum effort would be appreciated by no one. It is in those very times that we should realize who will acknowledge our greatest efforts. Often, the difference between a great work and a mediocre one is more than the genius involved; it is the care and extra work that make the difference in the final result.

Take a moment to consider your present "job," whether it is doing homework, chores around the house, or working at an outside occupation. Are you giving it 100 percent? Ask God to show you specific areas where you can improve.

There will always be poor people in the land. Therefore I command you to be openhanded toward your brothers and toward the poor and needy in your land. —DEUTERONOMY 15:11

Have you ever been asked to return something that had been given to you? Or worse, have you ever been given something with "strings attached?" Jazz great Count Basie, whose birthday is today, learned a hard lesson about giving and receiving when living in Kansas City near the trumpeter known as "Lips" Page.

The two musicians were about the same size, but Basie did not have his wardrobe with him. The Count remembers, "So one night we were supposed to go out somewhere and I said I couldn't go because I didn't have anything to match up, and he said, 'That's okay. Why don't you borrow one of my suits?'

"I figured that would be great. Because he had three really sharp, truly great outfits. But I didn't know what I was getting myself into." Apparently his friend Page had not learned the principle of being openhanded with his giving.

"I couldn't get rid of him. Everywhere I went he was right there with me saying, 'Don't lean on that.' Or he'd say, 'Hey man, that chair is kinda dirty.' Or 'Basie, watch it sitting down.' He couldn't think of anything else all night but that suit of his I was wearing. That was one of the most uncomfortable evenings I've ever had in my life. I never was so glad to get back home and take off a suit."

If God asks you to give something, do it with an open hand, no strings attached.

In the Book of Acts, we read that the early Christians sold their possessions, took the money and "put it at the apostles' feet" (Acts 4:35). Choose something that you can sell, then give that money to your church.

Every prudent man acts out of knowledge. —PROVERBS 13:16a

Claude Debussy (1862–1918), perhaps the greatest of all French composers, was born on August 22, 1862. He was the foremost musician of what is usually called the Impressionistic period. His new harmonies created an entirely new way of composing and had an enormous influence on composers of the twentieth century.

Debussy wrote a good deal of orchestra music and much has entered the standard repertoire. Most everyone's favorite is his captivating *Afternoon of the Faun.* From its opening flute solo to its hushed ending, it is a delicate masterpiece. Others delight in *La Mer,* a beautiful depiction of the sea. Another marvelous work is his *Nocturnes,* with perfectly named movements: "Clouds," "Festivals," and "Sirenes," whose impression of Homer's Greece is supported by a "wordless" female chorus. That's right, no words, just singing "Ah" throughout, and it's exquisite.

Debussy made many mistakes in his life, but the care he showed in every detail of his composition cannot be faulted. He hated sloppiness and was very conscientious of every little sixteenth note. His writings are filled with dozens of themes that he did not think were good enough to use. This dedication to excellence meant that it took a great deal of time to finish a composition, but he never let deadlines or commissions cause him to create an inferior product.

Claude Debussy spent more than a decade composing his beautiful opera, *Pelleas et Melisande.* After its success, Debussy was approached by the director of a major opera company. He wanted to commission a new opera, but the composer explained that it might be a long time before the work would be completed. The official explained that there was no hurry, and that his company could wait three or four months. Debussy shrieked, "Three or four months?! It takes me that long to decide between two different chords!"

God doesn't want us to rush through a project just to get it done. He wants us to give our best, every time, even if it takes some extra time. He wants nothing but our best.

We are all tempted to give our second-best at times and to slop through a job. Make a habit of checking back over all you do, to see if it can be improved. Try this method on a chore or homework today.

"I am the Lord, the God of all mankind. Is anything too hard for me?" —JEREMIAH 32:27

Can God really do the impossible? Can He find an excellent instrument for a young musician who could not possibly afford one? Cellist Barbara Kavanaugh can testify that the Lord cares about every aspect of our lives—including our musical instruments.

Barbara began playing the cello at the age of nine. At first she rented a battered cello from her school, but as she soon advanced, a better instrument was needed. Unfortunately, her family of seven could not afford the thousands of dollars needed for such a purchase. It looked as though the young girl would have to settle for a very inferior instrument.

She and her mother prayed for God's help and guidance and kept their eyes on the classified ads in the newspaper. Then her teacher heard of an elderly lady who had a cello to sell. The instrument had been in the attic for many years and nothing was known about its condition.

Barbara and her mother went to see the old cello. The owner simply desired that the instrument be played and asked for only fifty dollars. They gratefully took it home. But at her thirteenth birthday party, the cello was accidentally broken. Wondering whether the old instrument was worth the price to fix it, they sent the cello to a reputable repair shop to have the damage appraised. Imagine her astonishment when she was told that it was a superb instrument worth thousands of dollars! God had more than answer their prayers—and this is the cello that she still uses professionally today.

We often pray for things but all too easily forget to praise God when prayers are answered. Start a prayer journal, writing down prayer needs and noting the answers as they come.

Blessed are they who keep his statutes and seek him with all their heart. —PSALM 119:2

Sunday is a wonderful day to go to church, worship with fellow believers, hear the Word of God preached, and enjoy fellowship with our friends. But if we are to heed the above Scripture, then we cannot abandon the Lord for the other six days. We need our relationship with Jesus to be for seven days each week, not just for one.

A Christian band has chosen its name to emphasize this point. Seven Day Jesus has had a tremendous ministry to young people in America, both in its recordings and its concerts. Even after the performances, the band members make a point of ministering to people. Drummer Kevin Atkins told *CCM Magazine*, "Things tend to be a lot more intimate one-on-one as opposed to a crowd situation. When you just talk to people, there's a genuineness that people appreciate and really need."

Yet a few years ago, this band went through a troubled time. Several members quit and its lost a record label's support. The group's leader, Brian McSweeney, needed encouragement badly. He received it by helping others, in this case another Christian band. He filled in on guitar for a number of Audio Adrenaline's concerts.

This change of scene was invigorating, and he learned from the chance to work with different musicians. McSweeney admits, "It was just what I needed, and I think if I hadn't done it, I might have just snapped and quit music altogether because I was at a really frustrated point." Seven Day Jesus was revitalized and the ministry was stronger than ever. Its leader declares, "I know I count my blessings every day for what we've got."

List the seven days of the week, with a different blessing God has given you for each day. Post the list and every day thank God for that blessing.

Jesus said, "Let the little children come to me, and do not hinder them, for the kingdom of heaven belongs to such as these."

—MATTHEW 19:14

On August 25, 1918, a boy was born in Lawrence, Massachusetts, who would become one of the greatest musicians of the twentieth century. Louis Bernstein, who later changed his name to Leonard Bernstein, could do it all. He was a masterful conductor, pianist, symphonic composer, and popular songwriter.

In 1943, Bernstein was the unknown assistant conductor of the New York Philharmonic. One day the orchestra was to play a concert for the national radio audience, but neither the guest conductor nor the regular conductor was available. At the last moment, Bernstein was called and did a remarkable job. Suddenly he was America's favorite son, and was in demand everywhere. His own compositions ranged from serious symphonies to musicals such as the celebrated *West Side Story.*

What would be the ultimate musical accomplishment for this master? For millions, the answer is crystal clear: his fifty-three televised "Young People's Concerts" broadcast from 1958 to 1972. Bernstein was personally responsible for turning an entire generation onto the joys of great music.

Conductors have sometimes been aloof figures who would never bother to give "kiddie concerts." But Bernstein gave each of the "Young People's Concerts" his very best effort. Who could ever forget the episode entitled "What Does Music Mean?" when he jokingly compared the Lone Ranger to William Tell and Don Quixote with Superman. The studio audience of children weas spellbound, and Bernstein clearly showed that he loved each one of them.

Young people are often bored with those who are younger still. But children are longing to learn more. Spend some time with a little one today, sharing your love of music.

One night the Lord spoke to Paul in a vision: "Do not be afraid; keep on speaking, do not be silent." —ACTS 18:9

John Hodges is a conductor who studied with the great Leonard Bernstein in the summer of 1982. Like his colleagues around him, Hodges had a tremendous respect for Bernstein's genius. But beyond that, Hodges had a Christian's love for his teacher, as well as a burden for his soul. He prayerfully sought an opportunity to share his own faith in Christ.

One night at a party, Bernstein remarked to the group, "Everyone has something that satisfies them. What satisfies me is conducting and composing, and I go back and forth between the two." Hodges later had a few moments alone with Bernstein and asked him, "Do those things really satisfy you?"

The great musician pondered a moment and shook his head, "No." Hodges then asked, "Do you think that if we have this desire that longs for satisfaction, could it be possible that there is nothing that will satisfy that desire?" Bernstein again answered, "No." He knew that there must be something that would satisfy his deepest desires.

Hodges was sensitive in his witness. Rather than battering him with preaching, he simply told Bernstein of a book that had helped him with such questions, called *Mere Christianity* by C. S. Lewis. Would he accept a copy as a gift? Bernstein replied that he'd be happy to read such a book, and Hodges gave him a copy before his time of training was over. He was unable to keep in touch with the most famous musician alive who traveled weekly over the globe. But John Hodges thanks God that he had even a little opportunity to spread the Good News.

C.S. Lewis is one of the greatest Christian writers of all time. Get a copy of his Chronicles of Narnia *or another of his books and start reading today!*

My comfort in my suffering is this: Your promise preserves my life.

—PSALM 119:50

When World War II broke out in Europe, the French composer Olivier Messiaen (1908–1992) joined the army to defend his native land. He had the misfortune of being captured in 1940 by the Germans while trying to escape on an old bicycle. Among his few possessions when he was sent to Stalag 8A were scores of Bach's Brandenburg concertos and others by Beethoven, Ravel, Berg, and Stravinsky.

Messiaen endured two long years in the prison camp, fighting off disease, starvation, and despair. His faith in God and his love of music gave him hope, which he tried to share with the other prisoners. To bolster their spirits, he arranged to have a short concert in the camp with the few instruments they could find.

Desperate for a taste of culture, or anything to remind them of better times, five thousand of the pathetic prisoners came to the makeshift stage. There sat several of their own: a cellist who held a battered instrument having only three strings, a clarinetist, and a violinist. Next to them stood a dilapidated upright piano. They would soon hear that it was horribly out of tune and many of its keys were broken.

Messiaen had composed the music for the event, and it bore the apocalyptic title "Quartet for the End of Time," which has been called one of the most important pieces of modern chamber music. For many in the audience, this would be the last music they would ever hear. Fortunately, the composer was released the following year. But he never forgot that performance, and Olivier Messiaen often asserted that his music had never been listened to with such attention and understanding as on that cold day in Stalag 8A.

Music has great powers to comfort. Can you give a musical gift to someone in need? Play, sing, or share a special recording with someone who is lonely or ill.

He has showed you, O man, what is good. And what does the Lord require of you? To act justly and to love mercy and to walk humbly with your God. —MICAH 6:8

Thousands in the late nineteenth century were brought to Christ through the ministry known as "Moody and Sankey." Dwight L. Moody was a powerful evangelist and often traveled with his gifted singer and accompanist, Ira Sankey. Sankey was born on this date in 1840. As a teenager he became a devout Christian. His father once said, "I'm afraid that boy will never come to anything; all he does is to run about the country with a hymnbook under his arm."

Although this father was wrong with such a negative prediction, he noticed correctly the boy's love of hymn singing. Sankey became one of America's great evangelistic singers and led huge choruses around the country at D. L. Moody's revivals. He compiled important collections of hymns and composed some of them himself, such as the famous song "The Ninety and Nine."

This hymn originated in evangelistic meetings in Edinburgh. On the second day, Moody decided to preach on "The Good Shepherd." At the sermon's conclusion, he turned to his friend Sankey and asked him to sing something fitting his topic in order to close the meeting. Sankey flipped through his trusty notebook but found nothing suitable. Then he remembered a poem he had recently clipped from a local newspaper. As thousands looked on, Sankey quickly pulled out the words of "The Ninety and Nine"—which until that moment had never been set to music—and made up the inspiring hymn as he was going along.

Even after his beautiful voice had brought him international fame, Sankey was quite humble about his gifts. He insisted, "I am no musician. I am no singer. I was never taught to sing. As to my singing there is no art or conscious design to it. I never touch a song that does not speak to me in every word and phrase. Before I sing I must feel, and the hymn must be of such a kind that I know I can send home what I feel into the hearts of those who listen."

Choose a poem or a favorite passage of Scripture. Make up a melody for the words, and sing it in praise of the Lord.

The proverbs of Solomon son of David, king of Israel: for attaining wisdom and discipline; for understanding words of insight.

—PROVERBS 1:1, 2

Stanley Konopka has been assistant principal viola in the Cleveland Orchestra since 1993. He is a strong Christian who came to the Lord through a great tragedy in his life, the divorce of his parents. His story shows the healing power of God's Word.

"No other time in my life was more pivotal than when I was nine years old. My parents filed for divorce, Christ entered my heart, and I started violin lessons. The divorce was devastating. As my family broke apart I became confident that I could count on no one and trust in nothing. But I thought that if only I would read the Bible and do what it said I would know God. I set this formula into action by reading something out of my children's Bible every night before bedtime.

"Very little seemed to apply or even make sense to me until I opened up to the Book of Proverbs. I began to read the first five or six chapters over and over every night. While grieving and despairing over my family's crisis, a profound image never left my mind: me, standing on a foundation with a large crack formed underneath me—and the Lord asking me to come to Him by walking right off the edge out into nothing.

"Proverbs chapter three rang in my ears as I continually confronted this troubling image: 'Trust in the Lord with all your heart, and lean not on your own understanding.' The Holy Spirit, along with the nightly bombardment of wisdom from God's Word, led me slowly but surely into taking that step out toward God. That step was into the only secure place there is, into the loving hands of our Creator. Serious music study began at school that very year and I found an incredible way to praise Him!

Read Proverbs 3 today, pick your favorite verse, and memorize it. Praise God for the wisdom available to us in His Word!

Even a child is known by his actions, by whether his conduct is pure and right. —PROVERBS 20:11

On this day in 1835, the great composer Felix Mendelssohn (1809–1847) became the director of the new Leipzig Conservatory. Only twenty-six years old, his genius was already renowned. He had composed symphonies, overtures, concertos, songs, and dozens of magnificent piano works.

Since this master lived to be only thirty-eight, much is written about his youth as a piano prodigy. The spiritual side of his upbringing, however, was full of conflict. His grandfather, Moses Mendelssohn, had been an important Jewish philosopher, yet the composer's father, Abraham, was somewhat uncertain in his beliefs. At first, his children were raised "without religion in any form," though his brother-in-law was strongly influencing him toward Christianity.

Once when he was a child, Mendelssohn ran home in tears from chorus practice. The chorus had been singing a passage from Bach's Saint Matthew Passion when another youth hissed mockingly, "The Jew-boy raises his voice to Christ!" Seeing his children tormented because of their religious heritage was too much for Abraham, and he had them baptized and raised in the Christian faith.

Yet Mendelssohn, far from resenting such a forced entry into the new faith, embraced it fervently his entire life. In his manuscripts this composer often penned ardent prayers. He championed the music of Bach, considering it "the greatest Christian music in the world." In fact, Felix Mendelssohn held one particular Bach chorus in such high regard that he wrote, "If life had taken hope and faith from me, this single chorus would restore all."

How much do you know about the faith of your family and ancestors? Try to find out what you can. But whatever you discover, remember that your personal relationship with Jesus is more important than a family tree of saints.

"How can you say to your brother, 'Let me take the speck out of your eye,' when all the time there is a plank in your own eye? You hypocrite, first take the plank out of your own eye, and then you will see clearly to remove the speck from your brother's eye." —MATTHEW 7:4, 5

Many young musicians go to a concert and find themselves envying the performers on the stage: "If only I could be up there." It may seemed glamourous from the audience, but any veteran performer will tell you otherwise. Like any profession, much of the music business means persevering through struggles and discouragements.

The name of a popular Christian band is taken from the above Scripture. Plankeye has a very progressive sound, and its performances bring a powerful message of the Gospel to thousands of young fans. But its members too have had to endure through difficult times.

On one tour, the trailer hitch snapped in half and their twenty-foot trailer full of equipment smashed into a wall. On another tour, guitarist Eric Balmer explained to *CCM Magazine,* "The roads were iced over and the truck slid off the road and down an embankment and was sitting at a tilt. I put on my jacket and beanie and jumped out of the truck and went about waist deep in snow! We spent the next half hour running in place to keep from freezing while we tried to CB for help. Finally, we ran about a mile back to a gas station. The police had to put up a roadblock so they could tow the truck out."

Yet the four men in Plankeye look for the spiritual blessings that accompany the ups and downs of music ministry. After one tour, in which they had played for crowds of two thousand to five thousand, Balmer admits, "It was a humbling experience to go back to playing for two hundred to five hundred people. I think we had higher expectations, and in a lot of ways our expectations were not satisfied. It forced us to continue to trust God and be thankful for what He has given us."

There is much in the Bible about perseverance, and Jesus specifically told us to persevere in prayer. Pray for the members of Plankeye, that they will continue its powerful ministry to their generation.

It is the glory of God to conceal a matter; to search out a matter is the glory of kings. –PROVERBS 25:2

"To search out a matter" is something all of us must do. Whether we face a small choice or a major life decision, each Christian is called to seek the Lord until His leading is found. In particular, when one door is suddenly closed, we must keeping searching until a new one opens.

For decades, Jim Reeves (1924–1964) was internationally known as one of America's greatest country singers. His smooth, deep voice recorded over eighty songs, which included many number-one hits. Yet Reeves never set out to be a singer. His first dream was to be a professional baseball player.

After playing for the University of Texas baseball team, Reeves was picked for a Saint Louis Cardinals farm team. This seemed like the beginning of a great career until a fateful game in Lynchburg, Virginia. Trying to slide into second base, Reeves badly injured his leg and, consequently, could never play baseball again.

What should he do now? Rather than lapse into depression or anger, Reeves immediately began the search for a new career. He found a job in radio as an announcer and became a successful radio personality. Late in his twenties he was persuaded to sing for a few records. One of them became a national hit, so Reeves put together a band and recorded another song that topped the charts. Finally, Jim Reeves had found his life's work—but it had taken some searching.

God's leading is not always easy for us to figure out. Sometimes we take turns or detours that we just don't understand or that may seem like the end of a dream (as did Reeves' injured leg). It may be, though, that God is leading us in an even better direction than we could imagine. We just need to have faith and keep searching.

Searching God's Word will yield a lifetime of treasures. Use a Bible concordance and look up several verses about music or another topic that interests you.

O Lord, open my lips, and my mouth will declare your praise.

–PSALM 51:15

Many people have heard of chant, perhaps even Gregorian chant, named for Gregory the Great, who was pope from 590 to 604 and who spent much of his papacy organizing the church's music. But have you heard of Ambrosian chant, named for Ambrose (340–397), the bishop of Milan? This great musician introduced the hymn and the antiphon into Christian worship services. Those who knew Ambrose wrote, "He devoted the greater part of the night to prayer, to the study of Scripture and the Greek Fathers; preached every Sunday and often in the week; was accessible to all, especially the poor and needy."

Ambrose was once questioned by Saint Augustine about the Roman custom of fasting on Saturdays, which was not the custom in Milan. When asked what he would do when he went back and forth between these two cities, Ambrose replied, "When in Rome, do as the Romans do," a response that has been repeated for fourteen centuries!

He was a good friend of the great Augustine (354–430), Bishop of Carthege (another music lover). Legend has it that when Ambrose baptized Augustine, the two of them ecstatically improvised together the celebrated hymn, "Te Deum laudamus" ("We Praise Thee, O God"). Ambrose believed that corporate worship is what holds a church together: "The singing of praise is the very bond of unity, when the whole people join in the single act of song."

In these days when many churches are caught up in arguments about music, let us recall the words of Ambrose: "Psalmody unites those who disagree, makes friends of those at odds, and brings together those who are out of charity with one another. Who could retain a grievance against the man with whom he had joined with singing before God?"

What style of music does your church use? Take a moment to pray for the music leaders of your church—that the music will bring all into "charity with one another," to the glory of God.

For, "Everyone who calls on the name of the Lord will be saved."

–ROMANS 10:13

Imagine for a moment that you are an extremely talented young tuba player. Now ponder: what would be your dreams? For most talented tubists, the ultimate musical dream would be to secure a job in one of the world's greatest orchestras and to spend the rest of your life playing the very best in orchestral literature.

That is exactly what happened to Chester Schmitz. As a young man he longed to play in a fine orchestra, but the competition was fierce. Most orchestras employ only one tubist, and when a new one begins the job he often stays for decades. Therefore, there are very few openings and many tubists competing for the position. Schmitz practiced exceptionally hard on his instrument and finally was rewarded with a position in the Boston Symphony Orchestra.

Yet the very fulfillment of his dreams left him unfulfilled. He remembers, "My life's dream of playing in a fine orchestra had already been realized. Nothing in my life seemed to be wrong, and yet there was this new emptiness inside of me. It had been there for days. Nothing I tried to do could fill that void.

"Now I sat with my tuba in Symphony Hall one afternoon in January 1973, and I said, 'Jesus, if You're real, please let me know.' Was it only a few seconds? Somehow, I KNEW He was there. He is REAL! Amazing! Twenty-six years later, I can tell you that He is faithful—and more real than ever!"

Only Christ could truly fulfill the void in Chester Schmitz's life. Only Christ can fill the void in your life. Have you asked Him in?

God answers the prayer for salvation at any time, in any place. Share this story with a friend today—it may be his or her day of salvation.

Though the Lord is on high, he looks upon the lowly."

—PSALM 138:6A

The country of Norway mourns this day, for on September 4, 1907, its greatest composer, Edvard Grieg, died. The state funeral was attended by thousands, as this humble man was dearly loved by his people. Many of his works, such as the *Peer Gynt Suite* or his celebrated *Piano Concerto in A Minor*, contain elements of Norwegian folk melodies. The conductor Hans von Bulow called Grieg the "Chopin of the North."

Far from being an aloof intellectual, Grieg was an unassuming musician with many good friends. Once he and his musical friend Frants Beyer went fishing. Grieg suddenly felt inspired and quickly wrote a theme on a slip of paper. While he was busy with a fish, the wind blew the paper into the water. His friend quietly retrieved it while Grieg wasn't looking and, noting the musical notation, began to whistle the theme. Grieg looked up sharply, "What was that?!" Beyer answered nonchalantly, "Just an idea I had." The composer's mouth fell open. "I just had the same idea myself!" His friend later confessed, and their fishing was interrupted by their laughter.

Grieg loved his native Norway and zealously promoted its music. He said that he longed to "know the nature of Norwegian folk tunes and my own nature." His government granted him a lifetime annuity so that he would have no financial burdens and could concentrate fully on composition.

He was admired in other countries as well, especially England, where he received honorary doctorates from both Oxford and Cambridge. Yet Grieg's modest character was never changed by the many honors and medals that were given to him. Only once did he say that such things were useful to him. He would place all his medals and certificates in the top layer of his trunk when traveling, noting, "The custom officials are always so kind to me at the sight of them."

Look up Norway in an encyclopedia or on the Internet. Read the history of King Olaf and how his country became a Christian nation.

We work hard with our own hands. —1 CORINTHIANS 4:12a

This is an appropriate Scripture for musicians, since music is made using our hands. (Apologies to singers, as well as pianists, organists, and harpists, vibraphonists, and drummers, who also use foot pedals!) And one of the hardest working musicians of the twentieth century was the Russian composer Sergei Prokofiev (1891–1953), who premiered his second piano concerto on this day in 1913.

Even if the name Prokofiev doesn't immediately ring a bell, you've probably heard of *Peter and the Wolf.* One of his most clever pieces, it uses themes for the different characters, human and animals. Prokofiev also excels in his larger orchestral ventures. He wrote seven symphonies—the popular *Classical Symphony* is indeed a classic—and the orchestral suites *Romeo and Juliet* (originally a ballet) and *Lieutenant Kijé.*

Few musicians in history can claim to have worked as hard as Prokofiev. A friend remembers, "I have seen Prokofiev for weeks on end in his little room furnished with an upright piano, a small table and a few chairs, composing for fourteen hours a day, not going to eat except occasionally."

His work at the piano often led him into trouble. Complaints from neighbors forced him to change lodgings a number of times. Once, the door opened to reveal a very angry civil officer with yet another order to move: "You have just played two hundred and eighteen times in secession the same wildly barbaric chord! Don't deny it! I was in the apartment below and I counted them. I summon you to vacate these premises."

Psalm 139 says that we are "fearfully and wonderfully made." Look at your hands—how many ways can you use them? Thank the Lord for the way He has made you.

"Freely you have received, freely give." –MATTHEW 10:8b

It was on this date in 1984, that the country star Ernest Tubb died. He was known throughout Nashville for his friendly, generous nature, and he spent much of his career giving a break to unknown but talented performers. Loretta Lynn, Jack Greene, Cal Smith, Tanya Tucker, and many others were indebted to Tubb, who was personally responsible for launching their careers.

Perhaps one of the reasons that Tubb worked so hard on behalf of young singers was that he remembered how much he was helped in his younger days. He had been a fan of the cowboy yodeler Jimmie Rodgers, who died in 1933. When Tubb was only twenty-three, he visited the late Rodgers' house and spoke with his widow.

Carrie Rodgers wanted to help the young man who had a wife and new baby. She called RCA and persuaded it to give Tubb a chance. Then she went a step further, loaning him her husband's favorite guitar for the recordings. Tubb was overwhelmed and deeply grateful.

Unfortunately, he tried harder to imitate Jimmie Rodgers' style than to simply be himself, and the RCA recordings failed. After three more years of obscurity and mounting bills, Tubb once more called on Carrie Rodgers. Agreeing again to help, she recommended him to Decca Records and this time it worked. His hit song "Walking the Floor Over You" launched his career for good. But he never forgot the help he had received, and when it was his turn to help a newcomer, Ernest Tubb was always ready.

There is so much that God gives to us that there is no way we could ever repay Him. What He wants us to do, however, is—like Tubbs—remember that we have received and then give to others.

Make a list of the teachers and others who have helped you the most. Now make a list of those who you can help. Call one today and offer your services.

"[The king must] not consider himself better than his brothers and turn from the law to right or to the left. Then he and his descendants will reign a long time." –DEUTERONOMY 17:20a

Many great musicians have other talents in addition to their musical gifts. Nevertheless, it is difficult to imagine many of them as the leader of a country. Can you conceive of Beethoven, Louis Armstrong, or Ringo Starr running a country—at least not for very long!

Yet this is exactly what happened to the renowned pianist Ignacy Jan Paderewski (1860–1941). After studying at the Warsaw Conservatory, he began a tremendous performance career, touring around the world. When his beloved Poland was finally granted independence in 1918, this musician was made its prime minister.

How did Paderewski feel about his two great careers, one as a concert pianist, the other as a head of state? Perhaps that can best be answered by an amusing incident that occurred in January 1919, just before the Versailles Conference.

As the head of Poland, Paderewski arranged to meet President Clemenceau of France. The first question the French president asked the Polish prime minister was, "Are you a cousin of the famous pianist?" Paderewski smiled and admitted, "I am the famous pianist." Clemenceau shook his head sadly, but in good humor: "And you, the celebrated artist, have become prime minister? What a comedown!"

Read Proverbs 17:22. What would life be like without humor? Tell a good joke to your friends or family today and see how laughter can brighten one's day.

Test everything. Hold on to the good. –1 THESSALONIANS 5:21

There are literally dozens of Bible verses on the subject of "holding on." As in the above Scripture, we are first instructed to test everything, to make sure we are on the right track. But once we know we are on the right track, we should plow through every discouragement and never be stopped.

In the early sixties, songwriters Harland Howard and Hank Cochran put together a song that they felt had great potential. But they went through almost unbelievable disappointments before they saw the fruit of their efforts. Harland's wife made a demo of the song in a converted garage studio, and the long quest began.

They took the song from label to label but received one rejection after another. Finally, a Decca producer named Owen Bradley thought it would be a good match for one of his popular singers, Brenda Lee. But when she heard it, she turned it down as "too country" for her voice. Owens then took it to another Decca artist, Patsy Cline (whose birthday is today), but she also refused to sing it.

The two songwriters' belief in their song gave Bradley the courage to keep going. He convinced the top Decca executives of the song's potential, and eventually Patsy Cline agreed to give it a try. The recording session went well, yet even then Cline did not think the song would sell. Yet the song "I Fall to Pieces" became her greatest hit and stayed on the country music charts for an amazing thirty-nine straight weeks. The songwriters were well rewarded for their uphill battle for the song in which they believed.

The Bible tells us clearly that we will all face many uphill battles. But the Bible also tells us that if we hold on to what is good—and persevere as Howard, Cochran, and Bradley did—we too will be rewarded.

Get a book about the lives of persevering missionaries. (The "Heroes of the Faith" series contains stories of many missionaries as well as other people of unwavering faith.) Keep it nearby and read a chapter whenever you can to see how the Lord works through the endurance of the saints.

"The foolish ones said to the wise, 'Give us some of your oil; our lamps are going out.' 'No,' they replied, 'there may not be enough for both us and you. Instead, go to those who sell oil and buy some for yourselves.' But while they were on their way to buy the oil, the bridegroom arrived. The virgins who were ready went in with him to the wedding banquet. And the door was shut."

—MATTHEW 25:8-10

Jesus' parable above teaches us lessons about time, preparation, and watchfulness. Most of us could do better at showing up on time—for church, for school, for our home curfews. Usually the consequences are not too serious, but sometimes a little mistake about time can cause very large problems.

In the fall of 1959, a jazz festival was held in the town of French Lick, Indiana. Bands from all around the country had been hired to play, and each one assigned a specific time, as the festival ran for several days. Only the most successful groups could afford to fly their members to Indiana, while the majority drove in cars, vans, and buses.

Elvin Jones, born this day in 1927, was asked to play drums in a quintet with Harry Edison, who had a contract to perform at the festival. He eagerly accepted but was rather surprised to learn of the traveling arrangements. All five band members were to drive the eight hundred miles in a station wagon, with Jones' drums strapped to the top of the car.

The trip was dreadful: eight hundred miles nonstop except for gasoline, most of it through rain and hail. Jones feared that his drums would be ruined. Finally the exhausted musicians arrived, and hurried out to perform. Imagine their faces when they heard the following greeting: "Where have you been? You were supposed to play yesterday!"

No one knows exactly when Christ will return. The Bible is clear that we are not to know. The Bible is also very clear that we need to be well prepared—always—for when He does come so that we don't "miss the show"!

Do you have trouble getting to places on time? If you do, try this. For the next week, take note of every time you're late getting somewhere, and keep track of how late you were (five minutes, fifteen minutes, etc.). At the end of the week, add up all that time. It may not seem like much when it's just a few minutes, but those minutes add up! Ask God to help you be more careful with your time.

Fathers, do not exasperate your children; instead, bring them up in the training and instruction of the Lord. —EPHESIANS 6:4

One real test of a Christian father is how much true attention he gives his children's interests. It may be easy to play ball together, but what if the son or daughter has a great love for something the father detests? For example, how many fathers who were full-time ministers would—for the love of a son—find themselves at a Christian rock concert?

That is what happened to the father of Scott Keifer, who performs with Code of Ethics, a Christian band that God has used to reach thousands of kids for Christ. When Keifer was younger and became a fan of the group known as Stryper, his father—a Baptist minister—could have hit the roof and forbidden him to bring such rock music into the house. Instead, he chose to understand, and the next Stryper concert found the two of them there together, eighth row center.

Another time, Keifer and a friend wanted to show his father what it was like to minister in a typical club. Would this Baptist preacher be scandalized to enter such a club? After the visit, he spoke with seriousness and humility: "Don't ever stop what you guys are doing to reach those kids. I could not walk in there and minister to those kids; they wouldn't listen to me."

Now that Code of Ethics is an established Christian band, Keifer and his father are closer than ever. He once gave this advice to his musical son: "If you ever feel your head's in a cloud and you're better than anybody, remember where you came from. You wouldn't be here without God." His son agrees, "I think that's the best way to keep your head about you, to remember that you're nothing without God."

A wonderful part of our Christian faith is that once we accept Jesus as our Lord and Savior, we are God's beloved children. Read John 1:12, 13 and thank God for His Father love for you.

How long will you lie there, you sluggard? When will you get up from your sleep? —PROVERBS 6:9

The words of the above Scripture—and many similar words—were surely heard countless times by the great Russian pianist and composer Anton Rubinstein (1829–1894). He was notorious for sleeping late, causing him to miss many important rehearsals and appointments. After years of trying everything, his wife finally discovered a method to cure her sleepy husband.

She had a large piano placed in the room directly above his bed. In the morning, she would play a loud, unresolved seventh chord, and run downstairs. Her husband despised unresolved chords, so he would get up, climb the stairs and resolve the music to the proper triad. While he was doing this, his resourceful wife stripped his bed of covers before he could fall back in it again!

Rubinstein's generous nature won him many friends, though his compositions were never considered good enough to win him many fans. Once, before conducting the premiere of his opera, he announced to the orchestra, "Gentlemen, if my opera is a success you must all come to my hotel room after the performance for a champagne dinner." Unfortunately, the opera was a decided flop, and Rubinstein dejectedly tramped back to his hotel alone.

Long after he had gone to bed, there was a knock at the door. "Who is it?" he shouted irritably. "It is I, Herr Rubinstein, the orchestra's double bass player" came the reply. When the composer asked what he wanted, the musician answered, "I have come for my champagne dinner." "What nonsense!" cried Rubinstein. "The opera was a ghastly failure!" To which he heard a timid, "Well, Herr Rubinstein, I like it."

Oversleeping can cause many problems. How we begin the day often sets the pace and tone for the rest of it. If we get up on time and start the day with a conversation with God, what a difference we'll see!

Getting up in the morning is difficult for many of us. Tomorrow morning, tell yourself that "this is the day the Lord has made; let us rejoice and be glad in it" (Psalm 118:24). Then thank the Lord for a brand-new day.

Brothers, stop thinking like children. In regard to evil be infants, but in your thinking be adults. —1 CORINTHIANS 14:20

As Christians we are aware that our intellectual abilities are unable to save our souls. Nevertheless, some of us are so concerned to "not lean on our own understanding," that we refuse to take time for thoughtful reflection. Believers are called to be good stewards of all God has given us, and this certainly includes our intellect.

One of the best thinkers in today's CCM world is Charlie Peacock. As a young musician he was sidetracked by drugs and alcohol, but when he hit bottom he found Christ. His life turned around, and he soon began to use his musical gifts to serve the Lord. Unlike many musicians who specialize in one area, Peacock has successfully played the roles of songwriter, singer, instrumentalist, producer, author, and speaker.

Perhaps his versatility results from his astute intellect. "I've always been searching for meaning," he admits. "Why am I here? What should I be doing? How can I contribute to the body of Christ?" Such thoughts have led Peacock to write many meaningful lyrics and to challenge other Christians to look at themselves. In 1990, he and his wife, Andi, founded The Art House, where artists, professors, theologians, and many others gather to discuss issues of art and faith.

Charlie Peacock is a leader in contemporary Christian music, but his leadership is not the world's way. "Any person who expects to lead has got to be the chief repenter," he reminds us. "You've got to be humbled by your own circumstances, your own sinful choices." When one is truly humble, he knows that all he has is God's gift—including his intellect. Thus, it can be developed without pride and used to God's glory.

Charlie Peacock's questions should be our own. "Why am I here? What should I be doing? How can I contribute to the body of Christ?" Write down your thoughts and ideas.

Therefore each of you must put off falsehood and speak truthfully to his neighbor, for we are all members of one body. —EPHESIANS 4:25

During the dark years of World War II, America was in great need of encouragement. Morale was low, rations were tight, and thousands of families had lost sons in battle. Music was a source of needed inspiration, and one of the most popular examples of this genre was "Praise the Lord and Pass the Ammunition," written by soldier-songwriter Frank Loesser.

The song was supposedly about the fleet chaplain of the Pacific Fleet, Father McGuire. He was stationed in Pearl Harbor during the terrible surprise attack of the Japanese on December 7, 1941. The lyrics vividly describe how the brave chaplain manned a gun himself after the gunners had been killed, and soon shouted, "We got one!" inspiring the soldiers nearby. The folks back home loved the song.

Unfortunately, many of the lyrics were very exaggerated and some were quite untrue. When the real Father McGuire finally heard the song, he was mortified. For he knew that by international law, chaplains with the armed forces are not allowed to fight. Furthermore, he knew that fifty-six Catholic chaplains were then prisoners of war in Japan and that there might be reprisals against them if the Japanese heard of the "fighting chaplain."

Father McGuire immediately arranged for a published interview. He knew it would end his reputation as a folk hero, but he had to protect his fellow chaplains. He stated, "I did not man a gun on December 7 or at any other time in my career in the navy." On that fateful day, he assisted the wounded and heard confessions. But he admitted that in the fury of the battle he "might" have said, "Praise the Lord and pass the ammunition."

Have you ever been given credit when you did not deserve it? Read Ephesians 6:14-18 and determine to live a life of honesty.

"Do you not say, 'Four months more and then the harvest'? I tell you, open your eyes at look at the fields! They are ripe for harvest."

—JOHN 4:35

Some Christians seem content to simply go to church on Sunday and perhaps put some money in the collection. Then there are those who are "radically saved," who see the commands of Christ and choose to follow Him every day of the week. The young men who formed the Christian band Skillet are of the latter type and have a vision for the harvest fields Jesus referred to in the above Scripture.

"There's no such thing as a nonradical Christian," points out John Cooper, who sings and plays bass for Skillet. "Being radical means understanding what your salvation is all about. It means you are no longer a slave to sin and death. You're a partaker of the divine nature."

With this high measure of commitment, the members of Skillet are unapologetically evangelistic. Cooper explains, "Skillet started on the premise that we wanted to see people get saved. We've been seeking ways to preach to people in a manner that's not offensive in a secular setting. We've always wanted to reach a secular audience. We want to reach kids who have never heard the Gospel or have heard of it but run away from God."

Guitarist Ken Steorts is even more aspiring as he asserts, "We hope to play a role in helping spark a worldwide revival." To this end, the members of Skillet proclaim the Good News within the framework of high-voltage rock music. Even their musical style is part of the message, as drummer Trey McClurkin declares, "We want to proclaim His name. What better way to do that than with intense music?"

Think of your circle of friends. How many non-Christians does it include? Make a "top priority" list of three to five non-Christian friends and determine to pray for them and for the opportunity to share the Good News with them soon.

He who gives to the poor will lack nothing, but he who closes his eyes to them receives many curses. —PROVERBS 28:27

Among the millions of casualties in World War II were many musicians. One of the most tragic examples is the composer Anton Webern (1883–1945). After Hitler had been defeated and the European war was over, Webern was accidentally shot and killed by an American soldier on patrol near Salzburg. The composer was walking past curfew and when challenged by the sentry to stop, Webern misunderstood the order, came toward the American in the dark, and was shot.

During his life, Webern was an extremely innovative composer, writing in the atonal style of his teacher Arnold Schoenberg. Webern's pieces are generally short and compact—the fourth movement of his *Five Pieces for Orchestra* takes only nineteen seconds! None of his complex compositions can be considered "popular," yet his work has had a profound influence on dozens of other twentieth-century composers.

Few students have ever found such a dedicated teacher. Schoenberg believed in Webern so much that he raised funds for him from friends. This excerpt is from an overwhelming letter of confidence and support: "He is in very dire need. Since I myself have very few rich acquaintances, I have myself repeatedly helped him out with fairly large sums (far beyond what I can afford). At the moment I could scarcely do more.

"You know Webern. You know that he is an extraordinarily gifted composer. You undoubtedly have a flair for remarkable people and must long ago have realized that he is one of them. Do help to keep him going!"

There are many great Christian relief organizations through which you can support a child in an underdeveloped country. Pray about it, talk with your family about it, then look into "adopting" a child.

"If I have denied justice to my menservants and maidservants when they had a grievance against me, what will I do when God confronts me? What will I answer when called to account?" —JOB 31:13, 14

The great Austrian composer Franz Joseph Haydn (1732–1809) produced an enormous amount of music. Many of his works have subtitles or nicknames, such as the "Frog" Quartet (because of a "croaky" sounding finale), which he composed on September 16, 1787.

For almost three decades, Haydn worked for the music-loving Prince Paul Esterhazy. This wealthy patron had his own private orchestra, but unfortunately, he was not a generous provider to all of his employees. In particular, he gave the orchestra members very little time away from work, so that they seldom saw their families.

The musicians went to Haydn with their troubles. He determined to make an impression on the prince that might persuade him to show mercy to the orchestra. Haydn finally had an idea and went to work immediately. Soon he invited the prince to see the premiere of a new symphony.

While Haydn conducted the work, the prince sat in his box delighted. Then two of the musicians stopped playing, snuffed out the candles on their music stands, and walked off the stage. Before the astonished prince could react, two more musicians, and then two more made their exits as well. The prince jumped to his feet, perplexed, and turned his attention to the conductor, who seemed singularly unruffled by these abrupt departures. Slowly it dawned upon the prince that Haydn had named this new piece the "Farewell" Symphony. Finally, only two violins were left playing, and the conductor himself began to gather his score and prepared to leave. The prince took the hint and grudgingly gave his approval to the musicians' request for extra time off.

Someday we will all be "called to account" for how we treated people around us—whether we are the boss or not. God wants us to treat all others with respect, dignity, compassion, and above all, love. Find a special way to show God's love to a family member today.

Gray hair is a crown of splendor; it is attained by a righteous life.

−PROVERBS 16:31

One of the most remarkable women in music history is Hildegarde von Bingen (1098–1179). As the tenth child in her family, she was pledged by her devout parents to the church, and from the age of eight she lived a monastic life. She rose to the position of mother superior and later founded a new convent of which she was the abbess.

Hildegarde saw many poetic visions and wrote both the music and the words to many beautiful chants—most of which have become well-known only in the late twentieth century. Her chant uses elements of folk music and contains innovations that include melodies that span two and a half octaves! Doubtless she is still singing praises in the heavens, as she died on September 17, 1179, at the age of eighty-one.

The Christ-centered words of her chants are profound and dramatic. Hildegarde's *Antiphon for the Redeemer* cries out to the Lord: "Pastor of our hearts, voice primordial, You spoke before the would was; we spring to hear. Yet now we languish, we are wretched and ill. Set us free! We beseech You, make us well."

In addition to the dozens of songs she composed, this amazing woman wrote many theological books, a book on medicine describing almost two thousand remedies, and a book entitled *Lingua Ignota* ("the unknown language"). This last work has yet to be decoded, and the language she created for it contains nine hundred words and uses an alphabet of twenty-three letters. When this unstoppable Hildegarde wasn't writing or managing thousands of nuns in convents, she was preaching the Gospel. We know of at least four extended mission trips she took in unconverted Europe when she was over seventy years old!

What a joy to the Lord was her life!

Do some research on Hildegarde and life in the twelfth century. Try to imagine living then. Praise God that we can learn from His people throughout the ages.

If you falter in times of trouble, how small is your strength!

—PROVERBS 24:10

Whether we like it or not, all of us are sometimes called on to perform when we don't feel ready. Perhaps you may be placed in an important position for which you haven't been trained or asked to complete an assignment when you know that there isn't enough time. Such difficult situations can actually bring out the best in us, as we turn to God and ask His help for the impossible.

In 1853, Costa Rica was a fledgling republic trying to assemble the basics of government. Government officials from both America and England were planning to pay a visit, and the new president was determined to make a good impression. Unfortunately, as the date approached, someone noted that the new country had no national anthem to play for its guests.

The president was not disturbed. He simply ordered his guards to find the best musician in the land and have him write the needed anthem. After some searching, the guards were directed by villagers to a man named Manuel Maria Gutierrez. He was taken at gunpoint to the presidential mansion. The president congratulated him on being chosen for such an honor. Nevertheless, Gutierrez pleaded, "But I've never written a tune in my life! I mostly play by ear."

His words infuriated the president, who threw the unfortunate musician into prison. He was told that he would remain there until the anthem was written. What could he do? It took three full days, but somehow Gutierrez scratched out a tune and hummed it to a local musician who could write it out for the instruments they had on hand. Manuel Maria Gutierrez was released, and the president was delighted with the new composition, which still serves as Costa Rica's national anthem today.

When we are faced with trying situations, God is ready and willing to give us the strength to make it through. We need to just ask Him for His help.

Have you ever felt that you might as well be in prison as to complete a particular assignment? Pray for guidance and endurance, take a deep breath, and plunge in.

He who walks with the wise grows wise, but a companion of fools suffers harm. –PROVERBS 13:20

The life of composer Richard Wagner (1813–1883) is surely one of the most puzzling in music history. Much of it was spent in self-indulgence and misery. As the Scripture above states, for a long time Wagner was "a companion of fools" and greatly suffered from the consequences.

In particular, this great composer allowed himself to be influenced by the atheistic philosopher Friedrich Nietzsche. For years Wagner admired the strength of Nietzsche's writings, and the two became well acquainted. But it could not last. Late in life Wagner turned to Christianity, and his old friend was stunned. In a letter dated September 19, 1869, Wagner tried to make Nietzsche understand his new beliefs, but to no avail.

Wagner's yearning for God continued to grow, and he later explained, "When I found this yearning could never be stilled by modern life, and realized once again that redemption was to be had only in flight from this life, in escaping from its claims upon me by self-destruction, I came to the primal fount of every modern rendering of this situation—to the man Jesus of Nazareth."

Nietzsche deserted the composer and later denounced him hysterically in a public article, "The Fall of Wagner." Nietzsche wrote, "Incredible Wagner has turned pious." He bitterly described his former friend's conversion by saying, "Richard Wagner, apparently the most complete of victors, fell suddenly, helpless and broken, before the Christian cross." But the composer refused to turn back and wrote a lengthy article about Jesus Christ, the "all-loving Savior," who was "born to suffer and die for mankind, redeeming the human race through His blood."

Nietzsche would be shocked to know that his words that were meant to belittle Wagner are actually a basic truth of Christianity, and that we all need to fall "helpless and broken, before the Christian cross." Only Christ could fill Wagner's yearning. Have you let Him fill yours?

Picture yourself helpless and broken before the cross. Then thank God for His amazing love for us.

Command them to do good, to be rich in good deeds, and to be generous and willing to share. —1 TIMOTHY 6:18

One of the most versatile singers in contemporary Christian music is Kathy Troccoli. She is one of the few artists whose songs have made the "top ten" in both Christian and secular charts, with such hits as "Everything Changes." Yet as busy as her vocal career keeps her, she has somehow found time to be "rich in good deeds" by being heavily involved with many serious Christian causes.

An outspoken advocate for many pro-life ministries, Troccoli has been a national spokesperson for the national Catholic youth organization LifeTeen. She was instrumental in the founding of A Baby's Prayer Foundation, which raises money for life-affirming organizations such as Crisis Pregnancy Centers and Teen Mother's Choice. Troccoli has also worked closely with Prison Fellowship, Feed the Children, and His Touch Ministries.

When asked about all this involvement, she humbly told *CCM Magazine*, "I don't think I'm any kind of special person because I've done some of these things. As a matter of fact, it's not like I've gone after them. They kind of came by my door, and I opened the door and said, 'Oh, okay, there's a need.' People always ask me, 'When did you get the call to do these things?' But to me, the need is the call."

Troccoli is simply a giver; she gives of herself to the church and to the world—in both her activities and in her music. She explains, "I'm not about just giving entertainment value, and I don't want to give Christianity-lite to people. It is important to leave them with something that will help them get through their days."

Take a moment to pray for the abortion crisis in our country. Pray for prolife ministries, for the young women who are making crucial decisions, and for the doctors involved in performing abortions. Remember, God loves all of us!

A prudent man keeps knowledge to himself, but the heart of fools blurts out folly. –PROVERBS 12:23

Strange things can happen when musicians of different musical backgrounds meet. Jazz players used to improvising can't understand classical musicians, who have to have all the music written out. Opera singers used to being heard over large orchestras can't understand why popular singers need a microphone. The list could go on and on.

Jazz guitarists and classical guitarists both play an instrument of six strings, but that seems to be the only similarity. Once a jazz guitarist was being rebuked by the band's leader for always tuning and retuning his guitar. When he answered by stating that all guitarists must constantly retune, he was rebuffed: "I just saw a concert by the renowned classical guitarist Andrés Segovia, and he didn't tune once!" (Segovia was considered the greatest classical guitarist alive.) The guitarist shook his head and said, "Some folk just don't care."

Another amusing incident involving Segovia took place in New York. A number of jazz guitarists banded together to form the Guitar Club. They placed amplifiers in all the main recording studios that could be used only by members. In this way they did not have to haul an amp into town for a recording session.

Jazz guitarist Don Arnone had just finished a session when he was told that the renowned Segovia was recording in the next studio. Arnone had vaguely heard of a great guitarist named Segovia, so he asked if he could drop in. The manager cried, "Oh no. No one gets in there. Orders from Segovia." So the frustrated Arnone shot back, "Okay, then tell him he can't use our amps!"

The Bible, especially the Book of James, has much to say about controlling our tongues. There's no quicker or easier way to make ourselves look foolish than by opening our mouths. Remember that the next time you're frustrated or ready to blurt something out. Don't make an "Arnone" mistake!

The Book of Proverbs has much to say about the importance of our speech. Look up Proverbs 12:25, 15:1, 16:24, 25:11, and try to be aware of the words you speak today.

In all their distress he too was distressed, and the angel of his presence saved them. In his love and mercy he redeemed them; he lifted them up and carried them all the days of old. —ISAIAH 63:9

Marshall Williamson has taught in the opera department of the Juilliard School for many years. He coaches some of the finest young singers in the world and has a tremendous influence upon them. He is also a man of great faith and has been a church organist since he was fifteen.

Living in New York City has many advantages for him, including the short walk to work as well as to his church. His talented students often perform nearby, and dozens of musical venues are at his disposal. But such city life also has its trials, as he found in March of 1999.

Williamson recalls, "My faith was put to the test when a taxi struck me from behind, smashing the right tibia bone just below the knee. As I lay in the middle of Broadway, all I could think was, 'Help me, Lord.' Dozens of kind New Yorkers (including a doctor) rushed to my aid and comforted me."

The doctors at the hospital worked carefully on Williamson's leg, and after many months of therapy he was able to walk again. It is a slower walk to Juilliard and to church, but he is deeply grateful for God's protection. Williamson learned that the Lord is always with us, even during periods of trial. He concludes: "The love of the Lord Jesus has stayed with me at all times—a very present help in times of trouble."

The Lord promises to be with us always, giving the grace and strength we need. Write down the ways God has shown you His care and his love.

But as for you, continue in what you have learned and have become convinced of. −2 TIMOTHY 3:14A

Matt Slocum had "become convinced of" God's call on his life in music ministry. He and Leigh Bingham formed a band they called Sixpence None the Richer. The name refers to an interesting passage from C. S. Lewis' *Mere Christianity,* which gives an illustration of God's love toward us: a child asks his father for a sixpence to buy him a birthday present. The father happily gives the money for his own present, though he is, of course, "none the richer" when he receives the gift.

Now that Sixpence None the Richer is a nationally established band, few people realize the dedication needed to keep going through many trials. It took seven long years before the big breaks came its way. It had many different band members as musicians joined and then left to pursue different interests.

After moving to Nashville, the group ran into even more problems. The recording label that signed the group had financial troubles, and the contract hassles were enormous. The band almost broke up under the strain. But Slocum would not let the vision die. He recalls this period: "We started developing this attitude that we'll do whatever it takes to make this work."

The breakthrough finally came in 1998. It was as if the world suddenly discovered Sixpence None the Richer. Record sales soared, and one of the group's works was even chosen as the theme song to a major Hollywood movie. The members were overwhelmed by their long-sought triumph and very grateful that they had not quit. Slocum reflects, "After seven years of lessons learned, I'm still just very thankful for the opportunity to make music, and I'm trying to take it in stride."

C. S. Lewis has been one of the most interesting Christian writers of the twentieth century. Rent the movie Shadowlands *to get an idea of his life.*

Therefore confess your sins to each other and pray for each other so that you may be healed. —JAMES 5:16a

Rich Mullins (1955–1997) was a Christian singer with a vision for Christlikeness. Long after he had achieved success in his music, he insisted on limiting himself to a very small income so that he could give the rest away. He often worked among the poor children of New Mexico's Navajo reservations, teaching music and the Bible.

A characteristic of Mullins' high spiritual maturity was the way he radically dealt with sin. By way of example, he once told the following story to *CCM Magazine*: "I was in Michigan, on my way to somewhere where I knew I ought not to be going. I started praying, 'Oh God, why don't You just make my car crash so I won't get there because I can't stop myself.'"

Then Mullins remembered the Scripture, "If we confess our sins, he is faithful and just and will forgive us our sins and purify us from all unrighteousness" (1 John 1:9). And another Scripture came to mind: "Confess your sins to each other and pray for each other so that you may be healed" (James 5:16a). Mullins decided, "I'm just going to stop and confess to the first preacher I see. The first church I go by, I'm going in there and I'm going to tell everything."

But Mullins realized that he needed to talk to friends rather than strangers. He immediately drove to Cincinnati, Ohio, and confessed his struggles with several good friends. He remembered, "It was one of the most liberating things I've ever done. It's not like I haven't been tempted since that time. I still have to make right choices. I still have to flee temptation. But the power of that sin was broken."

If you find yourself struggling with bad habits or desires, have the courage to speak to a friend, parent, or pastor. Like Rich Mullins, you will find God's grace and freedom.

When the Pharisees saw this, they said to him, "Look! Your disciples are doing what is unlawful on the Sabbath." —MATTHEW 12:2

Fault finding, such as illustrated in the above Scripture, is as old as Adam and Eve. It is much easier to find fault to point out in someone than to seek the good to praise in someone. Furthermore, the unfair criticism we sometimes receive can produce devastating pain in our lives. Perhaps we can learn from the great Finnish composer Jean Sibelius (1865–1957) on this subject.

When Sibelius was born, almost all classical music originated from Germany, France, and Italy—definitely not from Finland. His father died when he was only an infant, and the boy was raised by his mother and grandmother. Beginning music lessons at an early age, he wrote his first compositions when he was only ten.

Young Sibelius had to travel abroad for serious music study, which he received in Berlin and Vienna. He was always a diligent worker, and meticulous to every detail in his compositions. Once in Berlin, he arrived to hear a rehearsal of his *Symphony no. 2* and was told that one of the three needed trumpet players was absent due to illness. Sibelius stayed for a while, but finally burst out, "I can only hear the trumpet which isn't there, and I can't stand it any longer!"

This son of Finland came back to his beloved country in 1891 and remained there to create his greatest works, *Finlandia, The Swan of Tuonela,* the *Karelia Suite,* and the seven symphonies. He conducted the premiere of his *Symphony no. 3* on this date in 1907. Many thought his music should imitate the European masters, and he was not appreciated outside his own country for many years. But his Finnish style was eventually accepted by all, and he became a hero to his country. His attitude toward the much unjust criticism he received was once summed up by one of his students: "Never pay attention to what critics say. Remember, a statue has never been set up in honor of a critic!"

Sibelius was right; monuments are made to honor one who is admired. Think of someone you admire, and write down the reason why you believe this person is worthy of honor.

Cast your cares on the Lord and he will sustain you; he will never let the righteous fall. –PSALM 55:22

Much of Antonin Dvorak's (1841-1904) early life was an uphill battle. His parents struggled continuously to make ends meet, and they feared their son's musical ambitions were a sure ticket to poverty as well. Yet the young Dvorak dedicated himself to his calling as a composer, leaving home and working himself through Prague's Organ School. He could not even afford to rent a piano, much less buy one. Those days were later recalled as years of "hard study, occasional composing, much revision, a great deal of thinking, and very little eating." As a composer he remained virtually self-taught: "I study with the birds, flowers, God, and myself."

Dvorak persevered in his musical education, regardless of his handicaps. After his marriage, he continued to work hard, writing symphonies and chamber music in every moment he could spare from his large family, as well as from his teaching and conducting.

The "big break" of his career came when he met the famous composer Johannes Brahms. This older composer convinced his own publisher to distribute Dvorak's music, and he influenced musicians throughout Europe to play the young man's works. Dvorak's genius finally began to attract attention. He was selected to direct a conservatory in New York City, was given a huge salary, and was invited to conduct throughout the world. It was on this day in 1892 that the composer first set foot upon American soil.

Was the struggle through poverty and obscurity worth it? Of course it was, for Dvorak and for all of us who love his music. Now that we see the end of the story, it is easy to brush over the years of thankless toil and concentrate on the years of success. In the midst of poverty, Dvorak could not have seen the prosperity to come. He must have often doubted whether such results would come from all his labor. Dvorak realized, however, that the greatest mistake anyone can make is that of giving up.

When hard times come, as they did for Dvorak, we need to remember that we can give our troubles and worries to God and He will see us through.

Dvorak, a devout Christian, had a great love of nature. Take a walk today and enjoy God's creation.

"Therefore do not worry about tomorrow, for tomorrow will worry about itself. Each day has enough trouble of its own." –MATTHEW 6:34

Spiritual revelations can come to us when we least expect them. Maybe even in the practice room. This is what happened to violinist Mary Irwin while she was preparing for a major competition—one she did not believe she would win. After hours of practice, she began to reflect on the point of playing music.

"Why," she remembers asking herself, "would a career in music have anything to do with demonstrating to the world a commitment to glorifying God? What was the point of striving to be 'perfect' enough to win competitions, my idea of the way to success and acceptance? It was the day before the competition, and here I was—not practicing, but delving into some theological abstraction!"

Finally the revelation came, and Irwin was "immediately ushered into the presence of the Lord, where I just sat and cried with amazement and delight." The Lord showed her that "when a violinist performs a concerto, the most successful rendition will be executed when he or she is as completely present for every note as possible—not concerned with a mistake on page one or difficult passage coming up on page four.

"In essence, the musician is demonstrating to the world what it means to live life free of the past and the future; to live freely without condemnation or anxiety. The Lord has given musicians the ability to draw the world into glimpses of what life was meant to be—and what it will be again when Jesus returns. By 'forgetting ourselves in time,' we bring listeners opportunities to hear of the glory of God." And after all this was revealed to her, she won the competition as well.

What are you worried about that might happen in the future? Make a list of those worries, then pray through the list, offering each concern to the Lord.

But godliness with contentment is great gain. — 1 TIMOTHY 6:6

On this date in 1866, the Belgian violinist Eugene Ysaye received a wedding present: the new Violin Sonata in A Major by Cesar Franck (1822–1890), destined to become a staple of the repertoire. Throughout his life, Franck was a very content man, undisturbed by success or failure. His student and friend D'Indy remembered, "He aimed only at expressing his thoughts and feelings by means of his art, for, above all, he was a truly modest man. He never suffered from the feverish ambition that consumes the life of so many artists in the race for worldly honor and distinction."

Even when his compositions were belittled by the public, Franck was undisturbed. The first performance of his *Symphony in D Minor*—now a classic in every orchestra's repertoire—was a complete disaster. In spite of all the criticism, Franck was delighted at the premiere. One of his students, Pierre de Breville, wrote, "Going out we trembled to find Father Franck saddened by the coldness of the public. He was radiant." When his wife later questioned him about the audience and the applause, Franck, thinking only of the music itself, replied with a joyful countenance: "Oh, it sounded well, just as I thought it would!"

Franck was uncomplaining when the premiere of *Redemption* was bungled in 1873. He showed the same contentment when the *Third and Eighth Beatitudes* were botched by the orchestra during a festival in 1887. Franck always took the long-term view. "Of one thing I am certain," he told his wife, Felicite, at the end of the evening, "it is a very fine work." It was said that the finding of a single new chord was adequate to keep him happy the rest of the day.

This compliant attitude about his music did not represent any lack of confidence or an inactive lifestyle. Franck was a hard worker, composing by five thirty every morning. His secret was an inner knowledge of the true Judge of his music, his Lord and Savior. He worked in Christ's service alone, without the need for praise from men for his motivation.

Seeing the "long-term view" is a very Christian perspective. Prayerfully write down three to five goals you wish to accomplish in the next ten years. Check them periodically to see if you are on target.

Surely the Sovereign Lord does nothing without revealing his plan to his servants the prophets. –AMOS 3:7

Wolfgang Amadeus Mozart (1756–1791) was one of the great "musical prophets" of his day. His innovative compositions pointed the way to the Romantic music of the following century. On this day in 1789, he composed his celebrated *Clarinet Quintet,* featuring the instrument he championed and brought into the modern orchestra. Mozart also had a prophetic premonition of his own death, which occurred when he was but thirty-five years old.

The gift of such rare genius either brought him praise from his fans or the scorn of envious fellow composers. The first group included Franz Joseph Haydn, whose friendship with Mozart was untouched by even a hint of rivalry. Haydn's admiration for his colleague can be seen in a statement he made to Mozart's father, "I assure you before God, as an honorable man, your son is the greatest composer I know personally or by reputation."

Unfortunately, there were musicians in his time who could hardly conceal their jealousy of Mozart's amazing talent. After Mozart's early death, one of these was heard to say to another composer, "It's a pity to lose such a genius, but a good thing for us that he is dead. For if he had lived much longer, we should not have earned a crust of bread by our compositions."

Mozart himself was free from such pettiness, and he loved to praise talent when he found it. One of his most prophetic bits of encouragement was given to a young man of sixteen who had the opportunity to play for him. After hearing this unknown pianist perform, Mozart turned to his friends nearby with the words, "Keep your eyes on that young man. Someday he will give the world something to talk about." The boy's name was Ludwig van Beethoven.

The Bible is filled with prophecies. Look up some of the Old Testament Scriptures that tell of the coming of the Messiah—such as Isaiah 53. Jesus Christ fulfills them all.

A fool shows his annoyance at once, but a prudent man overlooks an insult. –PROVERBS 12:16

Buddy Rich, one of the great drummers of the twentieth century, was born on September 30, 1917. He had thousands of fans and admirers, but those who knew him well were cautious around Rich. He was a notorious practical joker, and some of his jokes went too far. One of his main victims was the singer Mel Torme.

Torme arranged to visit the jazz club known as Buddy Place in New York. After Rich's performance, the crowd went wild with excitement. Then the drummer stood at the microphone and introduced his friend to the audience, "Ladies and gentlemen, the absolute greatest—Mel Torme!" When Torme rose from his table he was met with absolute silence. The stunned singer looked dumbfounded for a few seconds, then the audience burst out laughing. They had been put up to the gag by Rich before his friend arrived.

But another joke turned out to be very unfunny. Torme was doing his closing show at a club with a packed house that wanted to hear him sing. Only twelve minutes into his performance, Buddy Rich appeared on the stage. He joked with the audience that his friend had been dieting, and "tonight, closing night, he deserves a little dessert." He slammed a lemon meringue into the singer's face.

Torme remembers, "Women shrieked out in surprise and disgust as their dresses were splotched with whipped cream and meringue. Men were furious to find their pants and jackets suddenly fouled by flying goop. Buddy laughed. I stood there covered in dripping lemon pie. My suit was ruined and so was the show." It is to Torme's credit that he apologized to the audience and left Rich without a word. Everyone was angry at Rich's prank, but his friend Torme never held it against him.

It could have been easy for Torme to stay mad at Rich and hold a grudge, but he chose not to. In the same way, we need to forgive those who have hurt us. It may not be easy. It may require a lot of prayer, but it is what God wants us to do.

Have you ever been involved in a sour joke—the giver or the recipient? If it was not resolved, get in touch with the other person and resolve the issue.

"The Lord does not look at the things man looks at. Man looks at the outward appearance, but the Lord looks at the heart."

—1 SAMUEL 16:7b

A very well loved contemporary singer in America is actually from Sydney, Australia. The songs of Rebecca St. James are teaching thousands of young people about the true ways of God, that His ways are not the world's ways. "Our society puts so much emphasis on the outside," she told *CCM Magazine*, "it's another one of those contradictions. God says, 'I don't care about what you look like on the outside. I care about your heart.' "

With a straightforward and bold style, St. James' best-selling albums are given such simple titles as *PRAY* and *GOD*. The message she brings is uncompromising: "Live radically for God. Read the Bible. Pray. Stand up for what you believe in and make a difference in your world."

Worldly standards are a topic that St. James deals with constantly. She points out, "In the Christian life there are lots of contradictions to the world. The world says, 'Serve yourself.' Jesus says, 'Follow Me, die to self.'" St. James insists, "I think one of our biggest problems as a generation is selfishness. We've been told over and over that life is about living for ourselves, doing whatever feels good. And that is so destructive; it's so damaging."

Prayer is another key topic in her music ministry. "I have people come up to me and say, 'Thank you for putting my prayers into song.' And Rebecca St. James is never far from evangelism, as she tells of a youth pastor she met at a concert: "He told me that four of his students came to the concert and gave their lives to God. Then they went home and six of their friends came to God as well. That's really what ministry is all about."

Whom have you judged by outward appearances? Ask for God's forgiveness and to allow you to see that person through His loving eyes.

"You will surely forget your trouble, recalling it only as waters gone by." —JOB 11:16

The Great Depression began with the stock market's crash in 1929 and brought terrible misery to millions. Jobs were scarce, breadlines were long, and many formerly wealthy people were selling apples on the street. Yet the very troubles of the Depression were the motivation that started country music singer and cowboy movie star Gene Autry on his way.

Autry was born in 1907, in the real cowboy town of Tioga, Texas. His powerful voice was first noticed while singing in the congregation of the Indian Creek Baptist Church, where his grandfather was the pastor. Autry loved music so much that on his eleventh birthday, his mother presented him with a guitar.

Although he tried several times to break into the music business, 1929 found him working on the railroad and singing for his own enjoyment. Things might not have changed for him if the Depression had not left him unemployed. Rather than accept despair, Autry acted with courage and traveled east with his guitar.

Victor Records heard him first, and soon he was making records with several other labels as well. In 1935, he recorded a national hit with "That Silver Haired Daddy of Mine." Hollywood then noticed Autry and made him famous in a number of successful cowboy movies. Indeed his troubles were now recalled "only as waters gone by." Gene Autry died on this date in 1998.

Think of an elderly person you admire, perhaps a grandparent, neighbor, or member of your church. Ask him or her to tell you about a troubled time in life, and if good later came from it. How does he or she feel about it now?

"Therefore I tell you, Do not worry about your life."

—MATTHEW 6:25a

The Hamburg Opera watched two musical rivals in 1705. One was Reinhard Keiser, famous in his day but now completely forgotten. The other was a young upstart named George Frederic Handel. To try and look better than the other, they each wrote operas about the same story and with the same title: *Nero*.

Who won this popularity contest? No one, not even the public. Both operas were complete flops. The music to Handel's work was lost and never rediscovered. Handel soon left Hamburg for Italy and then later for England, where he composed his finest music. Looking at the entirety of his life, how would one rate the importance of this Hamburg rivalry? Zero.

Yet at the time, when Handel was feverishly working on his opera *Nero,* the urgency of winning this competition must have seemed critical. How odd it would have seemed to him if he could have known that his opera would be a failure, the music would be lost, and it would not really matter. His musical talent would ultimately make him considered one of the greatest composers of all history.

When our competitive nature rises up in us or we find ourselves in contention with someone, we should stop and ask ourselves a few commonsense questions. "Why does this feel so important to me?" "In twenty years, will the outcome of this conflict make any difference?" "Is this really worth all the worry?" By prayerfully turning it over to God, we can let go of this situation and concentrate on the more meaningful aspects of our life.

What's your latest worry? Grades? Love life? Health? Reputation? To put it all in perspective, take a moment to read Jesus' words on the subject, found in the Sermon on the Mount: Matthew 6:25-34.

Let everything that has breath praise the Lord. Praise the Lord.

—PSALM 150:6

On this day in the year 1226, the humble Francis of Assisi went to be with his Savior. His entire adult life was spent in Christ's service, as he had been called to "rebuild My church." When others joined him in this pursuit, he taught them how to care for the sick, the lepers, and the outcasts, and he exhorted them to preach the Gospel to everyone. The first rule for his followers was "to follow the teachings of our Lord Jesus Christ and to walk in His footsteps."

Francis once prophesied to his first few followers: "Fear not, in that you seem so few and simple-minded. Preach repentance to the world, trusting in Him who has overcome the world, that His Spirit speaks through you. You will find some to receive you and your word with joy, if still more to resist you and mock you. Bear it all with patience and meekness. In a short time the wise and the noble will come to preach with you before princes and people, and many will be turned to the Lord. He has shown it to me, and in my ears there is a sound of the multitude of disciples who are to come to us out of every people."

Founder of the Franciscan order, this extremely humble man was also a great lover of music. He and his disciples sang praise to God every day, and a number of hymns have been attributed to his authorship. The best known is his wonderful "Song of the Sun." He composed it during a serious illness, and this hymn of praise is still sung centuries later:

All creatures of our God and King,
Lift up your voice and with us sing Alleluia, Alleluia!
Thou burning sun with golden beam,
Thou silver moon with softer gleam,
O praise Him, Alleluia!

Take a walk and look around you. Imagine all of God's creation praising their Creator. Join in with the "Alleluia!"

Remember the Sabbath day by keeping it holy. —EXODUS 20:8

Different Christians sincerely disagree on a number of issues. One of these concerns the Sabbath. Some celebrate it on Saturday, while most do on Sunday. Some take the Old Testament commands against working on the Sabbath very seriously. Other Christians, noting Jesus' example and words, do not. But nearly all believers recognize a "Sabbath principle," that we need to set apart times of regular rest as well as worship.

Mark Dumm has played violin with the Cleveland Orchestra since 1985. But as a young Christian in music school, he was very concerned with this topic. He had an important private lesson each week with the great violinist Joseph Gingold. But this lesson was always on Monday.

Should he refrain from practicing the very day before his lesson? Such unprepared lessons would surely become a waste of time, both for student and teacher. But Dumm couldn't get around the feeling that the Lord was calling him to do this and that he should trust God for the results. Finally he tried it. The next day, Mark was astonished to have an excellent lesson. In fact, Gingold told him, "This is the best lesson you've ever had."

Notice that Dumm believed that God had specifically called him for this "Sabbath practice rest." He has never tried to put this conviction on any other Christians. Many times believers play performances on Sunday, and often of the finest Christian music. This is an area where every believer needs to hear the Lord for himself.

Whatever your specific belief about the Sabbath, we all need time to rest. Find a quiet place, put aside the busyness of life, and "Be still, and know that I am God" (Psalm 46:10) for the next fifteen minutes.

A fortune made by a lying tongue is a fleeting vapor and a deadly snare. —PROVERBS 21:6

The great violinist and composer Giovanni Battista Viotti (1755–1824) is known as the founder of modern violin technique. It was said that any violin put into his hands would sound beautiful. One day in Paris this compliment was put to an amusing test.

Viotti and his friend Ferdinand Langle were walking on the Champs Elysees when they heard a strange noise. Neither could quite recognize it, until they approached its source—a poor man playing an old violin made of tinplate. Viotti was delighted and told his friend, "Did you ever dream of such a curiosity! I say, Langle, I must possess that instrument."

When the man was asked if he would sell it, he hesitated, stating that it was made for him by his nephew. "Well," answered Viotti, "I will give you twenty francs for your violin. You can buy a much better one for that price. But let me try it a little." The master took the instrument and made such wonderful music that a crowd soon gathered. Langle seized the moment and passed around a hat, which was soon full. They gave the entire contents, plus twenty francs, to the astonished beggar.

But he shot back, "Stay a moment. Just now I said I would sell the violin for twenty francs, but I did not know it was so good. I ought to have at least double for it." The obliging Viotti gave him the extra sum and walked away with his purchase. In a moment he felt a pull at his sleeve. A workman said to him, "Sir, you have paid too much for that violin. As it was I who made it, I can supply you with as many as you like at six francs each."

Was Viotti being generous, or was he being cheated? Use your imagination and think of an ending to this story. But remember, God wants us to always speak the truth from our hearts.

The integrity of the upright guides them. —PROVERBS 11:3

The Russian composer Nicolay Rimsky-Korsakov was a man of humility and integrity. When he was first asked to teach composition at the Saint Petersburg Conservatory, he protested that he did not have the skills needed. When they still insisted on hiring him for the post, he worked every night for months in areas where he felt he was weak.

Rimsky-Korsakov is known for his suburb orchestration, such as seen in his *Scheherazade,* the *Capriccio Espagnol,* and the *Russian Easter Overture*—based on the chants of his beloved Orthodox Church. But as a member of the "Russian Five"—the other four composers were Cesar Cui, Alexander Borodin, Mily Balakirev, and Modest Mussorgsky—he spent much time encouraging the music of his native land. In his role of composition professor, he was always known for encouraging and inspiring his students.

An example was told by Alexander Gretchaninov, a composer who one day showed one of his early compositions to Rimsky-Korsakov. When Gretchaninov admitted that he was himself displeased with this work, Rimsky-Korsakov asked why. "Because it resembles Borodin a little too much." "Don't be afraid if your music looks like something," he was told, "just beware if it doesn't look like anything!"

When he believed in someone's cause, his integrity never allowed him to compromise. In 1905, the students at the conservatory protested several governmental policies, and Rimsky-Kosakov sided with their efforts even though it cost him his job. On this day in 1909, he premiered his opera *The Golden Cockerel* in Moscow. As it dealt with the problems of the Russian government, it was soon banned. Again, his integrity stood firm, and he would not change a single note. Rimsky-Korsakov was later reinstated to his position at the conservatory, but he never bowed to the government's pressure against him.

Praise God that the American government is designed to give its citizens freedom. Let us always be thankful for our liberties. Ask God's guidance for those in positions of leadership.

When we are cursed, we bless; when we are persecuted, we endure it.

—1 CORINTHIANS 4:12b

When we are attacked, the natural reaction is to fight back. Indeed, it takes a strong person to "turn the other cheek" or simply walk away. But as Christians, we are called to an even higher standard: to bless those who curse us.

In the 1960s, Harry Carney was playing in Duke Ellington's orchestra during its annual European tour. While staying in Switzerland, Carney and his friend Ray Nance went to a watch and jewel shop near their hotel. They looked at a number of items but decided not to make a purchase.

A few minutes after they left the store, someone discovered that three precious jewels were missing. The store immediately concluded that surely "those two black people" were the thieves. They pursued the two musicians, who were window-shopping nearby. Carney and Nance were apprehended, searched by the police, and interrogated at the police station. They were held until the shopkeeper came back to report that the jewels were found—a salesgirl had simply misplaced them.

Neither the police nor the shopkeeper apologized to the abused musicians. Did they seek revenge? Carney has the last word in the story: "I thought of the poor shopkeeper who had unjustly suspected us. I could imagine how bad he must have felt about it all. Well, I went back to that shop. I bought the most expensive watch that I could find. The man in the shop looked happy, and so was I." Harry Carney died October 8, 1974.

Carney could have justly demanded his rights. Instead he chose to bless. If you are feeling bitter about an unfair event in your life, ask God's grace so that you can forgive and then bless the offender.

Whatever your hand finds to do, do it with all your might.

—ECCLESIASTES 9:10a

The lifestyle of the ultrasuccessful may appear glamorous to outsiders, but behind the scenes it is usually filled with a great quantity of work. For example, any thorough reading about the Beatles immediately reveals what hard workers they were. While they were idolized by millions, every day they were busy writing, rehearsing, recording, and performing.

This work ethic was established long before they became a household name. In the months prior to their first albums, they played in a club in Hamburg, Germany. Paul McCartney recalls, "In Hamburg, we'd work eight hours a day, while most bands never worked that hard. So we had developed our act, and by the time we came to America, we had all that worked out." And that "eight hours a day" was performing, hour after hour before indifferent audiences.

It was a humbling experience. "When we started off in Hamburg, we had no audience," Paul explains. "People would appear at the door of the club while we were on stage and there would be nobody at the tables. The minute we saw them, we'd just rock out, and we'd find that we got three of them in. We were like fairground barkers."

Does this sound like the Beatles, the most successful rock band in history? Yet this humbling experience was only a prelude to victory—as it usually is. Before they left Hamburg, their fortunes began to improve. "We eventually sold the club out," Paul recalls with a smile, "which is when we realized it was going to get really big." Within a short time, they would be known throughout the world. But they never quit working.

God wants—and expects—His people to work with all our might and to never quit working. Though we may not realize it at the time, He sees our perseverance and is well pleased. We will be rewarded—as the Beatles so obviously were—for our hard work.

Of course, no one enjoys a humbling experience. Read Matthew 23:12. Do your tasks today with a humble attitude, knowing that God will hold you up.

Do not forsake your friend. —PROVERBS 27:10a

The great composer Robert Schumann (1810–1856) was a friend to many in need. His own best friend was his beloved wife, Clara, who was one of the finest pianists in Europe. She not only premiered his works, but encouraged and inspired many new efforts. In the year after their marriage, he composed over one hundred beautiful songs as well as many other works.

The world owes Schumann a debt for discovering and supporting many younger composers. As the editor of the publication *Neue Zeitschrift fur Musik,* his promotion of various composers often saved them from obscurity. Schumann considered his foremost task "to promote those younger talents."

He called Brahms, "the one chosen to express the most exalted spirit of the times in an ideal manner." Concerning Chopin, he wrote, "Through him, Poland has obtained a seat and vote in the great musical parliament of the nations." Concerning almost unknown Schubert, he wrote, "It would require whole books to show in detail what works of pure genius his compositions are." And his friend Mendelssohn was called, "the Mozart of the nineteenth century, the most brilliant musician, the one who sees most clearly through the contradictions of this period, and for the first time reconciles them."

Schumann would bravely stand up for his friends when they were not available to defend themselves. Once, the famous pianist Franz Liszt was at his house for a musical soiree. During supper Liszt made several negative comments about Mendelssohn, who was not present. Schumann rose from the table, seized Liszt by the shoulder, and shouted, "How dare you talk like this of our great Mendelssohn." The rebuke staggered Liszt, who quickly exited.

While God may not want us to attack another person, such loyalty is something we should try to imitate. True friends can be hard to find. When we do, we need to stick with them!

Schumann even supported his own competitors. Who are you in competition with? Pray that God will help you see that person as another child of God and not just a competitor.

Saul replied, "You are not able to go out against this Philistine and fight him; you are only a boy, and he has been a fighting man from his youth." —1 SAMUEL 17:33

As David learned in the above Scripture, there are always people who seem ready to discourage a young person with a vision. Howard Goodman, the head of the renowned gospel group the Happy Goodman Family, had a similar problem finding encouragement when he was beginning to play the piano.

The young boy loved to show up early for Sunday morning worship, to play a few minutes on the church's piano. But the church pianist was his "discourager" and complained to the pastor, "That Goodman boy is nothing but a pest. Ever since he joined the church he's been fooling around with this piano. Last Sunday we couldn't get him in his Sunday School class because he wanted to sit here and pick at the keyboard. Preacher, if you don't do something about it, I'm going to."

She did. One Sunday when the boy was playing a hymn, the piano lid was violently slammed down on his fingers! He was told, "Don't you ever touch that keyboard again." "I'm sorry, ma'am," Goodman answered, holding his throbbing fingers, "but how am I ever going to learn to play unless I . . ." She cut him off, "Learn indeed! The likes of you don't ever learn nothing. What makes you think you could ever learn the piano anyway? You'll never amount to anything so get out of here and don't come back."

Could any young child survive such a devastating rebuke? Howard Goodman refused to give up. Fortunately, his father soon was able to buy him a broken-down piano of his own. This boy who would "never amount to anything" wrote dozens of wonderful songs and performed all over the world. The Happy Goodman Family won many honors and tributes, including both Grammy and Dove awards. Not bad for a boy who was told, "The likes of you don't ever learn nothing."

Has someone ever discouraged your dream, or do you have a friend in that situation? Read about people like Albert Einstein or Helen Keller, who were able to succeed despite being given much discouragement. And always listen to God's voice first.

"For we cannot help speaking about what we have seen and heard."

—ACTS 4:20

The Happy Goodman Family is one of the best-loved groups in gospel music. When the family members appear in public, they do not simply "perform," they minister the Gospel. Only once did a promoter make the mistake of trying to "tone them down."

Before a concert in Fort Worth, Texas, the promoter, W. B. Knowlin, told the Goodmans, "You can't talk on stage tonight. Nothing but singing. No testimonies, just sing. No preaching. These people paid their money to hear you sing, not preach." Howard Goodman did not argue. He simply turned to his crew and said, "That's fine. Boys, go tear our equipment down."

The hall was almost filled, and the words spread like wildfire that the Goodmans were not performing. People demanded their money back at the box office, and soon the promoter went running toward the Goodmans. "What's going on here, Howard?" he called out. Goodman answered calmly, "Well, W. B., we're leaving. If the Happy Goodmans can't tell these people about Jesus, then there ain't no cause for us to be here." "You can't do that!" the promoter shouted. "Oh, yes, we can," replied Goodman, "and we are. Unless, that is, you want us to do the program you booked us to do, to let these people hear the Happy Goodman Family, not some sugar-coated version of us."

"Can you not do it my way?" pleaded Knowlin. "No, we can't," insisted Goodman. "If we're on that platform and one of our group feels that the Lord wants us to say something, we have to be free to do it." The promoter eventually relented and the show went on. As Vestal Goodman explains, "We're gonna sing about Jesus. We're gonna talk about the song, and we're gonna talk about the Lord, salvation, and healing. We'll do whatever the Lord tells us to do."

Are you as happy about Jesus and being a Christian as the Happy Goodman Family is? Tell a friend today what Jesus means to you and what He can mean to him or her.

Jesus answered them, "It is not the healthy who need a doctor, but the sick. I have not come to call the righteous, but sinners to repentance."

—LUKE 5:31, 32

The Christian group known as dcTalk (Kevin Smith, Toby McKeehan, and Michael Tait) created a national sensation with its song, album, and tour entitled *Jesus Freak*. Its message was straightforward and bold: "I don't really care if they label me a Jesus freak." The group's music is loved by thousands of Christians, and yet its mission is clearly to seek the lost.

McKeehan explained their missionary zeal to *CCM Magazine*: "That is exactly where we want to be. We want to be missionaries to a generation so we have to understand the culture and live in the culture on a day-to-day basis before the people are even going to listen to us."

"To me, that is the Great Commission," echos Tait. "To go into the world and not be of the world but in the world because you physically are. You have no choice. And so when we do music, it is great if Christians enjoy it. It is great if it encourages them along in their walk, and it changes their lives. But Jesus didn't hang out in the churches all the time. He hung out in the weird places, and He hung out with people who were ostracized by society and the freaks because they were the ones that needed to hear."

The three members of dcTalk have courageously taken the Gospel into the most secular arenas, including television appearances on the "Tonight Show," "Arsenio Hall," and "Entertainment Tonight." That is their call, as McKeehan states, "We know that Christians will be entertained and hope that they will be encouraged. Hopefully, they will be challenged and edified, but at the same time that is not our focus. What dictates what we do is the call of Christ to go into the world and share our faith."

How would you react to being labeled a "Jesus freak?" Make a list of some of the things Jesus has done for you and thank Him for His love.

The Lord detests the thoughts of the wicked, but those of the pure are pleasing to him. —PROVERBS 15:26

Many of the commands in the Bible are concerned about our actions, that we always do what is right. But the above Scripture teaches us about our thought life—what we think about. In the same way that we (hopefully!) would not eat foods that are destructive to our bodies, we need to be careful as to what we put into our minds.

Folksinger/songwriter Woody Guthrie realized that what we sing about is also important. Much of his life was spent traveling among the rotten shacks and tents of poor migrant workers, and he did all he could to encourage them in their plight. Guthrie wrote hundreds of songs for them to sing, always very careful as to their content.

"I hate a song that makes you think that you are not any good. I hate a song that makes you think that you are born to lose. Bound to lose. No good to anybody. No good for nothing. Because you are too old or too young or too fat or too slim or too ugly or too this or too that. Songs that run you down or poke fun at you on account of your bad luck or hard traveling.

"I am out to fight those songs to my very last breath of air and my last drop of blood. I am out to sing the songs that make you take pride in yourself and in your work. And the songs that I sing are made for the most part by all sorts of folks just about like you."

What a wonderful attitude! God wants us to think pure thoughts so that we will please Him, but He also wants us to think pure thoughts because those thoughts will influence how we act, what we do, and how we treat others. May we—like Woody Guthrie—try to encourage those around us.

Our thoughts influence what we say to those around us. Memorize the above Scripture and use it to replace discouraging or negative thoughts that come your way.

Go to the ant, you sluggard; consider its ways and be wise!

—PROVERBS 6:6

No one could ever accuse Hans von Bulow (1830–1894) of being a sluggard. He was one of the finest and most diligent musicians of the nineteenth century. Both a concert pianist and a conductor, he presented the premieres of many works now in the standard repertoire.

As a conductor he was notoriously exacting. Long before the "podium tyrants" like Arturo Toscanini, Von Bulow expected the very best from his players. They loved him but were often exasperated by him. During a rehearsal of Beethoven's *Symphony no. 9*—when the tympanist was playing very loudly—Von Bulow turned to him and said, "Forte." The drummer obliged, but Von Bulow again shouted, "Forte!" Now the drummer was nearly bursting the vellum. The conductor stopped the orchestra and said, "Forte, not fortissimo."

At another time, Von Bulow's orchestra performed this same masterpiece, which he loved dearly. At the conclusion of the hour-long symphony, the audience burst into applause. But he stopped them and said, "I am touched by your delight of this work of genius. I shall perform it again here and now!" When a few people rose from their seats, he politely asked them to be seated as he had already arranged to have all the exits locked.

In the area of being prepared, he was matchless. Concerning his piano practicing, he gave a principle which has been repeated by hundreds of musicians ever since: "If I stop practicing one day, I notice the difference. If I stop two days, my friends notice it. If I stop three days, the public notices it."

God notices the difference too. He wants and expects nothing but our best. We need to be able to offer that in everything we do.

The above proverb points out that working diligently is using wisdom. Call or write the wisest person you know and request an interview. Learn how that person acquired such wisdom and apply what you learn to your own life.

The trumpeters and singers joined in unison, as with one voice, to give praise and thanks to the Lord. Accompanied by trumpets, cymbals and other instruments, they raised their voices in praise to the Lord and sang: "He is good; his love endures forever." Then the temple of the Lord was filled with a cloud, and the priests could not perform their service because of the cloud, for the glory of the Lord filled the temple of God. —2 CHRONICLES 5:13, 14

Bill Gaither is certainly one of the great names in Christian music today. He and his wife, Gloria, have recorded more than forty albums and written hundreds of songs. Yet one of their most noteworthy achievements was as facilitators. In 1991, Gaither began calling many of the gospel music groups together for a "Homecoming" recording.

It began as an ordinary recording session at the Masters Touch studios in Nashville. Present were the Gaithers, Vestal and Howard Goodman, Brock and Ben Speer, Eva Mae LeFevre, J. D. Sumner, Mike English, Mark Lowry, Jake Hess, Larry and Rudy Gatlin, and others from the gospel music world. As Vestal Goodman remembers, "It became obvious after about ten minutes that this was not going to be an ordinary recording. Everyone could sense the Spirit of the Lord in that studio."

The session began, with one perfect take after another. After listening a few minutes, Jake Hess said, "Something special is happening here. I have never felt such a strong presence of the Spirit in a room in my entire life." As the singing continued—long after the scheduled recording—tears flowed from many of the performers' eyes. One singer, deeply moved, admitted, "I haven't always lived up to what I have sung, but by the grace of God, I want to from now on."

Hours went by, but no one wanted to stop. Gaither kept the audio- and the videotapes rolling. At one point, Larry Gatlin said, "This is the most amazing experience I have ever had!" When it was finally over, Gaither knew he had captured something very special. After showing the videotape to selected friends, Gaither was contacted by the Christian Broadcasting Network for a national airing. The show was repeated many times. It was a time of sovereign anointing, and everyone involved with it would never be the same.

Spend some time today singing praise and thanks to the Lord.

A friend loves at all times. —PROVERBS 17:17a

After two days in a coma—during which he clutched a cross in his hand—the French composer Charles Gounod died on October 17, 1893. Today he is best remembered for his great opera *Faust,* but in his time he was known as much for his friendliness and love toward others as he was for his music. His friend Henry Tolhurst wrote that "those who knew him best describe him as a good and sincere man . . . a lovable man, a 'gentleman' in the fullest sense."

This was a man who had a genuine love for people and an infectious sense of humor. Even strangers who came into contact with Gounod were put at ease by his friendly manner. While walking through Paris he once heard a street-organ grinding out one of his arias at breakneck speed. "Ah, friend," he smiled, "not so fast! Look, let me turn the handle." The street musician was too amused by this stranger to stop him, and then the notes were played at the proper speed. "This is the tempo," Gounod told him, "and let me tell you, my good fellow, I wrote it."

Gounod clearly valued his friends far more than worldly wealth. An offer of one million francs to go on an American tour did not tempt him to leave those he loved, even temporarily. He had many prominent composers for friends, particularly Cesar Franck and Jules Massenet, with whom he shared both compositional talents and a kinship of faith.

Gounod's friends included many younger musicians, whom he helped and encouraged in their careers. He gave Claude Debussy a recommendation that enabled him to find work as an accompanist. Gounod wrote him many warm letters, telling him, "You have genius, young fellow." He was a continual encouragement to the composers Eduard Lalo, Georges Bizet, Henri Busser, and many others—even when he did not agree with their musical styles. When he needed a copyist, he insisted on employing an old musician who had been poverty-stricken. Gounod paid him generously and treated him as an equal, welcoming him as an honored guest at his dinner table.

In John 15:12, Jesus says, "My command is this: Love each other as I have loved you." Make a list of seven people from your family and friends. Next to each name, write down a way that you can show that person love. Try this for one week and you, too, will be blessed.

Then Caleb silenced the people before Moses and said, "We should go up and take possession of the land, for we can certainly do it." But the men who had gone up with him said, "We can't attack those people; they are stronger than we are." —NUMBERS 13:30, 31

For any given situation, you can usually find people who will give you completely different advice. Like the above Scripture, there will be those who tell, "You can do it," and others who insist, "It can't be done." Whom will you believe?

Wynton Marsalis, who celebrates his birthday today, is known as a great trumpeter in both jazz and classical circles. A well-known aspect of his style is "making it sound easy." He has a very natural, lyric sound, which seems to indicate that he was born to play the trumpet. Yet he remembers receiving both encouragement and discouragement at the beginning.

Marsalis tells of a time when his father was playing trumpet with some of the world's top jazz players: "I was about five or six, and Miles Davis, Clark Terry, Al Hirt, and my father were sitting around a table at Al's club in New Orleans—this was when my father was still working in Al's band. My father, just joking around because there were so many trumpet players sitting there, said, 'I better buy Wynton a trumpet.' "

Al Hirt generously agreed with, "Ellis, let me give your boy one of mine." The youth's eyes must have opened wide when he heard of such an offer, but Miles Davis gave a different opinion. "Don't give it to him. Trumpet's too difficult an instrument for him to learn." To this comment, Wynton Marsalis has only one word: "Ha!"

Conflicting advice is all around us. When you don't know what to believe, turn to God's Word and pray for specific guidance.

Whom do you think you would agree with in the above story, Al Hirt or Miles Davis? Thank God for the people who have been an encouraging "Al Hirt" in your life.

"Could you men not keep watch with me for one hour?" he asked Peter. —MATTHEW 26:40b

The most vital part of our Christian walk is having a "quiet time" alone with the Lord. In these times, our relationship with God is strengthened, and we are equipped to know and do His will. But in our busy lives, it is often a struggle to find the time we need to be alone with our Savior.

Mothers with young children are surely the busiest people in our society. But if you have little children and, like singer/songwriter Crystal Lewis, have a successful music career as well, the pressures can be overwhelming: finding enough time to get everything done and using it carefully can be almost impossible. One of her songs asks, "How can I combat a complacent state of mind? I need a reminder of the wrong of wasted time."

Lewis is humbly transparent about her own battles in this area of time management, she explained to *CCM Magazine*. "That's probably the thing I struggle with the most, and I know I'm not alone." With the kids, the house, the travel, the recordings, the rehearsals, the concerts, what is it that sometimes gets lost? "Usually, it's my quiet time," she concedes.

She also gives us the answer of finding the time, which involves sacrifice on our part. In one hectic time of her life, "I couldn't seem to fit in devotion time with the Lord. I was convicted of that. Through Scripture I have found that it really does require sacrifice. I grew up in an upper-middle-class family, and sacrifice was not something I was totally acquainted with. There's far more to being a Christian than going through the motions. God really desires to spend time with me."

The verse "Give, and it will be given to you" (Luke 6:38) can apply to much more than money. How about the giving of your time to God? Starting today, schedule a quiet time every day with the Lord. He will bless your efforts, and you will accomplish everything else you need to do.

Live in harmony with one another. Do not be proud, but be willing to associate with people of low position. Do not be conceited.

—ROMANS 12:16

Today is the birthday of Charles Ives (1874–1954), one of America's greatest classical composers. His faith and his musical genius are inseparable. He set to music numerous psalms, and he borrowed extensively from gospel hymn tunes, often highlighting them in the most unusual musical circumstances. From his orchestral compositions to his multifarious chamber music, more than fifty different hymn tunes are "quoted," such as "Jesus, Lover of My Soul," "Just As I Am," and "What a Friend We Have in Jesus."

Ives' complete works contain dozens of religious titles and references, from "The Revival Service" to "General William Booth Enters into Heaven." People close to the composer knew him as deeply religious and very strict on matters of morality. Ives reserved a particular fondness for ordinary people. "He was always interested in the underprivileged and physically handicapped," one biographer recalled. "He had a sincere interest in anyone who needed help."

Ives never sought fame from his music. In his later years, when his genius was finally being proclaimed, he seldom appeared at performances of his own work. Sometimes years would go by before he heard his works performed, and many more years passed before their genius was understood and appreciated. His *Third Symphony* was not played until thirty-five years after it was written. When it finally emerged from obscurity, it won the Pulitzer Prize for Music. This great composer actually spent his days as an insurance executive.

Ives could have had fame as a great musician or wealth from his career, and he chose neither. Ives' prosperous insurance company could have made him a millionaire many times over, but he insisted on being paid only what was required to meet his family's needs. He also refused to accept money derived from his musical works, objecting to copyrighting his compositions. Charles Ives did finally submit to the usual copyright procedures but arranged that the profits his music earned would go toward aiding the publication of younger composers.

Ives' compositions are extraordinarily advanced and often mind-boggling to hear. Find a CD of his works and hear the music of this great Christian composer.

Praise him with the sounding of the trumpet. —PSALM 150:3

Do you recognize the name John Birks Gillespie, who was born on this day in 1917? Perhaps not, but you surely will know of "Dizzy" Gillespie. He played the trumpet with tremendous power and had a sound all his own. Part of this came from his singular trademark: he played a trumpet with the bell facing up at a right angle to the rest of the horn.

How did he get such a unique idea? Did he experiment for years with the physics of sound? Actually, it began at a birthday party in 1953 for his wife, Lorraine. Gillespie was scheduled to play a show that night, so all friends were invited to the club afterward. His trumpet was left on the stage standing straight up on its stand. While he was out, there was some horseplay on the stage, and someone accidentally fell back onto the horn. Instead of it falling over, the bell bent, sticking up into the air.

Everyone thought that Dizzy was be furious when he returned and saw the mangled instrument, but he kept a cool head. "It was my wife's birthday and I didn't want to be a drag. I put the horn to my mouth and started playing it. I played it, and I liked the sound. The sound had been changed and it could be played softly, very softly, not blarey." He played it the rest of the night, but had it straightened the next day. But then he pondered, "Wait a minute, man, that was something else!"

Gillespie decided to go for it. "I contacted the Martin Company, and I had Lorraine, who was an artist, draw me a trumpet at a forty-five-degree angle and send it to the Martin Company. I told them, 'I want a horn like this.' 'You're crazy!' they said. 'Okay,' I said, 'I'm crazy, but I want a horn like this.' They made me a trumpet and I've been playing one like that ever since."

Have you ever had something "bad" happen only to find it was a "blessing in disguise?" Read Romans 8:28, and remember that God is always in control.

We wait for the Lord; he is our help and our shield. —PSALM 33:20

Conductor Delta David Gier knows what it is to wait for the Lord. Now he has worked for the Metropolitan Opera House and with the New York Philharmonic. Yet for several years after his formal musical training was over, Gier had to wait through a soul-searching time when he had trouble finding work.

Beginning in music as a trumpeter, Gier began conducting at the Interlochen Music Festival. He talked with every guest conductor who came through and learned all he could from them. One of them, Semyon Bychoz, gave him much advice and encouragement. Later, Gier attended the Tanglewood Music Festival and finally won a Fulbright scholarship to study abroad.

It looked as if a great future lay ahead. Then the picture changed as open doors for young conductors were very few. Through the years of waiting for opportunities, Gier somehow found the motivation to keep his musical skills sharp. At last, he was invited to audition for the New York Philharmonic. The time beforehand became a serious regiment of music study and prayer.

Gier's first chance with this major orchestra went beautifully and confirmed God's call on his life. He remembers walking out of Carnegie Hall afterward and praising God, saying, "I'm never going to doubt His call again." Some time later, Gier again met Semyon Bychoz, who is now conducting the Orchestra de Paris. When told that he had encouraged Gier fifteen years ago to go into conducting, the older maestro smiled and said, "It must have been very good advice!"

How well do you wait? We live in a very fast-paced, electronically controlled world that promotes speed and busyness. The next time you find yourself feeling impatient as you wait, use the time to talk to God.

I remember the days of long ago; I meditate on all your works and consider what your hands have done. —PSALM 143:5

Many times the Scriptures encourage us to remember those who have gone before us. This principle is just as important in the world of music. For example, guitarist Phil Keaggy may be a top player in contemporary Christian music, but he is also well versed in the classics—and the music of the past has a powerful influence on his present music.

Keaggy declares, "Music is powerful. It communicates things that words can't express. There are thoughts and images that contain meaning without the articulation of actual words. I am so moved by some of the passing phrases of Edvard Grieg, Ralph Vaughan Williams, Chopin, Debussy. Their music is timeless; it speaks to every generation."

Musician Magazine listed Keaggy among the "Greatest 100 Guitarists of All Time," but he is much more interested in God's praise than in man's. He writes, "I really feel that there is some spirituality involved in music. We are spiritual beings, and before we grew in intelligence, as youngsters, we had meaning, and we had worth as spirits—these created persons whom God breathed the breath of life into. Somehow music has a way of touching that part of us."

Putting the past and the present together, Phil Keaggy notes, "As I have watched the Christian music industry mature and grow, I've been both encouraged by its energy and at once found myself taking comfort and solace in things that have lasted. I have learned to appreciate my musical and religious heritage and have found myself with a deepening respect for form, the liturgy, and antiquity—as well as the spontaneity of youth and how both can be immediate and meaningful ways to convey eternal things in a disposable age."

Keaggy says that music "communicates things that words can't express." Play a recording of your favorite beautiful music and meditate on God's greatness.

He who loves a pure heart and whose speech is gracious will have the king for his friend. —PROVERBS 22:11

Felix Mendelssohn (1809–1847) was a child prodigy as both a pianist and a composer. His parents encouraged his talents but did not spoil him; he had to rise at five in the morning for a full day's work. Some of his best works were composed while still in his teens, such as the beautiful *Midsummer Night's Dream Overture.* It was on this day in 1818 that Mendelssohn made his Berlin debut as a pianist—at the age of nine.

This brilliant musician was a devout Christian and studied the Bible with great care. His knowledge of biblical principles allowed him to find great success in working with people, such as when he founded the Leipzig Conservatory of Music. His gracious "people skills" also made him a great favorite of royalty, especially in the palaces of England.

Mendelssohn was greatly admired by Prince Albert and Queen Victoria, who was an amateur singer. Once Mendelssohn visited them and coaxed the prince into performing on the organ. The composer later wrote his mother that he played "so charmingly and clearly and correctly that it would have done credit to any professional." Then the queen sang several of Mendelssohn's songs, "really quite faultlessly, with charming feeling and expression."

At the conclusion of another such musical visit, the queen approached the composer and said, "Now, Dr. Mendelssohn, you have given me so much pleasure; is there nothing I can do to give you pleasure?" He could have asked for anything! But, being a simple family man, he replied that he would like to see the royal children and their rooms. The queen was delighted and conducted the tour herself. Those who followed them noted that they seemed like two typical parents, giving each other tips on the raising of children.

Get up at five o'clock tomorrow morning and begin your full day's work. See how much more you can get done in a day when you begin it early. Then at the end of the day, thank God for all He enabled you to do.

My times are in your hands; deliver me from my enemies and from those who pursue me. —PSALM 31:15

The piano has more excellent concertos written for it than for any other instrument. And with this celebrated literature, perhaps the most beloved favorite is Tchaikovsky's *Piano Concerto in B-flat Major*. Yet it was not always so universally admired. Its premiere in Russia was a marked failure. It was on October 25, 1875, that this masterpiece was given its American premiere in Boston, Massachusetts.

Peter Ilyich Tchaikovsky (1840-1893) was quite sensitive to the rejection of this beautiful piece. He first took it to Nikolay Rubinstein, the finest pianist in Moscow. The composer remembers: "I played the first movement. Never a word, never a single remark. . . . I gathered patience and played to the end. Still silence. 'Well?' I asked, and rose from the piano.

"Then the torrent broke from Rubinstein's lips. Gentle at first, gathering volume as it proceeded, and finally bursting into the fury of a Jupiter. My concerto was worthless, absolutely unplayable! The passages so broken, so disconnected, so unskillfully written, that they could not even be improved. The work itself was bad, trivial, common. Here and there I'd stolen from other people—only one or two pages were worth anything, the rest had better be destroyed."

Tchaikovsky was crushed and left the room. Yet his integrity told him that he had composed an excellent piece. Later Rubinstein went to him, and "seeing how upset I was, repeated that my concerto was impossible, but said if I would suit it to his requirements he would bring it out at his concert. 'I shall not alter a single note,' I replied." Today, music lovers everywhere are grateful to Tchaikovsky for not buckling under such criticism.

Find a recording of Tchaikovsky's Piano Concerto in B-flat Major. As you listen to it, imagine the scene between Tchaikovsky and Rubinstein. Be encouraged by Tchaikovsky's belief in his work, and know that your times are in God's hands.

Each man should give what he has decided in his heart to give, not
reluctantly or under compulsion, for God loves a cheerful giver.

—2 CORINTHIANS 9:7

On the title page of a piece of music, next to the title of the composition, you will usually see the words, "Music by . . ." (the composer).
Yet there are often others involved in the actual formulation of the song who
are unnamed—and usually unpaid as well. Nevertheless, there are those songwriters
of integrity who believe that everyone who takes part in the songwriting should
take part of the payments. Kendall Hayes is such a songwriter.

This Kentucky songwriter once wrote a song he called "Walk on By," but no
one was interested in buying it. Something seemed to be missing from the song,
but Hayes couldn't put his finger on it. Then one day another songwriter, Gary
Walker, had a four-word idea. He suggested simply adding the phrase "wait on
the corner" at a certain place in the song. Hayes had to admit that it worked perfectly.

Soon after this, the new "Walk on By" was recorded by singer Leroy Van
Dyke. The result was phenomenal. It stayed number one on the country music
charts for an amazing nineteen weeks, and later crossed over to the pop charts as
well. The top selling song for 1961, it sold more than any other country song
between the years 1960 and 1995! "Walk on By" became one of the top ten
country music records of all time, and made Hayes a fortune in royalties.

Many songwriters would have left Gary Walker's four-word contribution
unrewarded, or perhaps paid him a one-time fee. But that was not Kendall
Hayes' way. There was no legal requirement for such a payment, yet Hayes insisted on giving Walker a full one-fourth of all the royalties the song earned. Not too
bad for four words!

The Bible calls us to tithe—to give one-tenth of what we earn to God.
If you don't already tithe, do so—cheerfully—with your next paycheck and
see how God blesses you.

"The man who had received the five talents went at once and put his money to work and gained five more." —MATTHEW 25:16

When Jesus told the above parable, the word "talents" referred to a certain type of money. But the modern word "talents"—meaning gifts, skills, genius, artistry—is derived from this very parable. Indeed, it is clear that when God gives talents to someone, he or she is expected to work with them to make them more fruitful.

Cellist Alan Harrell has been given many talents from the Lord. Today he plays with the Cleveland Symphony Orchestra and teaches at the Christian Performing Artists' Fellowship's MasterWorks Festival. But before he found his first orchestra job, he had to learn the lesson of always preparing his talents.

Hearing that a certain orchestra had a cello opening, Harrell asked to audition even though he was not very well prepared. The process was grueling. The preliminary auditions began at 10 A.M., but he had to wait until 5:30 P.M. to play. Harrell made it to the semifinals, which began the next evening at 7:30, again waiting, this time until 10:00. Making it to the finals, he was scheduled to play at 10:30 the following night. This time, he waited until 1:30 A.M. to play. He then had to wait until four in the morning for the results—only to find that he wasn't hired.

Rather than feel defeated, Harrell began a year of solid preparation. When another cello job opened up, this time in the prestigious Cleveland Orchestra, he was ready. The first round began at 9 A.M. He breezed through the rounds quickly and by 2 P.M., he had won the position. Harrell's talents had been put to work and he was now being rewarded.

All of us need to plan ahead and prepare ourselves. Write down a current goal, and then list step-by-step the approach you will take to reach that goal. Commit all these plans to the Lord.

These are the things you are to do: Speak the truth to each other.
—ZECHARIAH 8:16a

Having helpful and supportive friends should be a blessing. But as the Czech composer Ernst Krenek found out, they had better stick to the truth. In the late 1930s, he fled the Nazis in Europe and settled in America. He was an old friend of George Antheil, a composer who then lived in Hollywood. Antheil and composer Ben Hecht had a wild experience trying to persuade the film tycoon Sam Goldwyn to hire Krenek for a movie score.

Antheil and Hecht marched into Goldwyn's beautiful office and exclaimed that the greatest composer in the world had just moved into town. Goldwyn was skeptical: "Is that so? What's his name?" When they told him, he replied, "Never heard of him. What's he written?" They answered that Krenek had written one of the world's most successful operas, *Jonny Spielt Auf.* Goldwyn answered, "Never heard of it."

The two friends were becoming worried now, so they tried a new tactic. Antheil said, "He wrote *Threepenny Opera,"* which was actually composed by Kurt Weill. Goldwyn only replied, "Never heard of it." Hecht ventured, "He wrote *Rosenkavalier."* (This was by Richard Strauss.) Goldwyn brightened; he had heard of *Rosenkavalier* somewhere. Hecht continued, "And *Faust,* too! Krenek wrote that." (Actually, Gounod did.) "No kidding!" said Goldwyn, impressed. Perhaps Krenek might get the job after all.

Hecht tried one too many: "And *La Traviata,* too." (Composed by Verdi.) Suddenly Goldwyn exploded, "So he wrote *La Traviata* did he? Just bring that guy around here so's I can get my hands on him! Why, his publishers almost ruined me with a suit just because we used a few bars of that lousy opera. We had to retake half the picture for a few lousy bars!" His two friends made a hasty retreat, and Ernst Krenek never did work for Sam Goldwyn.

God tells us to always speak the truth—for good reason! The lies of Krenek's well-meaning friends cost him a job and could have cost him more if they hadn't stopped when they did. It never pays to lie.

Think of a friend you can help today, but remember to always speak the truth.

Moses said to the Lord, "O Lord, I have never been eloquent, neither in the past nor since you have spoken to your servant. I am slow of speech and tongue." The Lord said to him, "Who gave man his mouth? Who makes him deaf or mute? Who gives him sight or makes him blind? Is it not I, the Lord?"

—EXODUS 4:10, 11

Mel Tillis is a major player in the country music business. In 1976, he won the Country Music Association's Entertainer of the Year award and has became one of the top twenty-five charting performers in country music history. Yet this great singer/songwriter had a tremendous obstacle to overcome: Mel Tillis was a stutterer.

As a young man, he had worked hard to partially overcome this serious speech impediment. He could sing without difficulty and could speak clearly enough from a prepared text. But the stutter appeared in normal speaking, and few people gave Tillis a chance at real achievement. After trying unsuccessfully to make it as a songwriter in Nashville, he gave up and moved his family to his hometown of Pahokee, Florida.

The stuttering continued to plague him, and finding a job was difficult. Finally he became a traveling salesman for a cookie company, but without much success. Tillis recalls, "I worked for three weeks and didn't sell one cookie." At one point he was so discouraged that he tried telling himself, "mind over matter." As he drove the cookie truck around Florida, he turned those words over and over until they became "Heart over Mind." Soon he was humming a new song with these words.

He finished the song, wrote two more, and decided to try again in Nashville. This time, all three songs were recorded by country singers and became big sellers. Tillis continued to write hit songs for others and to work on his speech problem. Finally, in 1970, Tillis himself recorded "Heart over Mind," and the response was overwhelming. This poor, stuttering cookie salesman had conquered his obstacles and even successfully branched out into comedy, acting, and writing.

Regardless of the obstacles we may face, we need to remember that the Lord made us. He gave us all our abilities, and He wants us to remember that.

Do you have a problem that seems unconquerable? Try Tillis' technique: "heart over mind." Read the above Scripture again and listen to a recording of Tillis' song. Put your trust in the Lord for a solution.

Devote yourselves to prayer, being watchful and thankful.

—COLOSSIANS 4:2

On October 30, 1826, Ludwig van Beethoven finished his last *String Quartet, Op. 135*. He had created dozens of masterpieces like this one, in a life that was seldom happy. He had been lonely, for he had remained a bachelor (though not by choice). Beethoven proposed to several different women, all of whom admired his genius but clearly perceived that his erratic personality would make him an outrageous husband.

Indeed, his untamable ways give us many amusing stories. Once, at the height of his fame, a police officer mistook him for a tramp as he wandered outside the city of Baden. Placing him under arrest, the officer must have rolled his eyes as Beethoven loudly protested, indignantly declaring his identity. He almost had to spent the night in jail, but a local musician came to his rescue, identifying the unkempt vagrant as the great Beethoven.

This composer may have been misunderstood by the world, but he knew that he was understood by his Maker. He once wrote, "I have no friend; I must live by myself. I know, however, that God is nearer to me than others. I go without fear to Him; I have constantly recognized and understood Him." To his friend, the Grand Duke Rudolf, Beethoven wrote, "Nothing higher exists than to approach God more than other people and from that to extend His glory among humanity."

Beethoven also knew how to pray, and his relationship with God was deeply personal: "In whatsoever manner it be, let me turn to Thee and become fruitful in good works." In the midst of frustration and discouragement Ludwig van Beethoven turned to God to make sense out of life's unfairness: "Therefore, calmly will I submit myself to all inconsistency and will place all my confidence in Your eternal goodness, O God! My soul shall rejoice in Thee, immutable Being. Be my rock, my light, forever my trust!"

The next time you are feeling lonely, listen to Beethoven's String Quartet, Op. 135, and think about Beethoven's comment that "God is nearer to me than others." Ask God to be near to you and to help ease your loneliness.

"For I know the plans I have for you," declares the Lord, "plans to prosper you and not to harm you, plans to give you hope and a future."

—JEREMIAH 29:11

Millions have been uplifted by the beauty of Michael Card's music. Thousands have seen this talented performer in concerts all over the world. But few have noticed something peculiar about his excellent guitar technique. Although Card is naturally left-handed, he doesn't restring his guitar as other left-handers do; he literally plays a standard right-handed guitar turned upside down!

The reason for this unorthodox style? As a young boy in Nashville, he simply picked up a guitar in the way that seemed right for him. There was no teacher available to tell him otherwise, and the rest is history.

Even though he was without an instructor to correct or encourage him, Card continued to hone his talents. While working on a master's in biblical studies he wrote his first song, and much of his work is designed to present the power of Scripture through music. He asserts, "My songs are interpretations of the Bible." Card now has recorded almost twenty albums, including *The Final Word, Coram Deo, Unveiled Hope,* and a children's album, *Come to the Cradle.* Furthermore, he has composed well-known songs for other Christian artists, such as the moving "El Shaddai," made famous by Amy Grant.

Most of us could find excuses for not working with the gifts God has given us. Many are without money, or training, or contacts, or "the breaks," or . . . But others determine to persevere despite the odds and find a way to be used in the Lord's work.

Michael Card uses his music to share biblical truth. Ask God how you can best share His Word with someone you know.

"Be dressed ready for service and keep your lamps burning."

—LUKE 12:35

A professional bassoonist must be an expert in "being prepared." Julie Gregorian of the Baltimore Symphony Orchestra explains that even the different bassoon reeds are part of her preparation. She has many reeds for the different music she plays: some are best for staccato, legato, soft attacks, bright sound, dark sound, and different registers. Yet each reed requires hours of construction, scraping, and "playing in."

Gregorian's position in the orchestra is that of assistant principal bassoon. This means she has to prepare herself for parts that she may or may not actually play. "I am responsible for stepping in at the last minute in case of emergency. That means I must have a reed that is appropriate for the music and be familiar with the all the parts. If I only prepared myself for the pieces that I knew I had to play, I might find myself in a very uncomfortable position."

A typical example: Recently Gregorian was scheduled to play only one piece on the orchestra's weekly program. Nevertheless, she duly practiced all the Bassoon I parts one evening before going to bed. "Early the next morning, the phone rang and I quickly learned that my section leader had a bad case of the flu and the principal job was mine all week! It felt rewarding and exciting to be prepared."

Julie Gregorian's conclusion? "As Christians we prepare ourselves by reading and studying the Bible and 'rehearsing' how we should behave in hypothetical situations. However, how often are we prepared for what the Lord has in store for us? As each day unfolds, new and sometimes unexpected events occur. When Jesus calls us to serve, it is rewarding and exciting to be prepared!"

Only God knows your future. Pray that you will be prepared for what He has in store for you. And determine to do everything with all your might, as for the Lord.

*My brothers, if one of you should wander from the truth and some-
one should bring him back, remember this: Whoever turns a sinner from
the error of his way will save him from death and cover over a multitude of sins.*

—JAMES 5:19, 20

On this day in 1830, the young composer Frederick Chopin
(1810–1849) set off from his native Poland to captivate Europe with his
music. Only twenty years old, Chopin tearfully said farewell to his beloved
family. As his mother embraced him, she whispered, "Frederick, thou wilt be a
great musician. Thy Poland will be proud of thee."

His family had given him a strong heritage of Christian faith. Even while
Chopin lived in the salons of Paris, with temptation ever present, his parents
continued to pray. Their letters to him encouraged him through this difficult
time away from home: "Your old father and mother live only for you and pray
God every day to bless and keep you."

For a time this gifted musician was led astray by the notorious French
woman novelist who called herself George Sands. Their stormy romance caused
tremendous pain for both of them. When it finally ceased, Chopin's health,
which had never been strong, began to fail completely. His body rapidly gave way
to tuberculosis, which the medical practices of his day could do little to cure.

In the last few weeks before his death, the Abbe Jelowicki, who had known
the composer for many years, was sent for. This devout clergyman had spent
years praying for Chopin, and he now led him back to the Lord. After confessing
his faith in Christ, Chopin had four days of spiritual renewal. A few of his final
words were: "Oh, how good God is! I love God and man. I am happy so to die;
do not weep, my sister. My friends, do not weep. I am happy." He clasped a cross
and placed it on his heart, confessing his thankfulness: "Now I am at the source
of Blessedness."

*Many believers keep a "prayer list" of things and people they need to
pray for. Make such a list yourself—including your family members—and be
faithful to pray for them regularly.*

When a man makes a vow to the Lord or takes an oath to obligate himself by a pledge, he must not break his word but must do everything he said. —NUMBERS 30:2

Today's story should have had a happy ending, instead of a sad one. It concerns the opera composer Vincenzo Bellini (1801–1835), whose birthday is today. As a young but poor musician in Naples, Italy, he was hired to teach music to the daughter of the president of Italy's supreme court. Bellini and the girl, Maddalena, fell in love and wanted to marry.

Bellini knew that her famous father would never consent to his daughter marrying an unknown musician, so he worked with great diligence composing his first opera, *Adelson e Salvini*. After its successful production, the composer asked her father for her hand. Bellini was rebuffed by the great man, and the two young lovers were deeply grieved.

Bellini tried to encourage Maddalena, "Before I shall have written ten operas, your parents will be only too glad to offer me your hand." "It takes a long time to write ten operas," she said sadly. "Only a few years," Bellini answered, "and we are young and can wait." Each made vows never to belong to another.

Soon his second opera was performed with great applause, and Bellini moved to Milan. He wrote a string of fabulous operas that made him famous and wealthy. One day he received an excited letter from Maddalena informing him that her father had now given his consent to the marriage. Alas! The very operas that impressed the girl's father had gone to Bellini's head. His next opera kept him so busy that he scarcely bothered to answer her. They never met again, and Maddalena soon died of a broken heart. Bellini himself died at the age of thirty-three, a short time after the premiere of his tenth opera, *I Puritani*.

This love story is a rather extreme case of a broken vow, yet it illustrates the seriousness of staying true to one's word. Read Proverbs 12:19 and ask God for His strength to always stand by your word.

A rebuke impresses a man of discernment more than a hundred lashes a fool. —PROVERBS 17:10

Music is such a personal art form that it is often very painful to hear criticism of one's performance. Yet a truly fine musician realizes the importance of receiving good advice, and using it to improve. An interesting example of this can be seen in the life of the blind country singer and pianist Ronnie Milsap.

In the early 1970s, the young man was already making hit recordings. But he was still in the process of finding his own style. One day between Memphis recording sessions, Milsap sat at the piano and sang an old song—unaware that anyone was listening. When he finished, a man came forward and encouraged the singer with a number of compliments. But he also offered some advice: "Stop trying to sound like Elvis Presley."

Rather than taking offense at the stranger's meddling, Milsap thanked him and took this advice to heart. It was not until some time later that he found that his listener and critic had been Elvis himself! Milsap found his own style and recorded a string of number-one hits and won the Country Music Association's Male Vocalist of the Year award three times.

It is fascinating how one blessing can lead to another. In 1977, Milsap was voted CMA's Entertainer of the Year. When the blind singer accepted the coveted award, he gave a heartwarming speech praising the virtues of his wife. A penniless songwriter named R. C. Bannon was watching the ceremony on television from his mobile home. He was so moved by Milsap's speech that he wrote a song entitled "Only One Love in My Life." Later, this very song became one of Ronnie Milsap's greatest hits.

God truly does work in mysterious ways. We never know how our words—of encouragement or rebuke—might affect another person. Ask God to help you be careful with all of your words.

How well do you receive a constructive criticism? Memorize Proverbs 17:10, and remember it the next time criticism comes your way.

" 'The glory of this present house will be greater than the glory of the former house,' says the Lord Almighty." —HAGGAI 2:9

There is truth in the old saying: You have to break some eggs to make an omelet. Sometimes we must allow something to die before something far better can emerge. This was found true by several young Christian musicians as their band, Villanelle broke up and a new band was formed called Smalltown Poets.

Keyboardist Danny Stephens explains, "We completely started from scratch. New songs, a new style that was more in the modern rock vein than we'd been wanting to play, a new outlook, some new players. But more than anything else, a new commitment to excellence. God really laid it on our hearts that He wanted us to take our music ministry to the next level."

Part of that "commitment to excellence" is being obedient to God's call. "We really believe that God is a big God," asserts guitarist and singer Michael Johnston. "We've come to a point in our lives and with our dreams and our career that we don't want to limit God at all. He's given us a vision and opened our eyes to so many things that we would never have imagined. Obedience is at the core of everything we do."

By "everything," they don't simply mean their songs, but their entire ministry, their performances, and their relationships. "Our goal, whenever we leave a place, is that we want the audience to feel loved. We want them to know that our relationship with God is the most important thing in our lives. We want them to see that—not only from how we respond to them as a band, but by the way we interact with each other on stage."

Have you ever suffered a loss and later good came from that loss? What did you learn? Praise God for giving you a heart of wisdom.

The Lord turned to him and said, "Go in the strength you have."

—JUDGES 6:14a

When the Lord gave Gideon the above command, He illustrated a principle of leadership. The true leader must attempt the task even if no one else follows. A person who leads must not waver if those who follow are wavering. The leader must continue onward, with whatever strength he or she has at hand.

An amusing example of this occurred one night when jazz trumpeter Pee Wee Erwin and his band were scheduled to play on an NBC live radio broadcast from New York. The band was not due to perform for some time, so Erwin gave the members a break. He waited in the studio while the other musicians went downstairs and out into the night air.

There must have been some confusion about the time of the broadcast. Erwin was shocked to see the announcer suddenly give him the cue that meant they were on the air! The trumpeter quickly sent someone to look for his band, then he grabbed his trumpet and ran to the bandstand alone. Just then the announcer said, "And now, from Nick's in Greenwich Village, Pee Wee Erwin and his band."

To stall for time, Erwin said to the announcer, "What do you suggest?" His reply didn't help very much, "It's your show. What can you do?" The trumpeter suggested, "How about a few bugle calls?" The announcer rolled his eyes. "That's hardly Dixieland! What else can you offer?" As he racked his brain for ideas, he saw his band scrambling through the doors. Erwin smiled in relief. "Well, I'll start the theme song and we'll see if we can build a band over the airwaves." He remembers: "I went into the 'Tin Roof Blues,' the house theme, and by the end of the verse and the first chorus we had the full band—winded and flushed but complete, back on the stand."

If God is calling you into a position of leadership, He'll give you the strength and the people you need to accomplish your task. It may not seem that you have a "full band," but if it is His calling, the Lord will make it happen.

History has repeatedly shown how an idea, followed by action, has accomplished the impossible. If you have an idea and believe that it is from the Lord, "go with the strength you have." Perhaps you should consider starting a prayer group or Bible study with your friends.

He makes me lie down in green pastures, he leads me beside quiet waters. —PSALM 23:2

Joseph Henry Gilmore (1834–1918) wrote many fine hymns, but he was also a preacher and teacher at several seminaries. In the spring of 1862, when America was caught in the tragedy of the Civil War, Gilmore was preaching at the First Baptist Church in Philadelphia, Pennsylvania. At that time in his life, he was "especially impressed with the blessedness of being led by God, of the mere fact of His leadership altogether apart from the way He led us, and what He was leading us to."

After giving a sermon on this subject, he was invited to a friend's nearby home. Yet he could not stop thinking about this new revelation of God's leadership. Finally, "the blessedness of God's leadership so grew upon me that I took out the pencil, wrote the hymn just as it stands today, handed it to my wife, and thought no more of it."

That hymn, "He Leadeth Me," is still loved today. But it might have soon been forgotten had not his wife mailed it to a religious publication, the *Watchman and Reflector*. It printed the words, which were read and set to music by the renowned hymnologist William Bradbury. He published it without Gilmore's knowledge in the 1864 collection entitled *The Golden Censer*.

A few years after its publication, Gilmore was to preach in the Second Baptist Church in Rochester, New York. He arrived early, and, "on entering the chapel, I took up a hymnbook, thinking, 'I wonder what they sing?' The book opened at 'He Leadeth Me,' and that was the first time I knew that my hymn had found a place among the songs of the church." He first asserted that someone else added the refrain. But years later, "I found among my deceased wife's papers the original copy of the hymn, and was surprised to find that I wrote the refrain myself."

Psalm 23 is perhaps the most beloved chapter of the Bible and has inspired many songs. Compose your own melody to these words and thank your Shepherd for His loving guidance.

Do not be like the horse or the mule, which have no understanding but must be controlled by bit and bridle or they will not come to you.

—PSALM 32:9

Animals and musicians have worked together for years. The cat of Domenico Scarlatti (1685–1757) once walked across his keyboard and inspired the theme of his "Cat" Sonata. In 1947, a mockingbird perched on a flagpole near the National Symphony Orchestra's outdoor bandstand and insisted on singing along with the vocal soloists. Rather than object, the members of the orchestra voted to admit the mockingbird as an "honorary member" of the NSO.

Some animal stories are difficult to believe. In 1888, a Kentucky piano teacher claimed to have taught a monkey to play the piano. Supposedly the hairy student became so advanced that he managed to turn the pages of the music with his tail!

A bit more documentation is available for Anna, the operatic horse. For many years this faithful animal always pulled the triumphant chariot in the Metropolitan Opera's productions of Verdi's *Aida*. For years after her death in 1940, operagoers asserted that whenever one of the singers in *Aida* sang flat, the horse would neigh at the correct pitch to help them.

Perhaps the most ridiculous "musical animal" story concerns Sharkey the Seal. This creature was trained to play the song "Where the River Shannon Flows" on a series of horns for a national radio broadcast on March 6, 1941. Unfortunately, Sharkey never got the chance. The lawyers at ASCAP (the American Society of Composers, Authors, and Publishers) would not allow that song on the air, due to some obscure legal problem. Sadly, it was the only tune in the seal's repertoire, but at least Sharkey was still paid her fee of a few small fish.

God can speak to us and teach us through just about anything or anyone. What might God be teaching you through an animal in your life? If you don't have a pet, look up several Scriptures referring to animals, and see what examples they give us.

Though one may be overpowered, two can defend themselves. A cord of three strands is not quickly broken. —ECCLESIASTES 4:12

Since music is experienced through the sense of hearing, it seems the ultimate tragedy for a composer to become deaf, as happened to Beethoven. Yet would it not also be tragic to be a blind composer? Composing great symphonies requires notation, and the ability to write down the sounds inside you so that others can play them. How could this be done by a composer without the gift of sight?

This was the situation of the composer Joaquin Rodrigo (1901–1999), who wrote the most famous of all guitar concertos, the *Concierto de Aranjuez*—premiered on November 9, 1940. It has been performed and recorded by every classical guitarist imaginable; Christopher Parkening recently said that he has performed it more than one thousand times! Rodrigo composed still more for this genre: the *Fantasia para un Gentilhomme* (for guitar and orchestra), the *Concierto Madrigal* (for two guitars and orchestra), and the *Concierto Andaluz* (for four guitars and orchestra).

When people hear these wonderful and complex compositions, they are usually amazed to learn that Rodrigo had been blind since the age of three. How did he write down such large orchestral works? With the help of his wife, the Turkish concert pianist Victoria Kamhi. He dictated each note to her, and she painstakenly notated the entire orchestration, playing it back for him on the piano.

Without her patience and diligence, these masterful concertos would have never been heard. Doubtless there were times when she might have rather been practicing her own music instead of helping her blind husband. Yet it was her servant's heart—combined with her husband's genius—that gave the guitar world the pinnacles of their repertoire.

Find a recording of a Rodrigo guitar concerto (a library is a wonderful source for hearing all types of music). As you listen, close your eyes and enter Rodrigo's world. Say a prayer of thanksgiving for the gift of sight and hearing.

Jesus said to them, "The kings of the Gentiles lord it over them; and those who exercise authority over them call themselves Benefactors. But you are not to be like that. Instead, the greatest among you should be like the youngest, and the one who rules like the one who serves. —LUKE 22:25, 26

November 10, 1862, saw the Russian triumphant premiere of Verdi's dramatic opera *La Forza del Destino* in Saint Petersburg. By the time of this Russian premiere, Giuseppe Verdi (1813-1901) was the most famous opera composer in history, and his fame would equal that of many of the top movie stars of today.

Even the organ-grinders on the streets played the latest Verdi arias. Once the composer moved to Moncalieri and showed a visiting friend two full rooms of these hand organs. He explained, "When I arrived here, all these organs were playing airs from *Rigoletto, Travatore,* and my other operas from morning to night. I was so annoyed that I hired the whole lot for the season. It cost me about a thousand francs, but in all events I am left in peace."

Sir George Henschel, the founding conductor of the Boston Symphony Orchestra, was asked by the composer to mail him some musical scores. "Without the slightest suspicion of conceit or affection he said, 'Oh, simply address it, "Maestro Verdi, Italy." ' "

His quiet humility is best related by a friend who was with him after the overwhelming success of his opera *Otello.* While the audience was wildly applauding, "He appeared as the only restrained person in the theater. Rather than bursting with pride, Verdi was unruffled, though somewhat embarrassed by the continuing bedlam. Throughout the entire event, he was as composed as he is on a country walk." Giuseppe Verdi was called for an unprecedented twenty ovations that night, yet his expression was calm and unassuming throughout. Despite his renown, he remained humble.

Jesus is the ultimate picture of humility and servanthood, and His is an example we should try to follow in every area of our lives.

If at all possible, go to a performance of one of Verdi's operas. If that's not possible, find a recording of one to listen to. Ask God to give you such measure of humility in your successes.

Do everything without complaining or arguing, so that you may become blameless and pure, children of God without fault in a crooked and depraved generation, in which you shine like stars in the universe.

—PHILIPPIANS 2:14, 15

Peter Keynote is an outstanding violist with the New York Philharmonic. As a Christian, he is in a position to minister to many musicians and has found that many of his colleagues suffer from a bitter, critical attitude. "This attitude may be difficult for many people to understand and yet is a common ailment among symphony orchestra musicians. A critical spirit is common to all men, and yet as Christians we need to believe that our lives are guided by the Lord and that He is accomplishing His purposes."

As an illustration, Keynote cites his own experience. "I auditioned for the New York Philharmonic while in the doctoral program at the Juilliard School of Music. I had no idea why I was in the Philharmonic, other than I had won the audition and was playing in a world-class orchestra. Had 'I' really won the audition, or was this one of those divine appointments from the Lord?

"For me, I've had to learn valuable lessons about being thankful, humble, and content in all things. I've learned that the real joys in living lie beyond the inherent difficulties in one's life. For example, a problem with a coworker is actually an opportunity for leaning more heavily on the Lord and His strength. Late nights out each week, as hard as they can be on family life, can be a blessing in that there are added extra hours at home during the day. And there are opportunities each day for witnessing to the grace and love of our Lord and Savior, Jesus Christ.

"It is clear that the Lord is in control, and He puts us where He needs us, both for our own spiritual development and for the benefit of those He is calling to His Kingdom. I believe that the Lord has called me to this profession and that my job is to please Him in all that I do and to serve Him with the gift he has given me. With God at the helm, I can rest assured that my job is more than a job. It is a calling, and not one to be ignored."

To "do everything without complaining or arguing" is not natural for most of us. As you go through your day today, write down every time you complain about something. (Just becoming aware that we're complaining is the first step toward stopping.) At the end of the day, look over your list, then think of all that God has done for you and offer Him a prayer of thanks.

As a prisoner for the Lord, then, I urge you to live a life worthy of the calling you have received. —EPHESIANS 4:1

It is so very important to realize one's calling. We each have a universal calling to follow Christ, but we also have individual calls to specific service. Some of us, like singer/songwriter Jennifer Knapp, have a double call, both to serve the body of Christ at home and to serve on the mission field in other lands.

First, Knapp points out, "It's important to me in my ministry to the church to encourage the body of Christ not to forget our dependence on God. I've seen people around me lose their passion for God, even though they're in church. So that's an important thing for me to communicate, having that honesty with God, because that's what He wants."

Knapp's music ministry has already given her a Dove Award for New Artist of the Year. She believes that any rewards that come from one's ministry are proportional to one's obedience to the Lord. "It's great to feel that I've been obedient to God and to still be surprised by all the new ways that He keeps using that obedience."

Another way Jennifer Knapp is obedient to the Lord is in world missions— even with a concert schedule of up to two hundred performances annually. For four consecutive years she has done mission work in Eastern Europe. "It's important for me to remember that my first priority as a Christian is to serve, not to be served. Missions makes that really obvious, because I'm serving next to people who care more about my ability to use a hammer than my ability to use a guitar."

God cares more about our obedience than any of our abilities. Think of one specific area in which you need to be more obedient. Spend time praying about that area and obey the promptings of your heart.

"If only you would be altogether silent! For you, that would be wisdom." —JOB 13:5

On this day in 1868, the great Italian composer Gioacchino Rossini died. He was so loved that his funeral procession consisted of six thousand mourners, accompanied by four military bands and a chorus of four hundred voices. His many operas—such as *William Tell* and *The Barber of Seville*—dominated Europe for the first half of the nineteenth century and are frequently performed today.

Rossini was an amazingly prolific musician, with a number of curious habits. The composer Sir Arthur Sullivan once visited him and found him writing a short piece of music. Sullivan inquired what composition the master was working on, to which Rossini answered very seriously, "It's my dog's birthday and I write a little piece for him every year."

His generosity was well known, and unemployed musicians were constantly going to him for help. He usually gave them the money they needed, but some could be rather bothersome. On one occasion, a man interrupted the composer's rest and asked to audition for him. Rossini asked, "What instrument?" and was told, "The drum, monsieur! And if you would let me play for you . . ." "Oh, no thank you," replied the composer, "and besides, we have no drum here." The man was ready, "But I have brought mine with me."

Rossini resigned himself to the coming torture. The musician brought in a huge drum and announced, "I have the honor of playing for you the overture to *La Gazza Ladra.*" After playing the deafening roll which opens the overture, the percussionist said, "Monsieur, here are now sixty bars' rest. We will pass over them, and . . ." But Rossini insisted, "I beg you to do no such thing! Please count them!"

As a busy and successful composer, Rossini had a difficult time finding the rest he needed. Our ears and minds need times of quiet as well. Find a place of quiet today, and listen to what the Lord may say to you.

The heart of the discerning acquires knowledge; the ears of the wise seek it out. —PROVERBS 18:15

When you are still in school, it may seem that you will never get through. The years of schooling stretch so far that it is easy to forget the critical importance of education. Yet much of your adult life is determined by how well the foundation of knowledge has been established in early life.

A man who learned this rather dramatically is James Houston Davis, better known to country music lovers as Jimmie Davis. Born in 1902 in extreme poverty, Davis was one of eleven children of a Louisiana sharecropper. His parents had little money, but they did endow their child with an understanding of the way out of poverty: education.

Jimmie Davis walked two miles to school, usually singing the gospel and country songs he loved. One of the few lads in his impoverished area to finish high school, he somehow managed to continued his education at the Soule Business College in New Orleans and at Louisiana College in Pineville. It wasn't until college days that this youth ever saw a library, yet Davis persevered until he received a master's at Louisiana State University.

The result of this determination was lifelong. Many of his college bills were paid by singing on the side, and in 1935, he signed a contract with Decca Records. For the next decade, he recorded a number of hits, including the classic "You Are My Sunshine." In 1944, this became his campaign song as Jimmie Davis became Louisiana's governor. Later Hollywood made a feature film on the life of this poor sharecropper's son, who knew the value of a good, hard-earned education.

God gave us our minds. He expects us to use them.

Imagine what your life would be with no education. Go to the library and read Up from Slavery *by Booker T. Washington. Praise God that you live in a time when education is so accessible and when career choices are so varied.*

For you yourselves know how you ought to follow our example. We were not idle when we were with you. —2 THESSALONIANS 3:7

All of us need to be aware of our witness to the world. As Christ's ambassadors, we are His living portrait before the world, and our witness can have a great influence on the lives of others. Sometimes our best witness is one of hard work and diligence. If we commit ourselves to excellence for Christ's sake, the world can witness the integrity of the Gospel working in our hearts and lives.

After seeing a great orchestra perform, have you ever pondered how the standards of excellence have risen as high as they are today? In Mozart's time, the Mannheim Orchestra was considered one of the best merely because the members could all crescendo together! Even early recordings of the renowned Toscanini display mistakes that would never be allowed today. How has such progress been made?

The answer usually has to do with specific individuals who have a vision for excellence and will not compromise their standards. Once such musician was the composer/conductor Christoph Willibard Gluck, who died this day in 1787. Today he is best known for his opera reforms, but he also reformed the way musicians rehearse together.

At that time, the musicians in opera orchestras often had a slipshod approach to their work. Few operas had more than a cursory rehearsal and were seldom together with the singers. But Gluck often insisted that his orchestra repeat passages up to thirty times until they were perfected. He worked his performers harder than anyone had ever dared. The players respected rather than resented this practice, and by the end of Gluck's life, the musical standards throughout Europe had vastly improved—mostly due to his example.

We may not be able to change the world all at once, but by doing our best for God, and setting an example of a commitment to excellence, we never know whom we might influence.

Striving toward perfection should always be our goal, both musically as well as spiritually. Read Philippians 3:14, and set your heart on the goal of Jesus Christ.

For he grants sleep to those he loves. —PSALM 127:2b

On this day in 1905, Eddie Condon was born. This jazz great was more than just a guitarist and banjoist. He was a producer of fantastic concerts and a promoter of what came to be called the Chicago style of jazz. Everyone knew Condon as a "down to earth" fellow with no pretensions. When asked about the "art form" of playing jazz, he answered wryly, "Canning peaches is an art form."

One of his unknown talents was discovered late one night at a hotel in Manassas, Virginia, when his band was playing in a jazz festival in that city. Condon's hotel room was between the rooms of his friends Al Rose and Bob Greene. Rose relates, "I'd gotten a full hour of shut-eye when a sudden loud and eerie noise set me rigidly upright in bed. I deduced that someone had broken into Condon's room and was in the process of pulling his fingernails out."

Rose put on a bathrobe and raced into the hall. Bob Greene had also left his room on the same errand. They tried the knob to Condon's room but it was locked. They knocked loudly, but the horrible sounds continued. They were preparing to break down the door when they saw Condon's wife, Phyliss, coming down the hall with an overnight bag. She greeted them with a cheery, "Good morning, boys. Trouble getting to sleep?"

"Eddie's in trouble!" they shouted, but she only smiled. "No, he's all right." She explained, "He's just singing. He sings in his sleep." She then explained that he always had to rent an extra room for her at hotels so she could get some sleep—which was never possible near her husband's "concert."

Have you ever been deprived of sleep? Stay up an hour later tonight, or get up an hour earlier tomorrow, and see what a difference even one hour can make in how you feel. Thank God that He gives you the precious gift of sleep.

Resist the devil, and he will flee from you. —JAMES 4:7B

On this day in 1912, the Russian composer Igor Stravinsky, "while having an excruciating toothache," finished his best-known composition, *The Rite of Spring.* Some years later he became a devout Christian and spoke very openly of his convictions. In an interview in Brussels, the composer stated, "The more one separates oneself from the canons of the Christian church, the further one distances oneself from the truth."

Stravinsky had strong opinions about the purpose and use of music. "The church knew what the psalmist knew: music praises God. Music is as well or better able to praise Him than the building of the church and all its decorations; it is the church's greatest ornament." When asked if one must be a believer to compose church music, Stravinsky attested, "Certainly, and not merely a believer in 'symbolic figures,' but in the Person of the Lord, the person of the devil, and the miracles of the church."

The composer certainly loved his Orthodox Russian Church, yet he wrote music for all denominations. Stravinsky wrote *Three Sacred Choruses* to be used in its liturgy, telling his friend the work was "inspired by the bad music and worse singing in the Russian church." Harboring no sectarian prejudice, he also wrote a Catholic mass which, he believed, "appeals directly to the spirit." Other works based on sacred texts include *The Flood, The Tower of Babel, Abraham and Isaac, Requiem Canticles, Sermon, A Narrative and a Prayer, Threni, Canticum Sacrum,* a *Credo,* an *Ave Maria,* and a *Pater Noster.*

In his work, Stravinsky found expression for his views on Christian doctrine. He seemed especially preoccupied with the nature of evil, writing, "As Satan's falsetto aria with flutes is a prolepsis of Christianity, Satan must now be shown as anti-Christ." Stravinsky continued to make a thought-provoking theological observation, noting that Lucifer is "inclined to take his position for granted, which is why true Christians can overcome him."

Stravinsky spoke of the "canons of the Christian church." Read the Apostles Creed and ponder the fundamental truths of our Savior and His church.

To the weak I became weak, to win the weak. I have become all things to all men so that by all possible means I might save some. I do all this for the sake of the gospel, that I may share in its blessings.

—1 CORINTHIANS 9:22, 23

Mark Mohr is a musical missionary to a difficult mission field. After coming to Christ at the age of seventeen, he became the founder of the world's first Christian reggae band, named Christafari. He decided that he needed to get a foundation for his ministry with solid biblical training. "Some of the best advice I was ever given was to go to Bible college so that I could be theologically and doctrinally sound," he recalls.

Such training has proved essential, as Christafari primarily performs in secular surroundings for unbelievers. For example, Christafari was the first Christian band to be featured on the Reggae Sunsplash Tour. Now Mohr has become an ordained minister, and he has written excellent materials for the reggae crowd, clearly pointing to Christ as the Messiah. For this Mohr is often persecuted by the very ones he is trying to reach.

Once in a Cleveland hotel lobby, a reggae artist from Jamaica attacked Mohr for his stand on Christianity. Mohr was punched in the neck and then slashed with a knife. Police were soon on the scene, but Mohr declined to press charges. "I felt the Lord leaning on my heart," he asserts, "that I could not expect (his attacker) to understand the God of forgiveness and grace if I did not first demonstrate that myself."

For those Christians who may wonder at the appearance of Mohr and his band—complete with reggae dreadlocks—he refers them to 1 Corinthians 9:22. He states, "In that passage Paul says, 'I have become all things to all men so that by all possible means I might save some.' That's why we wear our dreads. That's why we play this kind of music. They gain us access to a lot of places other people can't go. And once we're there, we preach that Jesus Christ is the only Way."

Take a moment to pray for Mohr and the members of Christafari—for their protection, strength, and courage to share the truth of the Gospel.

Finally, brothers, whatever is true, what is noble, whatever is right, whatever is pure, whatever is lovely, whatever is admirable—if anything is excellent or praiseworthy—think about such things. —PHILIPPIANS 4:8

Christina Smith was appointed principal flutist of the Atlanta Symphony Orchestra in 1991, fulfilling her lifelong dream to play in a great orchestra. A native of Sonoma County, California, she began her flute studies at the age of seven. By the time she was fifteen, she was already appearing as a soloist with major orchestras. When she graduated from the Interlochen Arts Academy in 1989, she claimed the academy's highest honor, the Young Artist medal. After only two years at the Curtis Institute of Music, she won her principal position in Atlanta.

Smith gives God the credit for her amazingly successful career. In demand at many secular music festivals, she still finds time to play and teach at the Christian Performing Artists' Fellowship's MasterWorks Festival. "Music has always been a way for me to praise God," she explains. "I played in my church choir every Sunday for about fifteen years, and this has given me a great perspective on music as it relates to Christianity and life in general."

Playing principal flute in a major orchestra when you are scarcely in your twenties can be very stressful. How does Smith deal with the stress levels all around her? "I was given a note with Philippians 4:8 printed on it. I keep it in my flute case, and look at it every day and before every rehearsal. It helps to keep negative thoughts away and gives me the peace of Christ."

Christina Smith is now passing on her Christian principles to the next generation of young flute players. "I have had some wonderful moments sharing with several of my students. Whatever particular aspect of music they are struggling with—from technique to performance to progress—when I try to encourage them, I always come back to the real reason I play music: to glorify God and to develop and share the great gift He has given me."

Make a list of the stress factors in your life. Read Philippians 4:8. Now make a list of the positive factors in your life, those that are "true, noble, right, pure," etc. Think on those things!

"A student is not above his teacher, but everyone who is fully trained will be like his teacher." —LUKE 6:40

Today in 1864 saw the premiere of the Mass in D Minor by the Austrian composer Anton Bruckner (1824–1896). His powerful music is now loved by millions, but he was very unappreciated in his own time. He once admitted, "They want me to write in a different way. I could, but I must not. Out of thousands I was given this talent by God, only I. Sometime I will have to give an account of myself. How would the Father in Heaven judge me if I followed others and not Him?"

This gentle composer was deeply loved by his music students. They knew that the public had generally rejected his music in favor of Wagner's and that Bruckner had despaired of ever receiving the recognition he deserved. So they found an amusing way to encourage their teacher, using his dog, who was named Mops.

While Bruckner was away, his students "trained" the dog. One of them relates how "we would play a motif by Wagner, and as we did so, would slap Mops and chase him. Next we would start Bruckner's *Te Deum,* and while this was playing we would give Mops something to eat. He soon showed a convincing preference for the *Te Deum!"* After considerable training they were ready for their fun.

One day the students said to Bruckner how much better his music was than that of Wagner: "Why, even a dog would know that you are a greater composer than Wagner!" As their astonished teacher watched, they played the Wagner melody and the dog howled and ran out of the room. Then they played Bruckner's *Te Deum,* and Mops returned wagging his tail. It was soon clear what they had done, but their teacher was deeply touched by their loyalty. The love that he had always shown his students had come back to touch him.

This story illustrates how a prank can be used to encourage rather than to humiliate. Think of a humorous way to bless a member of your family.

I long to see you so that I may impart to you some spiritual gift to make you strong—that is, that you and I may be mutually encouraged by each other's faith. —ROMANS 1:11, 12

Steven Curtis Chapman's many songs have encouraged millions of Christians around the world. His vibrant faith finds expressions in his public performances, and he has particularly inspired the young believers of America to be strong in the Lord. One day, he himself received a new lesson in encouragement.

Chapman was invited by Chuck Colson, the founder of Prison Fellowship, to visit Michigan State Prison. They were to meet a man who had become a Christian fourteen years before when he had arrived on death row. As they walked through the rows of hardened criminals, Chapman determined to bring an encouraging word into this troubled atmosphere. He later explained to *CCM Magazine*:

"Then we came around a corner, and it was like a blinding light in the midst of this death row. We came around to this cell, and this guy's smile just blinds me. He comes up real close to the bars and says, 'Chuck Colson! I heard you guys were coming! I'm so excited, I've just been praying!' He's got his Bible open and he says, 'Man, I've been praying for you guys. Ya'll just be string out there! It's hard out there! I know it's got to be hard to follow God out there on the out-side, but you just keep singing to people about Jesus!'

"It was unbelievable!" Chapman remembers, "It just blew my mind. I was thinking, 'Wait a minute! We're supposed to be coming to encourage you, and you're sitting there encouraging us!' "

Sometimes we may feel that we are always on the "giving end" of things. But the Lord has ways of giving back to us, to keep us from growing weary. Even as we determine to give to others, God will arrange others to give to us—as He did for Steven Curtis Chapman, whose birthday is today.

Do you feel that you aren't in a position to be able to encourage some-one else? Take example from this story: even a man who was on death row was able to encourage others in a profound way. Now, who can you encourage today?

It is not good to eat too much honey, nor is it honorable to seek one's own honor. —PROVERBS 25:27

A most unique composition in music history was premiered today in 1928. Maurice Ravel's Bolero, which the composer whimsically called "a piece for orchestra without music," is played by every major orchestra today. It is a seventeen-minute crescendo based on a single theme without development, but with a fantastic orchestration. In a classic understatement, the composer modestly said, "Once the idea for using only one theme was discovered, any conservatory student could have done as well."

Ravel was a quiet musician who did not put himself forward or concern himself with the opinions of others. An interesting example of his humility concerns the premiere of another of his pieces, the *Values Nobles et Sentimentales*. It was placed in an unusual concert in which the program concealed the composers' names for each piece that was performed. The audience was to hear each work and guess the identity of the composers.

After hearing the *Values Nobles et Sentimentales*, the audience was divided. Some thought that Ravel had composed it, while others believed it to be by Satie, Kodaly, Selva, Szanto, or other lesser-known composers. Ravel himself remained completely calm and showed no reaction to the other listeners.

Near Ravel were a number of his most loyal supporters. They agreed among themselves that the *Values Nobles et Sentimentales* was surely by a different composer. In order to show their fidelity to Ravel, this group unwittingly began to jeer his own composition. It must have amused him inwardly, but the modest musician displayed no outward emotion whatsoever at this strange reception to his new piece.

We need to be loyal to our friends, not for what they accomplish, but for who they are. Write a letter or e-mail a friend you haven't seen in a while, and give that person an encouraging Scripture to read.

Let us run with perseverance the race marked out for us.

—HEBREWS 12:1B

Since musicians and athletes carefully use their bodies in their work, they are especially vulnerable to a career-shattering injury. It is very difficult to fully recover from an injury and to keep life going as before. How much worse to try and keep going after having been severely injured twice.

Dave Dudley would eventually have a thriving career in country music, but he began his adult life in the world of baseball. His fastball and his curve were phenomenal, and he was soon in the major leagues. Just when it seemed that baseball would be his life, a serious arm injury abruptly stopped his dreams. After all the high expectations, Dudley needed a new career.

An old friend remembered that the fastball pitcher had always played guitar and asked him to perform on a local radio station. This was such a success that Dudley was soon given his own show. Forming a trio, he began to record and to attract the attention of the country music world. By 1960, he was on the verge of receiving a major contract when he was hit by a car. Bedridden for six months, he must have wondered if the baseball disaster would be repeated.

By the time Dudley recovered, the contract possibilities had evaporated. Again he was forced to start from scratch. After playing a series of small venues, he discovered a song he liked and found a studio to record it at his own expense. This song, "Six Days on the Road," became very popular with truckers, who told their friends about it. Radio stations found their phones deluged with requests. Without the advantages of a major label or publicity agency, Dave Dudley's homemade recording became an overnight hit and spent twenty-one weeks on the national charts. It had been worth the perseverance.

There are many ways in life that God wants us to persevere—in relationships, in studies or work, in taking care of our bodies. The most important, however, is our spiritual perseverance and developing our relationship with Him. How persevering are you?

David was told that he would be king of Israel. Yet in the years that followed, he had to conquer many discouraging obstacles. Read 1 Samuel chapters 20–24, noting each obstacle he had to overcome. Ask God for that same spirit of determination.

Now the tax collectors and "sinners" were all gathering around to hear him. But the Pharisees and the teachers of the law muttered, "This man welcomes sinners and eats with them." —LUKE 15:1, 2

Jesus often shocked the "religious" people of his day by showing love to the unlovable and being a friend to the sinner. A Christian band that follows in His footsteps is called Grammatrain, and it reaches thousands in its concerts who would not normally attend a church meeting. A key to Grammatrain's success is its insistence upon high standards—both musical and spiritual.

For example, look at the words to its songs. Guitarist and vocalist Pete Stewart maintains, "I'm very dissatisfied with unclever lyrics. I rewrite them until I feel like I'm not gonna be ashamed of them later. We put so much effort into our music that to not put an equal effort into the lyrics would be a horrid crime. The message of Christianity deserves so much more than a mindless little cliché that rhymes. It's the most important and inspiring message of all time, and it deserves the most thoughtful and inspiring lyrics we can produce."

The members' heart for souls comes directly from their life experiences. Drummer Paul Roraback tells his story, which should convict each of us: "When I became a Christian, when I started to turn my life around for the Lord, I came out of a group of people who were stoners, smoked weed, did mushrooms and stuff. And I went to a youth group and it was the loneliest time of my life, because my pot-smoking friends wouldn't hang around me because I was a Christian, and these so-called new 'Christian' friends wouldn't hang out with me because I had long hair and I was definitely different from them.

"That was the hardest point in my life, hanging on to my Christianity, because I really had to make sacrifices. And I think some of the things we sing about reach out to those people who are going through that stage where they're not feeling loved by other Christians. We want them to know that they are being let down by people, but God will never let them down."

Have you ever been disappointed by a friend? At some time, we all have been let down by others. If you are still hurting from such an experience, ask God to fill your heart with His forgiveness.

"Do not judge, or you too will be judged." —MATTHEW 7:1

On November 25, 1960, a daughter was born to Gloria and Burton Paine Grant who would become a teenage sensation. The release of her first album, simply entitled *Amy Grant,* made her an immediate success. After the resounding sales of the album *Age to Age,* with its megahit "El Shaddai," Amy Grant became the undisputed queen of contemporary Christian music throughout the 1980s.

Later, she believed that God was calling her to expand into the secular world instead of just serving within Christian circles. She was not in any way renouncing her deep faith, but simply felt called to reach out beyond the walls of the church. She once explained, "I see myself as a sort of combination performer and evangelist. I hope people enjoy my singing, but at the same time their lives are affected by the words."

Nevertheless, some of the reactions by the Christian public were very negative, revealing that her former fans felt somewhat betrayed by Grant. Others were outraged at what they considered a lowering of moral standards, yet few took the time to listen to her unwavering witness for Christ. Once she was challenged by a well-meaning young father who gave her a bouquet of flowers with a note reading, "Turn back. You can still be saved if you repent what you've done." The singer was soon in tears. Yet she courageously continues to produce music from her heart, which is loved by thousands of believers and unbelievers alike.

Have you ever been accused or condemned unjustly? It is extremely painful, but our reaction can be a gauge of our spiritual maturity. Do we fight back? Or do we trust that God will bring us through? After those times, we should remember the pain so that we won't do the same and will avoid the temptation to condemn others.

Make a list of anyone you know whom you do not like very much. Write down your reason(s) for not liking them. Ask yourself: Is this just? Is this showing the love of Christ? Now find a practical way to bless those on your list.

For who is God besides the Lord? And who is the Rock except our God? —PSALM 18:31

On Christ the solid Rock I stand,
All other ground is sinking sand.

The words of this grand hymn were written by Edward Mote (1797–1874). This Londoner was not raised in a Christian environment, as he recalls vividly, "My Sabbaths were spent in the streets at play. So ignorant was I that I did not know there was a God." Fortunately, someone cared enough to take the youth to church. Under the preaching of John Hyatt, Mote gave his life to Christ and began writing hymns to celebrate his newfound faith.

In 1834, he felt compelled to write a hymn on the "gracious experience of a Christian." After finishing the first four verses, he met a friend, Brother King, "who informed me that his wife was very ill, and asked me to call and see her." Mote visited their home before their church service and was told that the couple always sang a hymn before church. When Brother King could not find his hymnbook, Mote offered, "I have some verses in my pocket. If you like, we could sing them."

The two men sang the new hymn and the dying woman enjoyed it so much that Mote was impressed to publish the verses. This has become one of his best-loved hymns. In 1852, Mote entered the Baptist ministry full-time and pastored a large, growing congregation.

Through his efforts, a beautiful new church was built, and his congregation expressed its appreciation by offering him the deed. He answered, "I do not want the chapel; I only want the pulpit. And when I cease to preach Christ, then turn me out of that!" Just before his death, Edward Mote again spoke of the solid Rock: "The truths I have preached I am now living upon; and they will do to die upon."

God is referred to as "the Rock" in both the Old and New Testaments. Write a paragraph on what this image means to you.

Great peace have they who love your law, and nothing can make them stumble. —PSALM 119:165

Wes and Shannon Nance have learned to pray their way through many an audition. Meeting as students at the Eastman School of Music, today they both play in the Rochester Philharmonic Orchestra. But the audition process was very grueling, as Wes recalls: "Ask any orchestra musician, and they will tell you how much they loathe auditions. Whether you are behind the screen, or on stage with the committee and the music director, it's hard to play your best at an audition, let alone to have fun and enjoy playing your instrument."

God taught them both something very real at Shannon's audition. "Shannon was warming up for the first round and was quite nervous, even shaking a bit in her bow arm and left hand—not good for a violinist! I felt God quietly ask, 'What are you afraid of?', and I asked Shannon that question. There were several answers: afraid she wouldn't play well, that she'd be embarrassed, but also intimidated by the committee—many of whom knew her and had high expectations."

Wes turned to Psalm 119 and read the entire psalm aloud. Many of its comforting promises spoke to them, and when he got to verse 165, the peace of God descended on Shannon: "Great peace have they who love your law, and nothing can make them stumble." Her hands stopped shaking and she went on to win the audition.

Which was more important, the job or the lesson learned? Wes states, "The end result was much less important than what God had spoken to both our hearts during the audition process. To this day neither of us will forget what God taught us through one psalm in a tiny practice room at the Eastman School of Music."

Psalm 119 is almost a love poem between the psalmist and God's Word. Read the entire psalm, writing down particular verses that have strong meaning for you. Thank God for His continual support and peace.

Fix these words of mine in your hearts and minds.

—DEUTERONOMY 11:18a

On this day in 1829 was born Anton Rubinstein, one of nineteenth- century Russia's greatest pianists. He founded the Imperial Conservatory in Saint Petersburg, while his brother Nikolay founded the Moscow Conservatory. Anton Rubinstein was not only an extraordinary pianist, but also a conductor, teacher, and a prolific composer. The conductor Hans von Bulow called him "the Michelangelo of Music."

Rubinstein was one of the first internationally known musicians to tour America. In 1872–73, he gave 215 recitals in the United States, including many concerts in the Old West. He remembered with amusement one such performance in a cowboy town used only to traveling minstrel shows. An hour before the concert, a worker (who had no idea what a concert pianist was) stuck his head into Rubinstein's dressing room and said, "Don't you think, boss, it's about time to have your face blacked?"

One aspect of Rubinstein's recitals that astonished his audience was his practice of performing without music in front of him. With his phenomenal memory, he performed 140 major works for piano from memory—a feat that has never since been attempted. The thousands of notes were truly fixed in his heart and mind.

If a person can put such time and effort into memorizing pieces of music, shouldn't we work to fix God's Word in our minds and hearts? Millions of Jews have memorized whole books from the Pentateuch, and their reward has been great blessing. Let us follow this example and "hide God's Word in our hearts."

Do you think you could memorize an entire chapter of Scripture? Certainly you can, one verse at a time. Start with the short but wonderful first chapter from the letter of 1 John—only ten verses!

We want each of you to show this same diligence to the very end.

—HEBREWS 6:11a

Today is the birthday of Gaetano Donizetti (1797–1848), known for his many comic operas. He composed almost seventy operas, and many are still performed today. Yet with all his success, this composer kept both a humble spirit and a sense of humor. When asked which of his operas he thought was the best, he answered, "How can I say which? A father always has a preference for a crippled child, and I have so many."

Donizetti must surely rank as the fastest composer in history. His finest masterpieces seldom took more than a week for him to compose. He was once asked by the conductor Sir Charles Halle whether it was true that the composer Rossini wrote *The Barber of Seville* in two weeks. Donizetti, thinking that this would be a long time for composition, answered, "I quite believe it, he has always been such a lazy fellow." The conductor recalled, "I confess that I looked with wonder and admiration at a man who considered that to spend a whole fortnight over the composition of an opera a waste of time."

Donizetti was so diligent in his work that people would come to him for help in emergency situations. When a theater manager in Milan was let down by another composer, he immediately asked Donizetti. Explaining that he needed an opera in two weeks, he begged the composer to rework an older work. Donizetti shot back, "Are you making fun of me? I am not accustomed to patching up my old operas, let alone another composer's. I'll give you a new opera in fourteen days."

His librettist, Felice Romani, was sent for. "I'll give you one week to prepare the text. It must be set to music within fourteen days. Let's see which of us has guts!" The challenge was accepted, and the result, *L'Elisir d'Amore,* is often called Donizetti's greatest work.

Are you known as a fast worker? The next time you have a "time crunch," spend a moment in prayer to God, who never gives us more than we can handle.

One of the servants answered, "I have seen a son of Jesse of Bethlehem who knows how to play the harp. He is a brave man and a warrior. He speaks well and is a fine-looking man. And the Lord is with him." Then Saul sent messengers to Jesse and said, "Send me your son David, who is with the sheep."

—1 SAMUEL 16:18, 19

Have you ever wondered whether young David was nervous the first time he was asked to play before the king of Israel? He had no idea of his future, that this king would become his enemy and that he eventually would be king himself. David was simply a young boy suddenly thrown into the courts of the high and mighty. It took courage to play those first harp pieces.

Many centuries later, another young musician named Shelly Manne had a similarly intimidating experience. Still a teenager, he had played drums for only a year when he was asked to substitute for the professional drummer Dave Tough, who was ill. The club was named Hickory House in New York, and Manne was thrilled to have such an opportunity at a "real" job.

It happened that the great Benny Goodman went to the Hickory House that night to hire Dave Tough for an important performance in Washington, D.C. the next day: the President's Ball. But Goodman found that Tough was sick, listened for a while and then left. While the band was taking a break, young Manne was called to the phone. He was shocked to find that it was Benny Goodman himself.

"Yes, Mr. Goodman," he stammered. "You wanna go on the road with my band?" the voice said. Manne almost dropped the phone, but managed a "Sure!" He was told where to meet them at the train station. Manne remembers his first meeting with the historic band. "Here they come: Cootie! Georgie Auld! Charlie Christian! Helen Forrest! Man, I was really going berserk! I was scared!"

On the train, the agitated drummer was approached by Benny Goodman. "What are you worried about, kid?" "Well," Manne hesitated, "I haven't seen the music book or anything." "You've been listening to my music for years!" laughed Goodman and walked away. That confidence set Shelly Manne at ease, and the performance was a great success.

So much time and energy is wasted when someone is nervous. Memorize Philippians 4:6, 7. Concentrate on these verses when you are in a similar situation.

Delight yourself in the Lord and he will give you the desires of your heart. —PSALM 37:4

Being the principal cellist in a major orchestra is a tremendous challenge. Anne Martindale Williams, who has this position in the Pittsburgh Symphony Orchestra, has learned to take her challenges to the Lord. One particular problem she had to recently face is one common to all string players: the overwhelming price of fine string instruments.

"I had found the 'cello of my dreams,' " Williams explains. "The only problem was that it was very expensive—almost three times the cost of my house!" (If this seems unbelievable to nonstring players, consider that some Stradivarius instruments cost well over one million dollars.)

Months passed as the financial matters were worked out. The loan details were settled, yet the only way Williams could have the new cello was to trade in her old one. A string player can become very close to her instrument; she had played this one for years. "This was the cello bought for me in college by my parents—which I would really miss!" she explained. Nevertheless, she agreed to the painful trade-in deal.

Yet God had a better way, as Williams remembers, "On the way back from Chicago (where I had reluctantly turned in my instrument) I stopped to visit friends on a beautiful farm in central Pennsylvania. I told them how sad I was to have to trade in my cello in order to purchase the wonderful new one. Can you believe it? Right on the spot, they said that they would like to give me a check in order to buy back my cello—it was redeemed!" Anne Martindale Williams concludes: "The Lord truly supplies all our needs in the least expected ways!"

Can you imagine yourself in a major symphony orchestra? The next time you see one in performance or rehearsal, take a moment to pray for the musicians—that God will use the beauty of music to bring them closer to the Lord.

Make it your ambition to lead a quiet life, to mind your own business and to work with your hands, just as we told you.

—1 THESSALONIANS 4:11

Franz Schubert (1797–1828) spent most of his short life destitute and struggling. Born in Vienna to a penniless schoolmaster and his wife, Schubert never received a thorough musical education. But financial hardship never diminished his enthusiasm to compose. It is astonishing to see how many hundreds of compositions came pouring out of his imagination—songs, symphonies, chamber music, masses, and piano works, dozens of which are considered standard repertoire today.

Schubert often referred to his faith in his letters, acknowledging that his talents were a gift from God. In 1825, he wrote home describing the way worshipers responded to a new hymn he had composed. It "grips every soul and turns it to devotion," he wrote. Concerning his audience, he remarked that it "wondered greatly at my piety." He concluded, "I think this is due to the fact that I have never forced devotion in myself and never compose hymns or prayers of that kind unless it overcomes me unawares; but then it is usually the right and true devotion."

In 1816, Schubert began to keep a diary, noting odd thoughts that occurred to him in solitude. Mired in poverty, he once wrote, "A man endures misfortune without complaint, but he feels it the more acutely. Why does God endow us with compassion? The world resembles a stage on which every man is playing a part. Approval or blame will follow in the world to come." His daily difficulties must have turned Schubert's longings toward God: "It sometimes seems to me as if I did not belong to this world at all."

Yet his cheerful personality and strong work ethic kept him composing masterpiece after masterpiece. He even went to bed with his glasses on so he could begin working as soon as he awoke! When a friend once came into his room and saw it littered with manuscripts, Franz Schubert simply explained, "When I finish one piece, I begin another."

Play a recording of Schubert's music and ponder his faith as well as your own. Thank God for the gift of music and how it can inspire our devotion to God.

David also said to Solomon his son, "Be strong and courageous, and do the work. Do not be afraid or discouraged, for the Lord God, my God, is with you." —1 CHRONICLES 28:20a

On this day in 1908, the *Symphony in E-flat* by the English composer Sir Edward Elgar was premiered. Elgar was the first successful composer from the British Isles in over two centuries. This symphony was very well received, and the conductor Han Richer declared it "the greatest symphony in modern times, and not only in this country."

Elgar had a dream, an incredible idea. In the words of musicologist Percy M. Young, "It may be seen that Elgar chose to set to music virtually the whole of the New Testament—or at least so much of it as would with music give such total effect." The composer himself wrote, "It has long been my wish to compose an oratorio which should embody the calling of the Apostles, their teaching (schooling) and their mission, culminating in the establishment of the church among the Gentiles."

After many years of preparation, Elgar began this monumental project. The first part of the massive trilogy, *The Apostles,* appeared in 1903. Three years later, Elgar finished the second New Testament oratorio, *The Kingdom.* These two works are intricately linked. *The Apostles* is about the period when Jesus walked the earth and closes with His ascension; *The Kingdom* continues the story, telling of the church in Jerusalem. It was Elgar's intention that the two works be performed on consecutive evenings. Concerning the work's climactic *Great Commission,* Ian Parrott wrote, "Here the apostles, filled with zeal, go out into the world to preach, and the composer's music has the same urgency and exaltation."

Unfortunately, Elgar did not complete a third oratorio for his trilogy. Many years later, the last theme he ever wrote, however, was called "The Judgment," the name he had given the final part of the project. Sir Edward Elgar gives us an inspiring example of a man with a vision, and his great oratorios *The Apostles* and *The Kingdom* continue to move their audiences with the message of the Gospel.

Elgar's dream was to tell the story of Jesus Christ in music. How could you creatively tell the story in your own way? Write down a few ideas, and be prepared to tell this wonderful story to those around you.

But we have this treasure in jars of clay to show that this all-surpassing power is from God and not from us. —2 CORINTHIANS 4:7

When we see a successful performer or group of performers, we are usually unaware of the long road of getting to where they are today. Usually this road is filled with hard work, specific training, and tremendous perseverance. Although there may be turning points, the climb is generally a gradual one in which steadfastness of mission is a key ingredient.

The band known as Jars of Clay has traveled such a road. The name of the group is taken from the above Scripture. The members felt that such a name would help keep them humble, reminding them that all they have has come from God. They met when they were all majors in contemporary Christian music at Greenville College in 1993. They wrote a few songs for fun and to satisfy the requirements of a recording studio class.

One of them noticed an advertisement in *CCM Magazine* for a national talent contest. They were among the ten finalists chosen, and their performance on April 27, 1994, at the Gospel Music Association Spotlight Competition won them the grand prize. Record companies began to contact Jars of Clay, and the group members eventually signed with Essential Record. In 1995, the band took its first real tour and released its first album. The following year, a single named "Flood" became a number-one hit on both Christian and secular radio stations. The album itself sold over two million copies.

The mission for Jars of Clay remains consistent: "We want very much to be about ministry and sharing Christ. We see our music as a tremendous gift from God to help us do that." When asked to describe what is behind their songs, the members respond: "Christ our Savior, and how holy and blameless He is, the contrast of God and man; the whole image of the jars of clay, how fragile that is, how easily broken—yet God entrusts His Savior in us."

If you were to start a Christian group, musical or otherwise, what name would you choose? Think of your favorite Scriptures and write down a few possibilities.

"The Lord who delivered me from the paw of the lion and the paw of the bear will deliver me from the hand of this Philistine." Saul said to David, "Go, and the Lord be with you." —1 SAMUEL 17:37

Few musicians in history have had such a "David and Goliath" experience as violinist Arthur Hartmann (1881–1956). As a young man, he and his friend Rene Ortmans visited Eugene Ysaye (1858–1931), the most celebrated master of the violin. When they arrived, Ysaye was practicing from memory the *Violin Concerto in F* by Lalo, and the two younger musicians were enthralled with his playing.

Hartmann knew the composition very well and noticed that in a number of passages Ysaye played different notes than the composer had written. He was pondering this as Ysaye finished playing and demanded of him, "Well? What do you think?!" The youth remembers, "I was too confused to be able to say the right words and dreaded to contradict him. I blurted the words which accomplished just that! I answered, 'Oh, it is marvelous, only it isn't quite right. It isn't that . . . it isn't accurate.'

"What! he roared like a bull that has just been stabbed. Ysaye turned to the other violinist and bellowed, 'Rene, did you hear that? Rene, this pig has the effrontery to tell me that it wasn't right!' " Hartmann was mortified. Then Ysaye thrust his violin at him and yelled, "Rene, now you are going to see something! This pig is going to play the *Concerto in F* of Lalo for me!" Hartmann recalls that he was "paralyzed with terror as this infuriated Goliath towered over me."

No amount of apology would pacify Ysaye, so Hartmann reluctantly took the violin. Unprepared as he was, the young man began the concerto. Ysaye watched him closely, at first with menace, but more and more with approval. When Hartmann finished the first movement, the old master admitted, "He is right. I must look through the score a little after lunch." He gave Hartmann a slap on the back, and commented, "He is brave. He has talent. We will have lunch together."

What "Goliath" are you facing? Read what Jesus had to say about having a "mustard seed faith" to face such a Goliath (Matthew 17:20). Ask God to increase your faith in that situation, and live this day in confidence in Him.

Who are you to judge someone else's servant? To his own master he stands or falls. —ROMANS 14:4a

On December 8, 1950, the President of the United States, Harry S. Truman, wrote a letter to the *Washington Post* newspaper. It was addressed to Paul Hume, a music critic. He had given an unfavorable review of Truman's daughter, who had just performed in a recital. The President began, "Mr. Hume, I have just read your review of Margaret's concert. . . . Some day I hope to meet you. When that happens you'll need a new nose, and a lot of beefsteak for black eyes. . . ." Music critics don't always bring out the best in people.

One critic accidentally made a composer's career, however. When Jacques Offenbach (1819–1880) premiered the operetta *Orpheus in the Underground,* a powerful critic named Jules Janin told all of Paris that he loathed the work! He attacked *Orpheus* with such enmity that Offenbach must have been sick with heartache reading his newspaper. But the fury of Janin's critique had the opposite effect from that which the critic desired. Everyone had to see what had prompted such outrageous criticism, and soon every performance was sold out. Incidentally, the public disagreed with the critic; the people adored the music, and the incident made Offenbach rich and famous.

Perhaps the worst (of many) critic stories concerns the Russian composer Sergei Prokofiev (1891–1953). The music critic Leonin Sabaneiev reviewed the premiere of Prokofiev's *Scythian Suite* in Saint Petersburg. As you might imagine, the critic wrote a terrible review, telling all of Russia what a wretched piece of music he had heard.

This time, the critic had gone too far. You see, he didn't bother to attend the concert and made up everything in the review. What he didn't know was that at the last minute Prokofiev's composition was removed from the program and never played! The newspaper was forced to print a lengthy letter from the composer, explaining that the critic could not have known the music since it was not yet published and its only copy was in Prokofiev's hands.

There are many Scriptures that forbid us to judge our neighbor. Read Matthew 7:1, Romans 2:1, 14:13, 1 Corinthians 4:4, 5, and James 4:12. Ask God to cleanse you of any critical spirit.

Speak to one another with psalms, hymns and spiritual songs. Sing and make music in your heart to the Lord, always giving thanks to God the Father for everything, in the name of our Lord Jesus Christ.

—EPHESIANS 5:19, 20

In 1993, pianist Hugh Sung joined the faculty of the Curtis Institute of Music in Philadelphia and has since become its director of instrumental accompaniment. Sung has lived in the "City of Brotherly Love" for most of his life, making his debut as a concerto soloist with the Philadelphia Orchestra when he was only eleven. He entered the Curtis Institute as a student at the age of thirteen.

When asked how he became a Christian, Sung immediately tells of meeting a young girl, who later became his wife. "She was very sweet and outspoken. The first thing she said was, 'I am a Christian'—almost like she was rubbing it in my face! I was very sympathetic, saying, 'Well, I have been there, and I'm very open-minded.' For the first time, someone really answered my questions. In my church questions were considered rebellious and blasphemous. She tried to answer what she could, and when she couldn't, she honestly said, 'I don't know.'"

Since he became a Christian, Sung has been used by the Lord in a wide variety of areas. In the summers, he teaches and performs at the Christian Performing Artists' Fellowship's MasterWorks Festival and always has excellent advice for young Christian performers:

• Do what the Bible says: find a good church, a good fellowship with strong, biblically based teaching.

• Be grounded in God's Word. Be in a situation where you can consult with people who are mature and whose opinion you can trust.

• Work at what God has given you: there is no excuse for a lack of discipline. God will give you the wisdom to see where He has gifted you.

• Have the attitude that no matter where you are, no matter what situation God places you in, you can work for God's greater glory and enjoy Him through it!

Choose a favorite psalm and read it aloud. Try singing it. Now try singing the words, "Making music in your heart to the Lord." Praise God for the gift of music.

"He went to him and bandaged his wounds, pouring on oil and wine. Then he put the man on his own donkey, took him to an inn and took care of him." —LUKE 10:34

December 8, 1980, was a day when much of the music world was in shock. For on that day a deranged young man shot and killed John Lennon outside his New York apartment. The event prompted millions to remember the many songs Lennon and the other Beatles had made famous.

Fifteen years before this tragedy, the Beatles were the undisputed kings of the popular music world. Their latest movie, album, and hit song were each entitled "Help," and all were smash hits. The Fab Four were already wealthy men, and to their millions of fans it must have surely seemed that the Beatles had everything this world could offer.

Yet within all the publicity and concerts, the Beatles were just four men with problems and needs like anyone else. John Lennon later recalled that he was truly "crying out for help" when he wrote the song "Help." His plight will certainly sound familiar to many: he was depressed because of an inability to lose weight.

Lennon remembers, "You see the movie: He—I—is very fat, very insecure, and he's completely lost himself. And I am singing about when I was so much younger and all the rest, looking back on how easy it was. . . . I was fat and depressed and I was crying out for help."

And yet, who could tell? Of all the thousands around him, who knew about his pain? If only, during such a period of anguish, someone nearby could have responded with the love of Christ. This story represents millions of similar situations, where people around us seem happy on the outside, but internally are crying out for help. Are we sensitive enough to realize it? Are we ready to respond to the needs around us like the Good Samaritan in the opening Scripture?

Do you or someone you know suffer from a weight problem? Read 1 Samuel 16:7. Ask the Lord for the ability to see people (ourselves) as He does—from the heart.

Let us not become weary in doing good, for at the proper time we will reap a harvest if we do not give up. —GALATIANS 6:9

Most of us have been tempted to give up at one time or another. The goals we have before us may be many years from their fulfillment, and patience and perseverance are difficult to find. A key to reaching those goals, as seen in today's story, is to continue to do good in every situation we find ourselves in—even if that situation doesn't seem to have anything to do with the goals we seek.

The mother/daughter act of Naomi and Wynonna Judd has long been a staple in Nashville's country music scene. But in the early 1980s, they were simply more unknown singers trying to break into the music business. Songwriter Kenny O'Dell had written excellent material for them and the Judds had created a fine demo tape, but none of the recording labels showed interest.

With her music career on hold, mother Naomi Judd did some deep soul-searching. She had so much to give, but no musical outlet was in sight. So she decided to go back to the profession in which she was trained and accepted a job as a nurse at the Williamson County Hospital. She might not be singing, but at least in this way she could minister to those in need.

She was working one day in the emergency ward, when a girl was admitted who had been in an automobile accident. It happened that this was the daughter of Brent Maher, a top record producer at RCA. During the time that his daughter was recovering Naomi Judd was caring for her and eventually gave her a copy of the Judds' demo tape. A few weeks later, Brent Maher called and asked the Judds to sing for RCA. Soon the mother/daughter team had their long-sought recording contract, and the rest is history.

Naomi Judd pursued a dream and then laid it aside. God fulfilled it in a way she could not have predicted. Take heart if you have a dream unfulfilled, and read 1 Thessalonians 5:24.

"But you will receive power when the Holy Spirit comes on you; and you will be my witnesses in Jerusalem, and in all Judea and Samaria, and to the ends of the earth." —ACTS 1:8

A composer who took the above words of Christ very seriously was born this day in 1908—Oliver Messiaen. His innovative compositions and illustrious career were spent in the core of the secular music world. Yet without compromise, he used his compositions, his speeches, his teaching, his writings, and his interviews as an opportunity to be a witness for Christ.

Consider the opening of a typical speech he made in Amsterdam, given to a group of secular musicians: "I've been asked to deliver a confession of my faith, that is, to talk about what I believe, what I love, what I hope for. What do I believe? That doesn't take long to say and in it everything is said at once: I believe in God. And because I believe in God, I believe likewise in the Holy Trinity and in the Holy Spirit (to whom I've dedicated my *Messe de la Pentecote),* and in the Son, the Word made flesh, Jesus Christ (to whom I've dedicated a large part of my works)."

Messiaen spoke with the same conviction to music critics as he would have in a conversation with his church. Yet all of his biographers, including those who did not share Messiaen's faith, express a profound admiration for the uncompromising message of the man and his music.

Oliver Messiaen was a man with strong convictions concerning his Savior. He stated, "The Resurrection is the cause and the root of our hope." His emphasis was the central point of all Christian faith, Jesus Christ: "He appears to us—came to us and tried to make Himself comprehensible in our language, in our sensations, in our attitudes of mind. That's the most beautiful aspect of the Godhead: the mystery of the Incarnation, and that's why I'm a Christian."

Messiaen was excellent at his work and bold in his faith. In your current position—whether as a student or professional—how can you make known your faith in Christ? Write down several ideas and try one today.

For Christ's love compels us, because we are convinced that one died for all, and therefore all died. —2 CORINTHIANS 5:14

The breathtaking voice of Yolanda Adams is well known in gospel music today. Her versatile style results from a wide variety of influences, "everything from Stevie Wonder to Beethoven." But the secret of her convincing performances and recordings is in her supreme devotion to serving Christ.

Adams reminds us that we need to be focused on our specific calling. "If you are so busy trying to do everything for God, then you are out of your place. Because then you're doing someone else's job. And He never requires us to do someone else's job in order to get His stuff done because He's big! He's huge! He don't need your stuff—for real—to run His world. All He asks you to do is to be in place so you can serve and receive."

She is very clear on her own purpose, which is to bring the Gospel to those in the world. Adams recently said, "And I understand why it is so important to get the message out to everybody. Not just for a few people in the church walls, but for everybody hanging out of the church." When questioned if she has simply "gone secular" and left the fold, Adams is resolute: "Do they really think anything could change my love for God?"

It is her love for God that compels Yolanda Adams to bring her music to unbelievers who need to hear the Gospel. "I need to be in a place where my message can be heard by everyone. I understand my purpose. I understand what I was put here for. I take that on every day of my life."

We, too, need to focus on God's priorities for us. Pick up a pencil and prayerfully prioritize those things God has called you to do this year.

"Not everyone who says to me, 'Lord, Lord,' will enter the king-dom of heaven, but only he who does the will of my father who is in heaven." —MATTHEW 7:21

It is one thing for people to ask Jesus Christ to be their Savior. It is quite another for them to then make Christ their Lord, to dedicate them-selves fully to following Christ and striving to always do His will, as Jesus says in the above Scripture. This is the message of the Christian band known as Three Crosses, which began in 1994.

The two founders of this group, Steve Pasch and Ralphie Barrientos, both well understand the need to be a fully dedicated believer—because of their own backgrounds. Both were saved for some time before they truly turned all their lives and problems over to God. In their case, the sin that held them back was alcoholism, as Pasch admits, "I was saved in 1992, but it was two more years before I was totally broken and got dead serious about being sober. I asked the Lord to take the addiction from me, and He totally turned my life around."

God soon called them to deliver the message of serious dedication to Christ through their music. Both were already professional secular musicians, but their ignorance of the Christian music scene did not deter them. "We didn't know anything about Christian music. We just wanted to write songs to praise and honor God. We each were seasoned writers, but this felt very different from any-thing we had ever done . . . like God was really using us."

Hundreds of concerts and several albums later, Three Crosses is still being used to proclaim the Gospel. "God has given us a message for people who know who Jesus is but don't really know Him as their Savior. We can speak honestly to that situation, because that's where we came from." It is amazing to see how God uses us when we overcome our sins. We can help others to overcome their sins when we dedicate our lives to doing "the will of our Father in heaven."

Are you fully dedicated to serving Jesus Christ? Ask the Lord to reveal specific ways in which you can increase your dedication to Him.

But from everlasting to everlasting the Lord's love is with those who fear him, and his righteousness with their children's children—with those who keep his covenant and remember to obey his precepts.

—PSALM 103:17, 18

Most of us are so busy with today that we seldom ponder the yesterdays of our parents, grandparents, and all those who went before us. Yet their lives are a part of our lives, and all that they were helped to form what we are today. Whether we know much about our family heritage or not, each of us has roots in our ancestors—and how we live our lives will deeply affect our children and grandchildren, someday.

Janet Paschal, a beautiful voice in the CCM world, learned this lesson from her grandfather. "He was the first one in my family to accept Christ," she says proudly. "He was totally unbending. He chose to follow Christ. Period." The strong faith of this man continues to influence Paschal's ministry.

She tells of his Christlike life: "He, too, was a carpenter. He literally and figuratively built the little church I grew up in. He was always remodeling, adding to, and updating the tiny building that housed his evangelistic fire. But more than that, be built dreams and goals in the hearts of those of us who watched him drive nails and pour foundations. He erected a standard that we can only aspire to. He showed us the Gospel day after day, so it was only consequential that he preached it on Sundays."

This grandfather literally passed his faith on to "children's children," and has inspired her to do the same. Paschal declares, "I conclude simply that, for me, there is no other way but to follow Christ. To study Him. To pursue Him. He has carved a place in my heart that yearns for Him."

Spend some time thinking about your place in your family tree. Write down any important truths that were passed down to you. Now write what you desire to pass on to your children someday.

"Therefore go and make disciples of all nations, baptizing them in the name of the Father and of the Son and of the Holy Spirit, and teaching them to obey everything I have commanded you. And surely I am with you always, to the very end of the age." —MATTHEW 28:19-20

December 14 is the birthday of the renowned classical guitarist Christopher Parkening. He has a remarkable testimony. Parkening's career soared in his early twenties, with recordings, awards, and world tours making him a household name. Yet he began to feel an emptiness that fame and fortune could not answer. To the astonishment of the music world, he suddenly retired in his twenties. His only plans were to spend the rest of his meaningless days fly-fishing.

Parkening later came into contact with the claims of Jesus Christ and became a devout Christian. While learning about Christ, he began to wonder about the rest of his life. Surely God did not want him to spend it only fly-fishing. Concluding that his principle gift was music and that he should be using it for God's glory, Parkening dusted off his guitar and began to reenter the music world.

The result was tremendous, and almost immediately he found himself at the top of his field. Now he was using every opportunity to share the Gospel. After every master class, Parkening gives a time for the students to hear his testimony. His life has been used to touch thousands with the life-changing message of the Good News.

Why has God given us talents? Is it just to make money, to have an ego-driven career, to receive praise from others? Or is it to make us a useful vessel for the work of the Lord? Christopher Parkening has told me repeatedly, "We will be able to do many things in heaven, but the one thing that we will not be able to do in heaven is preach the Gospel—so we had better do it now!"

Think of a non-Christian you know who has similar talents or tastes as yourself. Invite that person to do something that you both enjoy, and ask God for a Spirit-led opportunity to share the love of Christ.

Like arrows in the hands of a warrior are sons born in one's youth. Blessed is the man whose quiver is full of them. They will not be put to shame when they contend with their enemies in the gate. —PSALM 127:4, 5

The great Czech composer Antonin Dvorak (1841–1904) did not fit the stereotype of the eccentric lone musician. After becoming world famous with such masterpieces as the *New World Symphony,* Dvorak remained a simple, modest family man. He cherished his wife and many children and savored their company even as he composed. Instead of retreating to the solitude of a private study, Dvorak often worked at the kitchen table. Surrounded by the aroma of bread baking in the oven and the din of children chasing noisily through the house, Dvorak accomplished some of his best composing.

A revealing picture of Dvorak's home life is given by a student who recalled, "His children were permitted to invade his studio at all times, even while the composer was at serious work. My daily lessons were usually taken with the accompaniment of grimacing boys and girls hidden behind articles of furniture, or appearing at unexpected moments in doorways out of their father's sight."

Perhaps a reason Dvorak had such a tender love of his family was because he endured the tragedy of having children who died young. His first daughter lived only two days. A few years later the Dvoraks had two children and suffered a double misfortune. Their ten-month-old daughter accidentally found a solution of phosphorus (used for making matches), drank it, and died. Less than a month later, their three-year-old son contracted smallpox and died on Dvorak's thirty-sixth birthday. The couple was left childless.

Happily, the Dvoraks had many other children, who were deeply loved. When abroad in his musical travels, the composer wrote letters to his children encouraging them to go to church often and "pray fervently." His love and pride in his children found their way into many letters to his friends, including the following announcement given with a new symphony to his publisher in 1885: "You might be interested to know that there is another new opus in our family (a boy)! So you see a new symphony and a boy as well! How is that for creative energy?"

What does it mean to be blessed? Look up the definition, then write a definition in your own words. Though you may not be blessed with children yet, thank God for all the blessings He has given you.

Though I walk in the midst of trouble, you preserve my life; you stretch out your hand against the anger of my foes, with your right hand you save me. The Lord will fulfill his purpose for me; your love, O Lord, endures forever—do not abandon the works of your hands. —PSALM 138:7, 8

Happy Beethoven's birthday! In music schools around the world, students and teachers alike are celebrating with "Ludwig parties." Anyone who has ever read Charles Schultz's wonderful "Peanuts" cartoons knows the piano player Schroeder walks around for weeks beforehand with a sign reading, "Only ___ more days until Beethoven's birthday!"

Unfortunately, this composer's life did not include many celebrations. As a talented but still unknown youth, Beethoven was mistreated and ignored. Once he visited Prince Lobkowitz and mentioned that he was in need of financial patronage such as Goethe and Handel enjoyed. He was told, "My dear young man, you must not complain. For you are neither a Goethe nor a Handel, and it is not to be expected that you ever will be." The humiliated composer turned away in silence.

Later in life, Beethoven's deafness also led to many painful incidents. When he tried to conduct a rehearsal of his *Symphony no. 7*, he got lost and the rehearsal fell apart. Everyone in the orchestra stopped playing, but the conductor, deaf and unaware of the problem continued to conduct. Finally, a friend scribbled a note: "Please do not go on; more at home." Beethoven read the note hastily, then raced out of the opera hall. He did not stop running until he reached his home, where he threw himself on the sofa and buried his face in his hands.

What does one do in such agonizing moments? Beethoven took his pain to his Lord. He had an intimate relationship with God and spoke about Him openly, even in an age that was becoming increasingly agnostic: "It was not a fortuitous meeting of chordal atoms that made the world; if order and beauty are reflected in the constitution of the universe, then there is a God." His own desire was to serve the Lord in peace. In an important letter, Ludwig van Beethoven expressed his hope of finding tranquillity and fulfillment in composing for "a small chapel" where he would dedicate his works to "the glory of God, the Eternal."

We need to turn to the Lord in our own times of trouble. Make a list of comforting Scriptures and post them where you can see them every day.

The shepherds returned, glorifying and praising God for all the things they had heard and seen, which were just as they had been told.

—LUKE 2:20

Have you ever heard of a macaronic? It is a song that combines two or more languages. The original text to the carol "Good Christian Men Rejoice," takes us all the way back into fourteenth-century Germany. It was composed of both Latin (the language of the church) and German (the language of the common people). The two languages intertwined throughout, created rather unusual combinations, as in the first two lines:

LATIN: "In dulci jubilo," (In sweet jubilation)
GERMAN: "Nu singet und seyt fro!" (Now sing and be joyful!)

According to an old legend, a Dominican monk named Heinrich Suso heard this song being sung by a band of angels. (These angels apparently spoke good German and Latin!) The monk was so enraptured by this sound that he joined with the angels in ecstatic dance. As one of today's most jubilant Christmas carols, it still animates those who sing or hear it.

This song has been popular for many centuries. The German composer Michael Praetorius (1571–1621) used the theme for several compositions. At a Moravian mission gathering in Bethlehem, Pennsylvania, in 1745, this hymn was sung in thirteen languages simultaneously. It was like Acts, chapter two, all using the same melody!

Good Christian men, rejoice With heart and soul and voice;
Give ye heed to what we say: News! News! Jesus Christ is born today!

Fortunately, those of us who are bewildered outside the English language have an excellent arrangement we can sing, too. The British musician John Mason Neale (1818–1866) produced the rendition that we sing today. His text combines the essence of both the Latin and the German and conveys the joy every Christian feels from the proclamation: "Christ is born today!"

Find a copy of "Good Christian Men, Rejoice" and sing the entire carol. Praise God for the gift He gave us at Christmas.

He who is kind to the poor lends to the Lord, and he will reward him for what he has done. —PROVERBS 19:17

On December 18, 1869, the American composer and pianist Louis Moreau Gottschalk died in Rio de Janeiro. His music was long forgotten after his death but has been discovered in the late twentieth century. His compositions are primarily for the piano, plus two rather exotic symphonies: *no. 1* is subtitled "A Night in the Tropics" and his *Symphony no. 2* is called "At Montevideo."

As this is the anniversary of his death, it should be mentioned that some newspapers apparently reported it a bit too early! An interesting letter survives in the composer's own hand: "I wish to speak of my death. This sad event took place in Santiago three months ago. I was carried off in three days by a frightful attack of black vomit. It is the newspaper of *Savana la grande* who tells it. But the *Revue de Villa Clara*, without doubt better informed, makes me succumb to an aneurism of the heart—which I much prefer, the aneurism being much more poetical than the vomit. I have written to these gentlemen, assuring them that I am still alive, and requesting them to publish my letter when it reaches them. The newspaper *Savana la grande* has already been at the expense of a lithograph of 'the deceased and ever to be regretted Gottschalk.' "

This talented musician played hundreds of piano concerts, up and down North and South America. In large cities, he often made arrangements for "monster concerts," so nicknamed because they used as many as fourteen pianos and twenty-eight pianists simultaneously! Nevertheless, his greatest fame was as a solo pianist.

In one of the many towns he performed in, a young lady who was seriously ill wanted to hear Gottschalk play. Her family met with the pianist after a concert and told of the girl's sickness. Immediately he arranged to have his grand piano taken to her humble home at his own expense. Louis Moreau Gottschalk played for hours near the enthralled girl's bedside, and she quietly died in rapture listening to the beautiful music.

There are always opportunities to be kind to the poor at this time of year. Get involved in a charitable project beyond tossing a few coins into a red kettle. Help deliver canned goods from a food drive or gifts to needy children. The Lord will thank you.

"Glory to God in the highest, and on earth peace to men on whom his favor rests." —LUKE 2:14

Some Christmas carols have been through several changes before reaching the form we now hear. Often, this process is helped by many different people, each adding his own contribution to create the final product. For instance, when Charles Wesley first penned the words to his popular carol in 1739, he called it "Hymn for Christmas Day," and the first line went, "Hark, how all the welkin rings!" ("Welkin" is an old English word referring to the heavens.) Fourteen years later, George Whitefield changed this line to the one we still sing, "Hark! the herald angels sing." Another minister, Martin Madam, changed the line, "Universal nature say, 'Christ the Lord is born today,'" to "With angelic hosts proclaim, 'Christ is born in Bethlehem.'"

Furthermore, it was more than a century later before Wesley's ten-stanza text would be sung to the tune we now recognize. When the song was first published in America (1857), the words had been set to the melody that is today associated with the hymns "Take My Life and Let It Be" and "Ask Me What Great Thing I Know." (It's amusing now to try to sing the words of "Hark! the Herald Angels Sing" to the tune to these hymns!)

How did Wesley's text eventually meet with the famous tune of Felix Mendelssohn, which we now sing? Still another helper was needed, an English church musician named William Cummings. He was familiar with both these words and an inspiring melody Mendelssohn had composed in a work for men's chorus and brass instruments. One day Cummings noticed how well the two went together and made the final modification of this Christmas classic.

Hark! the herald angels sing,
Glory to the newborn King.

As it takes many parts of a mosaic to make the whole, this hymn could not have found perfection without the collaboration of many.

Write a few lines expressing the true meaning of Christmas. Now try to fit them to a melody you know.

Consider it pure joy, my brothers, whenever you face trials of many kinds, because you know that the testing of your faith develops per- severance. —JAMES 1:2, 3

Being "put to the test" can be a trial for any of us. For a young musician, to be asked to sight-read difficult music in front of a crowd of celebrities could be a nightmare. Yet that is the very position that Felix Mendelssohn—composer of symphonies, concerti, sonatas, and the music to "Hark! the Herald Angels Sing"—found himself in while still a young boy.

The young musician was invited to a special party at the home of the poet and philosopher Johann Wolfgang von Goethe. Having heard of the youth's genius, Goethe went to him and said, "Now you shall play something." Mendelssohn played a Bach fugue and then a Mozart minuet, to everyone's delight.

But Goethe said, "Well come, you have only played pieces you know; but now we shall see if you can play something you do not know. I will put you on trial." The old man brought out a manuscript and set it before Mendelssohn. Again, the playing was faultless. Goethe smiled and said, "But I will give you something over which you will stick, so take care!" Another manuscript, splashed sloppily with ink blots, was presented. The boy laughed and said, "How is that written? Who can read it?"

Another musician nearby spoke up. "Why, Beethoven wrote that! He always writes with a broomstick, and passes his sleeves over the notes before they are dry!" While the others laughed, Mendelssohn became very serious and studied the untidy score. In his love for Beethoven, the boy played over the piece slowly, correcting several mistakes with a sudden, "No, so," and then announced, "Now I will play it for you." This time, the Beethoven composition was performed per- fectly, to the amazement and applause of all—especially Goethe.

God doesn't place trials in our lives to trip us up, make us fall, or cause us embarrassment. He allows us to face trials so that we may learn and grow, and our faith will be strengthened.

Mendelssohn knew that his "trial" would take serious study and slow, careful work. Think of a trial in your life, pray for guidance, and plan the strategy to pass the test.

When the angels had left them and gone into heaven, the shepherds said to one another, "Let's go to Bethlehem and see this thing that has happened, which the Lord has told us about." —LUKE 2:15

The carol "O Come All Ye Faithful" had humble beginnings. For years, hymnbooks simply listed it as "Adeste Fideles," composer unknown. But in 1946, an English vicar found several eighteenth-century manuscripts of the piece that bore its composer's signature, John Francis Wade.

This man was not a world-famous master, but an obscure music copyist and teacher. Born in England, he wrote the words and music to this classic in 1744, while living in Douay, France. Very little is known of his life; we are not even sure why he moved to France, though this village had become a refuge for those who suffered religious persecution during the Jacobite rebellion of 1725.

Perhaps as this dislodged Englishman considered the bitter divisions throughout the church of his day, his heart longed for the unity found in worshiping Jesus Christ. The hymn he composed is not addressed to the Lord, but to every Christian, repeatedly calling each of us to "Come and adore Him, Christ the Lord."

> O come, all ye faithful, joyful and triumphant,
> O come ye, O come ye to Bethlehem;
> Come and behold Him, born the King of angels;
> O come, let us adore Him, Christ the Lord!

Today this work of an uncelebrated Christian musician has been sung in over one hundred languages and is loved throughout the world. The English translation we sing was made in 1841 by Frederick Oakeley, an Anglican minister who wanted to improve the worship in his London church by finding little-known musical gems to enrich the worship services. John Francis Wade's vision of seeing brothers and sisters everywhere worshiping God has been fulfilled.

Read the Scripture Philippians 2:9-11. Kneel down and sing this carol, adoring Christ the Lord.

"Bless those who persecute you." —ROMANS 12:14

The German composer George Frederic Handel (1685–1759)—who wrote the *Messiah, Royal Fireworks Music, Water Music,* and many other masterpieces—composed his greatest music in England. Born into the Lutheran church, he later lived in Italy and worked with many Catholic musicians. After moving to England, he spent the rest of his life among Anglican believers.

Handel had a great faith in Christ and love for his fellow man. He also had a modest and straightforward opinion of himself and his talent. When a friend unwittingly commented on the dreariness of some music he had heard at the Vauxhall Gardens, Handel rejoined, "You are right, sir, it is pretty poor stuff. I thought so myself when I wrote it."

Nevertheless, in his time he endured many trials, sometimes instigated by fellow believers. Handel composed brilliant concert works, such as *Judas Maccabaeus, Messiah, Esther,* and *Israel in Egypt,* to take the Scriptures out of the church and into all the world. For this evangelistic outlook, he had to withstand very painful criticism. A devout believer and dedicated to his Christian faith, he was nonetheless reprimanded by the English church for performing biblical dramas in secular theaters instead of in churches.

The oratorio *Messiah*—which joyfully proclaims the deity and glory of Jesus Christ—came under fire by well-meaning clergymen. The powerful preacher John Newton (who wrote the famous hymn "Amazing Grace") stormily denounced the secular performances of *Messiah* from his London pulpit. He relentlessly pursued this topic for fifty-two consecutive sermons!

Handel's response? He was never known to bad-mouth his Anglican brothers, always showing love and respect for his adopted country. A friend remembered that Handel "would often speak of it as one of the great felicities of his life that he was settled in a country where no man suffers any molestation or inconvenience on account of his religious principles."

It is especially painful to be reprimanded by a brother or sister in the Lord. Yet Handel took seriously and practically the opening Scripture of this page.

Have you been hurt by a fellow believer? Have you shown forgiveness? If not, ask God for help and begin to reconcile and bless.

But the angel said to them, "Do not be afraid. I bring you good news of great joy that will be for all the people. Today in the town of David a Savior has been born to you; he is Christ the Lord. —LUKE 2:10, 11

Certain compositions seem to be especially inspired by the Lord. Both the words and the music to the hymn "O Little Town of Bethlehem" qualify for such distinction. The text was written by Phillips Brooks (1835–1893), who was known as a great preacher in his day. His tremendous ministry took place in Philadelphia and Boston, but his world-renowned Christmas carol began in 1865 with his trip to the Holy Land.

On Christmas Eve of that year, Brooks journeyed on horseback from Jerusalem to Bethlehem. He rode into the nearby fields, the traditional site of the shepherds who watch their flocks by night. That night he attended the service at the ancient Church of the Nativity, built by Constantine in 326 over the very place where Jesus is believed to have been born. The entire experience was so unforgettable that his memories were still vivid when he wrote this carol for the children of his Philadelphia Sunday School three years later.

O little town of Bethlehem, how still we see thee lie!
Above thy deep and dreamless sleep the silent stars go by:
Yet in thy dark streets shineth the everlasting light:
The hopes and fears of all the years are met in thee tonight.

Once the text was written, Brooks asked his organist Lewis Redner to compose its accompanying music. The music was due for a specific Sunday service, but on the preceding Saturday night the work remained unwritten. Redner later related how during the night he was awakened with an angelic melody in his ears. He quickly wrote it down, finishing the harmony the following morning. The composition was first sung by six teachers and thirty-six children. Today this lovely carol is sung by millions around the world.

Go outside and look at the stars in the sky. Imagine that you were one of the shepherds, looking at those same stars, then suddenly seeing a sky filled with angels. Sing "O Little Town of Bethlehem" and praise our Heavenly Father.

But I have stilled and quieted my soul. —PSALM 131:2a

This beautiful favorite of all Christian carols, which conveys so much peace to our hearts, would not have been written except that something broke down unexpectedly—a church organ.

Silent night! holy night!
All is calm, all is bright.

The scene was the village of Oberndorf in Upper Austria, Christmas Eve, 1818. Life was neither silent nor calm for Father Joseph Mohr of Saint Nicholas Church. He stumbled into the midst of every minister of music's nightmare: his organ would not work for the Christmas service. All the music that was planned would have to be scrapped. He had to find something to substitute, and quickly.

Father Mohr must have prayerfully quieted his soul, for he began to write out the words, "Stille Nacht . . . heilige nacht . . ." In a surprisingly short time he had penned a lovely poem. He hastily asked his friend Franz Gruber—village schoolmaster and church organist—to set the words to music. That evening, the service had a new song. The two men sang "Stille Nacht" as a duet, with Gruber accompanying on the guitar.

That could have been the end of an obscure story, but the organ still needed to be repaired, and God had further plans for this song. When the repairman Karl Mauracher arrived, he heard the song and asked for a copy. Mauracher shared this throughout the Tyrol countryside as he repaired other instruments, and it found its way to the Stasser family of Zillertal. This unusual family had the double occupation of making gloves and singing folk songs at fairs. In the Leipzig fair of 1831, the Stasser family sang "Stille Nacht," creating a sensation. Soon it would be known and sung throughout the world.

This Christmas, if we become overwhelmed with the pandemonium of this world—or if everything we had planned falls apart—let us follow Father Mohr's example. As the psalmist "quieted and stilled his soul," let us seek the Lord for His perfect peace and keep our eyes on Jesus this season.

Sit in a quiet, darkened room with nothing but the Christmas tree lights or other Christmas lights on. Read the second chapter of Luke aloud. Ask the Lord to help you keep His peace in your heart.

All hard work brings a profit, but mere talk leads only to poverty.
—PROVERBS 14:23

On December 25, 1734, J. S. Bach (1685–1750) presented his magnificent *Christmas Oratorio*, played in two Leipzig churches over the next twelve days. The musical creativity of Bach stands as a marvel through more than two centuries since his death. Yet the musician did not believe that he was singled out for unsurpassed genius. He told a student, "Just practice diligently, and it will go very well. You have five fingers on each hand just as healthy as mine."

When asked the secret of his genius, he answered simply, "I was made to work; if you are equally industrious you will be equally successful." It is doubtful whether anyone has matched Bach's industriousness. It took his music publisher forty-six years to go through his multitudinous scores, collect and publish them, and the completed edition filled sixty huge volumes.

Bach composed almost all his music while fulfilling dozens of other tasks: working as an organist, a conductor, a music director, a private instructor, even a teacher of Latin to young boys—not to mention raising a large family and moving from post to post. The inspiration and beauty of his music are abundantly apparent. Yet the real mystery of Bach's life as a composer concerns how he found the actual time to write it all and still more to have created so many masterpieces cherished throughout the ages.

Bach personified the Germanic Protestant work ethic. "I was made to work" could have been his life motto. In his final year of life, after an operation left him sightless, Bach frantically pursued the revision of his great choral fantasies. His productivity forged a musical legacy that Richard Wagner would someday refer to as "the most stupendous miracle in all music." He certainly was the most stupendous worker in all of musical history!

Suppose for a moment that Bach were to say to you personally, "I was made to work; if you are equally industrious you will be equally successful." Would you believe him? Would you even take him seriously? Take time to consider how you can be "equally industrious" with the talents that God has given.

"For nothing is impossible with God." —LUKE 1:37

Elizabeth Ostling is the associate principal flutist of the Boston Symphony Orchestra. She is also a devoted Christian who uses her talents to glorify the Lord: "I believe that I am not my own, but belong—body and soul, in life and in death—to my faithful Savior Jesus Christ, who has fully paid for all my sins with His precious blood."

Like thousands of other young flute players, Ostling enjoyed playing in her youth orchestras but wondered if she should consider music as a career. Even after being accepted to the exclusive Curtis Institute of Music, she questioned whether it would be possible to make a living on her instrument. There are hundreds of flute players and very few openings in orchestras.

When a flute position in the renowned Boston Symphony Orchestra became available, Ostling almost didn't bother to audition. Realizing that you can't win if you don't try, she decided to give it her all. Amazingly enough, she made it through the first round and again through the second. Her name was announced for the finals, but she could hardly believe it. Finally, she and one other auditioner were asked to perform with the symphony for two weeks each—and Ostling at last was selected.

Experiences like this have taught Elizabeth Ostling that God can do anything! She instructs her students at the Christian Performing Artists' Fellowship's MasterWorks Festival that, "It is vitally important for me—for any Christian—to have a personal relationship with Christ; praying and reading the Bible daily, as well as worshiping God in church and having fellowship with other believers. I am amazed at God's grace and am beginning to realize just how dependent I am on Him and that He is in control of my life."

How dependent are you on God? Start making a list of what He has done for you, beginning with your creation. Thank Him for His grace and love—and for every item on your list.

An honest answer is like a kiss on the lips. —PROVERBS 24:26

For years the Oak Ridge Boys were one of America's best loved gospel music groups. In the 1970s, when they began to record in the country music genre and let their hair grow long, many of their gospel fans deserted them. One of the Oak Ridge Boys, Bill Golden, felt condemned by all his old friends—until he met some with a heart full of Christ's love.

Howard and Vestal Goodman, of the Happy Goodman Family, were leaving a funeral service when they spotted Bill Golden walking toward them on the sidewalk. When Golden saw the couple, he hung his head and crossed the street to avoid meeting them. But the Goodmans wanted to see their old friend, so they crossed the street as well. Vestal called out, "Bill! Bill Golden! You stop right now!"

Both Howard and Vestal gave Golden a big hug, and then she asked, "Bill Golden, why did you cross the street to avoid us?" "Well, Vestal," he admitted, "I know a lot of people in the gospel industry are upset with us, and I was afraid you felt the same way." The Goodmans knew what it was like to have been unfairly judged, and they poured out a stream of love and counsel.

Vestal answered him, "Bill, you know better than that. Don't you ever be guilty of doing that again. I love you, and I love the Oak Ridge Boys. Now the only gripe I've got with you—and I'll tell you to your face—is that you've gone out there and given the devil a lot of ammunition to shoot you with. I don't mind how you wear your hair or what kind of music you do, but you gotta keep your life right with the Lord. You gotta watch where your steps take you and be careful what comes out of your mouth—because you're gonna need God." The friendship was renewed instead of severed, and Golden was encouraged rather than condemned.

Have you ever felt condemned by other Christians? If so, make sure that you're not giving them ammunition to shoot you with. Then memorize Romans 8:1 and praise God for His acceptance.

Yet, O Lord, you are our Father. We are the clay, you are the potter; we are all the work of your hand. —ISAIAH 64:8

As God is our ultimate Father, much of His love for us can be learned through a godly father. This was the experience of the singer/songwriter Twila Paris, who celebrates her birthday today. Her tremendous music ministry began with the inspiration given by her father, as she testifies, "He is an encourager like no one else I have ever seen in my life. And because of it, whenever I have sensed God calling me to do something, I have known I could do it."

Having a dad in full-time ministry has been a trial for some children, but not for Paris. "I've heard other ministers' kids talk about how they would hear their dad get up and preach, and then see a different person at home. Not us." They saw him daily in the Word, in prayer, and in worship. "We saw that, and we saw the consistent love that he had for our mom, for us, and for my grandparents who lived next door."

Paris' parents found ways to show love as they disciplined her. She recalls a time when she was young and secretly did something she knew they would not allow. Later, they confronted her about this, and she denied her guilt. But they continued to question her, and it finally came out with tears and a full confession.

Her parents dealt with the problem in a spirit of love, which included praying together. What Twila Paris remembers most about this incident is what happened a few hours later: "Dad came home with a new leather Bible that had my name imprinted on it. And in the front he wrote, 'To Twila, from Mom and Dad. In honor of one of those days when God shows His love to a child in need.' "

Not all of us have the blessing of a godly dad. Yet we can all be adopted as God's sons and daughters. Look in a concordance and read the verses on "God our father."

Be prepared in season and out of season. —2 TIMOTHY 4:2a

Some people have prepared so much over the years that when an opportunity comes they are "prepared for anything." An amusing example of this is the great jazz pianist Thomas "Fats" Waller (1904–1943). This man was so laid back from a lifetime of preparation that he drove record producers wild. Yet he always created fantastic records.

Eddie Condon was once hired by a record company in order to arrange the recording of Fats Waller and his band, to make certain that they were on time and prepared. Condon found Waller, who "was so amiable, so agreeable, so good-natured, that I felt ashamed of my mission. But I performed it: I asked Fats about making a record. A recording date? He'd be delighted, he'd be proud; just about any time. In four days? Fine. At Liederkranz Hall? Wonderful. At noon? Perfect."

The night before the session, Condon was horrified to find that Waller had not selected the music, pulled the band together, or rehearsed. Condon demanded, "After we get the band together, what shall we play?" "Why, we'll play music," Waller answered calmly. Condon stayed with him all evening but got no further. The next morning, Condon found that Waller was still sleeping at ten thirty. He shouted, "We're due at the studio at noon!" Waller yawned and said, "That's wonderful! That's perfect! Now let's see about a band. Look around for some nickels so I can make the telephone go."

Waller and several other musicians were soon in a cab heading for the studio. The pianist said, "Now here is what we are going to play." Humming a few tunes, he told each musician what part he was to play. They arrived at ten minutes before noon and completed an outstanding recording session. Afterward, one of the recording engineers (who had no idea of Fats Waller's "method" of preparation) was heard to say, "We must have some more of these dates. This is an excellent example of the wisdom of planning and preparation."

Do you have trouble feeling anxious about life? If so, part of the problem may be that you're not well prepared for the things that come your way. There is a calm confidence that comes from knowing your abilities and what you're doing. Prepare yourself today to serve the Lord by reading His Word and praying.

"Blessed are the meek, for they will inherit the earth."

—MATTHEW 5:5

When Jesus said the above words, He could have been speaking particularly of the Austrian composer Anton Bruckner (1824–1896). His music was under attack by critics for years, yet he never fought back and always kept his good humor. While he was composing his ninth and final symphony, he jokingly told Gustav Mahler, "I must at least finish, or I'll cut a poor figure when I appear soon before the good Lord and He says, 'Well, my boy, why did I give you so much talent if not to sing to My honor and glory? You have not done nearly enough with it!' "

Few composers have ever faced such long-term opposition from a hostile public. A director of the Vienna Conservatorium told Bruckner to give up on trying to compose and to throw his symphonies into a trash can. It became nearly impossible to have his works performed. The Vienna Philharmonic performed his *Symphony no. 1*, but it received such a cold response that the organization refused to play Bruckner's other works. The powerful music critic Eduard Handslick gave him horrible reviews whenever a piece was performed, calling one symphony "insatiable rhetoric."

Nevertheless, Bruckner continued to compose work after work, believing that his efforts would eventually be blessed. He was correct, and in the 1880s, all of Europe was won over. At length he was awarded an imperial insignia by Emperor Franz Joseph, who was ready to bestow upon Bruckner whatever he asked, even a royal pension. The composer's answer to this royal boon? Bruckner smiled and asked the emperor to stop Hanslick from continuing his wretched reviews!

God rewarded this composer's refusal to attack when he was attacked. The public came to love his great works and to even disdain those who disagreed. Indeed, at the premiere of his *Symphony no. 8*, the audience actually booed his old nemesis Hanslick and sent him scampering out of the concert hall! From a musical point of view, the meek composer Anton Bruckner truly did "inherit the earth."

Has there been a time when a "critic" has put down your efforts? Read Colossians 3:23, 24. Pray for that person and rest assured, knowing that your work is your best for the Lord.

And now these three remain: faith, hope and love. But the greatest of these is love. —1 CORINTHIANS 13:13

If Paul the Apostle were writing specifically to musicians, he might have worded the first three verses in 1 Corinthians, chapter 13 a bit differently:

"If I can sing better than Caruso, Pavarotti, Ella Fitzgerald, or Paul McCartney, but have not love, I am only a resounding gong or a clanging cymbal.

"If I can play piano better than Horowitz, guitar better than Segovia, violin better than Perlman, drums better than Buddy Rich, cello better than Casals, and if I can compose better than Beethoven, Bach, or Mozart, but have not love, I am nothing.

"If I have more sales than the Beatles, and have more fans than Elvis, but have not love, I gain nothing."

We have known hundreds of great musicians—indeed many of the living musicians in this book are good friends of ours—and seen the rising and falling of many music careers. Recently I visited with my dear friend Jerome Hines, who has had an extraordinary career for over forty years with the Metropolitan Opera. Now he is well advanced in years, and of course, no one is asking him to sing opera anymore. The spotlights are gone; what remains is love, God's love, that of his family and many friends. This will happen to most of us, no matter "how high we climb." (I must mention that Hines is a faithful Christian, who is deeply grateful to God for his life and very much looking forward to meeting with Him!)

Therefore, we conclude that whatever blessings come our way—no matter how wonderful the position or how gold or platinum the recording—all these things we strive after are absolutely nothing compared with God's love. We pray that in the coming year we will all strive more to know God and to show His unfathomable love to everyone around us. And whatever success or failure we may have next year, let us always remember that "the greatest of these is love."

—Patrick and Barbara Kavanaugh

Start your new year with a new dedication to God. Set aside time tonight or tomorrow to prayerfully consider specific ways in which you might know more of God's love and share it with others. Make next year the best yet in your walk with Christ.

This is not meant to be an exhaustive glossary, but contains many of the words mentioned in the text which concern the technical aspects of music. As much as possible, the definitions are given in laymen's terms.

A cappella (Lit. "in church style"): Singing without instrumental accompaniment.

Absolute music: Music which does not have a programmatic title, or depend on literary or other associations.

Accelerando: Increase the speed gradually.

Accent: A strong beat, normally the first beat of each measure; rhythmic stress at any place in a piece of music.

Accidental: A symbol placed before a note to raise or lower the tone, usually by a half step. Example: # b

Accompaniment: A part supporting the leading melody.

Acoustics: The branch of physics which studies the laws and phenomena of sound; also, the sound-affecting properties of an auditorium, concert hall, etc.

Ad libitum (Lit. "at will"): An indication telling the performer that he may employ a tempo or an expression that suits his pleasure.

Air: A song or melody. See Aria.

Anthem: A sacred choral composition, from the Anglican church tradition and with an English text. It began as an unaccompanied, contrapuntal motet, and later was accompanied by organ or strings.

Antiphonal: Two or more choruses or instrumental chords "against" each other, often placed at different parts of the concert hall, stage, or church.

Antiphon: Originally a chant using a short text from the Psalms and used on special feast days of the church, it later came to include other independent songs with Scriptural texts.

Aria: A composition for solo voice and instrumental accompaniment, often taken from an opera or oratorio.

Atonal: Having no fixed key; not centering on any distinct key.

Ballet: A dance composition accompanied by the orchestra, often employing a dramatic thread or story.

Bar: A vertical line dividing notes on the staff into measures, and indicating that the strong accent falls on the note or notes immediately following.

Baroque: The music or style of art which prevailed during the seventeenth and part of the eighteenth centuries, characterized by the use of grandiose and magnificent forms.

Bass clef (Also called the F clef): The sign indicating that F below middle-C is the fourth line of the staff.

Baton: A conductor's stick.

Beat: The regularly recurring pulse which constitutes a unit of rhythmical measurement in a musical piece.

Bel canto (Lit. "beautiful singing"): A style of singing made famous by Italian singers in the eighteenth century.

Cacophony: The dissonant effect produced by sounds which are combined in such a way that they are displeasing to the ear.

Cadenza: A brilliant passage for the solo voice or instrument formerly improvised by the performer but now usually written in the composition by the composer.

Camp Meetings: Popular forms of outdoor religious gatherings in nineteenth century America, often lasting for several days and characterized by fervent, emotional preaching and singing.

Cantata: A vocal composition in several movements for solo voices and chorus with instrumental accompaniment.

Canticle: A hymn with a biblical text similar to but not from the Psalms.

Capriccio: A lively and sometimes humorous instrumental composition written in free form.

Carol: A joyous song, originally a dancing song, for a special season of the year.

Chant: A sacred song in free rhythm with many words sung on the same pitch.

Choir: In vocal music, a group of singers performing in choral style.

Chorus: 1. A large group of singers. 2. The refrain of a song.

Christian music: Any vocal music which uses a text either from the Bible or words which reflect Christian faith and doctrine.

Chromatic: Melodies or harmonies based on the chromatic (semitone or 1/2 step) scale.

Clef: A sign placed at the left of each staff in music to fix the pitch of the lines and spaces. See bass clef, treble clef, and C clef.

Composition: 1. A piece of music created by the composer from his own imagination. 2. The name of a subject teaching the principles of composing.

Concert overture: A separate orchestral piece which is usually in sonata form and frequently programmatic.

Concertmaster: The leader of the first violin section of an orchestra.

Concerto: A work for one or more soloists and orchestra.

Concord: Sounds which by themselves give a sense of completion and repose.

Consonance: A combination of two or more tones that produce a pleasing effect.

Contrapuntal: Music composed in the style of counterpoint, using various simultaneously sounding musical lines.

Counterpoint: Refers to a type of composition with various simultaneously sounding musical lines.

Crescendo: Make gradually louder.

Debut: In music, the first public appearance of a performing artist.

Decibel: A unit for measuring the loudness of sound.

Decrescendo: Make softer.

Diminuendo: Make softer.

Dissonance: A combination of two or more tones that are out of their normal harmonic relation to one another.

Downbeat: The downward stroke of the conductor's baton indicating the first beat of a measure.

Duet: A composition for two performers, singers, or instrumentalists, with or without accompaniment.

Duration: A term referring to the amount or length of time a tone continues to sound.

Dynamics: The gradation or change in amount of loudness and softness in music.

Encore: A piece or performance repeated or added in response to the demands of a pleased audience.

Ensemble: 1. A group of musicians performing together. 2. General effect of music performed by a group of musicians.

Expressionism: A term borrowed from twentieth-century art to refer to music that presents inward feelings in unconventional forms.

Fanfare: A short flourish of trumpets or an imitation of their sound to introduce some special event or ceremony.

Fantasia: A composition free in form and feeling.

Finale: 1. The last movement of an extended work; sometimes given the title of a separate piece. 2. The concluding portion of an operatic act.

Fugue: A form of musical composition based on a melody (called the "theme" or "subject") which is taken up in turn by the different parts (or "voices"). Usually there are three or four voices, and each expresses the theme one after the other while all continue to develop the piece according to established rules for writing this kind of music.

Great Awakening: A series of revivals which took place during the first half of the eighteenth century in the American colonies. Sometimes the period of revival that took place in the Eastern United States during the middle of the nineteenth century is called the "Second Great Awakening."

Gregorian Chant: The form of liturgical chanting codified during the time of Pope Gregory the Great (590-604) and widely used for centuries, notably in the Roman Catholic church.

Harmonization: The arrangement of tones to create chordal harmony.

Harmony: The science of manipulating chords; applied to music produced by such manipulation.

Homophony: Music in which one part stands out and the others accompany in chord effects. The music is formed vertically, as opposed to polyphony where the parts move horizontally.

Hymn: A religious or sacred song to be sung by a congregation in public worship.

Hymnology: The study of the history and composition of hymns.

Imitation: The contrapuntal device of employing in one voice, a melodic or rhythmic figure which has been stated in another.

Impressionism: A term originally used in reference to a style of painting popular at the end of the nineteenth century. Impressionistic music creates descriptive effects or impressions by the use of harmonic devices based principally on the whole-tone scale. Debussy and Ravel were the two most famous composers of this school.

Improvisation: 1. Music spontaneously created directly from the imagination. Improvisation is widely used in jazz. 2. The title of a composition written to give the effect of its having been improvised.

Incidental music: Music played during the incidents and intervals of a dramatic work.

Instrumentation: The choice of instruments for a composition.

Interlude: Music designed to be played between acts of a play or opera, or between other pieces of music.

Intermezzo: A type of piano piece common in the nineteenth century.

Interval: The distance in pitch between two tones.

Intonation: Good or bad intonation refers to playing in or out of tune.

Introduction: A preliminary section.

Kapellmeister: Generally applied to the director of music in eighteenth-century choirs. Used in Germany to mean a conductor at the theatre or concert hall.

Key: 1. The particular system of tones and semitones constituting a scale and built on a selected tone (the tonic). The key note or tonic thus formed becomes the first note of the scale and becomes the name of the key. 2. The black and white digitals of the piano.

Legato: Indication that the passage is to be performed in a smooth and connected manner.

Libretto (It. "booklet"): The book of words of an extended choral composition, such as an opera, cantata, or oratorio.

Lied (Ger. "song"): Strictly used for the great number of art songs by German composers.

Lyrical: Adapted for singing expressively, songlike.

Lyrics: The words of a song.

Madrigal: An unaccompanied part-song setting of a short lyrical poem written in the language of the country.

Mass: Musical setting of the Roman Catholic worship service.

Measure: A group of beats set off by bar-lines.

Mode: Strictly, any mode or manner of arranging tones and semitones to form a scale. Generally refers to the ancient scales used for religious music.

Modulation: Passing from one key to another within a composition.

Monophony: Music composed of a single melodic line without harmony or accompaniment.

Motet: A sacred vocal composition in contrapuntal style without accompaniment, important from the thirteenth to the seventeenth centuries, and nearly always in Latin.

Motive: A brief theme or figure, either an integral part of a larger theme or the germinal ideal from which the theme develops.

Movement: A division complete in itself, forming part of an extended work.

Music drama: A form of music used by Wagner and others to distinguish their writings of continuous music combined with continuous drama from the known form that divided the music into operatic numbers.

Musicianship: A person's understanding of music, and ability and skill in performing it.

Mute: A device to soften or muffle the tones of a musical instrument.

Neoclassicism: A term used to designate a movement in the twentieth century to adapt the objective style of the Classical (and especially the Baroque) period to present-day melodic and rhythmic practices. Neo is a prefix meaning new.

Nocturne: "Night piece." A kind of piano piece popular in the nineteenth century. Typically melancholy with expressive melody.

Note and tone: In strict usage, note refers to the written symbol of a sound on a page of music; tone refers to the sound itself. However, the two terms are often used interchangeably.

Note: A sign used to represent the time value of a tone.

Octave: The interval of eight degrees. The lower and upper tone of the octave have the same letter name, and the upper tone having twice the number of vibrations as the lower.

Opera: A musical drama sung to the accompaniment of an orchestra.

Operetta: A light play of popular appeal with vocal and instrumental music, spoken dialogue, and, frequently, dancing.

Opus: "Work" of a composer. The numbers used with Opus indicate the chronological position of a composition, often with respect to publication.

Oratorio: An extended composition for vocal soloists, chorus, and orchestra, sung without costumes, scenery, or action. Usually of religious character.

Orchestration: The art of writing or scoring music to be performed by an orchestra.

Organum: The earliest attempts at part writing for voices, beginning in the ninth century. Based on plainsong, the parts progressed in parallel fifths and fourths.

Ornaments: Collective name for ornaments of expression. Usually indicated by specific signs in the score. Examples: trill, modent, and turn.

Overture: Instrumental music composed as a musical introduction to an opera, oratorio, or play. A concert overture is an independent composition often in sonata form with a title suggesting a pictorial or literary association.

Partita: A term used in the seventeenth and eighteenth centuries to mean suite of movements.

Passion: The story of Christ's death in an extended music setting.

Pedal: 1. A foot lever on the organ. 2. A foot lever on harp, harpsichord, piano, timpani, or organ. 3. A note sustained below changing harmonies.

Phrase: A musical clause composed of two or more measures.

Pianoforte: The full Italian name of the piano.

Pitch: The highness or lowness of a tone, determined by its frequency of vibrations per second. For example, the A above middle-C has 440 vibrations per second. The first seven letters of the alphabet are used as pitch names.

Plainchant: See Chant.

Plainsong: The name for Gregorian chant. Derived from cantus planus ("plain song")—that is, free or unmeasured chant—as opposed to cantus figuralis ("figured song")—that is, polyphonic, exactly measured music.

Polyphonic, polyphony: The combination of two or more melodies.

Polytonality: A twentieth-century system of writing music in several keys at once.

Postlude: A final number such as the organ selection at the close of a church service.

Praise chorus: Congregational songs made popular in the second half of the twentieth century, which contain a minimum of lyrics and usually employ a refrain-verse alternation form.

Prelude: A musical composition to be played before another composition, drama, or church service.

Program music: Music based on some scheme of literary or associative values, evoked by means of sound.

Pulse: The beat that underlies all music and helps determine its motion and speed.

Quarter tone: A microtone that is one half of a half tone.

Quartet: 1. A musical composition for four voices or instruments. 2. A string quartet in sonata form for two violins, viola, and cello.

Range: The limits of a voice, instrument, or melody with respect to pitch.

Recital: A musical performance by one individual or by a soloist and accompanist.

Recitative: A reciting, declamatory style of vocal music in imitation of speech. It originated in the early seventeenth century opera.

Reed: A thin strip of can, wood, or metal adjusted in an instrument to set an air current in motion.

Register: A certain part of the range of a voice or instrument. Also, in the organ, a set of pipes controlled by one stop.

Repeat: A section of a composition to be performed again can be indicated by a repeat sign. The performer is to return to the beginning or to the repeat sign in reverse.

Requiem: Mass or service for the dead; a memorial choral work.

Responsorial: A type of singing in which a soloist is answered by the choir, or vice versa.

Rest: A sign in musical notation that represents a pause or cessation in sound. Rests have the same value as notes of the same name.

Rhapsody: An instrumental composition irregular in form, often showing national characteristics.

Rhythm: The regular recurrence of like features in a composition; the organization of time elements of music.

Romanticism: A style of composition which places strong emphasis on the personal expression of poetic sentiment, particularly in the nineteenth century.

Rondo: A form often used as the final movement of a classical symphony in which the opening section is repeated alternately with other melodic material of a different character.

Sacred music: Any vocal music which uses a religious text. See also Christian music.

Scale: A succession of tones which is used as the basic material for writing a piece; developed from the modes.

Score: 1. Music in written or printed form, such as sheet music or a conductor's score. 2. The music of an opera, cantata, oratorio, ballet, symphony, concerto, or suite.

Secular music: Music other than that intended for religious or devotional purposes, either instrumental or with a non-religious text.

Semitone: A half-tone.

Serenade: Applied to music suitable for performance in the open air.

Solo: A piece or part of a composition played or sung by a single performer.

Sonority: Said of a sound in general. In modern music, "sonority" or "sonorities" may be used as a term to describe chords or any complex of simultaneous sounds that cannot otherwise be described with the terminology of conventional harmony.

Spiritual: A religious folk song, generally referring to the many Negro spirituals which originated in the southern United States.

Staccato: Quick, detached. The sign is a dot over or under the note.

Staff, stave: Five horizontal, parallel, and equidistant lines and the included four spaces upon which musical symbols are written. Historically, the staff, at one time or another, has had as few as one and as many as eleven lines.

Style: A characteristic manner of expressing ideas.

Subject: See theme.

Suite: 1. A set or series of instrumental pieces in various dance forms. 2. A set of movements rather loosely connected which may be assembled from an opera or ballet.

Symphonic poem: An extended one movement orchestral composition of no fixed form based on an extra musical idea, such as a story or a poem.

Syncopation: A rhythmic pattern in which the accent falls on the normally weak beat or portion of a beat.

Technic, technique: Mechanical training, skill, dexterity.

Tempo: Time; commonly used to mean pace or speed.

Theme: A melody of sufficient length and importance to form a musical idea. In fugues and sonatas this is known as the subject.

Time signature: See meter signature.

Tonality: A term used to describe music written in a tonic-centered key.

Transcribe: To arrange or adapt a piece for voice or instrument other than that for which it was originally written by the composer.

Transition: Passages which lead from one principal idea to another.

Transpose: Transposition. Putting a piece in another key (that is, level of pitch).

Treble: 1. Soprano. 2. Highest part in a vocal composition.

Trio: 1. A group of three performers. 2. Center section of the minuet or scherzo.

Tuning: The adjustment of strings or tubing to bring an instrument into tune.

Unison: A tone of the same pitch as a given tone; a higher or lower octave of the same tone.

Upbeat: 1. The raising of the conductor's hand indicating the last beat of a measure. 2. Unstressed note or notes beginning a composition before the first bar-line.

Variations: Changes given to a theme through harmonic, rhythmic, or melodic means.

Vibration: The rapid movement back and forth, as that of a vibrating string.

Vibrato: Slight fluctuation of pitch produced on stringed instruments or in the voice to increase the emotional effect of the sounds produced.

Virtuoso: A musician who has complete technical mastery of his instrument.

Vocal music: Music to be performed by singing voices, either as solo, small ensemble, or chorus.

Voice: 1. The human voice, comparable to a wind instrument, with the lungs supplying the wind. 2. Separate parts of a chord. 3. Parts in polyphonic compositions.

Whole step: Two half steps.

Whole-tone scale: A scale composed only of whole tones.

Word painting: A term used to mean the depiction of a text by some appropriate musical means to underline or emphasize the thing or sentiment in question.

Fischer, John—Apr 13

Francis of Assisi—Oct 4

Franck, Cesar—Sep 28

Franklin, Aretha—May 6

Franklin, Kirk—Jan 10

Furtwangler, Wilhelm—Jan 25

Gaither, Bill—Oct 16

Gershwin, George—Jul 11

Gier, Delta David—Oct 22

Gillespie, John Birks "Dizzy"—Jul 22, Oct 21

Gingold, Joseph—Oct 5

Glazunov, Alexander—Aug 10

Gluck, Christoph Willibald—Jul 2, Nov 15

Golden, Bill—Dec 27

Goodman, Benny—Feb 1, Jun 13, Nov 30

Goodman, Howard—Oct 11, Oct 12, Dec 27

Goodman, Vestal—Dec 27

Gorecki, Henryk—Jun 17

Gossec, Francois Joseph—Jan 17

Gottschalk, Louis Moreau—Dec 18

Gounod, Charles—Mar 19, Oct 17

Grammatrain—Nov 24

Granados, Enrique—Mar 24

Grant, Amy—Nov 25

Green, Keith—Jan 3

Green, Steve—Aug 1

Gregorian, Julie—Nov 1

Gregory the Great—Sep 2

Grieg, Edvard—Jul 15, Sep 4

Gruber, Franz—Dec 24

Guthrie, Woody—Oct 14

Gutierrez, Manuel Maria—Sep 18

Haig, Al—Jul 22

Hampton, Lionel—Jan 5

Handel, George Frederic—Feb 11, Apr 27, Jun 16,
    Oct 3, Dec 22

Happy Goodman Family—Oct 11, Oct 12, Dec 27

Harrell, Alan—Oct 27

Harris, Larnelle—May 16

Harrison, George—Feb 25

Hartmann, Arthur—Dec 5

Haydn, Franz Joseph—Jan 21, Mar 23, Jul 8, Sep 16

Hayes, Kendall—Oct 26

Hayward, Justin—Jul 29

Hecht, Ben—Oct 28

Heifetz, Jascha—Feb 2

Hendrickson, Steve—Jul 14

Hill, Harry—Jun 12

Hill, Kim—Apr 5

Hines, Jerome—Mar 3, Dec 31

Hirt, Al—Oct 18

Hodges, John—Aug 26

Howerton, Layton—Feb 8

Irwin, Mary—Sep 27

Ives, Charles—Oct 20

Jackson, Mahalia—Jun 27

Janacek, Leos—Jul 3

Jars of Clay—Dec 4

Joachim, Joseph—Jun 29

Joiner, Lee—Jul 6

Jones, Elvin—Sep 9

Josquin de Pres—May 4

Judd, Naomi—Dec 9

Judd, Wynonna—Dec 9

Kasica, John—Feb 23, May 31

Kavanaugh, Barbara—Aug 23, Dec 31

Kavanaugh, Patrick—Dec 31

Keaggy, Cheri—Jul 13

Keaggy, Phil—Oct 23

Keller, Linn Maxwell—Aug 7

Keynote, Peter—Nov 11

King, Wes—Jan 31

Knapp, Jennifer—Nov 12

Kochel, Ludwig von—Jan 13

Konopka, Stanley—Mar 6, Aug 29

Kraft, Jim—May 1

Kreisler, Fritz—Feb 2

Krenek, Ernst—Oct 28

Lambert, Lisa-Beth—Aug 3

Langlois, Roslyn—Jun 4

Leinsdorf, Erich—Feb 4

Lennon, John—Dec 8

Lewis, Crystal—Oct 19

Liszt, Franz—Jul 31

Lowry, Mark—Jun 24

Lully, Jean-Baptiste—Mar 22

Luscombe, Greg—Jul 19

Luther, Martin—Feb 18

Lyte, Henry Francis—Jun 15

Mahler, Gustav—May 27, Jun 23, Jul 20, Sep 19,
    Dec 30

Manne, Shelley—Nov 30

Marsalis, Wynton—Oct 18

Masen, Sarah—Apr 26

Mason, Lowell—Aug 11

Massenet, Jules—Feb 16

McCartney, Paul—Jun 18 , Oct 9

McGuire, Father—Sep 13

Mendelssohn, Felix—Mar 14, Jul 24, Aug 30, Oct 24, Dec 19, Dec 20

Merritt, Myra—Jul 30

Messiaen, Olivier—Aug 27, Dec 10

Milsap, Ronnie—Nov 4

Mitropoulos, Dimitri—Mar 1

Mohr, Joseph—Dec 24

Mohr, Mark—Nov 18

Monteverdi, Claudio—Aug 19

Mozart, Wolfgang Amadeus—Jan 13, Jan 16, Apr 4, May 19, Sep 29

Mullins, Rich—Sep 24

Nailed—Apr 19

Nance, Wes and Shannon—Nov 27

Neale, John Mason—Dec 17

Nelson, Willie—Apr 30

Nelson, John—Jun 17

Newsboys, The—Jan 19

Newton, John—Dec 22

Nicolai, Otto—Mar 28

Nikisch, Arthur—Aug 18

Nordeman, Nichole—Mar 31

Norman, Larry—Aug 8

Oakeley, Frederick—Dec 21

Offenbach, Jacques—Dec 6

Ormandy, Eugene—Apr 1

Ortmans, Rene—Dec 5

Ostling, Elizabeth—Dec 26

Owens, Buck—Aug 12

Paderewski, Ignacy Jan—Sep 7

Paris, Twila—Dec 28

Parkening, Christopher—May 25, Dec 14

Parker, Charlie—Mar 12, Jul 22

Paschal, Janet—Dec 13

Patty, Sandi—Jun 14

Paul, Les—Jun 9

Peacock, Charlie—Sep 12

Petra—Jul 5

Pettit, Warren—May 28

Phillips, Craig, and Dean—Apr 21

Plankeye—Aug 31

Plumb—May 8

Point of Grace—Jun 21

Porter, Cole—Jun 28

Poulenc Francis—Jan 30

Praetorius, Michael—Dec 17

Presley, Elvis—Nov 4

Prokofiev, Sergei—Sep 5, Dec 6

Puccini, Giacomo—Apr 25

Rachmaninoff, Sergei—Mar 13, Aug 5

Ramey, Gene—May 2

Ravel, Maurice—Mar 7, Nov 22

Redford, J.A.C.—May 14

Redner, Lewis—Dec 23

Reeves, Jim—Sep 1

Rice, Tim—Jan 9

Rich, Buddy—Apr 2, Sep 30

Rimsky-Korsakov, Nikolai—Oct 7

Rinkart, Martin—Apr 23

Rodrigo, Joaquin—Nov 9

Rogers, Roy—Mar 16

Rossini, Gioachino—Nov 13

Rostropovich, Mstislav—May 12

Rouse, Ernie—Jul 26

Rubinstein, Anton—Sep 11, Nov 28

Rubinstein, Artur—Mar 5

Rubinstein, Nikolay—Oct 25

Sankey, Ira—Aug 28

Satie, Erik—May 17

Scarlatti, Domenico—Jul 23, Nov 8

Schmitz, Chester—Sep 3

Schoenberg, Arnold—Jul 20, Sep 15

Schubert, Franz—Dec 2

Schumann, Robert—Oct 10

Scriabin, Alexander—Jan 6

Seeger, Pete—May 3

Segovia, Andrés—Feb 21, Sep 21

Seven Day Jesus—Aug 24

Shaded Red—May 18

Shostakovich, Dmitri—May 12

Sibelius, Jean—Sep 25

Silverstein, Joseph—Mar 11

Sixpence None the Richer—Sep 23

Skillet—Sep 14

Smalltown Poets—Nov 5

Smith, Connie—Aug 14

Smith, Bessie—Apr 15

Smith, Willie—Jun 7

Smith, Michael W.—Jan 22

Smith, Christina—Nov 19

Smith, Derek—Aug 17

Snow, Hank—May 9

Sperl, Tom—Mar 6

St. James, Rebecca—Oct 1

Starr, Ringo—Jul 7

Steinway, Heinrich Engelhard—Feb 15

Strauss, Richard—Feb 14, Jun 11

Stravinsky, Igor—Apr 18, Jul 4, Aug 19, Nov 17

If you want to learn more about combining music and Christianity, check out these resources.

Christian Performing Artists' Fellowship

The Christian Performing Artists' Fellowship (CPAF) is a non-denominational ministry dedicated to performing to the glory of God and to spreading the Gospel in the world of the performing arts. Begun in Washington, D.C. in 1984, it has grown to include over 1,000 members from over 50 different denominations. They have presented Christ-centered performances from Washington's Kennedy Center to Moscow's Bolshoi Theatre, from Dallas' Meyerson Hall to Bethlehem Square in Israel. *Christianity Today* notes that CPAF, "strives to bring the Gospel to a relatively overlooked group: the secular arts world." The *National Christian Reporter* calls CPAF members "missionaries," who are "all dedicated to bring the Gospel of Christ to those who might otherwise not hear it." The Christian Performing Artists' Fellowship is a registered non-profit, tax-exempt organization. All expenses are met by donations. For more information about CPAF call 888-836-CPAF (2723) toll-free.

MasterWorks Festival

The MasterWorks Festival is a world-class performing arts festival for young performers who want to use their talents for the glory of God. Its faculty contains some of the greatest Christian performers and teachers in the music world, including many in this devotional book. For one month, dozens of high school and college-age students come together for programs in orchestra, chamber music, piano, opera, theater, and dance. The mission of the MasterWorks Festival is to train Christian performing artists in two distinct areas: (1) Excellence in their performance skills, and (2) Excellence in their Christian walk and witness. The atmosphere of the festival is a combination of serious music making and studying with the joy of a dedicated Christian environment. Although the time is filled with rehearsals, performances, private lessons, and masterclasses, there is also time for devotionals, Bible studies, prayer meetings, worship, and fellowship. For more information about or applications for the MasterWorks Festival, call toll-free at 888-835-2723, or see the website at: www.ChristianPerformingArt.org.

MasterClass Bible Studies for Musicians

"MasterClass Bible Studies for Musicians" is a unique Bible study guide for musicians. It was designed by Patrick Kavanaugh and John Langlois. The Bible studies cover a great number of Scriptural topics related to the performing arts. The material applies Biblical principles to such issues as practicing, performing, relationships, nervousness, teaching, competition, and musical careers. These Bible studies are generally used in small groups, many of which meet in professional ensembles as well as music schools. The studies are designed to encourage maximum participation and fellowship in each group. As a service to Christian musicians, CPAF provides copies of the "MasterClass Bible Studies" free of charge. They can be printed from CPAF's website: www.ChristianPerformingArt.org.

DR. PATRICK KAVANAUGH is the Executive Director of the Christian Performing Artists' Fellowship (Washington, D.C.), and the Artistic Director of the MasterWorks Festival (New York). His doctorate is in Music Composition (from the University of Maryland), and he has also done extensive post-doctoral work in musicology, music theory, and conducting. As a composer, he is published by Carl Fischer, Inc., and licensed by Broadcast Music, Inc. (BMI). In addition to conducting many premieres of his own works, he is also the conductor of the Asaph Ensemble of Washington, D.C. Dr. Kavanaugh is the author of a number of books, including *The Spiritual Lives of the Great Composers* (Zondervan), *Raising Musical Kids* (Vine Books), *Music of the Great Composers* (Zondervan), *The Music of Angels; Sacred Music from Chant to Christian Rock* (Loyola Press), and *Spiritual Moments with the Great Composers* (Zondervan).

The mother of four sons, **BARBARA KAVANAUGH** has performed as a cellist in hundreds of solo, orchestra, and chamber music concerts. With over twenty years of private cello teaching experience, she has also worked with many orchestra and youth orchestra programs. She is currently the Director of Chamber Music at the MasterWorks Festival in New York. She maintains her cello studio in Northern Virginia.

Patrick and Barbara believe that God should be the center of our lives. We don't have to make a decision between God or music, but if God is at the center, everything else will be balanced and in proper perspective.

> *Let the word of Christ dwell in you richly as you teach and admonish one another with all wisdom, and as you sing psalms, hymns and spiritual songs with gratitude in your hearts to God. And whatever you do, whether in word or deed, do it all in the name of the Lord Jesus, giving thanks to God the Father through him.*
>
> **— Colossians 3:16-17**

If you would like to email the Kavanaughs with your comments about this book, they can be reached at KavanaughStudio@aol.com.